In the Name

of

Purpose

Sacrificing Truth on the Altar of Unity

In the Name of Purpose

Tamara Hartzell

"Thus saith the L%%ORD%%, Stand ye in the ways, and see,
and ask for the old paths, where is the good way,
and walk therein, and ye shall find rest for your souls.
But they said, We will not walk therein."
~ Jeremiah 6:16 ~

In the Name of Purpose: Sacrificing Truth on the Altar of Unity

Copyright © 2007 by Tamara Hartzell

Cover art by Karen Flaming.

Library of Congress Control Number:		2006908719
ISBN 10:	Hardcover	1-4257-3627-0
	Softcover	1-4257-3626-2
ISBN 13:	Hardcover	978-1-4257-3627-9
	Softcover	978-1-4257-3626-2

All rights reserved. This book is also available as a free e-book at http://www.inthenameofpurpose.org. The e-book may be freely copied and distributed provided that it is done so without any alterations and for non-commercial use only.

E-mail your questions to *inthenameofpurpose@sbcglobal.net*.

All Scripture quotations are taken from the *Authorized King James Bible*. Underlines added for emphasis.

This book was printed in the United States of America.

To order additional copies of this book, contact:
Xlibris Corporation
1-888-795-4274
www.Xlibris.com
Orders@Xlibris.com

36818

This book is gratefully dedicated to my parents for raising me in a church that grounded me in the truth and taught me to stand up for the truth.

Acknowledgments

To my beloved husband, for your faithful love, prayers, and tremendous support undergirding this long and burdensome task I give you my deepest love and gratitude.

To all who have supported me in various ways throughout and have made this work possible, thank you from the bottom of my heart.

To my precious Lord, absolutely nothing compares to the priceless privilege of knowing You, in daily life and for all eternity. Words are inadequate in expressing my deep gratitude for all that You are and all that You do. You are life's greatest Treasure.

> If I gained the world, but lost the Savior,
> Would my gain be worth the life-long strife?
> Are all earthly pleasures worth comparing
> For a moment with a Christ-filled life? . . .
> O the joy of having all in Jesus!
> What a balm the broken heart to heal!
> Ne'er a sin so great, but He'll forgive it,
> Nor a sorrow that He does not feel!
> If I have but Jesus, only Jesus,
> Nothing else in all the world beside—
> O then ev'rything is mine in Jesus;
> For my needs and more He will provide.
>
> —Anna Ölander, 1904[1]

Contents

Acknowledgments 6
Note to the Reader 11
Introduction 15
    ♦ Neutralizing Christianity 15
Part 1 ♦ The Purpose-Driven "Groundbreaking Manifesto" and "Blueprint" 21
  1. Which Light Are We Following? 23
    ♦ Who Is Worthy of Praise and Glory? 23
    ♦ The Holy Scriptures: God's All-Sufficient Light unto Our Path 24
    ♦ Man's "Light" Says Doctrinal Views Aren't an Issue in God's "Final Exam" 29
  2. Humanism Achieves Immense Popularity 34
    ♦ Many Driven into the Alluring "Light" of the Broad Way 34
Part 2 ♦ The Purpose-Driven "Spiritual Journey": It's "Not about You," or Is It? ... 39
  3. The Bible Is Clear 41
    ♦ God Takes 40 Days to Prepare People for His Purposes? 41
    ♦ *God's* Purposes are *Man*-centered? 46
  4. Purpose #1: You Were Planned for God's Pleasure 48
    ♦ Worship That Is about *You* Is Not Worship of *God* 48
    ♦ Offering the Strange Fire of Profane Music Is Not Worship of God 52
    ♦ "The Foolishness of Preaching" 58
  5. Purpose #2: You Were Formed for God's Family 64
    ♦ "The Local Church Is the Body of Christ" 64
    ♦ Is it Through the *Blood* of Our Redeemer *Jesus Christ* or the Life*blood* of a Local *Church* That We Have Spiritual Life? 69
  6. Purpose #3: You Were Created to Become Like Christ 73
    ♦ Which Is It, to Be like Christ or to Be like You? 73
    ♦ The Fruit of the Spirit, or the Fruit of Community? 74
    ♦ The Fruit of the Spirit, or the Fruit of Satan's Temptations? 75
    ♦ Instant Sainthood Through the Power of God vs Spiritual Formation Through Spiritual Disciplines 77
  7. Purpose #4: You Were Shaped for Serving God 84
    ♦ Serve God According to Who *He* Is, Not According to Who *You* Are 84

- Finding Healing Through *Our Wounds* or Healing Through *Christ's Wounds*? 93
- Airing Our Dirty Laundry Is *Not* Our Most Effective and Powerful Ministry in Serving God 95

8. Purpose #5: You Were Made for a Mission 97
   - Was Christ's Mission on Earth to Atone for Our Sins or to "Introduce" People to God So They Can Become His Friends? 97
   - Introducing People to *Which* God? 98
   - Introducing People to *God* by Telling Them Mostly about *You*? 100
   - "Mission Accomplished!" 104

Part 3 ♦ Counting All Things but Loss for the Knowledge of Purpose 109

9. "There Is One Thing You Could Do Greater than Share Jesus Christ with Somebody" 111
   - Starting a Purpose-Driven Church 111
   - Sharing the Message of Purpose with the World 113
   - The True Purpose of Life is "Becoming One with that Passive Spark of Divinity Longing for Actuality"? 117

10. Purpose-Driven "No Matter What it Costs" 126
    - Sacrificing Righteousness and Holiness 126
    - Sacrificing *the* Truth of *the* Faith 127
    - Sacrificing the Mind of Christ 132

Part 4 ♦ Leading the Masses into a Spiritual Awakening or a Unity of Spiritual Blindness? 139

11. "America's Most Influential Spiritual Leader" 141
    - "What in the World Are Our Pastors and Church Leaders Teaching Their Congregations?" 141
    - "Secular America's Favorite Evangelical Christian" 146
    - "Ministering to Hurting People [Is] More Important than Maintaining Purity" 154

12. The New Reformation: "A Whole New Paradigm Between Faith Communities" 158
    - Turning the First Reformation Upside Down 158
    - Interfaith "Spiritual Care" -- "Whatever it Takes!" 169

13. "Except the LORD Build the House, They Labour in Vain That Build it" 180
    - The Kingdom of *God* Is the *Narrow* Way 180
    - Is Rick Warren's P.E.A.C.E. Plan the Kingdom of God? 182
    - Saving Bodies at the Expense of Souls -- A Revolution for Global Christianity 187

Part 5 ♦ The Fulfillment of PEACE on Earth in the Name of Purpose................. 193
14. Declaring the End from the Beginning.. 195
    ♦ "The Global Peace Plan IS GOING TO HAPPEN" 195
    ♦ God's Global Judgment *Precedes* God's Global Peace 201
15. The Angel of Light's "Plan" for World Peace 208
    ♦ An Interfaith Kingdom of World Servers Working Together as ONE 208
16. "The Power of ONE".. 220
    ♦ "Together as ONE We Can Change the World"................................... 220
    ♦ The U.N.'s Goals: Uniting the World as ONE 221
    ♦ Interfaith "Bread for the World" Feeds the Hungry.............................. 223
    ♦ "Unity Comes from Purpose, Not from Anything Else"......................... 229

Part 6 ♦ "Then There Will Emerge the Universal Religion, the One Church, and that Unified Though Not Uniform Approach to God"................. 235
17. "One Truth," Many Theologies.. 237
    ♦ "A Portion of Truth, Great or Small, Is Found in Every Religious and Philosophical System" 237
18. "One God," Many Paths 240
    ♦ "The Religions are the Tributaries of One Great River"......................... 240
    ♦ Uniting All Gods into ONE Through Interfaith Prayer Services 246
19. "One Church," Many Expressions... 253
    ♦ "The Religion of the Future" 253
    ♦ The Body of Christ Transcends the Borders of *the* Faith of Christianity?....... 254
    ♦ Fundamentalism: An Enemy of the Universal Religion 258
    ♦ Finding One's Own Self-Empowering Religious Expression....................... 267
20. "One Divine Life," Many 'Little Christs' 272
    ♦ "That Which Will Eventually Reorganize Our Human Life Is the Presence in the World of Those Who Know Christ as Their Example, and Recognize That They Possess the Same Divine Life".. 272
    ♦ "A Leadership Model That Can Transform Your Life" 274
    ♦ Giving Heed to "the Fundamental Doctrines of the Ageless Wisdom" 280

Part 7 ♦ "The Last Gasp of Christendom" 291
21. Letting the Old Faith Crumble Away.. 293
    ♦ The Spiritual Transformation of Today's Christianity............................. 293
22. "A Radically Different Kind of Church" for "the New Age" 299
    ♦ "A Whole New Species of Church Is Emerging".................................. 299
    ♦ "Even the Term 'Christ' Carries Little Meaning"................................. 303

- ♦ "The Point of Interfaith Conversation Is Not to Decide Which Religious Propositions Are Right or Wrong" 309
- ♦ "The Most Important Factor Is Vision!" 313
- ♦ "Either Everything Is Worship—or Nothing Is Worship" 320

Part 8 ♦ "Take Heed Therefore That the Light Which Is in Thee Be Not Darkness" 327

23. Ripe for the Harvest 329
- ♦ Unity at All Costs 329

24. The Coming of the Universal "Christ" for the Many Who Are ONE vs The Coming of the Lord Jesus Christ for the Few Who Are His 334
- ♦ The Ultimate "Man of Peace" 334
- ♦ The Universal "Christ" and "World Teacher" 337
- ♦ "And it Was Given unto Him to Make War with the Saints, and to Overcome Them" 340
- ♦ "How, Where or When He Will Come Is None of Our Concern" 343
- ♦ Two Paths, Two Christs, Two Kingdoms, Two Eternities 347

25. People of Faith vs People of the Faith 350
- ♦ Mindlessly Following the Crowd 350
- ♦ "A New Religion Has Been Initiated, Which Is No More Christianity than Chalk Is Cheese" 354
- ♦ What on Earth Am I Here For? Keep *the* Faith! 357

Endnotes 365

Note to the Reader

In 2004, the devastating Asian Tsunami hit Indonesia and the surrounding regions. Non-existent and deficient warning systems contributed to its widespread destruction, which was triggered by a massive shift in the plates on the ocean floor.

Today, a tidal wave is sweeping through Christianity leaving spiritual destruction in its wake as it overtakes sleeping churches (not to mention seminaries, organizations, music and publishing industries, etcetera). This tidal wave has been triggered by a massive shift in the foundations of today's Christianity. As was the case in Asia, a deficient warning system is contributing to the destruction.

This "paradigm shift"—a new way of thinking about God and the world—is a massive shift in thinking from God's *absolute truth* to man's *relativism*. The destructive tidal wave that is following this shift is sweeping people away from *the* faith and into the New Spirituality that transcends religious barriers.

Yet in the midst of all this, only a relatively few number of people in the Church have been diligently trying to warn the Body of Christ, and local churches continue to transform into the image of the world. Claiming that warnings and exhortations are too "negative" and "judgmental," local churches often choose to malign and marginalize those attempting to warn them, and the warnings go unheeded.

A sign of the times, purpose-driven churches and pastors have referred to believers trying to warn them in such terms as "malcontents," "heresy hunters," "elitists," "fruit inspectors," "the vocal minority," "the opponents," and "blessed subtractions." The latter term refers to those who bless these purpose-driven churches by leaving them, so the churches can go with the flow without fear of scriptural admonishments and warnings.

I had already begun to research the Purpose-Driven Paradigm when my own church began the purpose-driven transformation. Knowing what the transformation entailed, my family left the church. I continued my research and wrote an introductory article to try and warn people who didn't see the deception. Later, I set out to complete the article which I intended to be only about 25 pages long. Yet as I collected information and addressed the deception in my article, it gradually grew longer and longer. What I had expected to be a one-month project on an article has turned into a one-and-a-half-year project on a book. This book is unconventional, but I have done my best to present a great deal of information that people in the deception appear to have missed. Still, this information barely scratches the surface of the whole new way of thinking pervading today's Christianity.

The amount of Scripture has been included because what Scripture says *is* the point. God's truth has been one of the casualties in the new way of thinking, and many people are simply unaware or don't remember what God's Word actually says. This lack of knowledge facilitates the spread of deception. The Holy Scriptures were written by God for all people, not just for theologians and pastors.

If you are among the readers who already know the Scriptures which have been included, give thanks to God for your knowledge of His Word. Instead of possibly feeling put off by my inclusion of Scripture's basics, keep in mind that these have been included for any readers who might not know them and who commonly will not take the time to look up all the provided references. I would much rather 'err' in including too much than not enough.

Compelled by the Lord and by a grieving heart to do more than merely watch as Christianity is increasingly overtaken by the flood of relativism, this book is offered from my heart for you to consider the larger picture and its danger.

The enemy has come in like a flood, and it is incumbent upon all watchful believers to faithfully sound the alarm in the manner in which God compels us. Warning the global Body of Christ is not a private matter. The alarm must continue to be sounded publicly regarding this very public and very real danger.

In addition, we are called to speak the truth in love, not to help people feel good in their error or worry about what people will think of us when we go against the tide. Warning people in the path of a destructive tidal wave is done by urgently proclaiming the truth, not by offering sugar-coated affirmations. Yet the pseudo-battle between "positive" and "negative" has people covering their ears to warnings about the departure from the faith.

Our battle is not against flesh and blood. It is **"against principalities, against powers, against the rulers of the darkness of this world, against spiritual wickedness in high places"** (Ephesians 6:12). We need to fight the battle for souls, not the battles our Adversary would have us fight to distract us.

The spiritual battle is intensifying as we near the end, and evil spiritual powers are coming out of the woodwork seeking whom they may devour. We do need to unite *in the truth of the faith* to fight the true battle -- the spiritual battle for souls -- before it's too late.

Time is running out. The tidal wave is gaining further ground, and there aren't enough people of status to sufficiently sound the alarm. It's time for the ordinary believers, the "blessed subtractions," to speak up. It doesn't take credentials and status to discern the times, to stand fast in *the* faith, and to help others do the same.

–*Tamara Hartzell, April 2006*

"But God hath chosen the foolish things of the world to confound the wise; and God hath chosen the weak things of the world to confound the things which are mighty; and base things of the world, and things which are despised, hath God chosen, yea, and things which are not, to bring to nought things that are: That no flesh should glory in his presence." (I Corinthians 1:27-29)

"For God, who commanded the light to shine out of darkness, hath shined in our hearts, to give the light of the knowledge of the glory of God in the face of Jesus Christ. But we have this treasure in earthen vessels, that the excellency of the power may be of God, and not of us." (2 Corinthians 4:6-7)

Introduction

Neutralizing Christianity

For millennia, Satan's Dream has been to be like God (see Isaiah 14:12-14), and his Vision is that of a deceived world following him in interfaith unity rather than following God in *the* faith. Scripture prophesies that Satan's Plan to turn his Dream and Vision into reality will climax in his two global leaders, the Antichrist and the False Prophet, who will rule over the three segments of society -- government, business, and religion. Their ability to work signs and lying wonders will easily convince the world to follow the Antichrist (e.g., see Revelation 13; 17; 19:20 and 2 Thessalonians 2:8-9).

A multitude of details to complete his Plan are already in place, and many more are coming together on a regular and frequent basis. His Plan will be the greatest deception ever to befall mankind. The Lord Jesus Christ Himself warned that this deception would be great enough to deceive even His own people (see Matthew 24:24 and Mark 13:22; also see 2 Thessalonians 2:3 and 1 Timothy 4:1). Obviously, in order for this to be the case, the deception would have to appear "scriptural" and as a way of "light" rather than darkness.

This masquerade is no problem for Satan who can transform himself into **"an angel of light"** and whose ministers can transform themselves into **"ministers of righteousness"** (see 2 Corinthians 11:13-15). Satan is adept at misusing Scripture to make things *seem* as if they are right. This Master Deceiver has had thousands of years to perfect his deceptions and to practice craftily leading people into questioning and rethinking what God has really said.

Christianity, a once vocal mouthpiece for God's absolute truth and obstacle to the completion of Satan's Plan, needed to be neutralized. Its warnings needed to be silenced. To do this, Satan needed to lure it away from the truth and into a new way of thinking so it would become deceived along with the world.

You may question, "How can the Master Deceiver accomplish such an 'impossible' task without Christians realizing what is going on and fleeing the deception?" We are often reminded of the lesson of how to boil a frog in a pot of water. The secret to keeping him from jumping out of the pot to safety is to ever so gradually transition the water around him from cold to the boiling point. Only in this way will he fail to notice the life-threatening situation.

Likewise, the purpose of the transition stage is to process man's thinking far enough so that he loses the ability to recognize that the transformation is not what he wants. Barring getting pulled out of the fire, he will be unwilling and then unable to flee or undo the process. As a result, the damage is done and the transformation becomes complete.

The Master Deceiver's devices include surgically extracting the truth out of today's Christianity, ultimately replacing the truth with error. The following transformations are included in this process:

- **Gradually Transform God's Absolute Truth into Relativism**. Entice Christians to question and rethink what God really said. This is easily done by producing books and "Bible" versions that incrementally change what God said. This way they won't notice they have been deceived into changing the message and following lies rather than the truth.
- **Gradually Transform Obedience to God's Truth into Pragmatism**. Entice Christians to believe that whatever "works" is acceptable to God. This way they won't notice they have been deceived into rethinking the world's ways as obedience rather than the disobedience God's Word says they are.
- **Gradually Transform the Gospel of Faith into a Gospel of Service**. Entice Christians to believe that service is the most important aspect of faith. This draws them into the zealousness of serving the world's temporal needs. This way they won't notice they have been deceived into devoting a dwindling amount of time and resources toward preaching the Gospel of Christ and bringing those in the world to faith in the Lord Jesus Christ.
- **Gradually Transform the Faith of the Narrow Way into a Faith on the Broad Way**. Entice Christians to believe that judging truth and error is unloving, divisive, and intolerant. This draws them into silencing those exercising discernment rather than those spreading heresy. This way they won't notice they have been deceived into a pursuit of unity with the world that has truly united them with the world.
- **Gradually Transform Man into "God."** Entice Christians to rethink the nature and role of both God and man and blur the distinction between them. This way they won't notice they have been deceived into encroaching upon that which belongs to God alone.

Top all this with presenting the broad way as the "Christian," "scriptural" way of living for God's purposes and bringing global transformation and peace to the world. The end result is the post-truth "paradigm shift" metastasizing throughout today's Christianity.

> *"For the time will come when they will not endure sound doctrine; but after their own lusts shall they heap to themselves teachers, having itching ears; and they shall turn away their ears from the truth, and shall be turned unto fables." (2 Timothy 4:3-4)*

Itching ears have turned everything upside down:

- Lies are called *truth*, and truth is called *error*.
- Heresy is called *faith*, and uncompromising faith in the truth is called *heretical*.
- Claiming we can only know very little about God (a denial of the abundant knowledge of God revealed in His Word) is called *humble*, and being faithful to the revealed knowledge of God is called *egocentric*.
- Learning "truths" of foolishness from the world is called *wisdom* and *staying relevant*, and following wisdom from God's Word of truth is called *quarrelsome* and *irrelevantly old-fashioned*.
- False prophets are called *vision casters*, and God's watchmen (who speak God's Word rather than a vision of their own heart and who warn of sin and judgment) are called *false prophets*, *doomsday prophets*, and *neo-Pharisees*.
- Heretics are called *recovering fundamentalists*, and fundamentalists (those who believe in the fundamentals of the faith, i.e., that God said what He meant and meant what He said in His Holy Scriptures) are called *false teachers*.
- Disobedience is called *serving God*, and obedience is called *sin* and elicits public rebuke from compromised pulpits.
- Affirming the Body in its worldly disobedience is called *building up*, and admonishing the Body to live in holy obedience is called *tearing down*.
- A gospel of works is called *a gospel of faith*, and living the true Christian faith is called *elitism*.
- Ungodliness is called *righteousness*, and godliness is called *legalism*.

- Living for self is called *living for God*, and living for God is called *self-centered*.
- Worshipping God in relativism and the unholiness of the flesh is called *faithfulness to Christ* and *becoming all things to all people*, and worshipping God in truth and the beauty of holiness is called *the last gasp of Christendom* and *aesthetic snobbery*.
- Unifying with the world is called *fulfilling God's Great Commandment of love*, and faithfulness to God and His Word is called *unloving divisiveness*.
- Quoting the world is called *teaching*, and quoting the Holy Scriptures is called *your opinion*.
- Unbelievers are called *Christians*, and true Christians are called *unchristian intolerants*.
- Putting community above Christ is called *Christianity*, and putting obedience to the Lord Jesus Christ above the local church is called *Churchianity*.
- Humanistic teachings are called *God-centered* and *not about you*, and true theology of God is called *self-centered dogmatism*.
- The word of man is called *truth*, and the Word of God is called *metaphor* and *stories*.
- Learning "truth" from other faiths who follow false gods is called *humility*, and preferring to learn spiritual truth only from the faith given in the true God's Holy Scriptures is called *pride*.
- Believing that every different perspective of Jesus is right is called *a celebration of Jesus* and *a celebration of mystery*, and believing only in the Lord Jesus Christ as set forth in the Holy Scriptures is called *mediocrity* and *narrow-mindedness* (although meant as criticism, it is accurate -- the Lord Jesus Christ's way of truth is called the *narrow* way for a reason).
- Believing that everyone has the right to interpret Scripture, doctrine, and faith in their own way (which is relativism and places Scripture under the 'authority' of man) is called *a celebration of diversity* and *humility*, and believing that these things are not of private interpretation but set forth by God through His Holy Spirit as absolute truth is called *intolerance* and *self-righteousness*.
- Denying the faith in favor of interfaith conversation and experience is called *love* and *grace*, and standing on the understandable certainty of the Lord Jesus Christ (i.e., believing the Word of God is true and contending for its truth) is called *hatred* and *religious bigotry*.
- Interfaith unity is called *a spiritual awakening*, and faithfulness to the faith is called *spiritual blindness*.

- The broad way is called *a way of light* and *world service*, and the narrow way is called *a way of darkness* and *selfish individualism*.
- Unity with the broad way is called *passion* and *holiness*, and separating from the broad way is called *fanaticism* and *cultism*.
- Uniting light and darkness is called *the way of love and service and truth*, and discerning the difference between light and darkness, truth and error, and right and wrong is called *negative judgmentalism, heresy hunting*, and *a critical spirit*.

"Woe unto them that call evil good, and good evil; that put darkness for light, and light for darkness; that put bitter for sweet, and sweet for bitter! Woe unto them that are wise in their own eyes, and prudent in their own sight! . . . Which justify the wicked for reward, and take away the righteousness of the righteous from him!" (Isaiah 5:20-21, 23)

This upside-down deception is devouring today's Christianity, through big churches and little churches, best-sellers and not so best-sellers, big movements and little movements, national conferences and local seminars, popular theologians and pastors and students, and so on and so forth. This deception is no respecter of status, size, or popularity. Rick Warren, who like everyone else is not immune to deception, just happens to be the founder and perpetuator of the largest and most popular and influential of the group. His Purpose-Driven Paradigm is even assimilating many of the other movements into its own.

In addition, his global Paradigm is even seeking purpose-driven "men of peace" from any religion and no religion to participate in the purpose-driven works of his P.E.A.C.E. Plan. His goal is to fight five global giants (which include "spiritual lostness") through *interfaith unity*. This upside-down deception is the result of falling for the broad way's method of synthesizing light and darkness into a new reality -- a "paradigm shift."

This new way of thinking about God and the world resembles the Angel of light's interfaith (New Age) New Spirituality. It attempts to unite the broad way with the narrow way but at the dire cost of increasingly disobeying and departing from *the* faith of the narrow way.

The narrow way of light that leads to life and the broad way of darkness that leads to destruction are the only two ways in life. These two ways are eternally separate and can only be synthesized into a *counterfeit* way of "light" and "life" that profanes God.

The Paradigm's purpose-driven interfaith unity cannot be separated from its "blueprint," *The Purpose Driven Life*. Definitions of basic purposes have been enlarged to facilitate a more inclusive and less offensive world view. Inevitably, this has laid the foundation for interfaith unity in the P.E.A.C.E. Plan.

Rick Warren may be highly regarded as "America's Pastor,"[1] but he is still a pastor in need of earnest prayer and true scriptural counsel from men of God. He has fallen for the enticing, deceptive "light" of the world's teachings and ways. Yet instead of trying to show him the error of his ways, today's Christianity has put him on a pedestal, made him out to be an untouchable, and followed him into his deception hook, line, and sinker.

In the name of purpose, truth is being sacrificed on the altar of unity.

"There is a way that seemeth right unto a man, but the end thereof are the ways of death." (Proverbs 16:25 & 14:12)

"Let no man deceive you with vain words: for because of these things cometh the wrath of God upon the children of disobedience. Be not ye therefore partakers with them. For ye were sometimes darkness, but now are ye light in the Lord: walk as children of light: (For the fruit of the Spirit is in all goodness and righteousness and truth;) proving what is acceptable unto the Lord. And have no fellowship with the unfruitful works of darkness, but rather reprove them." (Ephesians 5:6-11)

"But ye, beloved, building up yourselves on your most holy faith, praying in the Holy Ghost, keep yourselves in the love of God, looking for the mercy of our Lord Jesus Christ unto eternal life. And of some have compassion, making a difference: <u>and others save with fear, pulling them out of the fire;</u> hating even the garment spotted by the flesh." (Jude 1:20-23)

Part 1

The Purpose-Driven "Groundbreaking Manifesto" and "Blueprint"

• *Chapter One* •

Which Light Are We Following?

Who Is Worthy of Praise and Glory?

"I am the LORD: that is my name: and my glory will I not give to another, neither my praise to graven images." (Isaiah 42:8)

Rick Warren's *The Purpose Driven Life* has swept Christianity in global proportions. It is highly acclaimed with such lofty words of praise that used to be reserved for the Lord God and His Holy Scriptures. Only the Lord God and His Word have the power to set us free, to enable us to live godly lives that He intended, and to place our feet firmly on the right path. Nevertheless, these things have been now widely ascribed to Rick Warren, his book, and various aspects of his Purpose-Driven Paradigm.

Remember when the Lord Jesus Christ didn't have to share His glory for changing lives and setting people free? How times have changed in the humanistic new Paradigm. *The Purpose Driven Life* has had the following on its back cover[1]:

> **"Make sure you're not missing the point of your life—read this book!** *The Purpose-Driven Life* will guide you to greatness—through living the Great Commandment and the Great Commission."—Billy Graham and Franklin Graham

> "Timeless, profound, compelling, and transforming . . . Rick Warren's new, groundbreaking manifesto will set millions of people free to live the lives God intended. This is the book we've all been waiting for!"—Bruce Wilkinson

> **"If you only read one book on what life is all about—make it this one! This book is life-changing.** Rick Warren is absolutely brilliant at explaining our real purpose on earth and stating profound truths in simple ways . . . . Believe me, you'll never be the same after reading this! What a gift!"—Lee Strobel

"**Rick Warren has written a masterpiece of wise counsel for you.** Whether you are a seeker, a new believer, or a seasoned saint, let God use these pages to place your feet firmly on the right path!"—Max Lucado

In addition, above the previous quotes and across the top of the back cover in large capital letters, "A GROUNDBREAKING MANIFESTO ON THE MEANING OF LIFE" introduced the world to *The Purpose Driven Life*. According to these very words, Rick Warren's book *must* differ from God's Holy Scriptures because this claim itself is saying that this book is an original public declaration on the subject of the meaning of life.

Yet in the dedication, Rick Warren presumptuously asserts, "Before you were born, God planned *this moment* in your life. It is no accident that you are holding this book. God *longs* for you to discover the life he created you to live—here on earth, and forever in eternity."

First, God does not plan for anyone to hold this book or any book that will lead them astray from His truth. Second, Rick Warren is usurping the position that belongs to God's Word. God, in His great love, plans how to get *His Word* to everyone because it is *God's* Word that is the source of faith and salvation (see Romans 1:16, 10:17; and 2 Timothy 3:15-17). It is also *God's* Word that already very clearly sets forth the meaning of life—according to God's error-free and unchanging truth—to those who have ears to hear.

The Holy Scriptures: God's All-Sufficient Light unto Our Path

"Thy word is a lamp unto my feet, and a light unto my path." (Psalm 119:105)

"The entrance of thy words giveth light; it giveth understanding unto the simple." (Psalm 119:130)

Throughout His Word, God reiterates the absolute indispensability of being solidly and firmly grounded in our knowledge of God and His Holy Scriptures:

- God's Word is the source of the words of the Lord Jesus Christ which are *spirit and life* (e.g., see John 6:63).
- God's Word is the source of *true knowledge of the Lord Jesus Christ* (e.g., see Luke 24:27; John 5:39; Acts 18:28).
- God's Word gives us *faith* (e.g., see Romans 10:17).

- God's Word makes us wise unto *salvation* (e.g., see 2 Timothy 3:15; Romans 1:16; 1 Peter 1:25).
- God's Word gives us *understanding* (e.g., see Psalm 119:104, 130).
- God's Word shows us how to live by being a *lamp unto our feet* and a *light unto our path* (e.g., see Psalm 119:105).
- God's Word gives us the knowledge of God by which He has granted to us *all things pertaining to life and godliness through the knowledge of Him* (e.g., see 2 Peter 1:2-4; Colossians 1:9-10; Ephesians 1:17-19; 1 Corinthians 15:34).
- God's Word is *the foundation of true worship* because we must worship in spirit and in truth (e.g., see John 4:24, 6:63, 17:17).
- God's Word is given to us by God for *doctrine, reproof, correction,* and *instruction in righteousness* that we may be *thoroughly furnished unto all good works* (e.g., see 2 Timothy 3:16-17).
- God's Word is *the foundation of true scriptural discipleship*, which is following the Lord Jesus Christ in the faith by knowing, believing, and obeying the true doctrine of Christ (e.g., see Matthew 28:19-20; 2 John 1:9; 1 Timothy 2:4, 4:16; 2 Timothy 3:15-17; Ephesians 4:11-16; 2 Peter 1:2-8; and the rest of the New Testament).
- God's Word is *the foundation and definition of true service and ministry* which can only begin with following the Lord Jesus Christ (e.g., see John 12:26; 2 Timothy 3:16-17).
- God's Word is *the standard of true love* because we are to love in deed and in truth (e.g., see 1 John 3:18; John 17:17).
- God's Word is *the power of God unto salvation* and thus to be taken to the whole world as *the basis of all missions* (e.g., see Romans 1:16; Romans 10:17-18; 1 Corinthians 1:18-24; Ephesians 1:13; 2 Timothy 3:15; 1 Peter 1:23-25).
- God's Word reveals *true knowledge of self* (e.g., see Romans 3:10-23 and the rest of Romans; Hebrews 4:12).
- God's Word is *the source of the meaning of life* (e.g., see 2 Corinthians 5:15; Galatians 2:20; Ephesians 2:10, 4:13, 22-24; Philippians 1:21; Colossians 3; Revelation 4:11; and the rest of the Holy Scriptures).

The Word of God is so essential to every part of our lives that the Lord Jesus Christ equated it to the importance of food to our body and declared that we need to live **"by _every word of God_"** (see Luke 4:4 and Matthew 4:4). Yet people are filling up so much on man's word that they don't leave room to feast on God's, and scriptural illiteracy continues to mushroom.

No one knows better than God Himself how we are to prepare for eternity, what the meaning and purpose of life are, and how we can live an obedient and godly life of faith and holiness that pleases and glorifies Him. To truly please God in all of the purposes He has for us, we need to study and rightly divide God's Word of truth.

> **"Study to shew thyself approved unto God, a workman that needeth not to be ashamed, rightly dividing the word of truth." (2 Timothy 2:15)**

In the following quote, Rick Warren gives sound advice that should definitely be followed, but, sadly, he does not heed his own advice:

> "To discover your purpose in life you must turn to God's Word, not the world's wisdom. You must build your life on eternal truths, not pop psychology, success-motivation, or inspirational stories." (*The Purpose Driven Life – PDL*; p. 20)

Yet Rick Warren does indeed synthesize the world's "wisdom" into much of his Paradigm. A self-professing avid reader, he has admitted:

> "'I am a product of every book I've ever read . . .'"[2]

> "[W]e're trying to learn from anybody. What I am is a translator. I have an ability to simplify and synthesize. And so I learn from everybody." —Rick Warren[3]

> "We believe we can learn truth -- I've learned a lot of truth from different religions. Because they all have a portion of the truth."[4]

> "'I was just wired by God to see how things relate to each other. I'm a synthesizer and systematizer,' says Warren." —*USA TODAY*, 7/21/03[5]

> "'What I'm saying isn't new,' he [Rick Warren] says. 'I just synthesize ideas and translate them into simple language.'" —*TIME* Magazine, 4/18/05[6]

> "I am grateful to the hundreds of writers and teachers, both classical and contemporary, who have shaped my life and helped me learn these truths." (*PDL*; p. 5)

Would this latter quote from the dedication to *The Purpose Driven Life* include the "truth" he said he's learned from different religions? Near the end of his book after he has clarified his meaning and purpose of life as taught by these hundreds of people, Rick Warren further declared:

> "In this book I have passed on to you what others taught me about the purpose of life; now it's your duty to pass that on to others." (*PDL*; p. 309)

He has even said:

> "I believe I have the key to meaning and purpose in life with God, and I'm trying to share it with as many people as possible."—Rick Warren[7]

There is much that can be said about this quote, but suffice it to say that if Rick Warren himself has "the key" then we must go to *him* to get it, rather than to God and His Word.

As revealed in his material in *The Purpose Driven Life* as well as with the people and books he quotes and endorses, Rick Warren has indeed turned to the very things he says we should not. The door opened by Rick Warren's "key" is an entryway to the broad way of the world.

It is not possible to learn God's holy truth from ungodly and worldly sources because what these sources say about God must, by their very nature, be rooted in darkness. The Word of God makes it clear that the world and unbelievers *cannot know* the things of God. No *man* knows the things of God because they are spiritually discerned *through the Holy Spirit* (see 1 Corinthians 2:11-12, 14), and the unbelieving world cannot see, know, or receive the Holy Spirit (see John 14:17). Thus the wisdom of the world is foolishness (see 1 Corinthians 3:19).

No word of man, Christian or otherwise, should automatically be trusted as scriptural, especially since the Word of God makes it clear that false teachers will arise *among us* (e.g., see 2 Peter 2:1-3 and Acts 20:29-31). We need to make sure that every source of teaching we choose to listen to, whether verbal or written or otherwise, is in complete agreement with Scripture so that we are not drawn away from the truth.

God tells us in His Word that **"a _little_ leaven leaveneth _the whole lump_"** (1 Corinthians 5:6 and Galatians 5:9). In addition, synthesizing pure light with the impurities of the world's darkness results in an impure shadowy light, which *changes* the message. Nevertheless, and again usurping what belongs to God and

His Word of truth, Rick Warren makes a bold declaration about what hundreds of people have taught him, which he is passing on in his book:

> "You may have felt in the dark about *your* purpose in life. Congratulations, you're about to walk into the light." (*PDL*; p. 21)

Included in "the light" of Rick Warren's book is the following declaration, which further contradicts and negates his positive quotes regarding studying the Bible:

> **"The *last* thing many believers need today is to go to another Bible study**. They already know far more than they are putting into practice. What they need are *serving* experiences in which they can exercise their spiritual muscles." (*PDL*; p. 231; bold added)

This deceptive declaration provides insight into Rick Warren's "light," not to mention a lack of discernment. A lack of the true knowledge of God and His Holy Scriptures has become a full-force pandemic which is growing by leaps and bounds, and which precludes having "spiritual muscles." The growing Purpose-Driven Paradigm is itself evidence of this tragic pandemic. Yes, we do need to also be *doers* of the Word, but scriptural illiteracy has led to the opposite end of the spectrum:

> "... *they have a zeal of God, but not according to knowledge.*" *(Romans 10:2)*

True and accurate Bible study that *rightly divides* God's Word is exactly the single most important thing critically needed today.

> *"My people are destroyed for lack of knowledge: because thou hast rejected knowledge, I will also reject thee, that thou shalt be no priest to me: seeing thou hast forgotten the law of thy God, I will also forget thy children." (Hosea 4:6)*

Many aspects that belong to *God's* Word continue to be attributed to Rick Warren and *The Purpose Driven Life*, both in the claims surrounding them as well as in the book's content itself. Studying a book written by a *man* is neither the equivalent to nor a replacement for studying *God's* Word, regardless of how many scriptures it quotes. Yet, at the request of its writer, people and small groups are going through *The Purpose Driven Life* and other purpose-driven curricula over and over and over . . .

Rather than heedlessly rushing headlong (like lemmings to their destruction as the story goes) into "the light" of Rick Warren's Paradigm, we need to seriously heed the warnings of the Lord Jesus Christ Who said:

> *"The light of the body is the eye: if therefore thine eye be single, thy whole body shall be full of light. But if thine eye be evil, thy whole body shall be full of darkness. If therefore the light that is in thee be darkness, how great is that darkness!" (Matthew 6:22-23)*

> *". . . Can the blind lead the blind? shall they not both fall into the ditch?" (Luke 6:39)*

We need to conscientiously and warily make sure that the only *light* we are heeding is the true light of the Lord Jesus Christ and His uncorrupted, unchanging, absolute Word of truth. This is the only true and pure light unto our path.

> *"For with thee is the fountain of life: in <u>thy light</u> shall we see light." (Psalm 36:9)*

God's counsel includes the wisdom He gave King Solomon; wisdom which abounds in this proverb that needs to be heeded today:

> *"Cease, my son, to hear the instruction that causeth to err from the words of knowledge." (Proverbs 19:27)*

Man's "Light" Says Doctrinal Views Aren't an Issue in God's "Final Exam"

"*The Purpose-Driven® Life* is a blueprint for Christian living in the 21st century—a lifestyle based on God's eternal purposes, not cultural values. Using over 1,200 scriptural quotes and references, it challenges the conventional definitions of worship, fellowship, discipleship, ministry, and evangelism. In the tradition of Oswald Chambers, Rick Warren offers distilled wisdom on the essence of what life is all about." (*PDL*; back flap)

*T*he Word of God is our blueprint for godly living in *any* century, including the 21st century. The Word of God is also where we find the true definitions of worship, fellowship, and so forth. Yet Rick Warren's book has challenged and usurped the position and purpose of God's Word, clearly *in favor of* cultural values. His use of "over 1,200 scriptural quotes and references" does not refute this because his repeated twisting of scriptural quotes actually assists him in his challenge of the definitions of the rightly divided Word of God (examples will be addressed later).

Rick Warren's "blueprint for Christian living" claims to be "based on God's eternal purposes." Yet it challenges the Word of God in regards to doctrinal beliefs determining where a person will spend eternity:

> "One day you will stand before God, and he will do an audit of your life, a final exam, before you enter eternity . . . . Fortunately, God wants us to pass this test, so he has given us the questions in advance. From the Bible we can surmise that God will ask us two crucial questions:
>
> "First, '*What did you do with my Son, Jesus Christ?*' **God won't ask about** your religious background or **doctrinal views**. The only thing that will matter is, did you accept what Jesus did for you and did you learn to love and trust him? Jesus said, '*I am the way and the truth and the life. No one comes to the Father except through me.*' [endnote: John 14:6 (NIV)]
>
> "Second, '*What did you do with what I gave you?*' What did you do with your life—all the gifts, talents, opportunities, energy, relationships, and resources God gave you? Did you spend them on yourself, or did you use them for the purposes God made you for?
>
> "Preparing you for these two questions is the goal of this book. **The first question will determine *where* you spend eternity**. The second question will determine *what you do* in eternity. By the end of this book you will be ready to answer both questions." (*PDL*; p. 34; bold added)

There are other problems with these claims but, most importantly, please notice that in complete contradiction to God's Holy Scriptures, Rick Warren writes here that *doctrine* does not have a role in determining where a person spends eternity!

People tend to think that as long as someone quotes John 14:6 then that makes everything else okay. But the Lord Jesus Christ is ours as the way and the truth and the life *through faith*, and it is *the doctrine of Christ* that tells us what we are to *believe* about Who He is and what He has done for us. Without the doctrine of Christ none of the following can take place: We cannot believe in Christ, we cannot have faith in Christ, we cannot accept Christ or what He did for us, we cannot love and trust Christ, we cannot serve Christ, and we cannot spend eternity with Christ.

The doctrine of Christ is the *doctrine* of the Father (see John 7:16), and He knows His own plan of salvation. According to His Word, the doctrine of Christ is absolutely indispensable to having both the Father and the Son, and having the Son is absolutely indispensable to having eternal life:

> *"Whosoever transgresseth, and abideth not in the doctrine of Christ, hath not God. He that abideth in the doctrine of Christ, he hath both the Father and the Son." (2 John 1:9)*

> *"He that hath the Son hath life; and he that hath not the Son of God hath not life." (1 John 5:12)*

> *"He that believeth on him is not condemned: but he that believeth not is condemned already, because he hath not believed in the name of the only begotten Son of God." (John 3:18)*

> *"Take heed unto thyself, and unto the doctrine; continue in them: for in doing this thou shalt both save thyself, and them that hear thee." (1 Timothy 4:16)*

It simply cannot be overemphasized that without the *doctrine* of Christ we do not have the *Person* of Christ, which means that we do not have either God or eternal life. Thus Jesus Christ Himself warned that a person can call Him Lord and even do many wonderful works in His name but still not be saved (see Matthew 7:21-23). Lip service and works—"What did you do with my Son, Jesus Christ?" and, "Now what you do with your life on earth will determine where you spend eternity" (Rick Warren[8])—will never save anyone.

Apart from the right beliefs, all "good works" are in vain. This is why it is so crucially important to first examine our *beliefs* in the light of Scripture to make sure that what we believe is the true *doctrine* of Christ.

> *"I marvel that ye are so soon removed from him that called you into the grace of Christ unto another gospel: which is not another; but there be some that trouble you, and would pervert the gospel of Christ. But though we, or an angel from heaven, preach any other gospel unto you than that which we have preached unto you, let him be accursed. As we said before, so say I now again, If any man preach any other gospel unto you than that ye have received, let him be accursed. For do I now persuade men, or God? or do I seek to please men? for if I yet pleased men, I should not be the servant of Christ."* (Galatians 1:6-10)

Preparing people for eternity is an act of love. But it is not loving to lead people to believe they will be prepared for eternity by reading a book that, among other things, does the following:

- It skirts the true and full Gospel of Christ, which is *the* power of God unto salvation (see Romans 1:16).
- It tends to delete key phrases of essential truth from the verses that are quoted.
- It goes against 2 John 1:9 and leads its readers toward a false gospel of works—what we "do," not our doctrinal beliefs ("views"), determines our eternal destination.

Who *you* are and what *you* do is more important in the Purpose-Driven Paradigm than the doctrine of Christ that tells us Who *He* is and what *He* did and does. This is not about either preparing for eternity or serving God's purpose in this generation, which is another goal for his book. God has been reduced to merely the means to a *self*-centered end, which is *self*-significance.

> "There is no greater epitaph than that statement! Imagine it chiseled on *your* tombstone: That *you* served God's purpose in your generation. My prayer is that people will be able to say that about me when I die. It is also my prayer that people will say it about you, too. That is why I wrote this book for you. This phrase is the ultimate definition of a life well lived. You do the eternal and timeless (God's purpose) in a contemporary and timely way (in your generation). That is what the *purpose-driven life* is all about." (PDL; p. 318)

> "That's why spreading the Good News is so important; you only have a short time to share *your* life *message* and fulfill your mission." (PDL; p. 295; emphasis added)

Chapter One

It's not about the Lord Jesus Christ. It's about you. Thus what you *do* is more important than what you *believe* in the purpose-driven journey.

Choosing to go on this "spiritual journey" with Rick Warren who would prepare his followers for eternity apart from doctrine is unwise, to say the least! Yet right on the front flap of *The Purpose Driven Life* its readers are warned that this journey will *transform* their answer on life:

> "Rick Warren will guide you through a personal *40-day spiritual journey* that will transform your answer to life's most important question: *What on earth am I here for?*"

Which light are we following?

◆ *Chapter Two* ◆

Humanism Achieves Immense Popularity

Many Driven into the Alluring "Light" of the Broad Way

*I*n spite of the book's reported use of "over 1,200 scriptural quotes and references," *The Purpose Driven Life* has been founded very firmly on unscriptural man-centered theology, philosophies, and traditions. Yet Rick Warren's Purpose-Driven Paradigm and its "manifesto" are sweeping hundreds of thousands of churches around the world. A favored argument in support of this extremely popular Paradigm is: How can millions of people and church leaders and churches all over the world be wrong?

The subjectivity of man, rather than the absolute objectivity of God, is the basis of this man-centered argument. We are to prove all things according to the light of God's Holy Scriptures, *not* according to whether or not something is popular. The fact that hundreds of thousands of churches, tens of millions of people, and hundreds of millions of dollars are part of this movement says *absolutely nothing* about it being of God.

That a humanistic movement which twists Scripture in order to align with worldly "wisdom" is enjoying global popularity in churches is merely a sign of our times regarding the tremendous lack of knowledge in today's Christianity. Humanism has become so commonplace and accepted that not only are its teachings not even recognized as such any more, but they are actually believed to be centered around God instead of man!

To follow the majority simply because it is the majority leads to destruction.

- The majority -- every single person on Earth, excluding a mere eight people -- died in the global flood of God's wrath.
- The majority -- every Israelite over the age of 19, *including the religious leaders* and excluding a mere two people (the two faithful spies) -- died in the wilderness and were forbidden to enter the promised land. (This was the consequence of choosing to rebelliously listen to the word of the majority of the spies instead of to the *two* faithful spies telling them to trust and obey the word of God.)

- The majority of *religious leaders* -- **"_all_ the chief priests and elders of the people"** -- **"took counsel against Jesus to put him to death"** (Matthew 27:1).
- The majority of the multitude followed the persuading of their *religious leaders* to ask Pilate to **"destroy Jesus"** -- **"They _all_ say unto him, Let him be crucified"** (Matthew 27:20, 22).

Ultimately, to follow the majority is to follow the broad way that leads to destruction -- *many* are on this road, and only a *few* are on the narrow road that leads to life (see Matthew 7:13-14). Tragically, the *broad* way of destruction also includes *many* who call Jesus "Lord" and obviously believe they are Christians and that they are serving Jesus with their lives (see Matthew 7:21-23). This would clearly include church-goers of local churches.

> *"Not every one that saith unto me, Lord, Lord, shall enter into the kingdom of heaven; but he that doeth the will of my Father which is in heaven. <u>Many</u> will say to me in that day, Lord, Lord, have we not prophesied in thy name? and in thy name have cast out devils? and in thy name done many wonderful works? And then will I profess unto them, I never knew you: depart from me, ye that work iniquity." (Matthew 7:21-23)*

These *many* "Christians" (in name only) were wrong about the single most important thing in life. They believed they were following and serving the Lord Jesus Christ. But they were condemned by Him for all eternity because *they were wrong about how the Lord Jesus Christ wants to be followed and served.*

The *many* in this condemned group no doubt believed doctrine didn't matter. They no doubt believed they could pragmatically use any means that worked which were right in their own eyes to accomplish what they thought the Lord Jesus Christ wanted them to do. On the contrary, the Word of God is clear that we can only follow and serve the Lord Jesus Christ by believing the right things and by doing things *His* way (obedience). *Matthew 7:21-23 clearly proves beyond all shadow of doubt that the end does not justify the means.*

How can millions of people and church/religious leaders and churches all over the world be wrong? *Very easily*, as seen throughout Scripture. Along with the frog, they are boiling in the pot of transformation.

Not every transformation that occurs in life is a good thing.[1] Following the Purpose-Driven Paradigm, churches are pragmatically implementing change away from behaviors and teachings that are deemed exclusive, intolerant, divisive, and restrictive, in order to be attractive to the world. Rick Warren and his purpose-driven followers appear to be totally oblivious to the fact that their changes are increasingly uniting them with the broad way's *another* gospel and *another* Jesus and *another* spirit, and leading them away from the true Gospel of the true Jesus Christ.

The true Jesus Christ is the exclusive and divisive Rock of Offence and Stumblingstone that the world will never unite over but, rather, hates and stumbles over (e.g., see John 7:7; John 3:19-20; and I Peter 2:6-8). He is inclusive in the sense that all are welcome to come to Him, but they must come to Him in faith via His narrow way, and only a few are willing to do so. Many are they who hate Him and His narrow way which excludes all who refuse to believe and obey.

Contrary to what is being taught in the Purpose-Driven Paradigm, the world does not reject Christianity because the churches are doing a poor job of presenting Christ. The world rejects true Christianity because it *is* founded on Christ. Change Christianity to center it around the world, and the world will jump right in. But then what you are left with is no longer *Christ*ianity but merely an extension of the world into the churches.

Because the Rock of *Offence* is *offensive* to the world, neither He nor His Gospel will ever be popular. To take away what offends in order to preach an all-inclusive, tolerant, nonjudgmental Jesus is to preach *another* Jesus. We don't have the right to positively recreate the Rock of Offence into someone that pleases the world. Truth is positive and negative. To take away the "negative" is to take away truth. He tells us Who He is, and we either believe or we don't.

The Rock of Offence Himself said that He came to bring *division*. God's Word is a sword of absolute truth that divides those who are for it from those who are against it -- those who believe and obey it from those who do not. It divides the few who are on the narrow way from the many who are on the broad way.

> **"Suppose ye that I am come to give peace on earth? I tell you, Nay; but rather division." (Luke 12:51)**

> **"Wherefore also it is contained in the scripture, Behold, I lay in Zion a chief corner stone, elect, precious: and he that believeth on him shall not be confounded. Unto you therefore which believe he is precious: but unto them which be disobedient, the stone which the builders disallowed, the same is made the head of the corner, and a stone of stumbling, and a rock**

of offence, even to them which stumble at the word, being disobedient: whereunto also they were appointed." (1 Peter 2:6-8)

"Enter ye in at the strait gate: for wide is the gate, and broad is the way, that leadeth to destruction, and many there be which go in thereat: Because strait is the gate, and narrow is the way, which leadeth unto life, and few there be that find it." (Matthew 7:13-14)

Many today **"stumble at the word"** because they do not believe that God's unchanging, absolute Word is an eternal, living and powerful book of truth and wisdom that is equally alive and powerful in each and every generation. They especially do not believe that God's Word is equally alive and powerful in today's so-called "postmodern" generation; a more accurate term for today's world is "post-truth." This lack of belief drives many to find their meaning and purpose of life *not* in the pure, unadulterated Holy Scriptures written by God but, rather, in popular and corrupt man-centered books written by men that appeal to the flesh and the world.

◆ Part 2 ◆

The Purpose-Driven "Spiritual Journey": It's "Not about You," or Is It?

♦ Chapter Three ♦

The Bible Is Clear

God Takes 40 Days to Prepare People for His Purposes?

One of Rick Warren's premises for his book and the basis of his 40 Days campaigns (which have incrementally led churches into his global P.E.A.C.E. Plan that will be discussed later) is his assertion that:

> "The Bible is clear that God considers 40 days a spiritually significant time period. Whenever God wanted to prepare someone for his purposes, he took 40 days." (*PDL*; p. 9)

Forty-day time periods are only mentioned in the 66 books of the Holy Scriptures a mere 22 times:

- 4 of these are in reference to the 40 days it rained on the earth during the flood.
- 1 of these is in reference to the 40 days set by the Egyptians for embalming, which they did to Jacob.
- 7 of these are in reference to the two 40-day periods Moses spent with God on Mount Sinai.
- 2 of these are in reference to the 40 days the spies spent in the Promised Land.
- 1 of these is in reference to the 40 days Goliath challenged the Israelites.
- 1 of these is in reference to the 40 days Elijah took traveling to Horeb without eating, after an angel fed him.
- 1 of these is in reference to the 40 days Ezekiel had to lay on his right side bearing the iniquity of the house of Judah, each day representing a year.
- 1 of these is in reference to the 40 days the people of Nineveh were given to repent.
- 3 of these are in reference to the 40 days that Jesus was in the wilderness, tempted by the devil.

- 1 of these is in reference to the 40 days that Jesus was seen by His apostles after His resurrection.

All in all, there are only a handful of instances in Scripture where a 40-day period could possibly be construed as "spiritually significant." Scripture does not in any way justify Rick Warren's fallacious claims that "the Bible is clear that God considers 40 days a spiritually significant time period," and that "whenever God wanted to prepare someone for his purposes, he took 40 days." If this latter claim was true, then God has only prepared a handful of people, and everyone else in Scripture (and throughout history) was never prepared by God for His purposes!

Twisting Scripture to put spiritual significance on a 40-day time period is akin to occultic numerology. The Holy Scriptures are clear that transforming and life-changing power is found through the knowledge, belief, and obedience of the Lord God Himself and His Word. There are no 'magical' formulas or rituals that bypass this. Yet regarding his book Rick Warren confidently declares:

"The next 40 days will transform *your* life." (*PDL*; p. 10)

Eight examples are given from the Bible in an effort to justify his premises regarding 40-day periods (these examples are listed on p. 10 of *PDL*). Not one of his examples, which he has removed from their scriptural context, supports his unscriptural premises. However, some of these examples when examined in their scriptural context actually warn against following what the majority is doing.

- **"Noah's life was transformed by 40 days of rain."** The 40 days of rain were actually God's purpose itself. The 40 days brought the flood of God's *judgment* on the disobedient world and destroyed it. Thankfully, Noah did not follow the majority, or we would not exist. As a result of following God rather than the crowd, he had found God's grace (see Genesis 6:8). So God prepared Noah ahead of time in the years *preceding* the 40 days so that his life would be saved.

In addition, Scripture says nothing about these 40 days bringing about transformation in Noah's life, so why claim that the days it actually rained are more significant to Noah than the 150 days the waters prevailed upon the earth or the 370 days he was on the Ark?

- **"Moses was transformed by 40 days on Mount Sinai."** God's purpose was to deliver the Israelites from the oppressive Egyptians and then bring them into the Promised Land. Moses had already been obediently following God as a result of his transforming walk with God in the land of Midian. Rick Warren himself even wrote, "The Bible is filled with examples of how God uses a long process to develop character, especially in leaders. *He took eighty years to prepare Moses,* including forty in the wilderness" (*PDL*; p. 222; emphasis added)!

God specifically prepared Moses for His purpose not in the 40 days but in front of the burning bush. By the time Moses spent 40 days on Mount Sinai, God had already used Moses to fulfill the first part of His purpose. In addition, Scripture does not record that any transformation occurred in Moses' life on Mount Sinai to prepare him for God's purposes.

Food for thought: In neither of the two sets of 40 days on Mount Sinai nor in front of the burning bush did God reveal Himself to Moses in the context of community. He was *alone* when face to face with God. For Rick Warren to say that transformation occurred when Moses was on Mount Sinai *alone* is to contradict his own communitarian principles in *The Purpose Driven Life*!

Rick Warren's numerous internal inconsistencies and contradictions clearly reveal that his book is not firmly founded on the unchanging and consistent truth of the Holy Scriptures but, rather, is **"tossed to and fro, and carried about with every wind of doctrine"** (Ephesians 4:14).

Incidentally, when Moses was with God on Mount Sinai, Aaron had assisted the "community" in adopting the ways of the world in its worship. The result of their having **"turned aside quickly out of the way which I commanded them"** (Exodus 32:8) was God's severe judgment. About 3,000 men were killed, God blotted the names of those who had sinned out of His book, and then He plagued the people (see Exodus 32:28, 33, and 35).

♦ **"The spies were transformed by 40 days in the Promised Land."** The tragic truth is that the spies (excluding Joshua and Caleb who remained faithful to God in walking by faith and not by sight) were sinfully transformed by their 40 days of walking by sight and not by faith. The spies were frightened by what they saw during the 40 days they spied out the land God promised them. As a result, they frightened the Israelites and turned them *against* God's purposes (see Numbers 13:31-14:12).

God's *judgment* was the consequence of this 40-day transformation. God killed the spies with a plague because they tried to *thwart* God's purpose after their 40 days. God's preparation of all the spies was His word, yet only two spies believed and followed God. In addition, because the Israelites heeded the majority rather than the two who tried to get them to heed God's word, they were forbidden to enter the Promised Land for 40 years so that this generation could die off first (see Numbers 14:26-38). Yet nowhere does Rick Warren say the spies were transformed in anything other than a good way by their 40 days.

That these spies were transformed into plague-infested corpses should be heeded as a warning for those who think only good transformations can come out of 40-day regimes. In the name of purpose, churches are heeding the majority and are now walking by sight rather than by the faith and obedience of God's Word. What they see in the world (e.g., its successful pragmatic ways and aversions to "traditional" Christianity) determines how they "do church." By the way, anyone who thinks plagues are only for the Old Testament time period should carefully read Revelation 18:4.

♦ **"David was transformed by Goliath's 40-day challenge."** God's Word does not clarify how many days David actually sees Goliath. However, the *first* time that David sees Goliath he begins to speak up about killing him, so it is more likely that David saw only a few days, if not just one day, of Goliath's challenge (see 1 Samuel 17).

Contrary to supporting Rick Warren's premises, this passage is another example of 40 days being a *result* of sin: The Israelites (the majority) did not trust God and cowered before Goliath for an entire 40 days before David finally came and killed him in faith!

David had already been transformed by his walk with God (see 1 Samuel 13:14, 16:7, 13). When faced with Goliath, David said he knew God would deliver him into his hands because God had already enabled him to kill a lion and a bear (see 1 Samuel 17:32-37). God had prepared David *ahead* of time to fulfill His purpose of slaying Goliath and putting an end to the Israelites' 40 days.

♦ **"Elijah was transformed when God gave him 40 days of strength from a single meal."** This took place when Israel's leaders had led the people astray into the worship of false gods. Elijah had just killed the false prophets, and Jezebel threatened to kill him. After God's angel had given him two meals, Elijah traveled 40 days to Horeb, the mount of God. It was there at Horeb that he communed with God and told Him that God's children had forsaken His covenant, thrown down His altars, and killed His prophets. Although Elijah believed he was the only one left who was still following God, God let him know that He had reserved a remnant of 7,000 who had not bowed the knee to the false god the majority were following. (See 1 Kings 18-19.)

This 40-day period was near the end of Elijah's faithful service to God and were traveling days in between serving God and communing with God. Scripture does not say anything about these 40 days being a preparation of God's purposes or causing transformation in the life of Elijah. This is yet another example of adding to Scripture what God did not put in, which twists Scripture to fit man's purposes.

♦ **"The entire city of Nineveh was transformed when God gave the people 40 days to change."** When Jonah finally obeyed God and told Nineveh that it would be overthrown in 40 days if they did not repent, Scripture does not say that Nineveh waited the entire 40 days to repent. It merely records that after Jonah **"began to enter into the city a day's journey"** the people believed God and repented (see Jonah 3).

Yes, God chose to give them 40 days to repent, but the 40 days given to them were not the moving force behind Nineveh's "transformation." It was their belief and acceptance of the Word of God regarding their sin and God's impending judgment that caused them to repent. This should be thoroughly heeded today, as the signs of God's impending judgment rapidly increase in our own generation. Incidentally, the city's repentance put an end to the 40-day countdown to God's judgment.

♦ **"Jesus was empowered by 40 days in the wilderness."** Scripture has been abominably twisted in this choice for a supporting example of his premise. God's Word states that in the wilderness Jesus was **"being forty days tempted of the devil"** (Luke 4:2; see also Mark 1:13). Nowhere throughout all of Scripture does God even hint that being tempted by the devil *empowers* anyone! Besides, if these 40 days "empowered" Jesus physically, then the angels would not have needed to minister to Jesus immediately afterwards (see Matthew 4:11 and Mark 1:13). Furthermore, if these 40 days "empowered" Jesus spiritually, then Jesus would not have been fully God manifest in the flesh.

> *"And without controversy great is the mystery of godliness: <u>God was manifest in the flesh</u>, justified in the Spirit, seen of angels, preached unto the Gentiles, believed on in the world, received up into glory." (1 Timothy 3:16)*

> *"Beware lest any man spoil you through philosophy and vain deceit, after the tradition of men, after the rudiments of the world, and not after Christ. For in him dwelleth <u>all the fulness of the Godhead</u> bodily." (Colossians 2:8-9)*

To even hint that the devil and his temptations were a source of power for the Lord Jesus Christ is appalling, to say the very least! Contrarily, Jesus was already prepared when His 40 days of temptation came.

- **"The disciples were transformed by 40 days with Jesus after his resurrection."** Just before Jesus ascended into heaven, *after* the 40 days He was with the disciples, Jesus told them to wait in Jerusalem until they were ***"endued with power from on high"*** (Luke 24:49; see also Acts 1:3-9). On the day of Pentecost the disciples were transformed by the filling of the Holy Spirit, which was the preparation for God's purpose of using them to preach the Gospel of Christ to the world. It is important to note that Pentecost is a Jewish festival meaning "fiftieth" because it was celebrated on the 50th day. This example as well fails to support Rick Warren's claims.

Again, God's Word is clear that transforming and life-changing power is found through the knowledge, belief, and obedience of the Lord God Himself and His Word, rightly divided. Yet, grievously, Rick Warren has taken portions of the Word of God and twisted them, giving them new meanings apart from their Scriptural context. He does this throughout his purpose-driven "manifesto" and Paradigm in the attempt to justify his faulty premises and fulfill his purposes. Nevertheless, the masses have fallen in step behind him, his purposes, and his 40 Days campaigns. They have accepted Rick Warren's claims that his "spiritual journey" is all about God and His purposes.

God's Purposes are *Man*-centered?

"He [God] has clearly revealed his five purposes for our lives through the Bible." (*PDL*; p. 20)

"It's not about **you**." (*PDL*; p. 17; emphasis added)

*R*ick Warren's personal list of God's purposes for our lives consists only of the following five purposes, which he has clearly centered around "you":

PURPOSE #1: **You** Were Planned for God's Pleasure
PURPOSE #2: **You** Were Formed for God's Family
PURPOSE #3: **You** Were Created to Become like Christ
PURPOSE #4: **You** Were Shaped for Serving God
PURPOSE #5: **You** Were Made for a Mission

Looking at each of these five purposes, a basic understanding of elementary grammar clearly shows that *you*, not God, *are the subject*. In sentence structure, the subject is what the sentence is about. Regardless of his repeated claims to the contrary, each of the five purposes are about *you*—not only here but also in his descriptions of them.

According to his "manifesto," these five purposes can be summed up in worship, fellowship, discipleship, ministry, and evangelism. The God-centered *scriptural* definitions of these five things are indeed part of the many purposes God has for us. However, a great deal of man-centered theology and other unscriptural errors have been included in the purpose-driven definitions. *You*, not God, are the subject of this "spiritual journey." God is merely the means to purpose, meaning, and significance in life.

God's Word is clear that the nature of God is the basis for what He wants from us. Therefore, increasing our knowledge of God Himself also increases our knowledge of His purposes. Yet not much is said in *The Purpose Driven Life* about the nature of God. In a *man*-centered "spiritual journey," helping people deepen their knowledge of *God* isn't the primary issue.

Chapter Four

Purpose #1: You Were Planned for God's Pleasure

Worship That Is about *You* Is Not Worship of *God*

"Bringing enjoyment to God, living for his pleasure, is the first purpose of your life. When you fully understand this truth, you will never again have a problem with feeling insignificant. It proves *your* worth." (*PDL*; p. 63; emphasis added)

"Bringing pleasure to God is called 'worship.'" (*PDL*; p. 64)

"You only bring him [God] enjoyment by being you. Anytime you reject *any* part of yourself, you are rejecting God's wisdom and sovereignty in creating you." (*PDL*; p. 75; emphasis added)

Worship of *God* is not about being *you*. True worship of *God* is completely about the nature and worthiness of *God*, *not* about who *you* are or *your* worth. Furthermore, true worship of *God* is found in the fear and reverence that comes when *we* recognize and enjoy *God* for Who *God* really is, *not* when *God* enjoys who *we* are! Exactly *who* is worshipping *whom* in the purpose-driven definition of worship?

> "Give unto the LORD the glory due unto his name; worship the LORD in the beauty of holiness." (Psalm 29:2)

True worship of God that *pleases* God also consists of living a life of faith, righteousness, and obedience because *God* is worthy.

> "That ye might walk worthy of the Lord unto all pleasing, being fruitful in every good work, and increasing in the knowledge of God." (Colossians 1:10)

"I know also, my God, that thou triest the heart, and hast pleasure in uprightness . . . ." (1 Chronicles 29:17)

"So then they that are in the flesh cannot please God." (Romans 8:8)

Although the Lord Jesus Christ and His Word say otherwise, according to Rick Warren's counsel we are not to reject *any* part of ourselves. In fact, he admonishes us to realize that God Himself *wants* us to *worship Him* by unloading all of our sinful, fleshly emotions on Him, "holding back nothing" of what we feel:

> "In the Bible, the friends of God were honest about their feelings, **often complaining, second-guessing, accusing, and arguing with their Creator. God, however, didn't seem to be bothered by this frankness**; *in fact, he encouraged it*." (*PDL*; p.93; emphasis added)

> "**Tell God *exactly how you feel*.** Pour out your heart to God. **Unload every emotion** that you're feeling . . . . God can handle your doubt, anger, fear, grief, confusion, and questions." (*PDL*; p. 110; emphasis added)

> "To instruct us in candid honesty, God gave us the book of Psalms—**a worship manual, full of ranting, raving, doubts, fears, resentments,** and deep passions combined with thanksgiving, praise, and statements of faith. Every possible emotion is catalogued in the Psalms. When you read the emotional confessions of David and others, **realize this is how God wants you to worship him—holding back nothing of what you feel**." [!] (*PDL*; p. 94; bold added)

> "Can God handle that kind of frank, intense honesty from you? Absolutely! . . . What may appear as *audacity* God views as *authenticity*." (*PDL*; p. 94)

This aspect of Rick Warren's definition of "worship" is plainly all about *you*. We are free to be exactly who we are in the flesh, treat the loving Almighty Lord God far worse than dirt, and then proceed to the epitome of audacious *and* authentic defiance in referring to this as *worship*! *This* is what brings the Almighty Lord God *pleasure* and is what He is worthy of? *This* is part of Rick Warren's first and foremost purpose for why we are here.

> "Ye have wearied the Lord with your words. Yet ye say, Wherein have we wearied him? When ye say, Every one that doeth evil is good in the sight of the Lord, and he delighteth in them; or, Where is the God of judgment?" (Malachi 2:17)

> "The foolishness of man perverteth his way: and his heart fretteth against the Lord." (Proverbs 19:3)

God makes it clear throughout His Word that He is not even close to being *pleased* with, nor does He even remotely *encourage* "resentments," "ranting," "raving," "complaining," or "accusing" Him. Rick Warren's dangerous man-centered claim can only be derived at by twisting, ignoring, and taking unholy scissors to a multitude of Scriptures. "Candid honesty" or not, God does not "encourage" these sins, which these people, for example, definitely regretted (e.g., see also Numbers 11:18-20, 33):

> "And when the people complained, it displeased the Lord: and the Lord heard it; and his anger was kindled; and the fire of the Lord burnt among them, and consumed them that were in the uttermost parts of the camp." (Numbers 11:1)

> "Woe unto him that striveth with his Maker! Let the potsherd strive with the potsherds of the earth. Shall the clay say to him that fashioneth it, What makest thou? or thy work, He hath no hands?" (Isaiah 45:9)

> "Nay but, O man, who art thou that repliest against God? Shall the thing formed say to him that formed it, Why hast thou made me thus?" (Romans 9:20)

> "Moreover the Lord answered Job, and said, Shall he that contendeth with the Almighty instruct him? he that reproveth God, let him answer it. Then Job answered the Lord, and said, Behold, I am vile; what shall I answer thee? I will lay mine hand upon my mouth. Once have I spoken; but I will not answer: yea, twice; but I will proceed no further. Then answered the Lord unto Job out of the whirlwind, and said, Gird up thy loins now like a man: I will demand of thee, and declare thou unto me. Wilt thou also disannul my judgment? <u>wilt thou condemn me, that thou mayest be righteous?</u>" (Job 40:1-8)

These people will also regret their man-centered "frank, intense honesty" with God:

> "... Behold, the Lord cometh with ten thousands of his saints, to execute judgment upon all, and to convince all that are ungodly among them of all their ungodly deeds which they have ungodly committed, and of all their hard speeches which ungodly sinners have spoken against him. These are murmurers, complainers, walking after their own lusts; and their mouth speaketh great swelling words, having men's persons in admiration because of advantage." (Jude 1:14-16)

Contrary to leaders today, the apostle Paul gives genuine wise counsel that needs to be carefully heeded:

> "Neither let us tempt Christ, as some of them also tempted, and were destroyed of serpents. Neither murmur ye, as some of them also murmured, and were destroyed of the destroyer. Now all these things happened unto them for examples: and they are written for our admonition, upon whom the ends of the world are come. Wherefore let him that thinketh he standeth take heed lest he fall." (1 Corinthians 10:9-12)

On the other hand, following Rick Warren's counsel on how to "worship" will result in God's anger and displeasure, according to His Holy Scriptures. True worship kneels before the Almighty Lord God in awe and reverence for Who He is. This is the opposite of Rick Warren's man-centered "manifesto" that exalts who man is above the holy Lord God.

> "Exalt ye the LORD our God, and worship at his footstool; for he is holy." (Psalm 99:5)

> "God is greatly to be feared in the assembly of the saints, and to be had in reverence of all them that are about him." (Psalm 89:7)

> "Let all the earth fear the LORD: let all the inhabitants of the world stand in awe of him. For he spake, and it was done; he commanded, and it stood fast." (Psalm 33:8-9)

> *"And all the inhabitants of the earth are reputed as nothing: and he doeth according to his will in the army of heaven, and among the inhabitants of the earth: and none can stay his hand, or say unto him, What doest thou?"* (Daniel 4:35)

"Worship" mixed with the ugliness of man's fleshly emotions is anything but holy, and no one, least of all the Almighty Lord God, deserves to be treated in such an irreverent manner. Rick Warren has done exactly what he says we should *not* do:

> "But we cannot just create our own comfortable or politically correct image of God and worship it. That is idolatry." (*PDL*; p. 101)

I couldn't agree more. Yet *you* and *the purposes* of God, according to Rick Warren's personal understanding of them, continue to be placed above *the Person* of God. Anything placed above God Himself is idolatry, especially so when fear of God, reverence, truth, and holiness are sacrificed in the process. And that includes music.

Offering the Strange Fire of Profane Music Is Not Worship of God

> "The Church has sprung a leak and the world is leaking into the Church."
> —A.W. Tozer[1]

Music is just one more area in Rick Warren's worldly Purpose-Driven movement in which he has done exactly what he says we should *not* do. He has created his own comfortable image of God that lets him do what he likes:

> "God loves all kinds of music because he invented it all . . . You probably don't like it all, but God does! If it is offered to God in spirit and truth, it is an act of worship." (*PDL*; p. 65)

> "But God likes variety and enjoys it all.

> "There is no such thing as 'Christian' music; there are only Christian lyrics. It is the words that make a song sacred, not the tune." (*PDL*; p. 66)

First, "Christian lyrics" are increasingly man-centered and error-laden and as such would not be offered to God in spirit and in truth. Second, synthesizing

"Christian lyrics" with the profane noises ("tunes") that 'musicians' such as death metal bands and other bands in darkness create while they are stoned and blaspheming God, etcetera, would never make the songs from this wicked culture *sacred* and enjoyed by God! If you don't think "Christian music" is extreme enough to rival 'music' from cultures of darkness, then you have never had the displeasure, to put it mildly, of hearing modern "Christian" bands scream Jesus' name with a voice that sounds possessed, with a "tune" to match.

> *"[I]t takes all kinds of churches to reach all kinds of people . . . . In just the area of music alone, imagine all the styles of music needed to reach all the different cultures of our world."*—Rick Warren[2]

> "Warren's emphasis on approachable Christianity is reflected at Saddleback, where worshippers can choose from nearly two dozen services that feature different styles of live music, from heavy metal to reggae to hula."—*Associated Press*, 4/9/05[3]

Worldly music (complete with blatant secular lyrics) and "worship styles" that appeal to the flesh rather than the spirit is a big part of the purpose-driven transformation in churches. Purpose-driven "worship" is not about Who God is, therefore the "worship style" of today's churches must match *the people*:

> "What matters is that your worship style matches the people you are seeking to reach . . ."—Rick Warren[4]

> "'I'm never going to deny what I believe, but I've got to say it in a way that makes sense to the MTV generation in a postmodern world,' Warren says. 'Traditional churches think I'm changing the message, but all I'm doing is changing the method.'"—*Chicago Sun-Times*, 3/25/05[5]

> "I discovered that, of course, it takes all kinds of churches to reach all kinds of people. There is more than one way to grow a church and I say if you are getting the job done I like the way you are doing it. The only wrong way is the one way that you think that everybody should do it your way.

> "What I began to see is that God uses all kinds of styles, all kinds of methods, all kinds of formats to reach all kinds of people."—Rick Warren[6]

"The Purpose Driven model supports you as your church **matches the worship style of those you are targeted to reach** in the community."—PurposeDriven (Emphasis added)[7]

And what exactly is the "worship" style of the MTV generation?! No wonder church services today resemble the world! It is not the image of *Christ* that churches are deliberately conforming to. This is clearly *all about you*, or mankind.

> *"Professing themselves to be wise, they became fools, and changed the glory of the uncorruptible God into an image made like to corruptible man.... Who changed the truth of God into a lie, and worshipped and served the creature more than the Creator, who is blessed for ever. Amen." (Romans 1:22-23, 25)*

In *The Purpose-Driven Life*, Rick Warren says:

> "There is a right and wrong way to worship. The Bible says, 'Let us be grateful and worship God in a way that will please him.' [endnote: Hebrews 12:28 (TEV)]" (*PDL*; p. 100)

He even deleted the right way to worship from the verse he quotes on the subject. This verse specifically gives the right way, and thereby also the wrong way, to worship and serve God:

> *"Wherefore we receiving a kingdom which cannot be moved, let us have grace, whereby we may serve God <u>acceptably with reverence and godly fear</u>: For our God is a consuming fire." (Hebrews 12:28-29)*

The version he quotes even ends the verse with, "with reverence and awe," which he deleted. This deletion is consistent with today's man-centered "worship." The reverence and fear of God has obviously and purposefully been removed in order to cater to the unbelieving world.

> "Human wisdom delights to trim and arrange the doctrines of the cross into a system more artificial and more congenial with the depraved tastes of fallen nature; instead, however, of improving the gospel carnal wisdom pollutes it, until it becomes another gospel, and not the truth of God at all."—Charles H. Spurgeon[8]

The Lord God is not pleased with nor does He accept everything that is offered to Him in worship. He did not respect or accept Cain's offering (see Genesis 4), and He did not accept the **"strange fire"** offered to Him by Nadab and Abihu. In fact, He killed them with fire for offering it (see Leviticus 10:1-2). Whether or not they believed their offering was offered in spirit and truth was irrelevant. *What* they were offering was disobedience (therefore apart from truth) and was not considered by God to be an act of worship.

Likewise, modern "worship" is not worship in *spirit* and in *truth*; it is "worship" in the *flesh* and in *relativism*. "Worship" that "matches the people" so is tailored according to who the *unbelieving* world is rather than Who God is, is indeed creating one's own comfortable image of God to idolatrously worship. This has a great deal in common with the Israelites worship of the golden calf -- a worship style that led to the severe judgment of God resulting in the death of thousands and was then followed by a plague (see Exodus 32, especially verses 28 and 35).

God commands us to worship Him **"in the beauty of holiness"** (see Psalm 29:2 and 96:9). Rebellious refusal to separate from the things, beliefs, and ways of the flesh and the world and the profane is the opposite of holiness. Besides, offering profane things of the flesh to God—from "candid honesty" to "all kinds of music" and everything in between—is *always* about *you*, never about God.

> *"Be not deceived; God is not mocked: for whatsoever a man soweth, that shall he also reap. For he that soweth to his flesh shall of the flesh reap corruption; but he that soweth to the Spirit shall of the Spirit reap life everlasting." (Galatians 6:7-8)*

> *"Love not the world, neither the things that are in the world. If any man love the world, the love of the Father is not in him. For all that is in the world, the lust of the flesh, and the lust of the eyes, and the pride of life, is not of the Father, but is of the world. And the world passeth away, and the lust thereof: but he that doeth the will of God abideth for ever." (1 John 2:15-17)*

It's not how *the masses* view something that makes it right or wrong; it's how *God* views it. And God knows why the ways and things of the world please the world. God says in His Word, **"And be not conformed to this world"** (Romans 12:2) and, **"Let every one that nameth the name of Christ depart from iniquity"** (2 Timothy 2:19). Nevertheless, history continues to repeat itself -- **"but every man did that which was right in his own eyes"** (Judges 17:6 and 21:25).

In "Why We Are Lukewarm About Christ's Return," A.W. Tozer aptly described Christianity's predilection for things of the world:

> "Again, in these times religion has become jolly good fun right here in this present world, and what's the hurry about heaven anyway? Christianity, contrary to what some had thought, is another and higher form of entertainment. Christ has done all the suffering. He has shed all the tears and carried all the crosses; we have but to enjoy the benefits of His heartbreak in the form of religious pleasures modeled after the world but carried on in the name of Jesus . . . .
>
> "History reveals that times of suffering for the Church have also been times of looking upward. Tribulation has always sobered God's people and encouraged them to look for and yearn after the return of their Lord. Our present preoccupation with this world may be a warning of bitter days to come. God will wean us from the earth some way—the easy way if possible, the hard way if necessary. It is up to us."[9]

Charles Spurgeon also admonished:

> "Beware of the leaven of worldly pleasure, for its working is silent but sure, and a little of it will leaven the whole lump. Keep up the distinction between a Christian and an unbeliever and make it clearer every day . . . .
>
> "Avoid the appearance of evil. 'But we must not be too rigid,' says one. There is no fear of that in these days. You will never go too far in holiness, nor become too like your Lord Jesus. If anybody accuses you of being too strict and precise, do not grieve but try to deserve the charge. **I cannot suppose that at the last great day our Lord Jesus Christ will say to anyone, 'You were not worldly enough. You were too jealous over your conduct, and did not sufficiently conform to the world.'** No, my brethren, such a wrong is impossible. He Who said, 'Be ye therefore perfect, even as your Father which is in heaven is perfect,' has set before you a standard beyond which you can never go.
>
> "'Well, but,' says one, 'are we to have no enjoyments?' My dear friend, the enjoyments which are prepared for Christians are many and great, but they never include sin and folly. Do you call vice and folly amusements? . . .

"'But,' you say, 'I would greatly enjoy a little of the pleasures of sin.' Judge yourselves, then, to be falsely called children of God . . . .

"As for your Lord's work, be bound to the altar of Christ and be united for ever to Him, and I am sure you will not find that you are losers by giving up worldly pleasures." (Emphasis added)[10]

"For the grace of God that bringeth salvation hath appeared to all men, teaching us that, denying ungodliness and worldly lusts, we should live soberly, righteously, and godly, in this present world; looking for that blessed hope, and the glorious appearing of the great God and our Saviour Jesus Christ; who gave himself for us, that he might redeem us from all iniquity, and purify unto himself a peculiar people, zealous of good works. These things speak, and exhort, and rebuke with all authority. Let no man despise thee." (Titus 2:11-15)

"Christianizing" or "churching" things of the world, as well as pleasing the world under the guise of pleasing God, is still sowing to the flesh, and God is not mocked. People will reap what they sow. In "Feeding Sheep or Amusing Goats?" Charles Spurgeon further admonished:

"The devil has seldom done a cleverer thing than hinting to the church that part of their mission is to provide entertainment for the people, with a view to winning them.

"From speaking out as the Puritans did, the church has gradually toned down her testimony, then winked at and excused the frivolities of the day. Then she tolerated them in her borders. Now she has adopted them under the plea of reaching the masses . . . .

"If it is a Christian work, why did not Christ speak of it? 'Go ye into all the world and preach the gospel to every creature' (Mark 16:15). That is clear enough. So it would have been if He had added, 'and provide amusement for those who do not relish the gospel.' No such words, however, are to be found . . . .

"Then again, 'He gave some, apostles; and some, prophets; and some evangelists; and some pastors and teachers . . . , for the work of the ministry' (Eph. 4:11-12).

Where do entertainers come in? . . . **Were the prophets persecuted because they amused the people or because they refused?** . . .

"Again, providing amusement is in direct antagonism to the teaching and life of Christ and all his apostles. What was the attitude of the church to the world? Ye are the salt (Matt. 5:13), not the sugar candy—something the world will spit out not swallow . . . .

"Had Christ introduced more of the bright and pleasant elements into his mission, he would have been more popular when they went back . . . I do not hear him say, 'Run after these people Peter and tell them we will have a different style of service tomorrow, something short and attractive with little preaching. We will have a pleasant evening for the people. Tell them they will be sure to enjoy it. Be quick Peter, we must get the people somehow.' Jesus pitied sinners, sighed and wept over them, but never sought to amuse them.

"In vain will the Epistles be searched to find any trace of this gospel of amusement! Their message is, 'Come out, keep out, keep clean out!' . . . They had boundless confidence in the gospel and employed no other weapon.

"After Peter and John were locked up for preaching, the church had a prayer meeting but they did not pray, 'Lord grant unto thy servants that by a wise and discriminating use of innocent recreation we may show these people how happy we are.' If they ceased not from preaching Christ, they had not time for arranging entertainments. Scattered by persecution, they went everywhere preaching the gospel . . . . Lord, clear the church of all the rot and rubbish the devil has imposed on her, and bring us back to apostolic methods." (Emphasis added)[11]

"The Foolishness of Preaching"

When worship is no longer about *God*, preaching becomes "outdated":

"The *message* must never change, but the *methods* must change. If you change the message, you are a heretic . . . . At the same time, however, I also believe that if you continue to share it in an outdated mode, for instance, like a preaching style that was effective a hundred years ago, *you* are actually making the message watered down because people can't hear it."—Rick Warren[12]

"Are you being faithful to God's Word if you insist on communicating it in an outdated style? . . . I contend that when a church continues to use methods that no longer work, it is being unfaithful to Christ!"—Rick Warren[13]

Methods of relativism will inevitably change a message of absolutism. And this is exactly what is happening.

Unbelievably, preachers of "a hundred years ago," such as Charles Spurgeon, if alive today and preaching in their "outdated" "preaching style" would be considered guilty of *watering down the Gospel* and *being unfaithful to Christ*. Yet people today who cut gaping holes in the Gospel and change the message by changing the methods to cater to the unbelieving world *are highly praised, modeled after, and viewed as faithful to God's Word*!

Today's Christianity clearly doesn't realize that God's message and method are tied together because of the nature of *His light*, which is God Himself and His Word. Preaching the Word of God is God's message *and* method because it is in the light of *God*, not in the ways of the world, that mankind is enlightened in understanding His truth.

> "O send out <u>thy light and thy truth</u>: let <u>them</u> lead me; let <u>them</u> bring me unto thy holy hill, and to thy tabernacles." (Psalm 43:3)

> "<u>Being born again, not of corruptible seed, but of incorruptible, by the word of God</u>, which liveth and abideth for ever. For all flesh is as grass, and all the glory of man as the flower of grass. The grass withereth, and the flower thereof falleth away: But the word of the Lord endureth for ever. <u>And this is the word which by the gospel is preached unto you</u>." (I Peter 1:23-25)

> "Even the mystery which hath been hid from ages and from generations, but now is made manifest to his saints: To whom God would make known what is the riches of the glory of this mystery among the Gentiles; which is <u>Christ in you, the hope of glory: Whom we preach, warning every man, and teaching every man in all wisdom</u>; that we may present every man perfect in Christ Jesus." (Colossians 1:26-28)

> "That was the true Light, which lighteth <u>every man</u> that cometh into the world." (John 1:9)

Nevertheless, preaching is considered to be old-fashioned foolishness by today's leaders who prefer to follow the world's 'wisdom' and cater to the world's chosen wickedness. Yet God Himself is the One Who chose **"the foolishness of preaching"**:

> "<u>For the preaching of the cross is to them that perish foolishness;</u> but unto us which are saved it is the power of God. For it is written, I will destroy the wisdom of the wise, and will bring to nothing the understanding of the prudent. Where is the wise? where is the scribe? where is the disputer of this world? hath not God made foolish the wisdom of this world? For after that in the wisdom of God the world by wisdom knew not God, <u>it pleased God by the foolishness of preaching to save them that believe. For the Jews require a sign, and the Greeks seek after wisdom: But we preach Christ crucified, unto the Jews a stumblingblock, and unto the Greeks foolishness;</u> but unto them which are called, both Jews and Greeks, Christ the power of God, and the wisdom of God. Because the foolishness of God is wiser than men; and the weakness of God is stronger than men. For ye see your calling, brethren, how that not many wise men after the flesh, not many mighty, not many noble, are called: <u>But God hath chosen the foolish things of the world to confound the wise;</u> and God hath chosen the weak things of the world to confound the things which are mighty; and base things of the world, and things which are despised, hath God chosen, yea, and things which are not, to bring to nought things that are: That no flesh should glory in his presence." (I Corinthians 1:18-29)

The apostle Paul did not cater to what the Jews or the Greeks wanted. Even knowing that his message *and method* would be a *stumblingblock* and considered *foolishness* to them, he served God, not man, and preached Christ crucified whether they would hear or not. Obedience, not results, is the greater issue.

> "But God forbid that I should glory, save in the cross of our Lord Jesus Christ, by whom the world is crucified unto me, and I unto the world." (Galatians 6:14)

The apostle Paul's faithfulness was to God and to His Word, not to the world. This refusal to compromise led to his and the other apostles being **"made a spectacle** *unto the world,"* viewed as *"fools," "despised"* and *"defamed,"* and *"made as the filth of the world"* and *"the offscouring of all things"* (see I Corinthians 4:9-10, 13).

There is quite a difference between how the world viewed God's faithful back then who *"hazarded their lives for the name of our Lord Jesus Christ"* (Acts 15:26) and how it views many of Christianity's leaders today! The world loves getting its itching ears tickled, and compromising leaders today are quick to please, unlike the true apostles who refused to stop *preaching* the Lord Jesus Christ even when covered with bloody stripes.

> *". . . and when they had called the apostles, and beaten them, they commanded that they should not speak in the name of Jesus, and let them go. And they departed from the presence of the council, rejoicing that they were counted worthy to suffer shame for his name. And daily in the temple, and in every house, they ceased not to teach and preach Jesus Christ." (Acts 5:40-42)*

Unlike the leaders today who are afraid to offend anyone, the apostles suffered all of this willingly, refusing to be ashamed of the Rock of Offence and His truth that greatly offend the world.

> "<u>Be not thou therefore ashamed of the testimony of our Lord</u>, nor of me his prisoner: <u>but be thou partaker of the afflictions of the gospel</u> according to the power of God; who hath saved us, and called us with an holy calling, not according to our works, but according to his own purpose and grace, which was given us in Christ Jesus before the world began, but is now made manifest by the appearing of our Saviour Jesus Christ, who hath abolished death, and hath brought life and immortality to light through the gospel: Whereunto I am appointed a preacher, and an apostle, and a teacher of the Gentiles. <u>For the which cause I also suffer these things: nevertheless I am not ashamed</u>: for I know whom I have believed, and am persuaded that he is able to keep that which I have committed unto him against that day. Hold fast <u>the form of sound words</u>, which thou hast heard of me, in faith and love which is in Christ Jesus." (2 Timothy 1:8-13)

It is God's message *and* methods that save, not the world's. This is true in *every* generation. Tickling the world's itching ears and calling its ways "worship" will not change anyone's aversion to hearing the true message. Nor does this bring pleasure to God.

> ***"And he said unto them, Ye are they which justify yourselves before men; but God knoweth your hearts: for that which is highly esteemed among men is abomination in the sight of God." (Luke 16:15)***

In his generation, Tozer also faced "advocates of compromise" who sought to make the world "feel at home" in the churches:

> "Any evangelism which by appeal to common interests and chatter about current events seeks to establish a common ground where the sinner can feel at home is as false as the altars of Baal ever were . . . .
>
> "One of the most popular current errors, and . . . being carried on in evangelical circles these days, is the notion that as times change the church must change with them. Christians must adapt their methods by the demands of the people . . . . go along with them—give them what they want. 'The message is the same, only the method changes,' say the advocates of compromise."—A.W. Tozer[14]

Yet Tozer stood his ground against the crowd who insisted on the necessity of conforming to the times and finding common ground with everybody:

> "The fish that goes along with the current hasn't any trouble with the current, but as soon as he starts the other way the current gets sore at him. Just as long as you go the way the wind blows, everybody will say you're very fine and commend you for being deeply religious. If you decide to go God's way instead of the way the wind blows they'll say that your roof leaks or that something has happened to you that you're a fanatic. You can go along with the times or you can be like Zechariah and Elizabeth and refuse to go along with the times. Personally I've decided that a long time ago. They say that if you don't conform to the times and find a common ground for getting along with everybody that nobody will listen to you. The more I'm nonconformist the more people want to hear me."—A.W. Tozer[15]
>
> "I've been told that I've missed the boat but I reply that I wasn't trying to catch that boat. That boat and a lot of others like it can go on without me and I'll be quite happy. We can conform to the religion of our times if we want to.

"I weigh 145 pounds dripping wet, but I stand here to tell you that I'm a nonconformist, twice born, and a rebel and I will not conform to the times. Up to now I've been able to get a hearing and refused to conform to the times. But if a day ever comes when to conform to the times is the price you have to pay to be heard, then I'll go out and start where I started before on the street corner and preach there. But I won't conform to the times.

"They say you are supposed to do it. They say, 'Don't you know we have the same message but it's just different times we're living in.' I know the voice of the serpent when I hear it. The hiss of the serpent is in that and I recognize that. So we can either conform or we can withdraw from the whole business, and Paul says, 'From such turn away.'"—A.W. Tozer[16]

"Heresy of method may be as deadly as heresy of message."—A.W. Tozer[17]

The unfruitful works of darkness used to be warned against by Christianity's leaders. Now, Christianity largely dismisses the earnest warnings of the few with laughter or antagonism or marginalization, while it participates in the works of darkness and calls them "worship."

"Only let your conversation be as it becometh the gospel of Christ: that whether I come and see you, or else be absent, I may hear of your affairs, that ye stand fast in one spirit, with one mind striving together for <u>the faith of the gospel</u>." (Philippians 1:27)

"Wherefore gird up the loins of your mind, be sober, and hope to the end for the grace that is to be brought unto you at the revelation of Jesus Christ; as obedient children, not fashioning yourselves according to the former lusts in your ignorance: but as he which hath called you is holy, so be ye holy in all manner of conversation; because it is written, Be ye holy; for I am holy." (1 Peter 1:13-16)

"Thus saith the Lord, thy Redeemer, the Holy One of Israel; I am the Lord thy God which teacheth thee to profit, which leadeth thee by the way that thou shouldest go. O that thou hadst hearkened to my commandments! then had thy peace been as a river, and thy righteousness as the waves of the sea." (Isaiah 48:17-18)

◆ *Chapter Five* ◆

Purpose #2:
You Were Formed for God's Family

"The Local Church Is the Body of Christ"

*T*here definitely is a global transformation taking place. Rick Warren's extremely popular Purpose-Driven Paradigm is greatly facilitating the transformation of *Christ*ianity into *Church*ianity; his comments about Jesus Christ notwithstanding. Christ is being replaced with community.

Because true *Christ*ianity follows *Christ*, Jesus Christ is the foundation of what is done and taught. On the other hand, *Church*ianity is about "doing *church*," so the church is the focus of everything that is done and taught. Following the same path as Roman Catholicism, today's Churchianity is increasingly propagating the false gospel that complete salvation is only found in and through belonging to *a church*.

> "*A* church family identifies you as a *genuine* believer. I can't claim to be following Christ if I'm not committed to any specific group of disciples." (*PDL*; p. 133; emphasis added)

Think carefully about this. In other words, we can *only* be genuine believers *who follow Christ* if we commit to a local church! On the contrary, the true and unchanged Gospel of Christ clearly declares that *faith* in the Lord Jesus Christ—not faith + commitment to a local church—is the means by which we become followers of Christ. So by *continuing in His Word* we are truly His disciples.

> "**Then said Jesus to those Jews <u>which believed on him</u>, <u>If</u> ye continue in <u>my</u> <u>word</u>, <u>then</u> are ye my disciples indeed.**" (*John 8:31*)

Nevertheless, Churchianity prefers defining the Body of Christ as the local church, rather than as individual believers in the Lord Jesus Christ.

"Acts of Mercy was founded on four spiritual pillars: . . .

"The local church is the Body of Christ, and is the best instrument to accomplish Christ's ministry in the world."—Rick and Kay Warren, Founders of Acts of Mercy[1]

Again, think carefully about this. If this "spiritual pillar" was true, then the Body of Christ would only exist in local congregations, and anyone not part of a local church would only be deceiving themselves into thinking they are genuine believers following Christ. In other words, this pillar supports Rick Warren's previous unscriptural declaration in *The Purpose-Driven Life*.

But this pillar goes even further because *un*believers easily slip into membership of local churches, and according to Rick Warren "every church is filled with pagans."[2] So if "the local church is the Body of Christ," then the Body of Christ would be filled with "pagans"!

Contrary to what is being disseminated, individual *churches* are not the Body of Christ—the Lord Jesus Christ's true Church. This is especially so as a result of this worldly Purpose-Driven Paradigm, which is working very hard to help unbelievers ("the unchurched") feel comfortable in its churches so they will keep coming.

The true Body of Christ consists only of each and every *individual* person, scattered all over the world, who is a true believer in the Lord Jesus Christ and truly born again by God's definition found in God's Word. The Body of Christ does not consist of a group of people who decided to meet together in the same local church building and commit to a *relationship* with each other, despite whether there is any adherence to God's truth.

"The importance of helping members develop friendships within your church cannot be overemphasized. *Relationships* are the glue that holds a church together."—Rick Warren[3]

"God wants his family to be known for its love more than anything else. Jesus said our love *for each other*—not our doctrinal beliefs—is our greatest witness to the world . . . .

"Relationships must have priority in your life above everything else." (*PDL*; p. 124)

Churches that are "filled with pagans" are unable to rely on the Holy Spirit to keep them together since unbelievers and pagans cannot know or receive Him. So like communities and churches in other religions (faiths), such as Mormonism, they must rely on *relationships* within these churches to keep them together. Incidentally, Mormonism developed as it similarly pedestaled and followed its own founder and leader Joseph Smith. Paul Proctor, Christian columnist for NewswithViews.com, perceptively draws the comparison:

> "The Latter Day Saints have been selling themselves like this for years - hiding their heresy behind a friendly facade of family, familiarity, amusement and marketing; like craftily using The Bible and its touching stories on television to promote The Book of Mormon as if the two go hand in hand. No wonder their churches are growing like weeds!
>
> "Baptists call them a cult; yet, when The Purpose Driven Life is presented as a companion to the Bible by a Southern Baptist pastor and his publishing company, it is proclaimed a miracle of God because of its wondrous bounty of tasty tares! And, I have no doubt that just as many newly converted Mormons, as Purposites would be ready and willing to tell you how much their lives have been dramatically changed and transformed by the writings of Joseph Smith, as those who credit Rick Warren for his teachings."[4]

It's all relative in the realm of relationships, experiences, and pragmatism.

Twisting God's Word to implement "a human relationship paradigm" is a denial of what God repeatedly and clearly said throughout His Holy Scriptures. Dean Gotcher, founder and director of the Institution for Authority Research, describes this process well:

> "The leadership of the church is shifting its paradigm from didactic to dialectic in addressing the problems found in its own fellowship and in the world. Tools utilized by Satan in his deception of Eve are being utilized by the Church Growth agenda today. **What makes this process so lethal is its utilization of scriptures to cover its agenda. It no longer focuses upon translation** which is built upon the word 'Is', it has moved through interpretation which is built upon the phrase 'I feel,' to where it is now *extrapolation* (picking and choosing and then redefining) from the word of God those scriptures which justify its desired outcome, that being

the rebuilding of the church on a human relationship paradigm." (Bold added)⁵

God never separates love from the truth, which includes His doctrine, and never elevates relationships above His Word. On the contrary, the Lord God has magnified His *truth* above *even His own name:*

> *"I will worship toward thy holy temple, and praise thy name for thy lovingkindness and for thy truth: for thou hast magnified thy word <u>above all thy name</u>." (Psalm 138:2)*

With relationships (community) given top priority, as is evidenced throughout the Purpose-Driven Paradigm, the broad way's relativism and pragmatism inevitably become the prevailing "new way of thinking and acting." But on the narrow way, relationships never supercede the truth, which is a sword of division. In actuality, exalting human relationships "above everything else" can *prevent* a person from being a true disciple or follower of Christ:

> *"Suppose ye that I am come to give peace on earth? I tell you, Nay; but rather division: For from henceforth there shall be five in one house divided, three against two, and two against three. The father shall be divided against the son, and the son against the father; the mother against the daughter, and the daughter against the mother; the mother-in-law against her daughter-in-law, and the daughter-in-law against her mother-in-law." (Luke 12:51-53)*

> *"But whosoever shall deny me before men, him will I also deny before my Father which is in heaven. Think not that I am come to send peace on earth: I came not to send peace, but a sword. For I am come to set a man at variance against his father, and the daughter against her mother, and the daughter-in-law against her mother-in-law. And a man's foes shall be they of his own household. He that loveth father or mother more than me is not worthy of me: and he that loveth son or daughter more than me is not worthy of me." (Matthew 10:33-37)*

> *"If any man come to me, and hate not his father, and mother, and wife, and children, and brethren, and sisters, yea, and his own life also, he cannot be my disciple." (Luke 14:26)*

There is no true unity apart from the truth and belief in it. The Lord Jesus Christ even acknowledged this in His prayer in John 17 about believers being one. This prayer is one which many leaders in Christianity reference while commonly and conveniently leaving out the key aspects of His prayer regarding *belief* and *truth*, such as:

> *"Sanctify them through thy truth: thy word is truth . . . . Neither pray I for these alone, but for them also which shall believe on me through their word; that they all may be one . . ." (John 17:17, 20-21)*

This truth is reiterated in the following Scripture:

> *"But we are bound to give thanks always to God for you, brethren beloved of the Lord, because God hath from the beginning chosen you to <u>salvation through sanctification of the Spirit and belief of the truth: whereunto he called you by our gospel</u>, to the obtaining of the glory of our Lord Jesus Christ. Therefore, brethren, stand fast, and hold the traditions which ye have been taught, whether by word, or our epistle." (2 Thessalonians 2:13-15)*

Jesus Christ's true Church is bound together in godly unity for all eternity *by the Holy Spirit, through a common belief in the truth*, not by human efforts of focusing on common ground and striving toward "right relations." Only the *individuals* who are true believers *within* that local church building are part of the true Church, the true Body of Christ. To refer to local churches, that consist increasingly of unbelievers (which includes nominal "Christians"), as the body with which we must remain connected is to not understand what the Body of Christ truly is.

Through faith in the Lord Jesus Christ, God becomes our Father and adopts us into *His* family as His children (e.g., see John 1:12; Galatians 3:26, 4:4-6; and Ephesians 1:3-7). We never have to worry about being "orphans" because our Father promises that He will never leave us nor forsake us (e.g., see Hebrews 13:5), and His family is eternal.

Nevertheless, in *The Purpose Driven Church* in a chapter on membership (p. 314)—as well as in his Ministry Toolbox Issue for September 21, 2005 titled, "Turning attendees into a part of the family"[6]—Rick Warren declares:

> "A Christian without a church family is an orphan."

But the message hasn't changed, or so they keep telling us.

Is it Through the *Blood* of Our Redeemer *Jesus Christ* or the Life*blood* of a Local *Church* That We Have Spiritual Life?

*I*n Churchianity, commitment to a local church is imperative.

> **"The Bible says a Christian without a church home is like an organ without a body**, a sheep without a flock, or a child without a family. It is an unnatural state. The Bible says, *'You belong in God's household with every other Christian.'* [endnote: Ephesians 2:19b (LB)]" (*PDL*; p. 132; bold added)

Actually, Rick Warren's first instance of "the Bible says" has no endnote because this is *not* what God's Word says! Going ahead and claiming "the Bible says" when it does not say so is scriptural malpractice. His second instance of "the Bible says" is from one of the versions that has changed God's Word.

> *"For through him we both have access by one Spirit unto the Father. <u>Now therefore ye are</u> no more strangers and foreigners, but fellowcitizens with the saints, <u>and of</u> the household of God."* (Ephesians 2:18-19)

Because of our faith in the Lord Jesus Christ, the Holy Spirit indwells us and makes us a part of the household of God, the true Body of Christ, which is not the local church. Fellowship with other believers, which is important, does not require *a local church* for it to take place. Yes, fellowship in a local church is ideal, when there is one available that isn't trading in the Word of God for popular false doctrines sweeping Christianity today. But man-centered, purpose-driven Churchianity takes committing to a local church to a whole new level in its replacement of Christ with community.

> "You *must* be connected to a church fellowship **to survive spiritually**."—Rick Warren's 40 Days of Community Workbook (Emphasis added)[7]

> "*Any* organ that is detached from the body will not only miss what it was created to be, **it will also shrivel and die quickly**. The same is true for Christians that are uncommitted to any specific congregation."—Rick Warren (Bold added)[8]

"If an organ is somehow severed from its body, it will shrivel and die. It cannot exist on its own, and neither can you. Disconnected and **cut off from the lifeblood of a local body, your spiritual life will wither and eventually cease to exist.** [endnote: Ephesians 4:16 (no version listed)]" (*PDL*; p. 131; emphasis added)

The local churches are not the source of "lifeblood" that gives life to our spirit! Ephesians 4:16 says absolutely nothing of these outlandish claims. If our spiritual life ceased to exist because we didn't attend a local church, then the local church would be God's redeeming agent in salvation.

Contrarily, *true* spiritual life is the eternal life we are given when our spirit is born again. *True* spiritual life is the life that Jesus Christ lives in us through His indwelling Holy Spirit, when we receive God's free gift of salvation by *believing* the Gospel of Christ. This true spiritual life is sustained by the Lord God, not by the local church! And if this life ever ceased to exist, that person would have no salvation. It is through the *blood* of our Redeemer *Jesus Christ*, not the life*blood* of a local *church*, that we have spiritual life and are delivered from death. But "the message hasn't changed"!

> *"For the law of the Spirit of life in Christ Jesus hath made me free from the law of sin and death. For what the law could not do, in that it was weak through the flesh, God sending his own Son in the likeness of sinful flesh, and for sin, condemned sin in the flesh: that the righteousness of the law might be fulfilled in us, who walk not after the flesh, but after the Spirit . . . . <u>And if Christ be in you</u>, the body is dead because of sin; but <u>the Spirit is life because of righteousness</u>." (Romans 8:2-4, 10)*

> *"I am crucified with Christ: <u>nevertheless I live; yet not I, but Christ liveth in me: and the life which I now live in the flesh I live by the faith of the Son of God</u>, who loved me, and gave himself for me. I do not frustrate the grace of God: for if righteousness come by the law, then Christ is dead in vain." (Galatians 2:20-21)*

In addition, rather than the pure and sinless life and blood of Jesus Christ, look at the "lifeblood" that Rick Warren would have us depend on for our spiritual life:

> "There will never be a perfect church this side of heaven, because *every church is filled with pagans, carnal Christians, and immature believers.*"—Rick Warren (Emphasis added)[9]

> "Can you see God's wisdom in creating the church, *a family full of mentors and models for our benefit?* This is why being connected to a small group is so crucial to spiritual growth. It's a regular opportunity to learn from each other."—Rick Warren's 40 Days of Community Workbook (Emphasis added)[10]

Thank God that our spiritual life and growth do not depend on the local church, as Rick Warren claims, but on our faith in *the pure and holy*, Almighty Lord God and His eternal truth. *He* is the One Who sustains us.

> ***"As newborn babes, desire the sincere milk <u>of the word</u>, that ye may grow thereby: if so be ye have tasted that the Lord is gracious." (1 Peter 2:2-3)***

But the gross Scripture twisting and replacing God with community continues:

> ***"For <u>in him</u> we live, and move, and have our being . . ." (Acts 17:28)***

> "God challenges us to **create <u>a community</u>** where we love like our lives depend upon it (*1 Peter 1:22*, Msg), and **where we can each 'live and move and have our being'** (*Acts 17:28*, NIV)."—Rick Warren's 40 Days of Community Workbook (Parentheses in the original; emphasis added)[11]

Rick Warren is engaging in scriptural malpractice to support his unscriptural Shepherding-Discipleship beliefs.

> "A related benefit of a local church is that it also provides the spiritual protection of godly leaders. God gives shepherd leaders the responsibility to guard, protect, defend, and care for the spiritual welfare of his flock . . . .

> "Satan loves detached believers, unplugged from the life of the Body, isolated from God's family, and unaccountable to spiritual leaders, because he knows they are defenseless and powerless against his tactics." (*PDL*; pp. 135-136)

According to God's Word, the armor of God is given to us to stand against Satan and defend against ***"<u>all</u> the fiery darts of the wicked"*** (see Ephesians 6:11-17). Furthermore, the armor of God *only* includes truth, righteousness, the Gospel of peace, faith, salvation, and the Word of God. *Nowhere* is the armor of God said to include "the life of the Body" or the "spiritual protection" of "shepherd leaders." This is because God is about *Christ*ianity, not *Church*ianity.

On the other hand, Shepherding-Discipleship advocates, who very much want control over Christians, would love to have us believe that if we don't attend a local church we are not genuinely "following Christ." They would love to have us believe that apart from local churches we "are defenseless and powerless" and won't "survive spiritually." In order for them to gain control over the masses, the masses need to be coerced or intimidated into replacing *Christ*ianity with *Church*ianity. Incidentally, immediately following the previous quote regarding being "unplugged" is the heading, "IT'S ALL IN THE CHURCH."

♦ *Chapter Six* ♦

Purpose #3:
You Were Created to Become Like Christ

Which Is It, to Be like Christ or to Be like You?

> "Discipleship is the process of conforming to Christ. The Bible says, *'We arrive at real maturity—that measure of development which is meant by 'the fullness of Christ.''* [endnote: Ephesians 4:13 (Ph)] Christlikeness is your eventual destination, but your journey will last a lifetime." (*PDL*; p. 219)

Rick Warren refers to this third purpose as "discipleship." The *Lord Jesus Christ* is the foundation of the *Scriptural* definition of discipleship, which is to grow in *the knowledge of Him* so that we can believe, follow, and obey Him in *the faith*. Although the version he quotes even includes them, Rick Warren chose to leave out *unity of the faith* and *the knowledge of the Son of God* from the verse he quotes above in discussing what discipleship is.

Conforming to the image of God's Son requires the *knowledge* of God's Son. Ephesians 4:13 actually says:

> *"Till we all come in the unity of the faith, and of the knowledge of the Son of God, unto a perfect man, unto the measure of the stature of the fulness of Christ."*

The very next verse elaborates on the reason for this indispensable knowledge in true discipleship:

> *"That we henceforth be no more children, tossed to and fro, and carried about with every wind of doctrine, by the sleight of men, and cunning craftiness, whereby they lie in wait to deceive; but speaking the truth in love, may grow up into him in all things, which is the head, even Christ."* (Ephesians 4:14)

Although Purpose #3 says, "you were created to become like Christ," the purpose-driven life is really about becoming "more like you." Thus the knowledge of the Son of God has been largely omitted.

> "It [this book] is about becoming what God created you to be." (PDL; p. 19)

> "Besides, God made you to be you!" (PDL; p. 245)

> "God's gonna say, 'Why weren't you more like you? I made you to be you, and if you don't be you, who's gonna be you?'"—Rick Warren[1]

But "it's not about you."

The Fruit of the Spirit, or the Fruit of Community?

Even though Rick Warren says that growing to "Christlikeness" is accomplished through the Holy Spirit, he insists that it *cannot* occur in isolation. So the arm of the Holy Spirit is so short that He *cannot* work in an isolated believer, whom He inhabits? Again, *Christ*ianity is being transformed into *Church*ianity as community continues to be placed above Christ and His indwelling Spirit.

> "Real spiritual growth is *never* an isolated, individualistic pursuit. Maturity is produced through relationships and community." (PDL; p. 11)

> "Spiritual maturity is not a solitary, individual pursuit! You cannot grow to Christlikeness in isolation . . . . You need to be a part of a church and community. Why? Because . . . you can't practice being like Jesus without being in relationship with other people." (PDL; p. 176)

Jesus Christ is not our *model* that we are to *practice* being like. He is our *Lord* to Whom we are to obediently *surrender* so that He lives His fruit through us via His indwelling Holy Spirit.

Contrary to growing opinion, commitment and accountability to one's local church or community is *not* the same thing as surrendering to the Lord God and His will. Community does not give victory over sins. The all-sufficient and all-powerful Lord God does. He is not too small to help individuals spiritually mature and overcome their sins. Community is *not* more powerful than the Almighty Lord God.

"That he would grant you, according to the riches of his glory, <u>to be strengthened with might by his Spirit in the inner man</u>; that Christ may dwell in your hearts by faith; that ye, being rooted and grounded in love, may be able to comprehend with all saints what is the breadth, and length, and depth, and height; and to know the love of Christ, which passeth knowledge, <u>that ye might be filled with all the fulness of God. Now unto him that is able to do exceeding abundantly above all that we ask or think, according to the power that worketh in us</u>, unto him be glory in the church by Christ Jesus throughout all ages, world without end. Amen." (Ephesians 3:16-21)

The Lord God is not dependent on community to work in anyone because *His* work is based on Who *He* is, not on who *you* or we are. Yet Rick Warren's Purpose-Driven Paradigm is dependent upon community because his purpose-driven works and discipleship are about who *you* are, not Who *God* is. If they were about Who God is, he would never conclude that God is also dependent on temptation.

The Fruit of the Spirit, or the Fruit of Satan's Temptations?

"How, then, does the Holy Spirit produce these nine fruit in your life? . . .

"This next sentence is one of the most important spiritual truths you will ever learn: God develops the fruit of the Spirit in your life by allowing you to experience circumstances in which you're tempted to express *the exact opposite quality!* Character development always involves a choice, and temptation provides that opportunity." (*PDL*; p. 202)

"While temptation is Satan's primary weapon to destroy you, God wants to use it to develop you." (*PDL*; p. 201)

"In fact, he depends more on circumstances to make us like Jesus than he depends on our reading the Bible." (*PDL*; p. 193)

"Every time you defeat a temptation, you become more like Jesus!" (*PDL*; p. 203)

*Y*es, God does work everything out for good to conform those of us who love God to the image of His Son (see Romans 8:28-29). This is a wonderful promise, not a statement of God's *dependence* on circumstances or temptations to do so! Nowhere in the whole counsel of God does He say that circumstances are more important to our growth than reading His Word. Nor does the Holy Spirit need us to walk through temptation in order for Him to live His fruit through us. We are to walk in the Spirit and be led of Him (e.g., see Galatians 5:16-18), and in this way we defeat temptation when it does arise.

It all comes down to surrender -- bowing the knee to *the Lord* Jesus Christ and being willing to crucify the flesh with its affections and lusts, in His name (e.g., see Galatians 5:24 and 2 Timothy 2:19). Conversely, today's Christianity is giving new life to the flesh in the name of purpose-driven fellowship and unity with the world.

Rick Warren claims that God "depends" on circumstances in which we're tempted in order to develop the fruit of the Spirit in our lives and make us like Jesus. If these claims were true, then Satan the Tempter would have an essential role in conforming us to the image of *Christ!* God has absolutely no dependence whatsoever on temptation or on Satan to conform us to the image of His Son! The upside-down thinking of the new Paradigm continues.

Satan's work is to seek to *devour* us, not to merely "trip us up":

> "He [Satan] knows *exactly* what trips you up, and he is constantly working to get you into those circumstances. Peter warns, 'Stay alert. The Devil is poised to pounce, and would like nothing better than to catch you napping.' [endnote: 1 Peter 5:8 (Msg)]" (*PDL*; p. 206)

A very serious scriptural warning has been completely diluted here. A **"roaring lion" "seeking whom he may devour"** is not the same thing as "poised to pounce." Even playful kittens like to "pounce" when you're "napping"!

Again, the *fruit of the Spirit* is such because these characteristics are the fruit *the Spirit* manifests in us as He works in us in His mighty power, giving us the victory in resisting the devil, withstanding temptation, and making the right choices. And it begins with the knowledge of the Lord God.

> **"For whatsoever is born of God overcometh the world: and this is the victory that overcometh the world, even our faith." (1 John 5:4)**

> **"That the God of our Lord Jesus Christ, the Father of glory, may give unto you the spirit of wisdom and revelation <u>in the knowledge of him</u>: the eyes**

of your understanding being enlightened; that ye may know what is the hope of his calling, and what the riches of the glory of his inheritance in the saints, and <u>what is the exceeding greatness of his power to us-ward who believe, according to the working of his mighty power</u>." (Ephesians 1:17-19)

"Grace and peace be multiplied unto you through the knowledge of God, and of Jesus our Lord, according as <u>his divine power hath given unto us all things that pertain unto life and godliness, through the knowledge of him</u> that hath called us to glory and virtue: whereby are given unto us exceeding great and precious promises: that by these ye might be partakers of the divine nature, having escaped the corruption that is in the world through lust." (2 Peter 1:2-4)

Instant Sainthood Through the Power of God vs Spiritual Formation Through Spiritual Disciplines

"Contrary to popular book titles, there are no *Easy Steps to Maturity* or *Secrets of Instant Sainthood*." (*PDL*; p. 222)

Contrary to popular opinion, people do not have to go through a long process so they can become saints. That includes a proclamation of the Pope or through spiritual disciplines, neither of which can make one single person a saint no matter how much effort is put into the process.

True saints do indeed become *instant* saints through the power of God the moment Jesus Christ is believed in as Lord and Saviour. Behaving like saints also comes each time we obediently surrender to the immediate leading and power and work of God through His Holy Spirit living in us.

Amidst the multitude of contradictions in his book, Rick Warren rightly acknowledges that "you cannot reproduce the character of Jesus on your own strength" (*PDL*; p. 174). But he negates this statement in many places.

"Habits take time to develop. Remember that your character is the sum total of your habits . . . .

"There is only one way to develop the habits of Christlike character: You must *practice* them—and that takes time! There are no *instant habits*. Paul urged

Timothy, 'Practice these things. Devote your life to them so that everyone can see your progress.' [endnote: 1 Timothy 4:15 (GWT)]" (*PDL*; p. 221)

Scripture does not say this. We are told in 1 Timothy 4:15 to **"<u>meditate</u> upon these things; give thyself wholly to them; that thy profiting may appear to all."** Furthermore, **"these things"** refers back to things such as giving **"attendance to reading, to exhortation, to doctrine,"** as well as being **"an example of the believers, in word, in conversation, in charity, in spirit, in faith, in purity"** (verses 12, 13). In addition, verse 16 says:

> **"Take heed unto thyself, and unto <u>the doctrine</u>; continue in them: for in doing this thou shalt both save thyself, and them that hear thee."**

But God has His ways of putting the handwriting on the wall. The first verse of this chapter includes what Timothy is being asked to seriously think about:

> **"Now the Spirit speaketh expressly, that in the latter times some shall depart from the faith, giving heed to seducing spirits, and doctrines of devils." (1 Timothy 4:1)**

"Seducing spirits" and **"doctrines of devils"** are behind the popular yet occultic mysticism often included as "spiritual disciplines." The following quote is a continuation of Rick Warren's previous quote on "practice these things":

> "If you practice something over time, you get good at it. Repetition is the mother of character and skill. These character-building habits are often called '*spiritual disciplines,*' and there are dozens of great books that can teach you how to do these." (*PDL*; p. 221)

First, remember that building and transforming our character is to "become like Christ" in this third purpose. So for him to advocate "dozens of great books" for this says that God's Holy Spirit and Holy Scriptures are insufficient in conforming us to the image of Christ and need help in this area.

Second, books in the area of "spiritual disciplines"/occultic mysticism are flying off the presses in today's bewitched Christianity. Occultic practices are also growing in popularity at conferences for church leaders. Rick Warren was one of the speakers at the National Pastors Convention 2004 where occultic methods of prayer (the labyrinth, contemplative prayer, and yoga) were featured and preceded his talk.[2] These occultic practices continue to be featured each year at various conferences for pastors and youth leaders, as well as at other events held in a seduced Christianity.[3]

Christian author Ray Yungen, who has studied religious movements for over twenty years, goes into detail warning of the dangers of these practices in his two excellent books, *"For Many Shall Come In My Name": How mainstream America is accepting the 'Ancient Wisdom' teaching and what this foreshadows*, and *A Time of Departing: How Ancient Mystical Practices are Uniting Christians with the World's Religions*.[4]

The god of the realm of false spirituality, who is also **"the god of this world"** (see 2 Corinthians 4:4), has severely deceived people into believing that certain practices referred to as "spiritual disciplines" (e.g., contemplative prayer, breath prayers, centering prayer, the silence, spiritual breathing, the labyrinth, and yoga) are "Christian" practices. The Master Deceiver who transforms himself into an **"angel of light"** (see 2 Corinthians 11:14) has had millennia to perfect the lying experiences that he derisively enjoys giving all who disobediently enter his counterfeit realm.

Regardless of the adamant yet deceived claims to the contrary, these occultic spiritual practices will never make us "like Christ." In addition, these things never have been nor will they ever be the fruit or the work of the *Holy* Spirit. This is self-evident in that although the world cannot receive or know the *Holy* Spirit (see John 14:17), *people in different religions (faiths) practice these <u>same</u> spiritual disciplines and methods of prayer with the <u>same</u> experiences and the <u>same</u> "fruit" that so-called "Christian" mysticism produces.*

The (New Age) New Spirituality and its disciplines of mysticism bypass theology/doctrine and go straight to experience, which is now being given greater authority than God's absolute Holy Scriptures. Mysticism is coming to the forefront because it is being used to bring all religions (faiths) together in the unholy unity of a false spirituality through unholy spirits.

Yet none of this has opened the eyes of today's Christianity to the fact that it has adopted the behavior of the Angel of light's broad way of darkness. The "light" of the New Spirituality, which has deceptively tried to veil its New Age foundation specifically to entice and please professing Christians, has taken Christianity by storm. No wonder it has become blind to the fact that its thinking and beliefs have changed away from the truth. Satan brings great deception on those who choose to enter his realm of lies via its various practices.

Incidentally, prayer is only a ritual in other religions (faiths). In the true faith of Christianity, it is simply talking to God. We don't "practice" or "develop the habit" of talking to those we love! Turning prayer into a ritual or a method or a mystical practice denies Who God is and what He says about prayer.

> "One way [to 'pray all the time'] is to use 'breath prayers' throughout the day . . . You choose a brief sentence or a simple phrase that can be repeated to Jesus in one breath . . ." (PDL; p. 89)

> "With practice you can develop the habit of praying silent 'breath prayers' for those you encounter." (PDL; p. 299)

> **"Confession is 'spiritual breathing'. Exhale your sins, inhale God's love."**
> —Rick Warren (Emphasis added)[5]

Aside from the fact that *exhaling* your sins, etcetera, is sheer nonsense, "spiritual breathing" is an occultic method taught by Eastern gurus, such as Sri Chinmoy, for exhaling one's impurities (sins) and inhaling things of God. It is based on the Eastern belief in pantheism that All is One -- All is God and God is All.

> "We are all seekers, and our goal is the same: to achieve inner peace, light, and joy, to become inseparably one with our Source . . .

> "To live in joy is to live the inner life. This is the life that leads to self-realisation. Self-realisation is God-realisation, for God is nothing other than the Divinity that is deep inside each one of us, waiting to be discovered and revealed."—SriChinmoy.org[6]

> "When you breathe in, if you can feel that the breath is coming directly from God, from Purity itself, then your breath can easily be purified. Then, each time you breathe in, try to feel that you are bringing infinite peace into your body . . . .

> "Feel that you are breathing in not air but cosmic energy . . . and that you are going to use it to purify your body, vital, mind and heart . . . . It is flowing like a river inside you, washing and purifying your entire being. Then, when you breathe out, feel that you are breathing out all the rubbish inside you . . .

Anything inside your system that you call undivine, anything that you do not want to claim as your own, feel that you are exhaling . . . .

"When you have perfected this spiritual breathing, all your impurity and ignorance will be replaced by God's light, peace and power."—Sri Chinmoy Centre (Emphasis added)[7]

In *The Hindu-Yogi Science of Breath*, in a chapter titled "Yogi Spiritual Breathing," Yogi Ramacharaka also points out the goal of "spiritual breathing." Basically, it is to come to the realization or "consciousness" that the true "identity of the Soul" is Divine ("a drop from the Divine Ocean") and is connected with "the Universal Life" (i.e., All is One -- "at-one-ment with All").[8]

Occultic practices, which originate from *"doctrines of devils"* regarding universal energies and forces, do not suddenly become acceptable to the holy Lord God merely because churches have "Christianized" them and refer to them as "Christian." On the contrary, these practices have been designed by the evil spirit world to bring unity and "connection" with the god of this world, *"the God of forces,"* whom the Antichrist will honor (e.g., see Daniel 11:38-39).

Those who try to "Christianize" occultic practices are playing with *"strange fire."* It is not a coincidence that professing Christians who practice the occultic Eastern methods of "prayer" are being gradually drawn into the interfaith Oneness of the world and its (New Age) New Spirituality. This "New" Spirituality is actually based on the so-called "Ancient Wisdom."

The fruit of the unholy spirits who lie in wait to deceive all who enter the Angel of light's realm is destructive. Their ultimate goal is to get mankind to believe in its own divinity -- the ultimate defiance against the Lord God.

To further their goal, the spirit world approached Alice Bailey to spread its teachings (the Ageless/Ancient Wisdom). Bailey was a theosophist and occultist who "telepathically" channeled many teachings from one of her spirit guides known as "the Tibetan," or "the Master Djwhal Khul" -- "one of the Masters of the Wisdom."[9] (Appropriately, Bailey's Publishing Company, which is now called Lucis Trust, was originally named Lucifer Trust.)

Together, in numerous books, these two detailed "the Plan" of the spirit realm (a.k.a. "the Spiritual Hierarchy") for the coming New Age/New World Order/New World Religion and its (counterfeit) "Christ" and his kingdom (which will be elaborated on later). In fact, coining the term *New Age* has even been attributed to Bailey.[10] She and her spirit guide also detailed the methods and fruit of occultic practices, such as the following:

". . . **by surrendering himself to the life at the center** and there holding himself poised and still, yet alert, the light will break in and reveal to the disciple that which he needs to know. **He learns to express that inclusive love which is his major requirement and to let go the narrow,** one-pointed attitude which he has hitherto regarded as love. **He welcomes then all visions**, if they serve to lift and comfort his brothers; **he welcomes all truths**, if they are the agents of revelation to other minds; **he welcomes all dreams** if they can act as incentives to his fellow men. He shares in them all, yet retains his poised position at the center."—Alice Bailey & Djwhal Khul (Emphasis added)[11]

"**Contemplation has been described, as a psychic gateway**, leading from one state of consciousness to another."—Alice Bailey (Emphasis added)[12]

"In contemplation, a higher agent enters in. *It is the Soul that contemplates.* **The human consciousness ceases its activity and the man becomes what he is in reality - a soul, a fragment of divinity, conscious of its essential oneness with Deity**. The Higher Self becomes active, and the lower or personal self is entirely quiescent and still, whilst the true spiritual Entity enters into its own kingdom and registers the contacts that emanate from that spiritual realm of phenomena . . . .

"The man's consciousness, therefore, is no longer focused in that waiting mind, but has slipped over the borderland into the realm of spirit and he becomes literally the soul, functioning in its own realm, perceiving the 'things of the Kingdom of God,' able to ascertain truth at first hand . . ."—Alice Bailey (Bold added)[13]

". . . on the higher planes **we are all one**. One life pulsates and circulates through all . . . **This is part of the revelation which comes to a man who stands in the 'Presence' with his eyes occultly opened** . . . .

"Faith is lost in sight, and things unseen are seen and known. No more can he doubt, but he has become instead, through his own effort, a *knower*.

"His oneness with his brothers is proven, and he realizes the indissoluble link which binds him to his fellowmen everywhere."—Alice Bailey & Djwhal Khul (Bold added)[14]

Sadly, warning people to compare all subjective experiences with the final authority of God's Word is commonly dismissed with scornful and fallacious worldly reasoning. Subjective experience is now more important than truth to people and is even now viewed as "truth" itself. Refusing to acknowledge the dangers shows a tremendous lack of understanding of the occult and of the devices of our spiritual enemy.

The journey down this occult path will not lead to becoming "like Christ." But it will lead to the deceptive "awakening" of the "Christ consciousness" within, which is defined as the following by Ray Yungen in *A Time of Departing: How Ancient Mystical Practices are Uniting Christians with the World's Religions*:

"Christ consciousness
Taught by New Agers to be the state of awareness, reached in meditation, in which one realizes that one is divine and one with God and thereby becoming a Christ or an enlightened being."[15]

"Be sober, be vigilant; because your adversary the devil, as a roaring lion, walketh about, seeking whom he may devour." (1 Peter 5:8)

◆ *Chapter Seven* ◆

Purpose #4:
You Were Shaped for Serving God

Serve God According to Who *He* Is,
Not According to Who *You* Are

The purpose-driven SHAPE system is an unscriptural aspect of the Purpose-Driven Paradigm about which a book could be written. In fact, Christian author James Sundquist discusses it in his detailed book, *Who's Driving the Purpose Driven Church?: A Documentary on the Teachings of Rick Warren.*[1] Suffice it to say that whether deliberately or not, there are aspects of the SHAPE system that stem from Carl Jung, which Sundquist discusses. Jung's theories were deeply rooted in the occult and Gnosticism and became foundational to much of psychology.

Although psychology contains humanist philosophies that stand in direct opposition to the Word of God, it has nevertheless been blindly invited into Christianity by its leaders.[2] In spite of Rick Warren's statements against psychology, his SHAPE system (not to mention his Paradigm) actually contains a great deal of its man-centered philosophies and tools.

The gifts of *the Spirit* are manifested in us the same way as the fruit of *the Spirit*—through the direct working and power of the Holy Spirit Himself, within us and through us. But rather than relying on the Holy Spirit to minister through us in His power and in how He chooses to do so at any given time, this fourth purpose is about finding out who *you* are, listening to the inner promptings of *your* heart, assessing *your* gifts, *your* abilities, and *your* experience, and using worldly man-made tools to learn about *your* personality, so you can serve God accordingly. But trying to serve God according to who *you* are rather than Who *He* is leads to everyone doing what is right in their own eyes and in their own power.

Throughout *The Purpose-Driven Life* (as well as the Purpose-Driven Paradigm), Rick Warren shapes Scripture according to what he has to say by picking and choosing verses or phrases from certain versions with just the right wording that seems to support his statements at the time. Thus contradictions abound in his pragmatic Paradigm, as what he has to say changes according to the purpose of the immediate situation or topic. We are far better served when we see what Scripture has to say and then shape our premises and teachings accordingly.

In the previous purpose, Rick Warren quoted a verse from a version that claims our deceitful heart is "beyond cure." Yet in this purpose he says that listening to the inner promptings of this heart is the "H" in his SHAPE program for determining what ministry a person should have!

> "Jeremiah said, 'The heart is deceitful above all things and beyond cure.' [endnote: Jeremiah 17:9 (NIV)]" (*PDL*; p. 215)
>
> "SHAPE: Listening to Your Heart
>
> "The Bible uses the term *heart* to describe the bundle of desires, hopes, interests, ambitions, dreams, and affections you have." (*PDL*; p. 237)
>
> "Listening for inner promptings can point to the ministry God intends for you to have." (*PDL*; p. 238)

If a deceitful heart that is "beyond cure" is to be listened to in figuring out how best to serve God, then no wonder the worldly Purpose-Driven movement is walking so much in the flesh in how it is trying to go about its service of God. Yet this result fits with what Scripture actually says:

> **"The heart is deceitful above all things, and desperately wicked: who can know it?" (Jeremiah 17:9)**

This is why we are to grow in the knowledge of Who God is and study God's Word to show ourselves approved, instead of growing in the knowledge of who *we* are and doing what our heart—or manmade tests—tells us is right.

> **"A fool hath no delight in understanding, but that his heart may discover itself." (Proverbs 18:2)**

When we serve God according to Who *He* is, we understand that the holy and righteous God will not consider unholy and unrighteous works as service to

Him regardless of whether they are done in His name, regardless of whether people are following their heart or their abilities or their entire SHAPE, and regardless of whether an unbeliever happens to be "purpose-driven" and serving other people.

On March 22, 2005, Larry King interviewed Rick Warren and asked him:

> "You can, though, Rick, have a purpose-driven life and be an agnostic or an atheist, can't you? Still do good, still help others, still have purpose?"

Carefully notice Rick Warren's reply:

> "Absolutely, you can help other people. I believe that we were made for a purpose, and that purpose is really to know God and to serve God and to love God, and to serve other people by -- serve God by serving others. You know, you can't really serve God directly, Larry, not here on Earth. The only way you can serve God is by serving other people."[3]

Agnostics and atheists do not believe in God. If people who in God's book do not know, love, or serve God can still have a purpose-driven life, then the purpose-driven life is not about *God*, statements to the contrary notwithstanding.

Larry King then responded by asking:

> "Since you believe in God, if an agnostic or an atheist is doing good, God appreciates it, according to you, right?"

Again, carefully notice Rick Warren's answer:

> "God wants us all to be loving to each other, there is no doubt about that. In fact, Jesus wouldn't have made any distinction between someone who was of a different background. The issue was, do they love him and do they have a purpose? Are they following his purpose?"[4]

Refusing to believe in the truth of God's Word and of the Lord God Himself is neither following His purpose nor love or service for God regardless of the dedication with which one serves the world. People outside the faith are way beyond being of "a different background." They are enemies of God abiding on the broad way. No matter how "good" someone's works are, without *faith* it is impossible to please

God (see Hebrews 11:6), and this Scripture is not referring to any "faith" of other religions!

The Lord Jesus Christ is the *only* way to God, *including serving Him*. And there is no way to the Lord Jesus Christ apart from faith, which is believing and obeying the truth on His narrow way. Serving other people is the fruit of our serving God *directly* through faith, love, obedience, and truth. To do this, we must abide in the Lord Jesus Christ on His narrow way (see also Matthew 7:13-14):

> *"Abide in me, and I in you. As <u>the branch cannot bear fruit of itself, except it abide in the vine</u>; no more can ye, except ye abide in me. I am the vine, ye are the branches: He that abideth in me, and I in him, the same bringeth forth much fruit: <u>for without me ye can do nothing</u>. If a man abide not in me, he is cast forth as a branch, and is withered; and men gather them, and cast them into the fire, and they are burned." (John 15:4-6)*

The Lord Jesus Christ said that if we love Him we will keep His commandments (see John 14:15, 21, 23-24; and 1 John 5:3). Yes, He did summarize His commandments into loving God and loving our neighbors, but this does not eliminate obediently doing so in righteousness and holiness and truth.

Yet in the Purpose-Driven Paradigm, knowing and loving and serving God are being given broad definitions that allow other religions (faiths), which do not believe in the truth, to participate in its purpose-driven works of serving God "by serving other people."

> "It is inconceivable that a sovereign and holy God should be so hard up for workers that He would press into service anyone who had been empowered regardless of his moral qualifications. The very stones would praise Him if the need arose and a thousand legions of angels would leap to do His will.
>
> "Gifts and power for service the Spirit surely desires to impart; but holiness and spiritual worship come first."—A.W. Tozer[5]

> *"Now therefore fear the LORD, and serve him in sincerity and <u>in truth</u> . . ." (Joshua 24:14)*

> *"If any man serve me, let him follow me; and where I am, there shall also my servant be: if any man serve me, him will my Father honour." (John 12:26)*

> *"For the kingdom of God is not meat and drink; but righteousness, and peace, and joy in the Holy Ghost. For he that in these things serveth Christ is acceptable to God, and approved of men." (Romans 14:17-18)*

More often than not, the truth that our lives are to be grounded in righteousness and holiness has been excluded from Rick Warren's advice on how we are to live. This is a very serious omission from a book that is supposedly a "blueprint for Christian living." This "blueprint" also completely twists Scripture to support the unscriptural viewpoint that we are to serve God according to who *we* are:

> "God loves to use weak people . . . .
>
> "In fact, you have a *bundle* of flaws and imperfections: physical, emotional, intellectual, and spiritual . . . . Usually we deny our weaknesses, defend them, excuse them, hide them, and resent them. This prevents God from using them the way he desires.
>
> "God has a different perspective on your weaknesses. He says, 'My thoughts and my ways are higher than yours,' [endnote: Isaiah 55:9 (CEV)] so he often acts in ways that are the exact opposite of what we expect. We think that God only wants to use our strengths, but he also wants to use our weaknesses for his glory." (*PDL*; p. 272)

God does use our weakness for His glory, but *spiritual* flaws are included in his list of what God "wants to use"?! Furthermore, these categories are given as though no flaw within them could possibly be sin in need of repentance, and that God wants to use them regardless. The verse that he uses has been taken completely out of context and actually says *the opposite* of what he is trying to make it say:

> *"Seek ye the Lord while he may be found, call ye upon him while he is near: Let the wicked forsake his way, and the unrighteous man his thoughts: and let him return unto the Lord, and he will have mercy upon him; and to our God, for he will abundantly pardon. For my thoughts are not your thoughts, neither are your ways my ways, saith the Lord. For as the heavens are higher than the earth, so are my ways higher than your ways, and my thoughts than your thoughts." (Isaiah 55:6-9)*

Giving an entirely different meaning to what God wrote to suit one's purpose is scriptural malpractice. Yet this is done in the following quote as well:

> "Knowing and loving God is our greatest privilege, and being known and loved is God's greatest pleasure. God says, '*If any want to boast, they should boast **that they know and understand me** . . . . **These are the things that please me**.*' [endnote: Jeremiah 9:24 (TEV)]" (*PDL*; p. 87; ellipsis dots in the original; bold added)

His man-centered "blueprint for Christian living" has tremendously twisted this Scripture. With his deletions and ellipsis dots, he has given an entirely different meaning to what God delights in:

> "*But let him that glorieth glory in this, that he understandeth and knoweth me, that I am the* Lord *which exercise <u>lovingkindness, judgment, and righteousness</u>, in the earth: for <u>in these things I delight</u>, saith the* Lord.*"* (Jeremiah 9:24)

Sadly, there are numerous examples of Rick Warren omitting from his man-centered "blueprint" the God-centered truth that the righteous and holy Lord God wants us to love and serve Him in righteousness and holiness. That we are to be *holy* has been deleted from the *Message* that he frequently prefers:

> "The Message paraphrase says, '*Take your everyday, ordinary life—your sleeping, eating, going-to-work, and walking-around life—and place it before God as an offering.*' [endnote: Romans 12:1 (Msg)] Work becomes worship when you dedicate it to God and perform it with an awareness of his presence." (*PDL*; p. 67)

Romans 12:1 actually says:

> "*I beseech you therefore, brethren, by the mercies of God, that ye present your bodies a living sacrifice, <u>holy</u>, acceptable unto God, which is your reasonable service.*" (Romans 12:1)

Because we are to offer ourselves *holy* to God, this determines what behavior is acceptable in our "everyday, ordinary life." Merely offering up whatever we do in dedication to God is not acceptable unless what we do is holy. And nowadays, doing it "with an awareness of his presence" often means unholy contemplative spirituality.

> *"Follow peace with all men, <u>and holiness</u>, without which no man shall see the Lord." (Hebrews 12:14)*

> *"For the righteous* L<small>ORD</small> *loveth righteousness; his countenance doth behold the upright." (Psalm 11:7)*

> *"Righteousness shall go before him; and shall set us in the way of his steps." (Psalm 85:13)*

Judging what is righteous and holy is essential to serving God acceptably and for His glory. In addition, righteousness which is by faith in Jesus Christ is essential to being without offence in God's eyes:

> *"And this I pray, that your love may abound yet more and more in knowledge and in all judgment; that ye may approve things that are excellent; that ye may be sincere and without offence till the day of Christ; <u>being filled with the fruits of righteousness</u>, which are by Jesus Christ, unto the glory and praise of God." (Philippians 1:9-11)*

Yet in quoting the verse above, Rick Warren chose to quote a version that deletes the specific fruit of *righteousness* from it:

> "Now, for the rest of your life on earth, God wants to continue the process of changing your character. The Bible says, 'May you always **be filled with the fruit of your salvation—those good things** that are produced in your life by Jesus Christ—for this will bring much glory and praise to God.' [endnote: Philippians 1:11 (NLT)]" (*PDL*; p. 56; bold added)

The righteousness which is by faith has also been deleted from the following:

> "The second reason Noah pleased God was that he trusted God, even when it didn't make sense. The Bible says, *'By faith, Noah built a ship in the middle of dry land. He was warned about something he couldn't see, and acted on what*

he was told . . . . *As a result,* **Noah became intimate with God**.' [endnote: Hebrews 11:7 (Msg)]" (*PDL*; p. 70; ellipsis dots in the original; bold added)

Hebrews 11:7 actually says:

"By faith Noah, being warned of God of things not seen as yet, moved with fear, prepared an ark to the saving of his house; by the which he condemned the world, and <u>became heir of the righteousness which is by faith</u>."

Yet again, feel-good, man-centered teaching takes precedence over the whole counsel of God:

"God's motive for creating you was his love. The Bible says, 'Long before he laid down earth's foundations, he had us in mind, **had settled on us as the focus of his love**.' [endnote: Ephesians 1:4a (Msg)]" (*PDL*; p. 24; bold added)

In its entirety, Ephesians 1:4 actually says:

"According as he hath chosen us in him before the foundation of the world, <u>that we should be holy and without blame before him in love</u>."

". . . O my people, they which lead thee cause thee to err, and destroy the way of thy paths." (Isaiah 3:12)

God's path is never apart from righteousness (e.g., see Psalm 23:3); that is, all that is right in God's eyes, according to God's narrow way and absolute standard of truth and holiness. He never leads people in paths of *un*righteousness -- the fellowship and teachings and ways of the world and its broad way. The omissions from its "blueprint for Christian living" have clearly carried over into the behavior of the Purpose-Driven movement, which is more about pleasing and serving the world than God.

"Know ye not, that to whom ye yield yourselves servants to obey, his servants ye are to whom ye obey; whether of sin unto death, or of obedience unto righteousness? But God be thanked, that ye were the servants of sin, but ye have obeyed from the heart that form of doctrine which was delivered you. Being then made free from sin, ye became the servants of righteousness. I

speak after the manner of men because of the infirmity of your flesh: for as ye have yielded your members servants to uncleanness and to iniquity unto iniquity; even so now yield your members servants to righteousness unto holiness. For when ye were the servants of sin, ye were free from righteousness. What fruit had ye then in those things whereof ye are now ashamed? for the end of those things is death. But now being made free from sin, and become servants to God, ye have your fruit unto holiness, and the end everlasting life." (Romans 6:16-22)

Throughout His Holy Scriptures, the righteous Lord God of truth makes it clear what pleases Him and that His ways are not found outside righteousness and truth. So turning to an unholy, counterfeit "Bible" for help in this area isn't a wise place to look:

"Since pleasing God is the first purpose of your life, your most important task is to discover how to do that. The Bible says, '*Figure out what will please Christ, and then do it.*' [endnote: Ephesians 5:10 (Msg)]" (*PDL*; p. 69)

When the Holy Scriptures are rightly divided and studied to see what *God* actually says—instead of searched with tunnel vision to extract specific verses or phrases to 'validate' what *man* says—there is no need to "figure out" what pleases the Lord God. He makes it clear from Genesis to Revelation. True Scripture even makes it clear what pleases God *in this very sentence* from which Rick Warren extracted this verse:

"For ye were sometimes darkness, but now are ye light in the Lord: walk as children of light: (For the fruit of the Spirit is <u>in all goodness and righteousness and truth;</u>) <u>proving what is acceptable unto the Lord</u>." (Ephesians 5:8-10)

But yet again, righteousness and truth have been deleted from his "blueprint for Christian living."

"What thing soever I command you, observe to do it: thou shalt not add thereto, nor diminish from it." (Deuteronomy 12:32)

His "blueprint" is full of holes and can only build an unstable, faulty Paradigm. And this Paradigm is leading people to believe that adopting the behavior of the world is acceptable to God because the world's way "works" in "reaching" the world. Besides, this broad way of the world is itself being portrayed as *God's* way of "righteousness" and "service" by many corrupt books claiming to be the scriptural mouthpiece for God.

Incidentally, Rick Warren's use of Noah as an example of a life that pleases God opens the door to further man-centered problems:

> "Fortunately, the Bible gives us a clear example of a life that gives pleasure to God. The man's name was Noah . . . .
>
> "The Bible says, 'Noah was **a pleasure** to the Lord.' [endnote: Genesis 6:8 (LB)] . . . **Because Noah brought pleasure to God, you and I are alive today**." (*PDL*; pp. 69-70; bold added)

This Scripture actually says, ***"But Noah found grace in the eyes of the Lord."*** This is *not* the same thing. The man-centered, unscriptural change to God's Holy Scriptures denies our sinfulness and desperate need for God's *grace*. It is because of the grace of God that we are alive today!

Finding Healing Through *Our Wounds* or Healing Through *Christ's Wounds*?

Christianity today has gotten too used to the many per-versions of the Bible. It seems to have forgotten what God actually says in His uncorrupted Holy Scriptures so no longer sees the error in what it is reading and doing. A fitting example of this, as well as of the grave error of attempting to serve God according to who *we* are rather than according to Who *He* is, is the following:

> "God wants you to have a Christlike ministry on earth. That means other people are going to find **healing in your wounds**. Your greatest life messages and your most effective ministry will come out of your deepest hurts. The things you're most embarrassed about, most ashamed of, and most reluctant to share are the very tools God can use most powerfully to heal others." (*PDL*; p. 275; emphasis added)

A "Christlike ministry" means that people will find healing in *our wounds*? In addition, please notice that our wounds include things we are "most ashamed of," which includes sins! Christ was wounded to heal us of our sins, but now the most powerful tool to heal others is either our sins or the sins of others that wounded us? The poison has become the cure, and the cure has become the poison. Everything is upside down.

Rick Warren's claims are a very grievous usurping of the work that belongs to the Lord Jesus Christ alone and a denial of His all-sufficient and finished work on the cross through *His* wounds and death.

> *"Jesus answered and said unto them, Ye do err, not knowing the scriptures, nor the power of God." (Matthew 22:29)*

The rejection of the Man of Sorrows continues.

> *"He is despised and rejected of men; a man of sorrows, and acquainted with grief: and we hid as it were our faces from him; he was despised, and we esteemed him not. Surely he hath borne our griefs, and carried our sorrows: yet we did esteem him stricken, smitten of God, and afflicted. But <u>he</u> was <u>wounded</u> for our transgressions, <u>he</u> was bruised for our iniquities: the chastisement of our peace was upon <u>him</u>; and with <u>his</u> stripes we are <u>healed</u>. All we like sheep have gone astray; we have turned every one to his own way; and the LORD hath laid on him the iniquity of us all." (Isaiah 53:3-6)*

> *"Who his own self bare our sins in his own body on the tree, that we, being dead to sins, should live unto righteousness: <u>by whose stripes ye were healed</u>. For ye were as sheep going astray; but are now returned unto the Shepherd and Bishop of your souls." (1 Peter 2:24)*

The unscriptural claims that people will find healing in *our wounds* are based on the foolishness of worldly 'wisdom' that prefers to follow Jesus as "model" or "pattern" or "example" rather than as *the Lord* and *Saviour*. Quite the contrary, as we obediently follow the Lord Jesus Christ and allow Him to live through us in righteousness and godliness and truth, people will see a *difference* (not similarities) between us and the world, because of *His life* in us. In fact, if they believe His Gospel, they will find healing in *His* crucifixion wounds, *His* truth, *His* power, and *His* life.

Yet today, putting a man-centered psychological and physical band-aid on the world to fix it and bring it "recovery" is given greater importance than telling people how to become totally brand new and achieve victory through the all-sufficient Lord God.

"But my God shall supply all your need according to his riches in glory by Christ Jesus." (Philippians 4:19)

Airing Our Dirty Laundry Is *Not* Our Most Effective and Powerful Ministry in Serving God

*U*nbelievably, as we have begun to see, a psychological band-aid oozing from sin's wounds is the preferred method of "ministry" in purpose-driven living.

> "If you really desire to be used by God, you *must* understand a powerful truth: The very experiences that you have resented or regretted most in life—the ones you've wanted to hide and forget—are the experiences God wants to use to help others. They *are* your ministry! . . .
>
> "You have to stop covering them up, and you must honestly admit your faults, failures, and fears. Doing this will probably be your most effective ministry." (*PDL*; p. 247)
>
> "Your greatest life messages and your most effective ministry will come out of your deepest hurts. The things you're most embarrassed about, most ashamed of, and most reluctant to share are the very tools God can use most powerfully to heal others." (*PDL*; p. 275)

Since when is airing our dirty laundry and focusing on the sin and darkness of our lives *our ministry* for God? And since when is our dirty laundry more powerful than the Gospel of Christ? This is the fruit of corrupting and twisting Scripture. Yet Rick Warren claims:

> "If Paul had kept his experience of doubt and depression a secret, millions of people would never have benefited from it. Only shared experiences can help others." (*PDL*; p. 248)

What "millions of people" have benefited from the apostle Paul's supposed "experience of doubt and depression"? It is obvious in the Holy Scriptures that the apostle Paul's most effective ministry was preaching the Gospel of the Lord Jesus Christ. Besides, contentment belies doubt and depression. This man of God who was clearly filled with the *faith* and *joy* of Christ also said, **"for I have learned, in whatsoever state I am, therewith to be content . . . I can do all things through Christ which strengtheneth me"** (Philippians 4:11, 13). Knowing the Lord Jesus Christ Himself is the only thing that can give true help to others.

The ludicrous claims in these quotes must be why in modern "testimonies" people go on and on and on about the darkness and sins in their lives. They tend to say little, if anything, about God or the Gospel of Christ anymore, except maybe as an afterthought in the last few seconds with a generic, ". . . and God made my life better." But now "testimonies" are even replacing any comments about what *God* has done for them with all that their *church* is doing for them. This is just one more example of how *Church*ianity and community are replacing *Christ*ianity as people focus on who *they* are instead of Who *God* is.

◆ *Chapter Eight* ◆

Purpose #5:
You Were Made for a Mission

Was Christ's Mission on Earth to Atone for Our Sins or to "Introduce" People to God So They Can Become His Friends?

"The Bible says, '*Now we can rejoice in our wonderful new relationship with God—all because of what our Lord Jesus Christ has done for us in making us friends of God.*' [endnote: Romans 5:11 (NLT)]" (*PDL*; p. 86)

ick Warren's chosen version for this verse has greatly watered down the tremendous truth of all the Lord Jesus Christ has done for us. This Scripture actually says:

"And not only so, but we also joy in God through our Lord Jesus Christ, by whom we have now received the atonement." (Romans 5:11)

Friendship with God is one of the precious privileges we receive through the death of His Son, our Lord Jesus Christ. But it is because His sacrificial death on the cross was the *atonement*—God's required price and payment for our sins—that we have salvation and peace with God. Thus we are reconciled with God when we believe in the Lord Jesus Christ. It is His *atonement* that says ***"it is finished,"*** thereby completely excluding works so that we cannot add one single thing to what the Lord Jesus Christ has done for us. He paid the *full* price for our sins.

Rick Warren, who says his aim is to prepare people for eternity, has chosen to quote from a version that *deletes* the means of salvation from the verse above. Yet without His atonement for our sins, we would have no hope of ever being anything but the enemies of God. Because of the tremendous love of God for us, the true "mission" of Christ was that He came to earth *to die for our sins* so that we don't have to. Everything else He did was extra.

Yet preferring to put a man-centered spin on his purpose-driven "manifesto," Rick Warren says the following:

> "**The mission Jesus had while on earth is now *our* mission** because we are the Body of Christ. What he did in his physical body we are to continue as his spiritual body, the church. **What is that mission? Introducing people to God!** The Bible says, '*Christ changed us from enemies into his friends and gave us the task of making others his friends also.*' [endnote: 2 Corinthians 5:18 (TEV)]" (*PDL*; p. 282; bold added)

Sadly, Rick Warren repeatedly undermines his stated goal of preparing his readers for eternity by either ignoring the pertinent context (such as in this previous quote of 2 Corinthians 5), or by deleting key phrases of Scripture from the verses he quotes, or by choosing corrupt versions that have already done so.

Reportedly, one of the reasons for changing the "language" of the Gospel (but not the "message," mind you) is that today's generation can't understand Christianity's so-called outdated words. Well of course they can't, given the dumbed-down teaching they're being handed. Yet Christianity's leaders actually think they are going to resolve this lack of understanding by *catering* to this dumbing down process. In actuality, they are facilitating the departure from the faith.

Rick Warren's Paradigm largely reduces Jesus Christ's "mission" on earth to *introducing* people to God and *modeling* the purpose-driven life and the purpose-driven P.E.A.C.E. Plan. This generic feel-good emphasis on Jesus as "model" rather than as the Lord and Saviour is one with which most religions (faiths) have no problem.

Introducing People to *Which* God?

No one can come to God apart from the Lord Jesus Christ. Because "introducing people to God" is relative according to *which* God one believes in, there can be an eternal difference between "introducing people to God" and preaching the Gospel of Christ. For example:

> "Across America pastors and Christian leaders are allowing representatives of the Islamic faith to freely speak in their pulpits. This happened at Willow Creek Community Church, the largest church in America, where a Muslim man named Faisal Hammouda was allowed to share the pulpit. During the interview with Pastor Bill Hybels, Hammouda claimed: 'As a matter of fact, we, all of us, believe in Jesus. **I believe in Jesus. I believe in Mohammed and all the prophets. So *our mission here is to introduce people to God*.**' He also

stated, 'We believe in Jesus more than you do, in fact.'"—Editorial, *Voice of the Martyrs* (Emphasis added)[1]

This *Muslim* agrees with Rick Warren's fifth purpose that his "mission" is "to introduce people to God"! Yet he is introducing people to the false god and false "Jesus" of Islam.

Yet in Christianity today, we are increasingly being taught that Muslims believe in the same God Christians believe in. This couldn't be further from the truth. Muslims are required to follow the teachings of Islam that their god Allah *has no son*. Neither is the false god of Islam a Godhead consisting of the Father, Son, and Holy Spirit. The false "Jesus" of Islam was never crucified or sacrificed for our sins or resurrected, and he is nothing more than merely another *human* prophet along with "Mohammed and all the prophets." Their god is *not* the true God, and their "Jesus" is *not* the <u>Son</u> of God, the Lord Jesus Christ -- God manifest in the flesh.

Christians today who blindly accept the propaganda that "Allah" is simply the word for "God" in their own language have been dangerously deceived into equating the true and living God with a false god. "Allah" is no more just a word for "God" than "Baal" is just a word for "lord." And anyone who knows the Old Testament knows what the Lord God thought of Baal! Both Baal and Allah are the *names* of false gods who are not even remotely the true and holy Lord God Almighty.

The preferred feel-good, man-centered theology that desires interfaith unity is ignoring God's many warnings in His Holy Scriptures. For example:

> "That God would want me for a close friend is hard to understand, but the Bible says, '*He is a God who is passionate about his relationship with you.*' [endnote: Exodus 34:14 (NLT)]" (*PDL*; p. 86)

Exodus 34:14-15 actually says:

> **"For thou shalt worship no other god: for the Lord, whose name is Jealous, is a jealous God: Lest thou make a covenant with the inhabitants of the land, and they go a-whoring after their gods, and do sacrifice unto their gods, and one call thee, and thou eat of his sacrifice."**

In today's Christianity, covenants are being signed with Catholics, Mormons, and Muslims, as the focus switches from belief in the truth to a generic "relationship" with God. The drive to globally transform *Christ*ianity into an interfaith *Church*ianity continues at rapid pace. This is facilitated as the pragmatic leaders and the popular, mass-produced corrupt "Bibles" continue to take unholy scissors to God's Holy Scriptures.

Which God is the world being introduced to through interfaith unity? The jealous Lord God will not hold His peace for ever in this world that prefers man-centered relativism to the truth.

> *"The L*ORD *shall go forth as a mighty man, he shall stir up jealousy like a man of war: he shall cry, yea, roar; he shall prevail against his enemies. I have long time holden my peace; I have been still, and refrained myself: now will I cry like a travailing woman; I will destroy and devour at once."* (Isaiah 42:13-14)

Introducing People to God by Telling Them Mostly about You?

> "This is the essence of witnessing—simply sharing your personal *experiences* regarding the Lord . . . .
>
> "He [Jesus] wants you to share *your story* with others. Sharing your testimony is an essential part of your mission on earth because it is unique. **There is no other story just like yours**, so only you can share it. **If you don't share it, it will be lost forever**." (PDL; p. 290; emphasis added)

We are to be witnesses to *the truth*, to the Gospel of Christ. *His* story is completely unique, and if *His* Gospel is not shared with other people, *they* will be lost forever! Priorities are just a tad backward here! Nevertheless, *your* story is given greater importance than the Word of God:

> "Another value of your testimony is that it bypasses intellectual defenses. Many people who *won't accept the authority of the Bible* will listen to a humble, personal story." (PDL; p. 291; emphasis added)
>
> "You may feel you don't have anything to share, but that's the Devil trying to keep you silent. You have a storehouse of *experiences* that God wants to use to bring others into his family." (PDL; p. 289; emphasis added)
>
> "You may not be a Bible scholar, but you *are* the authority on your life, and it's hard to argue with personal experience. Actually, your personal testimony is

more effective than a sermon, because unbelievers see pastors as professional salesmen, but see you as a 'satisfied customer,' so they give you more credibility." (*PDL*; p. 290)

So the mission is to introduce people to *God* by telling them mostly about *you* because they won't accept or listen to *God's* Word—the Bible? If they don't want to accept or listen to the Word of *God*, then why would they want to be "introduced" to *God*?

The sad fact is that people who won't accept the authority of God's Word will not be willing to hear or believe in the Gospel of Christ to receive His salvation. But this tragedy is glossed over by the 'good news' that they will supposedly be willing to listen to *you* talk mostly about *you* and the new ultimate authority -- *experience*.

Consequently, you don't need to know much about the Bible to fulfill your purpose-driven mission because it's *your* unique story about your *experiences* that people want to hear. Subjective, relative experiences that easily can and do lead people astray have greater authority and credibility with people than the objective, absolute truth of God and His Word. Accordingly, Rick Warren neglects to even suggest comparing the lessons of your experiences with the unchanging truth of God's Word to make sure your experiences are not deceiving you, before you share them with others.

It used to be obvious that we can *only* be brought into the family of God through salvation by faith and that salvation *only* comes through the specific message of the Gospel of Christ. God's Word does not say that "our lives and experiences are the power of God unto salvation," nor does it say that "faith comes by seeing or hearing about the lives and experiences of others."

Yet sharing *our* story is largely what Rick Warren's fifth purpose is about. Again, God's Word says otherwise. It is not about *us* and *our* lives and *our* experiences:

> *"For I am not ashamed of the gospel of Christ: for <u>it</u> is the power of God unto salvation to every one that believeth; to the Jew first, and also to the Greek. For therein is the righteousness of God revealed from faith to faith: as it is written, The just shall live by faith." (Romans 1:16-17)*

> *"For we preach <u>not ourselves</u>, but Christ Jesus the Lord; and ourselves your servants for Jesus' sake. For God, who commanded the light to shine out of darkness, hath shined in our hearts, to give the light of the knowledge of the glory of God <u>in the face of Jesus Christ</u>. But we have this treasure in*

earthen vessels, that the excellency of the power may be of God, and <u>not of us</u>." (2 Corinthians 4:5-7)

"That the Gentiles should be fellowheirs, and of the same body, and partakers of his promise in Christ <u>by the gospel: whereof I was made a minister</u> . . . Unto me, who am less than the least of all saints, is this grace given, <u>that I should preach</u> among the Gentiles <u>the unsearchable riches of Christ</u>." (Ephesians 3:6, 8)

Incidentally, the Lord Jesus Christ is not a product to be bought and sold. The unbelievers that see church-goers as "satisfied customers" have more understanding than believers regarding the tremendous influx of money changers into these market-driven churches. Even so, it is no surprise that unbelievers would give more credibility to this *Church*ianity which centers around people and their perceived needs than they give to true *Christ*ianity which is founded on the Lord God and His Word.

> "By beginning with people's needs when you preach or teach, you immediately gain the attention of your audience . . . . A good **salesman** knows you **always start with the customer's needs, not the product**."—Rick Warren (Emphasis added)[2]

A.W. Tozer described today's Christianity perfectly:

> "The rise of a new religious spirit in recent years is marked by disturbing similarities to that earlier 'revival' under Constantine. Now as then a quasi-Christianity is achieving acceptance by compromise. It is dickering with the unregenerate world for acceptance and, as someone said recently, **it is offering Christ at bargain prices to win customers**. The total result is a conglomerate religious mess that cannot but make the reverent Christian sick in his heart."—A.W. Tozer (Emphasis added)[3]

Today's Christianity doesn't think twice about compromising in order to cater to itching ears that prefer storytellers to truth tellers.

> "Personal stories are also easier to relate to than principles, and people love to hear them." (*PDL*; p. 290)

People do indeed love to hear them. Scripture foretold today's refusal to hear the truth, but it does not say to give in to their desire and tell them stories when they won't listen to God's Word! It actually says the opposite:

"I charge thee therefore before God, and the Lord Jesus Christ, who shall judge the quick and the dead at his appearing and his kingdom; preach the word; be instant in season, out of season; reprove, rebuke, exhort with all longsuffering and doctrine. For the time will come when they will not endure sound doctrine; but after their own lusts shall they heap to themselves teachers, having itching ears; and they shall turn away their ears from the truth, and shall be turned unto fables." (2 Timothy 4:1-4)

Here's a good example of a fable, which reeks of the occult:

"Shared stories build *a relational bridge* that Jesus can walk across *from* your heart *to* theirs." (PDL; p. 290; emphasis added)

Regardless of the tremendous import ascribed to personal experiences and stories, and regardless of the sad fact that the world is not interested in hearing God's Word, the Word of God nevertheless unapologetically declares that it is **"the holy scriptures, which are able to make thee wise unto salvation through faith which is in Christ Jesus"** (2 Timothy 3:15). Unlike man, who has been bewitched away from the truth by man's philosophies and so-called wisdom, God, the One Who devised the means of salvation, knows what He is talking about.

The world is without excuse. It cannot hear or understand the preached Word because it does not want to, not because supposedly "outdated" methods are being used. It is the world's preference for its fleshly ways that lead to its deaf ears and blinded eyes and its hatred for the light in the words of the Lord Jesus Christ (e.g., see Matthew 13:15; Acts 28:26-27; John 3:19-20; 7:7; and 17:14).

Although faith comes by hearing the Word of God (see Romans 10:17), in those who hear it there still must be some faith that is *willing* to receive and respond to the Word. The preached Word of God will not profit those who have covered their eyes and ears, which Satan then exacerbates:

"But if our gospel be hid, it is hid to them that are lost: In whom the god of this world hath blinded the minds of them which believe not, lest the light

of the glorious gospel of Christ, who is the image of God, should shine unto them." (2 Corinthians 4:3-4)

"For unto us was the gospel preached, as well as unto them: but the word preached did not profit them, not being mixed with faith in them that heard it." (Hebrews 4:2)

Yet to cater to the unbelieving world, the "Good News" being spread today is a man-centered message designed to tickle itching ears.

> "In this book you have learned God's five purposes for your life on earth: He made you to be a *member* of his family, a *model* of his character, a *magnifier* of his glory, a *minister* of his grace, and a *messenger* of his Good News to others. Of these five purposes, the fifth can *only* be done on earth. The other four you will keep doing in eternity in some way. **That's why spreading the Good News is so important; you only have a short time to share your life message and fulfill your mission** . . . .
>
> "Question to Consider: As I reflect on **my personal story**, who does God want me to share **it** with?" (*PDL*; pp. 295-296; bold added)

It isn't the life of the Lord Jesus Christ that is the primary focus of the Purpose-Driven Paradigm.

> "sharing Christ: Learn how to enlist people in **the worldwide mission of sharing and reproducing *their* life**."—purpose driven church conference 2005 brochure (Emphasis added)[4]

The ravaging transformation of Christianity continues.

"Mission Accomplished!"

> "I pray that you will always be on the lookout to reach 'one more for Jesus' so that when you stand before God one day, you can say, 'Mission accomplished!'" (*PDL*; p. 288)

Chapter Eight

*F*irst, the mission of reaching one more for Jesus is not accomplished by sharing *our* personal story, sharing and reproducing *our* life, or getting as many unbelievers as one can into compromised worldly churches where the truth has been so watered down and twisted it is virtually unrecognizable—if it is even still given. It is giving them the solid truth, because apart from the truth of Christ and His Gospel these unbelievers will never be saved, or "reached" for Jesus.

Second, to stand before God one day and say, "Mission accomplished!" resembles proudly saying, "Look what *I* did for *you*, God!" Quite the contrary, we will be humbly falling on our faces before the infinitely holy Lord God overwhelmed with gratitude toward Him in the realization of the magnitude of all that *He* has done for *us*. And that includes God mercifully covering our ***"filthy rags"*** of seeming righteousnesses and hiding our lives in the Lord Jesus Christ so that only *His* true righteousness is seen!

But then, the purpose-driven life really is much more about *you* than it is about God.

> *"That's why* spreading the Good News is so important; *you only have a short time* to share *your* life *message* and fulfill your mission." (*PDL*; p. 295; emphasis added)

> "The Great Commission is *your* commission, and doing your part is the secret to living a life of significance." (*PDL*; p. 304)

The important motivation here in sharing the Gospel of Christ is so that before time runs out you can fulfill your mission and achieve significance. The significance, of course, comes from telling the world mostly about *you*! You were able to share *your* unique story before *it* was lost forever.

> "There is no greater epitaph than that statement! Imagine it chiseled on *your* tombstone: That *you* served God's purpose in your generation. My prayer is that people will be able to say that about me when I die. It is also my prayer that people will say it about you, too. That is why I wrote this book for you." (*PDL*; p. 318)

His purpose for writing this book was so that people will be able to say this about his readers when they die? In fact, what truly matters is that we live our lives focused completely on the Lord God Himself because we love Him, and because we want people to know and love the Lord God and speak words of praise about *the Lord God*! And the fact of the matter is, as Scripture often reiterates, when we do this, more often than not we will be persecuted and criticized rather than praised.

> *"Marvel not, my brethren, if the world hate you." (1 John 3:13)*

> *"Yea, and all that will live godly in Christ Jesus shall suffer persecution." (2 Timothy 3:12)*

> *"Blessed are ye, when men shall hate you, and when they shall separate you from their company, and shall reproach you, and cast out your name as evil, for the Son of man's sake. Rejoice ye in that day, and leap for joy: for, behold, your reward is great in heaven: for in the like manner did their fathers unto the prophets." (Luke 6:22-23)*

God's Word also assures us that when we stand up for the name of Christ, He is glorified even if we are reproached by people for doing so.

> *"If ye be reproached for the name of Christ, happy are ye; for the spirit of glory and of God resteth upon you: on their part he is evil spoken of, but on your part he is glorified." (1 Peter 4:14)*

However, if we water down the truth so much as to make it palatable and inoffensive to everyone who hears it, we need not worry about being reproached by man. But neither will Christ be glorified by us.

When focusing on God's *purposes*, the emphasis is not the precious *Lord God Himself* Who is the greatest Reward and Treasure a person could ask for. Rather, the emphasis becomes the significance of *our works* and what *we* do. As a result, the self-centered goal becomes an epitaph praising *our* works and then a self-*aggrandizing* entrance into the presence of our Self-*sacrificing* Lord and Saviour with the proclamation, "Mission accomplished!"

Basically, this is what the many do in Matthew 7:22. They try to get into heaven singing their *own* praises of their *own* **"many wonderful works,"** in essence saying, "Lord, Lord, look at all the things *we* did for *you*!" But it's not about us; it's about God:

"<u>Many</u>, O Lord my God, are <u>thy</u> wonderful works which <u>thou</u> hast done . . ."
(Psalm 40:5)

Here's a question to consider: Does the *Muslim* who claims to "believe in Jesus" and says "our mission here is to introduce people to God" already qualify according to the Purpose-Driven Paradigm to someday stand before God and say, "Mission accomplished!"? In the Paradigm's man-centered "spiritual journey," God is not going to ask him about his "religious background or doctrinal views." Even so, he claims to "believe in Jesus" more than we do!

At any rate, the Paradigm supports him by ascribing greater importance to knowing your purpose than knowing Jesus Christ.

◆ Part 3 ◆
Counting All Things but Loss for the Knowledge of Purpose

♦ *Chapter Nine* ♦

"There Is One Thing You Could Do Greater than Share Jesus Christ with Somebody"

Starting a Purpose-Driven Church

"*Nothing matters more* than knowing God's *purposes* for your life, and nothing can compensate for not knowing *them*." (*PDL*; p. 30; emphasis added)

"The *greatest* tragedy is not death, but life without *purpose*." (*PDL*; p. 30; emphasis added)

"Living on *purpose* is the *path to peace*." (*PDL*; p. 35; emphasis added)

"Knowing your *purpose* prepares you for eternity . . . .

"One day you will stand before God, and he will do an audit of your life, a final exam, before you enter eternity." (*PDL*; pp. 33-34; emphasis added)

These are not comments with a view to eternity. There are multitudes of people who have plenty of *purpose* in life but still die unsaved because they don't know the Lord Jesus Christ. Subjective "living on purpose" cannot save anyone or help anyone pass the so-called "final exam" or give anyone peace with the true God.

There is no greater tragedy than someone who dies without Jesus Christ as their Lord and Saviour. Jesus Christ does not become our Lord and Saviour merely because we believe we know God's *purposes* and are trying to live them. Jesus Christ becomes our Lord and Saviour because we know Who *He* is and *believe* in *Him* and then *He* lives *His* life in us (e.g., see Galatians 2:20).

People have gotten so purpose-driven in life that they have lost sight of the greatest privilege in the universe and the most *indispensable* knowledge -- knowing the Lord Jesus Christ *Himself*. Absolutely *nothing* compares to knowing our infinitely wonderful and awesome Lord. And when we know the Lord Jesus Christ *Himself*, everything else falls into place, including eternity. Self-significance, one of the goals of the purpose-driven life, is nothing but dung compared to winning Christ Himself!

> *"Yea doubtless, and I count all things but loss for the excellency of the knowledge of Christ Jesus my Lord: for whom I have suffered the loss of all things, and do count them but dung, that I may win Christ, and be found in him, not having mine own righteousness, which is of the law, but that which is through the faith of Christ, the righteousness which is of God by faith: that I may know him, and the power of his resurrection, and the fellowship of his sufferings, being made conformable unto his death." (Philippians 3:8-10)*

> *"And this is life eternal, that they might know thee the only true God, and Jesus Christ, whom thou hast sent." (John 17:3)*

It used to be obvious that the greatest thing we can do is tell others about the Lord Jesus Christ so they can have eternal life and the priceless privilege of knowing *Him* in this temporal life on earth and throughout eternity. Yet contrarily, although consistent with the previous quotes from his book, on November 2, 2003 Rick Warren actually stated the following in his Saddleback Church Service:

> **"Now you've heard me say many times that the greatest thing you can do with your life is tell somebody about Jesus and invite them to come to know him**. If you help somebody secure their eternal destiny that they spend the rest of their life in heaven, not hell, your life counts. Your life matters because nothing matters more than helping get a person and their eternal destiny settled. They will be forever ever grateful and thank you for the rest of eternity—thank you for telling me about Jesus Christ. **And I've always said that that was the greatest thing you could do with your life.** *I was wrong*. **There is one thing you could do greater than share Jesus Christ with somebody, and it is help start a church**. Because *a* church is going to outlast you and everybody else." (Emphasis added)[1]

The Purpose-Driven Paradigm's primary focus is not the Lord Jesus Christ Himself. In spite of adamant claims to the contrary, this is proven over and over throughout this *Purpose*-Driven Paradigm which commonly contradicts and negates any truth that has been given. Since *purpose* has become the be-all and end-all of life, today's Christianity has lost sight of the greatest privilege in the universe -- knowing and helping others to know *the Lord God*.

In a Paradigm in which purpose is preeminent, of course the churches started in lieu of giving the Gospel of Christ must be *purpose*-driven. Please do think about that:

> "I was told this last week by our international director, we now have purpose-driven churches in every nation in the world. Every nation. Think about that."—Rick Warren[2]

> "The purpose driven DNA is implanted in every cell of the Body of Christ."
> —Rick Warren[3]

Purpose, not God, is the center of *purpose*-driven. And whatever a person's or church's focus is, that is what they preach and teach.

Sharing the Message of Purpose with the World

*I*n support of his belief that telling others about Jesus Christ is *not* the greatest thing we can do, Rick Warren instead requires his followers to tell others about *his* message on the purpose of life. And to give added authority to his own required message he even throws in verses, which he extracted from their context in Scripture.

> "Now that you understand the purpose of life, **it is your responsibility to carry the message to others**. God is calling you to be his messenger. Paul said, '*Now I want you to tell these same things to followers who can be trusted to tell others.*' [endnote: 2 Timothy 2:2b (CEV)] **In this book I have passed on to you what others taught me about the purpose of life; now it's your duty to pass that on to others**. You probably know hundreds of people who do not know the purpose of life. **Share these truths** with your children, your friends, your neighbors, and those you work with. If you give this book to a friend, add your personal note on the dedication page.

> "The more you know, the more God expects you to use that knowledge to help others. James said, '*Anyone who knows the right thing to do, but does not do it, is sinning.*' [endnote: James 4:17 (NCV)] Knowledge increases responsibility.

But **passing along the purpose of life is more than an obligation**; it's one of life's greatest privileges." (*PDL*; pp. 309-310; bold added)

Rick Warren makes it clear that he believes God is calling us to be His messenger specifically in passing on *his* message on the purpose of life which he has been taught by "others," which he has now passed on to us in his book. According to him, this is our duty, responsibility, and obligation. He is so completely focused on his own understanding of purpose that he even goes beyond saying it is our duty and obligation. By putting James 4:17 where he did, he is clearly saying here that if we do not pass his message of purpose on, then we are *sinning*.

On the contrary, we are *not* to pass on unscriptural leaven from his book or any other source! The apostle Paul specifically wanted people to teach *the truth about Jesus Christ*, which he learned directly from Jesus Christ Himself. Yet Rick Warren would *require* us to teach the unscriptural, humanistic leaven of the world which he learned from "hundreds of writers and teachers."

What he is doing is scriptural malpractice, which is further evidenced in what immediately follows the previous quote regarding our "obligation" in passing along *his* understanding of the purpose of life:

> "Imagine how different the world would be if everyone knew their purpose. Paul said, '***If you teach these things*** *to other followers, you will be a good servant of Christ Jesus.*' [endnote: 1 Timothy 4:6 (CEV)]" (*PDL*; p. 310; bold added)

First, knowing your *purpose* has no power to change the world. It is being delivered from sin through knowing the Person of the Lord Jesus Christ and subsequently receiving the Holy Spirit to live in and through us that does indeed change people.

Second, Rick Warren is clearly trying to make the point in this section that we will be a good servant of Christ Jesus *if* we teach *these things*—what he learned from *hundreds* of people about the purpose of life—to other people. He has "the key," so according to him it is our "responsibility" and "duty" to pass it on.

Third, rightly dividing the Word of God does not consist of pulling out a phrase that seemingly supports your point when it is removed from its context. 1 Timothy 4:6 actually says:

> "***If thou put the brethren in remembrance of these things, thou shalt be a good minister of Jesus Christ, nourished up in the words of faith and of good doctrine, whereunto thou hast attained.***"

Rick Warren's Paradigm goes way outside the boundary of words of faith and good doctrine, which is inevitable when learning "a lot of truth from different religions." His "blueprint for Christian living" contains such a generic message of purpose that even those in other religions (faiths) have embraced its message of purpose-driven living. If his book was grounded in *"the words of faith and of good doctrine,"* it would not be acceptable to other religions or be popular in the world.

Nevertheless, he is so convinced his message is "the key" that near the end of his book he even summarizes teaching and modeling a purpose-driven life as *the work of Jesus* on earth. Yet the world hated Jesus and loves Rick Warren and his message.

> *"And this is the condemnation, that light is come into the world, and men loved darkness rather than light, because their deeds were evil. For every one that doeth evil hateth the light, neither cometh to the light, lest his deeds should be reproved." (John 3:19-20)*

> *"The world cannot hate you; but me it hateth, because I testify of it, that the works thereof are evil." (John 7:7)*

The Lord Jesus Christ brought light into the world, and the world hated His light and loved darkness. Now Rick Warren is bringing purpose-driven "light" to the world, and the world loves his "light." Think about it.

To cater to the world, the light of the Lord Jesus Christ must be removed to avoid His light's reproof, which is the very thing the world hated in the first place. This new message with the removed light is the message the world has opened its ears to:

> "The religious vision is uncomplicated and accepting: 'God wants to be your best friend.' Warren's Christianity, like his church, has low barriers to entry . . . .

> "It is tempting to interpret the book's message as a kind of New Age self-help theology. **Warren's God** is not awesome or angry and **does not stand in judgment of human sin**. He's genial and mellow."—Malcolm Gladwell, *The New Yorker*, 9/12/05 (Emphasis added)[4]

To remove the *judgment* of God is to remove the *throne* of God, and thus His *Lordship*; one does not exist without the other. It also removes Who the Lord God is in holiness and righteousness and justness and truth, among other attributes.

> *"But the L*ORD *shall endure for ever: he hath prepared his throne for judgment. And he shall judge the world in righteousness, he shall minister judgment to the people in uprightness." (Psalm 9:7-8)*

> *"And when he is come, he will reprove the world of sin, and of righteousness, and of judgment: of sin, because they believe not on me." (John 16:8-9)*

What the world sees is not the true Lord God or true Christianity because too many holes have been cut in the man-centered message it is being given. (By the way, Gladwell's article is clearly supported by Rick Warren's website Pastors.com which obtained permission to reprint it.[5])

The world may be very pleased with the holey message and new way of "doing church" in today's Christianity, but only temporarily. Its reaction will be quite different when it finds itself standing before the holy Lord God Who isn't anything like who it was led to believe in, and Who requires more than "knowing your purpose."

> *"Seek ye the L*ORD *while he may be found, call ye upon him while he is near: Let the wicked forsake his way, and the unrighteous man his thoughts: and let him return unto the L*ORD*, and he will have mercy upon him; and to our God, for he will abundantly pardon. For my thoughts are not your thoughts, neither are your ways my ways, saith the L*ORD*. For as the heavens are higher than the earth, so are my ways higher than your ways, and my thoughts than your thoughts. For as the rain cometh down, and the snow from heaven, and returneth not thither, but watereth the earth, and maketh it bring forth and bud, that it may give seed to the sower, and bread to the eater: So shall my word be that goeth forth out of my mouth: it shall not return unto me void, but it shall accomplish that which I please, and it shall prosper in the thing whereto I sent it." (Isaiah 55:6-11)*

> *"Jesus cried and said, . . . I am come a light into the world, that whosoever believeth on me should not abide in darkness. And if any man hear my words, and believe not, I judge him not: for I came not to judge the world, but to save the world. He that rejecteth me, and receiveth not my words, hath one that judgeth him: the word that I have spoken, the same shall judge him in the last day." (John 12:44, 46-48)*

Knowing the Lord Jesus Christ and His Word is clearly the most indispensable knowledge. Yet in purpose-driven living, knowing your purpose and sharing your message of purpose have priority, even if your message of purpose opposes God's purposes and truth.

The True Purpose of Life is "Becoming One with that Passive Spark of Divinity Longing for Actuality"?

> "When I wrote *The Purpose Driven Life*, I never imagined so many people would respond to its offer of hope and challenge. Using the book as a guide has enabled millions of people to discover the answer to life's most important question: What am I here for? I ended the book by asking readers, 'When will you write down your purpose on paper?' At that time I had no idea an essay contest about purpose would soon be established and provide the vehicle for *exactly what I hoped for*. Join me in celebrating this opportunity by writing an essay to share your message of purpose with us."—Rick Warren (Emphasis added)[6]

*G*od's purpose is for us to **"have no fellowship with the unfruitful works of darkness, but rather reprove them"** (Ephesians 5:11). Nevertheless, in 2004 Rick Warren joined the "distinguished panel" of five judges for The Power of Purpose Awards,[7] the worldwide essay competition to which he was referring in his previous quote.

This competition was sponsored by the interfaith, metaphysical John Templeton Foundation, which has the following objective:

> "*The objective of our Religious Foundations is to teach people that they are hurting themselves when they say they believe something.* What we should realize is we know almost nothing about God and therefore we should be eager to search and to learn."—John Templeton (Emphasis added)[8]

This Foundation of John Templeton is eager to learn from all religions. It funds projects such as "science research to supplement **the wonderful ancient scriptures of all religions**" (emphasis added) because Templeton believes that "relatively little is known about God through scripture."[9] Although he claims to be Presbyterian, his beliefs deny the Word of God:

> "Differing concepts of God have developed in different *cultures*. **No one should say that God can be reached by only one path**. Such exclusiveness lacks humility because it presumes that we can and do comprehend God. *The humble person is ready to admit and welcome the various manifestations of God.*"—John Templeton (Emphasis added)[10]

True to his belief that there is more than one way to God, Templeton has written the book *Wisdom from World Religions*, which is subtitled, "Pathways toward Heaven on Earth." His Foundation's website gives the following description of this book:

> "One of Templeton's most recent books, Wisdom from World Religions, assembles spiritual principles from sacred writings and from the teachings of Buddhism, Christianity, Confucianism, Hinduism, Islam, Jainism, Judaism, Sikhism, Taoism, Zen and Zoroastrianism."[11]

That he believes these religions are all pathways to heaven is only the beginning. His "wide-lens view of spirituality and ethics" also includes Metaphysics, such as "the New Thought movements of Christian Science, Unity and Religious Science" that "espouse a non-literal view of heaven and hell" and "suggest *a shared divinity between God and humanity*" (emphasis added).[12] Indeed, he has written about "our own divinity"[13] and has also said:

> "'The idea that an individual can find God is terribly self-centered. It is like a wave thinking it can find the sea.'

> "'The question is not is there a God, but is there anything else except God? **God is everyone and each of us is a little bit**.'" (Emphasis added)[14]

Templeton is "the visionary behind *The Power of Purpose Awards*."[15] And what is his goal? According to The Power of Purpose Awards website, "Templeton's goal has been nothing less than to *change mindsets about the concept of divinity . . .*" (emphasis added).[16]

Also according to this website, Templeton's essay competition was "a worldwide call for compelling and insightful essays to spark a new understanding of Purpose and unleash its Power to achieve noble goals."[17] Actually, it was not a "new" understanding of purpose that was ignited. It was a very ancient one, with roots in Gnosticism and Metaphysics, that seeks to unleash the power of the inner divinity and Oneness of all. Yet this is not at all surprising given the (New Age) New Spirituality beliefs and objectives of Templeton and his Foundation.

On The Power of Purpose webpage "ABOUT THIS COMPETITION," the "divine spark" within is mentioned three times.[18] The "divine spark" is panentheistic and gnostic, among other things. It refers to the pagan belief that nature and mankind are all a "spark" or a "fragment" of the ONE "God;" thus all of creation is divine since "All is in God and God is in All."

Even if a person was to read this synopsis of the competition without knowing this information ahead of time, enough information is given within it to convey this. The synopsis itself lets the readers know that "the divine spark" is "the idea that there is something of God's presence in each of us" and that it is in both humans and nature.[19]

This pagan concept is also referred to as "immanence"—a term Christians are deceptively being led to believe means merely that God is active in His creation. "Becoming one" with this inner divinity is the goal of Eastern enlightenment, which, not surprisingly, was presented as "the true purpose of life" in the essay that won the competition's $100,000 Grand Prize. The winner, August Turak (founder of the interfaith Self Knowledge Symposium), wrote in his essay:

> **"We must commit to becoming one with that passive spark of divinity longing for actuality** . . .
>
> **"Working toward this miraculous transformation, re-birth, or *inner alchemy* is the true purpose of life**. This transformation is what the West calls 'conversion' and the East 'enlightenment,' and is the fruit of our commitment to the authentically purposeful life that Father Christian described so well." (Emphasis added)[20]

Turak was introduced to his spirituality by the Zen Master he studied under. His "teacher, mentor, and life-long inspiration" is Richard Rose, who "always said that he found great wisdom in the writings of Theosophical Society founder Madame Blavatsky."[21] Turak's winning essay "Brother John" was a true story of his contemplative retreat at a Trappist monastery.[22] The monks there are "living a life of contemplative prayer according to the arduous Rule of St. Benedict"[23] (an arduous Rule of works that must be perseveringly followed to deserve salvation).

Contrary to Turak's claims, Eastern enlightenment is not in any way, shape, or form similar to the conversion or new birth of a new believer in the Lord Jesus

Christ. The former is by the power and deceptions of Satan. The latter is by the power and truth of God. The contemplative process of "becoming one with that passive spark of divinity" is an occultic "re-birth."

As noted earlier in chapter six, contemplative prayer is an occultic tool of the spirit realm designed to entice mankind into believing in this Oneness. Its underlying belief system is the pagan cousins of pantheism and panentheism -- God is/is in everything. This belief system teaches that "God" is not *outside* creation because he is not *separate* from anything. He is *within* creation giving Oneness to all.

Christian author Warren Smith was delivered from the New Age and has written books warning the Body of Christ on its dangers. In *Deceived On Purpose: The New Age Implications of the Purpose-Driven Church*, he writes:

> "When I was involved in New Age teachings and studying *A Course in Miracles*, I was taught that **the concept of 'Oneness' is inextricably linked to the understanding that God is 'in' everything.**" (Bold added)[24]

In his book, he discusses Rick Warren's own use of this teaching in his choice to quote Ephesians 4:6 from the *New Century Version* and also in the description of God in Saddleback's *Foundations* curriculum.

> "**The Bible says, '***He rules everything and is everywhere and **is in everything.**' [endnote: Ephesians 4:6b (NCV)]" (*PDL*; p. 88; bold added)

> "The fact that God stands above and beyond his creation does not mean he stands outside his creation. He is both transcendent (above and beyond his creation) **and immanent (within** and throughout his creation)."—*Foundations Participant's Guide* (Parentheses in the original; emphasis added)[25]

First, Ephesians 4:6 actually says, **"One God and Father of all, who is above all, and through all, and <u>in you all</u>,"** referring to **"the saints"** at Ephesus and **"the faithful in Christ Jesus"** (Ephesians 1:1). Second, these quotes, regardless of the intended meaning, are *foundational* tenets in paganism and should never be used in a "*Foundations*" course at any church or in any Paradigm claiming to be Christian (or in any book claiming to be a version of God's Word). In spite of the arguments that the intended meaning behind these two quotes is that God's "hand" is in everything or that God is "present" everywhere, that is *not* what these quotes say.

True to the Angel of light's purpose, churches today are presenting a synthesis of God immanent and God transcendent. And as they do, teachings on the "divine spark" (the "fragment" of God within all) are becoming more accepted.

"**The Eastern faiths have ever emphasized God immanent . . . The Western faiths have presented God transcendent** . . . Today we have a rapidly growing emphasis upon God immanent in every human being and in every created form. **Today we should have the churches presenting a synthesis of these two ideas** which have been summed up for us in the statement of Shri Krishna in the *Bhagavad Gita:* 'Having pervaded this whole universe with a fragment of Myself, I remain'."—Alice Bailey & Djwhal Khul (Bold added)[26]

". . . 'having pervaded this entire Universe with a fragment of Himself, He *remains.*' God is immanent **in** the forms of **all** created things; the glory which shall be revealed is the expression of that **innate divinity** in all its attributes and aspects, its qualities and powers, through the medium of humanity.

"On the fact of God and of man's relation to the divine . . . the new world religion will be based . . . . a fresh orientation to divinity and to the acceptance of the fact of God Transcendent and of **God Immanent within every form of life**.

"These are the foundational truths upon which the world religion of the future will rest."—Alice Bailey & Djwhal Khul (Bold added)[27]

Although *The Purpose Driven Life* has undergone numerous printings, as of its 46th printing no corrections have been made to Rick Warren's panentheistic declaration. His purpose-driven "manifesto" still reads, "The Bible says, 'He [God] . . . is in everything.'"

It used to be obvious to Christians that God is *not* immanent in everything. Even Richard Abanes, Rick Warren's biographer, has acknowledged in one of his books that "immanence, or the concept of divinity residing in all things" is a belief of pagans.[28] Apparently there was enough outcry over Rick Warren's lack of discernment in this area, that Abanes addressed it in his biography of him. Yet Abanes offers as a *defense*, "Warren's use of Ephesians 4:6 in *The Purpose-Driven Life* is an attempt to teach God's immanence"![29] Then after discussing God's "omnipresence," he continues his defense with a quote from a 1997 sermon in which Rick Warren himself even acknowledged:

> "God is not in everything. You hear this all the time. Everything is in God and God's in everything. That's a bunch of baloney! . . . God is not in everything and everything is not God. That is called pantheism."—Rick Warren[30]

According to Rick Warren's own sermon, the verse that he chose to quote from the New Century Version contains pantheism. So what happened? Why choose a perverted "Bible" version that quotes "baloney"?! What changed in him that led to his undiscerning choice to use an unholy "Bible" that sets forth a pagan tenet rather than Holy Scripture in this verse?

Abanes offers as a further defense that Rick Warren doesn't refer to everything as "divine" and isn't deliberately trying to teach pantheism. That may be true, but these statements are only rationalizations to cover the apparent refusal to make any retractions. At the same time, there's Rick Warren's choice to judge a competition that clearly presented these beliefs in its synopsis, not to mention in the beliefs of its visionary.

If the goal truly is to be scriptural, rather than a bridge between Christianity and the false beliefs of the world, then why is it that his actions are being defended and excused instead of corrected? Why is it so difficult to acknowledge the error and then make corrections in the new printings of the book? Why are Christian leaders and authors so willing to go against what they have previously believed and taught for the sake of defending error in this "whole new way of thinking and acting"?

> "When a man who is honestly mistaken hears the truth, he will either quit being mistaken or cease to be honest."—Unknown

The contradictions and changes continue. This is one example of many how teaching *sound* doctrine is becoming increasingly irrelevant in today's double-minded Christianity that speaks out of both sides of its mouth. People would be far better served contending for the faith than spending their time skirting the real issues and spin doctoring sin and error for the purpose of defending it.

Contrary to man's "baloney," neither God nor His divinity is in everything. Divinity, the essence of God, belongs to God and God alone. Some Christian leaders have fallen for the New Age teaching that our soul is a "divine spark," but our soul is not *divine*. Nor is being made in the image of God the same as being *divine*.

When God indwells believers of the Lord Jesus Christ, believers become **"one in Christ Jesus"** (see Galatians 3:28), but neither God nor His divinity becomes part of our nature. We are His *temple*, and He indwells us as a *separate* Being Who lives *His* divine nature through us, thus making us **"partakers,"** as stated in 2 Peter 1:4. God did not become "One" with the temple in Old Testament times, and He does not become "One" with us now.

The Almighty God shares His divinity with *nothing* and *no one*. Thus He alone is God and there is no "Oneness" with God for any part of His creation. No part of us ever has been nor ever will be divine. God alone is God. The belief that any part of mankind is divine or can become divine is a continuation of Lucifer's grave error who said that he **"will be like the most High"** (Isaiah 14:12-14).

Yet these beliefs are increasingly accepted in today's Christianity as the practices of contemplative spirituality become ever-more popular. And these beliefs are inseparable from the objectives of John Templeton, his Foundation, and his essay competition. Templeton must have been very pleased with Turak's winning essay in which "the true purpose of life" is to contemplatively transform ourselves by "becoming one" with our inner "divinity." His purpose of "chang[ing] mindsets about the concept of divinity" was served well by his five selected judges.

According to *Milestones*, a publication of the John Templeton Foundation, Turak's winning essay "was the *unanimous* first choice of the five judges in the essay competition" (emphasis added).[31] This winning essay had no mention of the Lord Jesus Christ or His Gospel. In fact, from Rome's false gospel of works to the (New Age) New Spirituality's false gospel of Oneness this winning essay *opposed* the Gospel of Christ. Nevertheless, *Rick Warren voted for it*. Nothing matters more than knowing your purpose.

The Power of Purpose Awards said in one of their e~LETTERs:

> "If our greatest global problem is spiritual emptiness—living without meaning and purpose—raising awareness through this new prize has been worth it tenfold."[32]

Rick Warren has similarly defined spiritual emptiness:

> "Spiritual emptiness -- billions of people don't know their purpose in life."—Rick Warren[33]

Apparently it doesn't matter which belief system your purpose in life is founded on. The message of purpose that he voted on sets forth a "true purpose of life" that is inseparable from the belief in immanence—i.e., that "God is in everything."

Even if Rick Warren had not voted for this essay, he still sat as one of five judges over the competition at which this essay won. His presence as judge for a metaphysical Foundation endorses the metaphysical winner. Which one of his five purposes did he fulfill in his fellowship with Templeton's unfruitful works of darkness:

- Was God worshipped or pleased by his endorsement of this interfaith Foundation of darkness?
- Was he helping anyone become part of God's family by supporting a Foundation that's working toward unifying the world's religions in interfaith unity?
- Was he becoming more "like Christ" by voting for a metaphysical essay espousing the inner spark of divinity and occultic inner alchemy as "the true purpose of life"?
- Was he serving God by serving the Foundations' godless objective of changing people's beliefs in God and divinity?
- Was he introducing anyone to the true God by promoting a competition whose visionary believes God cannot be found by individuals and that "God is everyone and each of us is a little bit"?

Where is the pastor who said:

> "Fundamentally, my role in life is to get people into heaven. And so I am spending all my time and energy on that, getting people into heaven."—Rick Warren[34]

Or does "getting people into heaven" have a broader meaning behind it that as yet remains under wraps? Using the broad way to reach people on the broad way does *nothing* for getting people *off* the broad way and into heaven! The immense popularity of this practice, which is the antithesis of the Gospel of Christ, reveals the dire state of today's Christianity. All this practice does is validate the broad way in the eyes of those on it as "another way" to God.

Is this what he wants to cooperate with and start doing? Is this what he wants to stop criticizing? Is this what he wants to be known for being *for*? The *Milestones* article that announced the "unanimous" vote closed with Rick Warren's comment as its final words:

> "Competition judge Warren added, 'I ended my book *The Purpose Driven Life* by asking readers, 'When will you write down your purpose on paper?' I had

no idea that an essay contest about purpose would soon be established, and provide the vehicle for *exactly what I hoped for.*'" (Emphasis added)[35]

In large letters across the top of the back cover of Richard Abanes' biography of Rick Warren is the following question that deserves a straightforward answer: "What Purpose Drives Rick Warren and His Message?" Although Rick Warren claims to be about God's purposes, God's eternal purposes are inseparable from the narrow way of the Lord Jesus Christ and His truth.

> *"And to make all men see what is the fellowship of the mystery, which from the beginning of the world hath been hid in God, who created all things by Jesus Christ: to the intent that now unto the principalities and powers in heavenly places might be known by the church the manifold wisdom of God, according to the eternal purpose which he purposed <u>in Christ Jesus our Lord</u>." (Ephesians 3:9-11)*

> *"For I am the* L<small>ORD</small>*, I change not . . ." (Malachi 3:6)*

♦ Chapter Ten ♦

Purpose-Driven "No Matter What it Costs"

Sacrificing Righteousness and Holiness

"If you will commit to fulfilling your mission in life **no matter what it costs**, you will experience the blessing of God in ways that few people ever experience. There is almost nothing God won't do for the man or woman who is committed to serving the kingdom of God. Jesus has promised, '*[God] will give you all you need from day to day if you live for him and make the Kingdom of God your primary concern.*' [endnote: Matthew 6:33 (NLT)]" (*PDL*; pp. 286-287; first brackets in the original; bold added)

Looking at the fruit of Rick Warren's Purpose-Driven Paradigm, "no matter what it costs" has already included the high costs of sacrificing truth, righteousness, holiness, and obedience to God. Indeed, *righteousness* has been deleted again in his very paragraph of declaring "no matter what it costs." The version that he chose to quote has deleted essential truth from Scripture:

"But seek ye first the kingdom of God, <u>and his righteousness</u>; and all these things shall be added unto you." (Matthew 6:33)

The Kingdom of God can only be sought through the righteousness of God because His Kingdom consists only of those who have been truly born again by the Holy Spirit through faith in the Lord Jesus Christ, thereby receiving His imputed righteousness.

Rick Warren's unscriptural claim that fulfilling your mission "no matter what it costs" will bring God's blessing in ways that only a "few people" experience is completely presumptuous and erroneous. God reiterates throughout His uncorrupted Holy Scriptures that His blessings are reserved for the *righteous*.

Sacrificing *the* Truth *of the* Faith

On November 22, 2004, in one of his interviews with Rick Warren, Larry King asked:

> "What is the purpose-driven life? And can non-Christians lead one?"[1]

Excellent question! Would the Lord Jesus Christ have "modeled" a life or taught others how to live a life that non-Christians (non-followers of Christ) could lead? And would this be "the work that brought glory to God"?

> "Jesus modeled a purpose-driven life, and he taught others how to live it, too. *That* was the 'work' that brought glory to God." (*PDL*; p. 310; emphasis added)

Regarding the work of God, the Word of God has this to say:

> **"Then said they unto him, What shall we do, that we might work the works of God? Jesus answered and said unto them, This is the work of God, that ye <u>believe on him</u> whom he hath sent." (John 6:28-29)**

There is a huge difference between Jesus being our "model" Whom we are to "imitate" in living a purpose-driven life and Jesus being our Lord and Saviour in Whom we are to believe and before Whom we are to kneel. Yet according to Rick Warren in this same interview, "*This book has enormous cross-over* and everybody's reading it" (emphasis added). "Does that mean that a Jew, a Muslim, an agnostic, an atheist could benefit from this book?" asked Larry King. To which Rick Warren replied, "If that's the question, sure. Anybody can benefit from it." He then proceeded to give an example of a Jewish lady passing it on to a Muslim lady.[2]

This would be fantastic if the saving, uncorrupted Gospel of the Lord Jesus Christ was actually in this book for the world to read so they could **"<u>believe</u> on him whom he hath sent."** But then the book would be offensive to the world instead of embraced by it.

The Purpose Driven Life is even praised on a website devoted to promoting Vijay Eswaran's book *In the Sphere of Silence*, which is overtly steeped in Eastern (specifically Hindu) religious beliefs and practices. The praise was part of a favorable review of Eswaran's book:

"Of late, books have come into the scene and continue to change or enrich lives. The bestseller, 'Purpose-Driven Life,' has *crossed religious boundaries* to be a handy practical guide to people." (Emphasis added)[3]

On December 2, 2005 during another of Larry King's interviews of Rick Warren, a caller identifying themself as of the "Jewish faith" commented that they were currently reading Rick Warren's book and asked him:

"I just wanted to know one question. How did you get a turning point to get your purpose-driven life?"

Notice that they did not see the need for the Lord Jesus Christ in their reading of his book, but merely getting one's "purpose-driven life." Likewise, Rick Warren didn't see the need to point that out. His typical feel-good, man-centered answer to the caller's question included nothing about the Lord Jesus Christ or the necessity of believing in Him as *the way* to God:

"I think it wasn't one turning point. I think over a period of time, as I began to study the Bible over and over, I kept seeing this concept that you are not an accident, that there are accidental parents, but there are no accidental children. There are illegitimate parents, but there are no illegitimate children.

"In other words, your parents may not have planned you, but God did. And honestly, it really doesn't matter whether your parents were good or bad or indifferent. The fact is the reason they were your parents is God chose them because they had just the right DNA that would create you.

"And God was more interested in making you than he was in their parenting skills, so they might have been terrible parents or they might have even abandoned you, and that concept that you're not an accident, you're made to last forever, you were made by God and for God, and until you understand that, life doesn't make sense."—Rick Warren[4]

The truth of *the* faith is being sacrificed in favor of feel-good, man-centered teachings that facilitate interfaith unity. It soon won't matter which religion's local church people attend, especially since it is believed that *all* religions (faiths) "have a portion of the truth." With this belief, what difference would it make in the new way of thinking which religion you decide to become "purpose-driven" in?

> "And by the way, **there's truth in *every* religion**. Christians believe that there's truth in every religion. But we just believe that there's one savior. We believe we can learn truth -- **I've learned *a lot* of truth from different religions. Because they all have a portion of the truth**. I just believe there is one savior, Jesus Christ."—Rick Warren (Emphasis added)[5]

Yet the Lord Jesus Christ said:

> "*Jesus saith unto him, I am the way, the truth, and the life: no man cometh unto the Father, but by me.*" (John 14:6)

Rick Warren's statement that "they all have a portion of the truth" actually negates the belief in "one savior" by denying that Jesus Christ is *the truth*. God's Holy Scriptures also specifically say that **"*truth came by Jesus Christ*"** (John 1:17). To say that truth is in other religions is to say that Jesus Christ is in other religions. This denies that *the* faith of Christianity is **"*the faith which was once delivered unto the saints*"** (Jude 1:3).

Without Jesus Christ, religions (faiths) have no portion of *the truth*. Jesus Christ cannot be parceled out. Furthermore, the doctrine of Christ which distinguishes between having the Lord Jesus Christ and having *another* "Jesus" or *another* "Christ" is not found in other religions (faiths). Jesus Christ, Who is *the* truth not *a* truth, said:

> "*. . . If ye continue in my word, then are ye my disciples indeed; and ye shall know the truth, and the truth shall make you free.*" (John 8:31-32)

> "*Howbeit when he, the Spirit of truth, is come, he will guide you into all truth . . .*" (John 16:13)

> "*Even the Spirit of truth; whom the world cannot receive, because it seeth him not, neither knoweth him: but ye know him; for he dwelleth with you, and shall be in you.*" (John 14:17)

The truth is not in any other religion (faith) because the Lord Jesus Christ is not in any other religion, and neither is His Word (the Holy Scriptures) nor the Holy

Spirit. Everything else is false and counterfeit and found on the broad way, not on the Lord Jesus Christ's narrow way of *the* truth of *the* faith.

Yes, the Lord Jesus Christ and His truth are divisive and exclusive of all who refuse to believe. He is Who He is, regardless of what people believe or want. People's beliefs do not determine Who He is. Rather, Who He is needs to determine people's beliefs. Time is running out. All who receive not the love of the truth will be sent strong delusion from God Himself so they will believe a damning lie (e.g., see 2 Thessalonians 2).

The Angel of light's purpose of uniting all people and religions (faiths) into a global interfaith unity will be completed by his coming false "Christ." The elimination of "non-essential" doctrines that divide the faiths, and the belief that all faiths have part of the truth actually further the Master Deceiver's work:

> "Today, slowly, the concept of a world religion and the need for its emergence are widely desired and worked for. **The fusion of faiths** is now a field for discussion. Workers in the field of religion will formulate the universal platform of the new world religion. It is a work of loving synthesis and will emphasize the unity and the fellowship of the spirit . . . . The platform of the new world religion will be built by many groups, working under the inspiration of the Christ . . . .
>
> "The churches in the West need also to realize that basically there is only one Church, but it is not necessarily only the orthodox Christian institution. **God works in many ways, through many faiths and religious agencies; this is one reason for the elimination of non-essential doctrines**. By the emphasizing of the essential doctrines and in their union will **the fullness of truth** be revealed. This, the new world religion will do . . ."—Alice Bailey & Djwhal Khul (Emphasis added)[6]

On July 21, 2003, *USA TODAY* reported:

> "Yet Warren's pastor-training programs welcome Catholics, Methodists, Mormons, Jews and ordained women.
>
> "'**I'm not going to get into a debate over the non-essentials**. I won't try to change other denominations. Why be divisive?' he [Rick Warren] asks, citing as his model Billy Graham, 'a statesman for Christ ministering across barriers.'" (Emphasis added)[7]

Notice that other religions (faiths), with either a false "Jesus" or no Jesus, are merely referred to here as "other denominations." Rick Warren's programs have been defended with the correction that Mormons and Jews were reputedly inserted here by USA TODAY.[8] Yet keep in mind that Mormonism is already considered a Christian "denomination" by a growing number of professing Christian leaders, as is Catholicism which is accurately included by USA TODAY because there are "Purpose Driven Catholics."[9]

Furthermore, it is good that Rick Warren is said to recognize that Mormonism and Judaism are other religions,[10] but, nevertheless, he taught his "preaching seminar" to the rabbis at the University of Judaism last June.[11] And this is the point! Doctrines are being set aside as non-essential in favor of watered-down purpose that transcends religious barriers and facilitates interfaith unity.

Although the Lord Jesus Christ said He came to bring **"division"** (Luke 12:51), "Why be divisive?" the world asks. "We won't join you on the narrow way of division and separateness, but why don't you join us on the broad way of unity and Oneness?"

Rick Warren was interviewed by The Dallas Morning News before he spoke at the Global Day of Prayer event,[12] held on May 15, 2005. He was asked:

> "You've become a very popular public speaker. As you've traveled, have you noticed any local differences in how your message is received?"

His response was:

> "Not at all . . . . It's *cross-cultural* -- I get letters from *Hindus*, from *Muslims*. [*The Purpose Driven Life*] didn't get niched as a *religious* book." (Brackets in the original; emphasis added)[13]

This latest quote follows the emerging pattern of interfaith unity. Hindus and Muslims are referred to here as being from different *cultures* not *religions*. This is another deceptive, inclusive, unifying trend in today's Christianity that has been growing as it increasingly merges with the broad way.

> "The Purpose Driven Church ministry philosophy is a transferable biblical process, successful in every culture, in every denomination, in churches of every size and shape."—PD Staff[14]

Because *The Purpose Driven Life* is based more on the teachings of the world than on the Holy Scriptures, this book did not get "niched as a *religious* book" and is therefore acceptable to those in different religions (faiths) or no religion. This negates its claims to prepare its readers for eternity.

The global transformation—transforming *Christ*ianity into a united *Church*ianity—continues unabated, as *the* truth of *the* faith is sacrificed in the name of purpose.

> "Purpose Driven's strategy dovetails easily into the polity of many denominations. We often describe it as a computer chip that can be used in *any form of computer.*"—PurposeDriven (Emphasis added)[15]

> "'Personal computers have brand names. But inside every pc is an Intel chip and an operating system, Windows,' Warren says. '*The Purpose Driven paradigm is the Intel chip* for the 21st-century church *and the Windows system* of the 21st-century church.'" (Emphasis added)[16]

The narrow way of the Lord God and His truth *cannot* be walked on by unbelievers. If it could, then God's Word would be a lie and salvation would be universal. If other religions (faiths) can be taught how to become purpose-driven, then God and His truth are not the center of the purpose-driven life. Besides, the exaltation of purpose above God and His truth has already been clearly evidenced in The Power of Purpose competition, which Rick Warren said was "exactly what [he] hoped for" when writing *The Purpose Driven Life*.

Incidentally, his statement that every PC has an Intel chip inside is not true; some of them have AMD chips. Similarly, the driving chip that would be universal in all churches can also be resisted. The Purpose-Driven Paradigm can be resisted by any person or pastor or church that cares more about walking in the Spirit and making disciples of the Lord Jesus Christ than being driven by an unscriptural Paradigm and making disciples of Rick Warren. Nevertheless, the "whole new way of thinking and acting" continues to metastasize.

Sacrificing the Mind of Christ

> "It has never been easier in history to fulfill your commission to go to the whole world. The great barriers are no longer distance, cost, or transportation. **The only barrier is the way we *think*.** To be a world-class Christian **you must**

make some mental shifts. Your perspective and attitudes must change."
(*PDL;* p. 299; bold added)

*R*ick Warren automatically assumes that Christians have the wrong perspective and attitudes. He has even stated that one of the problems with our perspective and the way we think is that we are thinking like *believers*, so we *must* mentally shift into thinking like *unbelievers*! Believe it or not, in an article titled, "We Must Learn To Think Like Unbelievers," he actually says:

> "The longer you're a believer, the less you think like an unbeliever . . . . Because I've been a Christian for most of my life, I think like a Christian. I don't normally think like an unbeliever. *Worse than that,* I tend to think like a pastor and that's even farther removed from an unbeliever's mind-set! That means *I must intentionally change mental gears* when seeking to relate to non-Christians."—Rick Warren (Emphasis added)[17]

In an interview with Pastors.com, he actually goes even further in a similar statement:

> "The secret of reaching unbelievers is learning to think like an unbeliever. But *the problem is* - the longer you're a Christian, the less you think like an unbeliever. And if you're a seminary-trained pastor, you're even more removed from unbelievers. **You think like a pastor, *not a pagan*. So you have to *intentionally learn* to think like an unbeliever again.** Paul says, 'I become all things to all men so I may, in some way, win some.'"—Rick Warren (Emphasis added)[18]

Nowhere in God's Word does the holy Lord God tell us that we are to conform our behavior and thinking to that of the *unbelieving* and *pagan* world so we can "relate to" or "reach" unbelievers! Not even in I Corinthians 9:22—a verse which is repeatedly twisted and abused by those who seek to justify their worldly behaviors—does Scripture say this.

Although Rick Warren goes on to say that the message is not to be compromised or changed, his changing methods do just that. In order to "intentionally learn to think like an unbeliever" and "a pagan," **"the mind of Christ"** which we have through the Holy Spirit (see I Corinthians 2:12-16) must be *set aside*. In the article, "We Must Learn To Think Like Unbelievers," Rick Warren also admits:

"I began Saddleback Church by going door-to-door for twelve weeks and surveying the unchurched in my area. I wrote down in my notebook five questions I would use to start Saddleback . . . .

"If they said yes [to 'actively attending any church'], I thanked them and moved on to the next home. I didn't bother asking the other three questions because *I didn't want to color the survey with the opinions of believers.*" (Emphasis added)[19]

According to his own admission, Saddleback Church has been deliberately founded on the opinions of unbelievers—who **"cannot please God."**

"But without faith it is impossible to please him: for he that cometh to God must believe that he is, and that he is a rewarder of them that diligently seek him." (Hebrews 11:6)

"For they that are after the flesh do mind the things of the flesh; but they that are after the Spirit the things of the Spirit. For to be carnally minded is death; but to be spiritually minded is life and peace. Because the carnal mind is enmity against God: for it is not subject to the law of God, neither indeed can be. So then they that are in the flesh cannot please God." (Romans 8:5-8)

Starting churches that please unbelievers (enemies of God) does not serve Christ.

"For do I now persuade men, or God? or do I seek to please men? for if I yet pleased men, I should not be the servant of Christ." (Galatians 1:10)

And giving greater importance to starting churches that please unbelievers than to telling them about the Lord Jesus Christ does not serve *the world*, either.

"Now you've heard me say many times that the greatest thing you can do with your life is tell somebody about Jesus and invite them to come to know him . . . . And I've always said that that was the greatest thing you could do with your life. *I was wrong.* **There is one thing you could do greater than share Jesus Christ with somebody, and it is help start a church.**"—Rick Warren (Emphasis added)[20]

The full impact of his final sentence in this quote—as well as of his earlier quote regarding not wanting "to color the survey with the opinions of *believers*"—is revealed in a statement Rick Warren made on May 23, 2005. It was at the Pew Forum's biannual Faith Angle Conference in a discussion on "Myths of the Modern Mega-Church." Providing further insight into his door-to-door survey that started his church, sadly and unbelievably he discloses the far greater importance of *Church*ianity over *Christ*ianity. Rick Warren admitted:

> "So then I asked myself, what kind of church are we going to be? And I decided, why don't we be a church for people who hate church? . . . And so I went out and for twelve weeks I went door to door, and I knocked on homes for about 12 weeks and just took an opinion poll. I had a survey with me. I just said, 'My name is Rick Warren. I'm not here to sell you anything, I'm not here to convert you, I'm not here to witness to you. I just want to ask you three or four questions. Question number one: **Are you an active member of a local church – *of any kind of religion* – synagogue, mosque, whatever?'** If they said yes, I said, **'Great, God bless you, *keep going*,'** and I politely excused myself and went to the next home. When I'd find somebody who'd say, 'No, I don't go anywhere,' I'd say, 'Perfect; you're just the kind of guy I want to talk to. This is great, you don't go anywhere. So let me ask you a question. Why do you think most people don't attend church?' And I just wrote the answers down. I asked, 'If you were looking for a church, what kind of things would you look for?' And I'd just list them. 'What advice would you give to me as the pastor of a new church? How can I help you?' So they'd say, 'I think churches exist for the community; not vice versa,' and I'd write that down."—Rick Warren (Emphasis added)[21]

What Rick Warren did here in starting his church shows the following:

- Starting a church supersedes giving the Gospel of the Lord Jesus Christ.
- Attending a local church of *any* religion (faith) supersedes knowing the Lord Jesus Christ for all eternity.
- Being *purpose*-driven supersedes helping others become a believer in the Lord Jesus Christ and gain eternal salvation.

Rick Warren was *purpose-driven*. Although the loving Lord God is **"not willing that any should perish, but that all should come to repentance"** (2 Peter 3:9), helping people come to a belief in the truth was not Rick Warren's intention—"I'm not here to convert you, I'm not here to witness to you." *His purpose* was to start a church based on the opinions of *unbelievers* only. Following God's purpose to help people believe would have defeated his own purpose.

But he even went the *opposite* direction of God's purpose. Regardless of the fact that these religions (faiths) are on the broad way leading to eternal destruction, he told them to *"keep going"* to their local churches *"of any kind of religion,"* and he praised and blessed these spiritually lost people for attending them. He definitely "intentionally change[d] mental gears when seeking to relate to [these] non-Christians"!

There is only one god who would be pleased with this behavior and whose purposes would be served with it. It isn't the loving Lord God of mercy and truth Who gives us His truth, salvation, and life on His narrow way -- where the *only* "religion" that is found is <u>the</u> *faith* of the Lord Jesus Christ.

> **"For this is good and acceptable in the sight of God our Saviour; <u>who will have all men to be saved, and to come unto the knowledge of the truth</u>. For there is one God, and one mediator between God and men, the man Christ Jesus." (I Timothy 2:3-5)**

In the new way of thinking, what difference does it make which religion's local church people belong to? After all, purpose-driven churches are more about who man is than Who God is.

Rick Warren's purpose-driven method of starting a church that will please unbelievers is popular:

> "This survey has been reprinted in dozens of books and articles. Several thousand churches have now used these 5 questions in their own communities. One denomination that I consulted with used these questions to start 102 new churches on a single day! If you haven't ever surveyed the unchurched in your area I strongly recommend that you do."—Rick Warren[22]

Now the global enormity of the purpose-driven method is even bringing in a "new reformation" on behavior and purpose.

> "In 1980, **a new kind of church was birthed that has impacted Christianity worldwide**. *The vision* has now been planted in more than 150 countries -

transforming millions of lives through tens of thousands of purpose driven churches around the globe.

> "The official inauguration of the global Purpose Driven movement will be celebrated at the anniversary of Saddleback Church in the 45,000 seat Angels Stadium. Our founding pastor, Rick Warren, will share our passion and vision for a new spiritual reformation in the 21st century. We believe April 17, 2005 will be remembered as a watershed moment in history." (Emphasis added)[23]

"Birthing" a new kind of church through interviewing enemies of God does not even come close to furthering *God's* Kingdom.

> ***"Except the LORD build the house, they labour in vain that build it . . ." (Psalm 127:1)***

Nevertheless, this new kind of church is being taken on its "spiritual journey" with Rick Warren as its guide. This new kind of church is being trained in his man-centered Paradigm's "groundbreaking manifesto on the meaning of life" -- its "blueprint for Christian living." And "no matter what it costs," this new kind of church is to be "the vanguard of a new reformation":

> "More than 400,000 churches have participated in the 40 Days of Purpose and 40 Days of Community modules that train their membership *in the Purpose Driven paradigm.*"—PD Staff (Emphasis added)[24]

> "Saddleback Church is now but one among thousands of purpose driven churches -- the vanguard of a new reformation. Together we are transforming the 21st century church through God's purposes."—PD Staff[25]

Part 4

Leading the Masses into a Spiritual Awakening or a Unity of Spiritual Blindness?

♦ *Chapter Eleven* ♦

"America's Most Influential Spiritual Leader"

"What in the World Are Our Pastors and Church Leaders Teaching Their Congregations?"

Simply being a Christian does not automatically immunize us from deception. It isn't *un*believers that Scripture repeatedly warns with: *"Take heed that ye be not deceived"* (Luke 21:8); *"Let no man deceive himself"* (1 Corinthians 3:18); *"Let no man deceive you with vain words"* (Ephesians 5:6); *"Let no man deceive you by any means"* (2 Thessalonians 2:3); *"But watch thou in all things"* (2 Timothy 4:5); *"Watch ye, stand fast in the faith"* (1 Corinthians 16:13); *"Be watchful, and strengthen the things which remain, that are ready to die"* (Revelation 3:2); *"Wherefore let him that thinketh he standeth take heed lest he fall"* (1 Corinthians 10:12); *"Therefore let us not sleep, as do others; but let us watch and be sober"* (1 Thessalonians 5:6); *"Therefore watch, and remember, that by the space of three years I ceased not to warn every one night and day with tears"* (Acts 20:31) . . .

Scripture's warnings are meant to be heeded. If Christians could not be deceived, then the Holy Spirit would be wrong about those who will *"depart from **the faith**"* (1 Timothy 4:1). On the contrary, the goal of the spirit world in eliminating truth, or what it views as "non-essential doctrines," is having tremendous success within an anything but watchful Christianity.

Baptist pastor Chuck Baldwin posted an article on June 2, 2005, titled, "Christians No Different from the World," in which he sadly and beseechingly reported the following:

> "Recently, pollster George Barna released his research regarding the beliefs and conduct of today's Christians. The results are shocking! According to Barna, **only 9% of America's born again Christians have a Biblical worldview**. Only 9%!
>
> "To determine a Biblical worldview, Barna used the following 8 point criteria:
>
> • Believing that absolute moral truths exist.

- Such truths are defined by the Bible.
- Jesus Christ lived a sinless life.
- God is the all-knowing, all-powerful Creator and still rules today.
- Salvation is a gift of God and cannot be earned.
- Christians have a responsibility to share their faith in Christ.
- Satan is real.
- The Bible is accurate in all its teachings.

"As any real Christian can see, these 8 points comprise basic Biblical truth. To think that more than 90% of born again Christians would deny any one of these fundamental truths suggests that the vast majority of professing Christians today have no clue as to what being a Christian really means.

"As a result, the obvious question that must be asked is, 'What in the world are our pastors and church leaders teaching their congregations?' It would appear that whatever they are teaching, **it isn't the Bible!** . . .

"George Barna summarized his findings by saying, 'Faith makes very little difference in their [Christians] lives: believers do not train their children to think or act differently [from the world] . . . .'

"The problem with America's Christianity today is that, for the most part, it doesn't exist! What passes for Christianity is instead an anemic, spineless, diluted substitute without convictions or principle . . . .

"No wonder that despite some 300,000 evangelical churches, scores and hundreds of television and radio ministries, and millions of professing Christians, our nation is still on a collision course with calamity! . . .

"George Barna's research suggests that **the real mission field may not be in heathen lands across the seas but in America's churches right here at home!**" (Brackets in the original; emphasis added)[1]

Additionally, an article from the November/December 2005 issue of the *AFA Journal* was recently posted by *AgapePress* titled, "A Strange Faith -- Are Church-Going Kids Christian?" This article underscores Pastor Baldwin's concerns as well as indicates the inroads of the (New Age) New Spirituality belief that all gods are ONE:

> "Barna, for example, after noting that 86 percent of teenagers claimed that they believed in God, asked, 'But what is the nature of the God they embrace?'
>
> "A strange god indeed, as it turns out. In his book, *Third Millennium Teens*, Barna revealed this stunning fact: **63 percent of church-going, supposedly Christian teens said they believed 'Muslims, Buddhists, Christians, Jews and all other people pray to the same God, even though they use different names for their god.'**
>
> "**In other critical areas of Christian doctrine – e.g., the divinity of Christ, the resurrection, the reality of absolute truth – the majority of church-going teenagers simply do not hold to views that are orthodox** . . . .
>
> "How could teenagers who go to church so often know so little – or at least *believe* so little – of the historic Christian faith? And whose fault is it? . . .
>
> "**Apparently, many church-going teens are not being challenged by the preaching and teaching of the true Gospel**. How else can one explain the overwhelming assumption among teens that they are Christian, when they clearly are not? . . .
>
> "Unless Christian leaders want to contemplate a future – much like that unfolding in Europe – in which their youth abandon Christianity in droves, **there must be a brutally honest re-examination of how we do church**." (Bold added)[2]

The masses are being led into a unity of spiritual blindness, thanks to purpose-driven leaders who believe the proper beliefs are already in place so all we need is a new Reformation of *purpose* and *behavior*.

> "**The *last* thing many believers need today is to go to another Bible study. They already know far more** than they are putting into practice." (*PDL*; p. 231; bold added)

"You see, **we know all the right things. We don't need a Reformation of belief** . . . . we need a Reformation of **not creeds** but deeds, **not beliefs** but behavior, to be doers of the word . . . . It's about our mission, and will we be the church."—Rick Warren (Emphasis added)[3]

This new way of "doing church" is so focused on man's teachings on *purpose* that God's teachings on *truth* are being destructively neglected. Christianity is being transformed into a religion of doers who don't know the truth.

Pastor Baldwin questioned, "What in the world are our pastors and church leaders teaching their congregations?" Another new survey by The Barna Group has revealed that Rick Warren's *The Purpose Driven Life* and *The Purpose Driven Church* are respectively the two "most helpful" books among pastors. And in the category for "most influential authors" among pastors, "not surprisingly, Rick Warren was king-of-the-hill in this listing . . ."[4]

Not only are pastors using his books to teach their congregations, but it repeatedly gets pointed out—and is easily seen on the Internet on many church sites—how pastors are using his *sermons* as well. Yet Rick Warren thinks he's improving pastors and making them into "a hero" by helping them out with his own sermons. The following quote, from *FORTUNE* magazine, is in reference to small-town pastors:

"'That guy's out flipping burgers or working as a mechanic during the week, and then, in four hours, trying to come up with something to say on Sunday . . . . If I can help that guy, *if I can move him from a C to a B preacher, so be it. I'll make him a hero.*'"—Rick Warren (Ellipsis dots in the original; emphasis added)[5]

What are our pastors teaching their congregations? Instead of men of God who studied the Word of God and faithfully spoke sermons as led by the Spirit of God, we now have clones of Rick Warren who buy and download the word of Rick Warren and "heroically" speak sermons as given by Rick Warren. Rick Warren is rescuing preachers from their "four hours" of having to study the Word of God and "trying to come up with something to say." Remember when the "Office" of preachers used to be called their "Study"? How times have changed in the new Paradigm.

Now, according to advertisements in Rick Warren's Ministry Toolbox™, pastors can "get help from Rick Warren himself!" (exclamation point in the original).[6] Contrary to one of these advertisements, sermons are not a "game":

"Looking for ideas for a holiday sermon this year? Check out these 34 holiday sermon transcripts from Rick Warren. Not only will you find Christmas sermons, but you'll be ahead of the game when Easter comes around!"—Rick Warren's Ministry Toolbox™, 11/23/05[7]

Sermons are supposed to be the timely messages of the Holy Spirit through the study of *God's* Word, not the reproduced messages of Rick Warren through the study of *his* words. Instead of sitting at the feet of the Lord Jesus Christ, pastors can sit at the feet of Rick Warren and pay to "get help from Rick Warren himself!"

"Are you looking for help to prepare a holiday message this year? **Get help from Rick Warren himself!** Click here to check out the special price . . ." —Pastors.com (Emphasis added)[8]

"Having to prepare sermons for holidays can often be difficult and sometimes even **distracting**. Let this great resource tool of 34 Holiday Sermon Transcripts help you. This CD rom contains some of Rick Warren's most effective HOLIDAY messages."—Pastors.com (Emphasis added)[9]

"The busyness of Christmas and New Year's can make sermon preparation difficult. This holiday season, we hope to make your preparation a little easier! . . .

"**34 holiday sermon transcripts for only $99 ($238 value!)** . . .

"Order one for yourself and others to give as Christmas presents!" —Pastors.com e-mail[10]

Incidentally, the Holy Spirit is free and perfectly effective. But He might as well go home because today's Christianity has laid Him off and replaced Him, which is clearly evidenced in the growing unity of spiritual blindness.

Rick Warren may include things such as Barna's 8-point criteria for a biblical world view in his teachings. But he so frequently waters down and contradicts and negates any truth he gives that his Purpose-Driven Paradigm is a huge part of the problem instead of part of the solution. Nevertheless, this Paradigm is being taught by hundreds of thousands of pastors to their churches and is being adopted and praised by governments and businesses and religions (faiths) of the world.

"Secular America's Favorite Evangelical Christian"

"'Rick Warren is arguably the most influential pastor in America.'" —RickWarren.com, quoting The Economist"[1]

"'The Purpose Driven Life is the epicenter of a spiritual shockwave taking root across America . . . It has become a movement.'"—RickWarren.com, quoting ABC News[12]

"'Business and political leaders across America are turning to Rick Warren for guidance.'"—RickWarren.com, quoting The Times (London)[13]

"'Movie stars and political leaders aren't the only ones turning to Rick Warren for spiritual guidance. Millions of people - from NFL and LPGA players to corporate executives to high school students to prison inmates - meet regularly to discuss The Purpose Driven Life.'"—RickWarren.com, quoting TIME[14]

"How do you explain a book by a pastor selling now over 25 million copies? And that's in English. The book has sold over 30 million copies worldwide." —RickWarren[15]

"More than three years after the book was published . . . it remains on the New York Times best-seller list. It has also been translated into 56 languages." —Newsweek, 12/15/05[16]

"Selling at up to 1 million copies per month, it [The Purpose-Driven Life] has been the best-selling new book in the world since 2003."—Christianity Today, October 2005[17]

". . . offers are regularly coming in from government, the business world, and even Hollywood, seeking Warren's help in understanding The Purpose Driven Life."—Florida Baptist Witness, 5/6/04[18]

"He [Rick Warren] also leads the Purpose Driven Network of churches, a global coalition of congregations in 162 countries. More than 400,000 ministers and priests have been trained worldwide, and almost 157,000 church leaders subscribe to the Ministry Toolbox, his weekly newsletter."—RickWarren.com[19]

"In the 1990s I trained about a quarter of a million pastors. It's now gone, as I said, to over 400,000 . . . and we're talking about all kinds of different groups, including priests in the Catholic church, and including rabbis."—Rick Warren[20]

"As a global strategist, Dr. Warren advises leaders in the public, private, and faith sectors on leadership development, poverty, health, education, and faith in culture. He has been invited to speak at the United Nations, the World Economic Forum in Davos, the African Union, the Council on Foreign Relations, Harvard's Kennedy School of Government, TIME's Global Health Summit, and numerous congresses around the world. *TIME* magazine named him one of '15 World Leaders Who Mattered Most in 2004' and in 2005 one of the '100 Most Influential People in the World.' Also, in 2005 *U.S. News & World Report* named him one of 'America's 25 Best Leaders.'

"As a theologian, Dr. Warren has lectured at Oxford, Cambridge, the University of Judaism, the Evangelical Theological Society, and numerous seminaries and universities."—RickWarren.com[21]

"One of the things you guys need to be aware of is the exploding purpose-driven movement on universities. And it's under the ground right now. But it is really starting to explode in universities. And actually Starbucks, near universities, are actually doing these *Purpose Driven Life* reading groups. And they actually – Starbucks asked me to write a little thing that they're gonna put on the back of their cups. It's a quote from *Purpose Driven Life*. It's gonna go on the back of Starbucks cups in April because so many of these *Purpose Driven Life* reading groups are using Starbucks places. And as a result I've accepted invitations. So this year I spoke at Harvard. I spoke at Oxford. I spoke at Cambridge. I spoke at the University of Judaism. I've got Yale coming up. And it's just amazing what's happened. It's a story you guys ought to be aware of."—Rick Warren[22]

"All of a sudden I'm going up on Capitol Hill and talking to guys. Producers in Hollywood are asking me to come up and discuss the book with eight or nine major studio producers."—Rick Warren[23]

"And then I flew to Philadelphia where this last weekend I was the chaplain for Live 8. Try being a chaplain for rock stars; that's a lot of fun. That's a lot of fun."—Rick Warren[24]

"During his 12-day tour ['marking the two-year anniversary of the book's release'], Warren will speak to a variety of East Coast audiences in 16 events about what he describes as 'the renewal of purpose happening in America -- the grassroots spiritual awakening that has been reported in dozens of national newspapers.' . . .

"Warren plans to use the tour to speak to different groups of what he calls 'cultural influencers,' including the media and entertainment industry in New York City, military and government leaders in Washington, D.C., and business leaders, philanthropists, psychologists, religious leaders and university students in other locations -- and the national convention for Mothers of Preschoolers in Nashville, Tenn., where three children's Purpose Driven books will make their debut . . . .

"Stops on the tour include:

"Sept 17 -- Washington, D.C., including an event at the Pentagon.

"Sept 19 -- West Point, N.Y. at the U.S. Military Academy."—*Baptist Press Staff*[25]

"That week [April 11, 2005], he [Rick Warren] joined Chuck Colson, founder of the world's largest prison ministry, in signing an historic partnership between Prison Fellowship and Purpose Driven to place 40 Days of Purpose and Celebrate Recovery into every prison in the world."—PD Staff[26]

"But then this last year it [40 Days of Purpose] hopped over and all of a sudden corporations started doing it, voluntarily. Coke corporation, Disney did it, Wal-Mart did it, Ford did it. All of the professional basketball and baseball teams."—Rick Warren[27]

"Another trend that I see is this 40 days phenomenon – this 40 Days of Purpose, which of course I'm right in the middle of . . . . it spread to corporations . . . and they started doing 40 Days of Purpose. And then it spread to all the sports teams. I spoke at the NBA All-Stars this year because all of the teams were doing 40 Days of Purpose. LPGA, NASCAR, most of the baseball teams – when the Red Sox were winning the World Series, they were going through 40

Days of Purpose during the Series . . . . *The Purpose Driven Life* is not just the best-selling book in American history; it's the best-selling book in about a dozen languages. It's in about 30 languages right now and that's why I was at this meeting last night with the Spanish ['in Miami speaking to this huge international convention of all of the Spanish-language publishers and they gave me the city key to Miami'].

"The next phase that you're going to see is we're actually doing citywide 40 Days of Purposes."—Rick Warren[28]

"Warren talks of turning Rwanda into 'the first purpose-driven nation.' . . .

"Warren says he was 'looking for a small country where we could actually work on a national model,' and Kagame [president of Rwanda], impressed by The Purpose-Driven Life, volunteered Rwanda in March. In July Warren and 48 other American Evangelicals, who have backgrounds in areas like health, education, micro-enterprises and justice, held intensive planning meetings with Rwandan Cabinet ministers, governors, clergy and entrepreneurs. One dinner was attended by a third of the Rwandan Parliament."—*Time*, 8/22/05[29]

". . . Rick Warren left Rwanda on the presidential jet to attend a meeting of African leaders in Senegal, then he went on to other meetings in Europe."
—*Christianity Today*, October 2005[30]

"I've had two state dinners in China in Tienanmen Square and People's Hall with their government, with the bureaucrats there, with the Cabinet members. I've actually had them in our home and had them in our church, and they've given me pretty much carte blanche in China for some reason. I don't know why they trust me . . ."—Rick Warren[31]

"My wife recently met with President Arroyo of the Philippines, and she said, 'We want to be the first purpose-driven nation.' She said, 'We have taken this book [*The Purpose Driven Life*] as a book for values and ethics, and we are requiring government leaders to read it. And they're teaching it in public schools.'

"I sat at a table the other day with the Minister of Commerce from Paraguay, and he didn't speak English. And I was trying to explain to his wife what I did, and I handed her my card, and she spoke English. When she finally translated the term 'purpose-driven' to her husband, he said, 'Oh, tell him I'm on day 38.' And he said, 'The President and I are going through this.' And I've heard this story a thousand times over around the world."—Rick Warren[32]

"Last night I signed a book for Viktor Yuschenko, who asked for a copy of *The Purpose Driven Life*. A few months ago, I signed a *Purpose Driven Life* for Fidel Castro, who asked for one . . . .

"I've probably signed books for, oh, probably 30, 40 different governmental presidents, you know, and I didn't ask them. They just asked me. So I'm interested in influencing influencers, but I'm not a politician."—Rick Warren[33]

[Regarding the Council on Foreign Relation's Influential Forum] "Each year, the Council organizes more than 200 events for members in New York and Washington, including . . . conversations with authors of important new books . . ."—Council on Foreign Relations brochure[34]

"September 12, 2005
A Conversation with Rick Warren
General Meeting
Speaker: Rick Warren
            Author, The Purpose-Driven Life, best-selling hardback in U.S. history. Called 'America's New People's Pastor' by Time Magazine"
            —Council on Foreign Relations, An Influential Forum[35]

"I spoke this morning with a representative from the organization that sponsored the Interfaith Prayer Breakfast [in conjunction with the United Nations' 60th Anniversary World Summit 2005], the Christian Embassy. According to him, there were around 200 'high level' delegates, including four presidents of foreign countries attending the event where Rick Warren spoke on Tuesday morning (13th) [September 2005]."—Ingrid Schlueter (producer and co-host of VCY America's Crosstalk Radio Talk Show)[36]

"The influence of the book keeps amazing me everyday as I get requests for autographed copies. I have signed books for 1) All the Supreme Court Justices

2) One for Fidel Castro (!) 3) One for the President of Peru . . . , and I even got a note saying that everyone on Air Force One was reading the book recently.

"But all this is not about us. God's intention is much bigger than the book. It's all about the global glory of God! We intend to leverage the attention that the Purpose Driven Life has garnered to bring about a whole new way of thinking and acting in the church about our responsibility in the world."—Rick Warren (Exclamation point in the original)[37]

"America's new superstar pastor wants to rebrand evangelical Christianity. He's got the management genius to do it. Here's where he's leading his troops . . . .

"**In part by campaigning for the job, Warren . . . has become secular America's favorite evangelical Christian.** This year he has spoken at Harvard, Oxford, Cambridge, the Aspen Ideas Festival, the Young Presidents Organization, a Pew Foundation forum for religion writers, and the University of Judaism. (The rabbis wanted to get his advice on how to increase their market share.) He has gone before the Council on Foreign Relations to pitch his newest idea: a breathtakingly ambitious project to mobilize American Christians to fight poverty, illiteracy, and AIDS in Africa.

"A protégé of management thinker Peter Drucker, Warren is also cultivating corporate executives. He calls himself Rupert Murdoch's pastor, he has entertained Jack Welch at his home, and he will meet Bill Gates at a *Time* magazine conference on global health, where they are both scheduled to speak. He also has forged ties with celebrity activists like Bono, who arranged to make him official pastor of the Live 8 concert last summer in Philadelphia. ('The only thing I remember about that concert is Linkin Park and a sweet smell in the air,' Warren joked to his congregation.) If a middle-aged Baptist minister can be said to possess that elusive quality called buzz, Rick Warren has it right now."—*FORTUNE* Magazine, 10/05 (All parentheses in the original; emphasis added)[38]

"Business experts also speak in reverent tones about one of the greatest branding leaders in a generation: Rick Warren of Saddleback Church.

"Rich Karlgaard, publisher of Forbes magazine, in 2004 declared Warren's 'The Purpose-Driven Church' the best book on entrepreneurship, business and investment he'd seen in years.

"Warren followed that with his mega-best-seller 'The Purpose-Driven Life.' His purpose-driven success has spawned a whole purpose-driven department at Saddleback . . . and Warren's friends tease him publicly about what might be coming next: purpose-driven toothpaste?

"Warren has his sights set much higher: making Africa the first purpose-driven continent."—*The Orange County Register*, 12/9/05[39]

"'**I've got a target**,' he [Rick Warren] says. '**It's called the globe**: The whole Gospel for the whole world.'"—*USA TODAY*, 7/21/03 (Emphasis added)[40]

"He's been often named '*America's most influential spiritual leader*' and '*America's Pastor*.'"—RickWarren.com[41]

"Bob Buford said just a few moments ago he [Rick Warren] is also perhaps the pivotal figure in American Christianity today."—David Gergen[42]

"Call it open-source evangelism. 'We're kind of the Linux of Christianity,' Warren says."—*FORTUNE* Magazine, 10/05[43]

*T*he Lord Jesus Christ made it clear that His narrow way is hated by the world. Yet Rick Warren's "purposes of God" are acceptable, and even "important," to other religions (faiths), Communists, the Pentagon, the U.S. Supreme Court, the Council on Foreign Relations, the United Nations, and the truth-hating world. Clearly, his purpose-driven message is too watered down to have enough of the Lord God's truth and Gospel to be recognized by the world. This does not bring "global glory" to God.

"I have given them thy word; and the world hath hated them, because they are not of the world, even as I am not of the world." (John 17:14)

"If the world hate you, ye know that it hated me before it hated you. If ye were of the world, the world would love his own: but because ye are not of the world, but

> *I have chosen you out of the world, therefore the world hateth you. Remember the word that I said unto you, <u>The servant is not greater than his lord. If they have persecuted me, they will also persecute you</u>; if they have kept my saying, they will keep yours also. But all these things will they do unto you for my name's sake, because they know not him that sent me." (John 15:18-21)*

> *"Then shall they deliver you up to be afflicted, and shall kill you: and ye shall be hated of all nations for my name's sake." (Matthew 24:9)*

> *"And ye shall be hated of all men for my name's sake: but he that shall endure unto the end, the same shall be saved." (Mark 13:13)*

On the other hand, tickle itching ears with man-centered teachings, and the world will love you.

> *"Woe unto you, when all men shall speak well of you! for so did their fathers to the false prophets." (Luke 6:26)*

In the name of purpose, the intention "to bring about a whole new way of thinking and acting in the church about our responsibility in the world" has been largely accomplished. *Change* is neutralizing today's Christianity. It used to be obvious that the message of Jesus Christ runs contrary to the world.

> "As soon as you try to turn the flock everybody says you're against everything. Of course, I'm against the devil, I'm against sin, I'm against worldliness, I'm against the flesh and I'm against Christianity that pretends to be Christianity and isn't. I'm against spiritual ignorance that tries to harmonize Christianity with the world. It's absolutely futile to try to do it.

> "There was a day when our religious leaders were made fun of and laughed at and opposed, even put in jail and driven out of town, but nowadays they are riding on the shoulders of the mobs and the multitudes because they are trying to make Christianity as much like the world as possible in order to win the world . . . . Don't we know that the message of Jesus Christ runs contrary to man and not in favor of man?"—A.W. Tozer[44]

Apparently not.

"Ministering to Hurting People [Is] More Important than Maintaining Purity"

*R*ick Warren believes that local churches that do not change according to his New Reformation are "dying." And not only are they "dying," but he says they are dying *on the vine*:

> "This reformation is all about how we act and operate in the world. It involves the key components of purpose, decentralization, lay mobilization, use of technology, and continuous learning. Churches that change are thriving and growing more effective. *Churches that refuse to change will miss the reformation, and are dying.*"—Rick Warren (Emphasis added)[45]

> "We've all heard speakers claim, 'If you'll just pray more, preach the word, and be dedicated, then your church will grow.' Well, that's just not true. **I can show you thousands of churches where pastors are doctrinally sound; they love the Lord; they're committed and spirit-filled and yet their churches are dying *on the vine*.**"—Rick Warren (Emphasis added)[46]

This statement completely disregards what Scripture says about "the vine." The Lord Jesus Christ said:

> *"I am the true vine . . . Abide in me, and I in you. As the branch cannot bear fruit of itself, except it abide in the vine; no more can ye, except ye abide in me. I am the vine, ye are the branches: He that abideth in me, and I in him, the same bringeth forth much fruit: for without me ye can do nothing." (John 15:1, 4-5)*

It is not the churches "on the vine" that need to be warned. Not every church that thinks it's alive actually is:

> *"And unto the angel of the church in Sardis write . . . I know thy works, that <u>thou hast a name that thou livest, and art dead</u>. Be watchful, and strengthen the things which remain, that are ready to die: for I have not found thy works perfect before God. Remember therefore how thou hast received and heard, and hold fast, and repent. If therefore thou shalt not watch, I will come on thee as a thief, and thou shalt not know what hour I will come upon thee." (Revelation 3:1-3)*

And it is not the churches that are refusing to change that need to be warned.

> *"My son, fear thou the* Lord *and the king: and meddle not with them that are given to change: for their calamity shall rise suddenly; and who knoweth the ruin of them both?" (Proverbs 24:21-22)*

These churches that are "thriving" in the Purpose-Driven Paradigm of change toward unity and diversity are filled with "pagans," etcetera. Nevertheless, they are deemed "healthy" as long as they are "purpose driven":

> "Every church is driven by something . . . But to be healthy, it must become purpose driven . . . .
>
> "No church is perfect but you can be healthy without being perfect."
> —Rick Warren[47]
>
> "Health doesn't mean perfection . . . . There will never be a perfect church this side of heaven, because every church is filled with pagans, carnal Christians, and immature believers.
>
> "I've read books that emphasize, 'You've got to reinforce the purity of the church.' But Jesus said, 'Let the tares and the wheat grow together, and one day I'll sort them out.'
>
> "We're not in the sorting business. We're in the harvesting business . . . .
>
> "Jesus demonstrated that ministering to hurting people was more important than maintaining purity. When you fish with a big net, you catch all kinds of fish."—Rick Warren[48]

So in other words, don't be concerned with destructive, unscriptural (and pagan!) doctrinal convictions and sinful behaviors. In the new way of thinking, purpose-driven ministry is more important than purity, obedience, or what a person believes. This clearly says that temporal issues are more important than spiritual ones. This is all upside down to God's Holy Scriptures. Besides, nowhere in all of God's Holy Scriptures does God even imply that unholiness is *healthy*!

> *"Having therefore these promises, dearly beloved, let us cleanse ourselves from all filthiness of the flesh and spirit, perfecting holiness in the fear of God." (2 Corinthians 7:1)*

Given all that we've seen so far, *clearly*, being purpose-driven in and of itself doesn't guarantee "health." When purity isn't part of one's purpose, conforming to the world is to be expected.

The parable of the tares of the field that Rick Warren refers to here in his justification of disregarding impurity has nothing to do with "maintaining purity" in the churches. Nor is this parable about ministering to "hurting people." The Lord Jesus Christ Himself explains this parable, so to change the interpretation is to change the Lord's words. (See Matthew 13:24-30, 36-43 for the whole parable and explanation given by Him.)

> *"<u>The field is the world</u>; the good seed are the children of the kingdom; but <u>the tares are the children of the wicked one</u>; the enemy that sowed them is the devil; <u>the harvest is the end of the world</u>; and the reapers are the angels. As therefore <u>the tares are gathered and burned in the fire</u>; so shall it be in the end of this world. The Son of man shall send forth his angels, and they shall gather out of his kingdom all things that offend, and them which do iniquity; and shall cast them into a furnace of fire: there shall be wailing and gnashing of teeth." (Matthew 13:38-42)*

The field where the tares are being sown is *the world*, not the church. *Of course* we're not supposed to sort the tares from the *world*. That is God's task at His judgment, which in this parable is the harvest. The tares in this parable are not "hurting people" who need to be gathered into the churches, ministered to, and harvested for salvation. These are the people who refuse to believe in the Lord Jesus Christ and will be harvested for God's judgment of fire. When this harvest comes, it will be too late for salvation.

It is scriptural malpractice to use this parable as an excuse for avoiding true scriptural discipline, exhortation, admonishment, correction, reproof, separation, and so forth, which are to elicit holiness and to help keep the churches and the Body of Christ obedient to the faith. Purpose-driven defenders cry foul repeatedly when they believe the critics of their Paradigm have taken Rick Warren's statements out of context. Yet it is amazing that they are largely silent, therefore don't appear to be bothered, when their Paradigm consistently takes *God's* Word out of context. Again, priorities are just a tad backward here!

The Word of God even declares the end result of twisting Scripture or going along with it:

> *"As also in all his epistles, speaking in them of these things; in which are some things hard to be understood, which they that are unlearned and unstable wrest, as they do also the other scriptures, unto their own destruction. Ye therefore, beloved, seeing ye know these things before, beware lest ye also, being led away with the error of the wicked, fall from your own stedfastness. But grow in grace, and in the knowledge of our Lord and Saviour Jesus Christ. To him be glory both now and for ever. Amen." (2 Peter 3:16-18)*

The only sure foundation is the truth, which is Christ Jesus Himself and the rightly divided Word of God. People tend to be lulled into a false sense of security when they automatically assume that books which quote Scripture are scriptural. Not seeing any need to be a Berean leads to a failure to notice when "Christian" books or other teachings are contrary to the truth, or when any truth they give is also negated, contradicted, twisted, and synthesized into error elsewhere.

> *"<u>Study</u> to <u>shew</u> thyself approved unto God, a workman that needeth not to be ashamed, rightly dividing the word of truth. But shun profane and vain babblings: for they will increase unto more ungodliness. And their word will eat as doth a canker . . ." (2 Timothy 2:15-17)*

♦ *Chapter Twelve* ♦

The New Reformation: "A Whole New Paradigm Between Faith Communities"

Turning the First Reformation Upside Down

"*The bottom line is that we intend to reinvent mission strategy* in the 21st century. This will be a new Reformation. The First Reformation returned us to the message of the original church. It was a reformation of doctrine - what the church BELIEVES. This Second Reformation will return us to the mission of the original church. It will be a reformation of purpose- what the church DOES in the world."—Rick Warren (Italics added)[1]

"Purpose Driven Ministries is *bypassing old distinctions* between denominations and nationalities and unifying the church worldwide." (Emphasis added)[2]

On May 15, 2005, Rick Warren's message for the Global Day of Prayer included a startling admission regarding his New Reformation:

"'The first Reformation was about belief; this one's going to be about behavior,' said Warren, pastor of Saddleback Church in Southern California and author of the best-selling *The Purpose-Driven Life*. 'The first one was about creeds; this one's going to be about our deeds. **The first one divided the church; this time it will unify the church**.'" (Bold added)[3]

A week later at the Pew Forum's Conference on May 23, 2005, Rick Warren elaborated on his purpose to undo the first Reformation:

"**The first Reformation actually split Christianity into dozens and then hundreds of different segments. I think this one is actually going to bring them together**. Now, you're never going to get Christians, of all their stripes and varieties, to agree on all of the different doctrinal disputes and things like that, but what I am seeing them agree on are the purposes of the church. And I find great uniformity in the fact that I see this happening all the time. Last week I spoke to 4,000 pastors at my church who came from over 100 denominations in over 50 countries. Now, that's wide spread. We had Catholic priests, we had Pentecostal ministers, we had Lutheran bishops, we had Anglican bishops, we had Baptist preachers. They're all there together and you know what? **I'd never get them to agree on communion or baptism or a bunch of stuff like that, but I could get them to agree on what the church should be doing in the world**."—Rick Warren (Emphasis added)[4]

Carefully consider Rick Warren's purpose here. The first Reformation was indeed about belief, and *it divided those who believed the true Gospel of Christ from those who believed a false gospel*—i.e., Rome's false gospel of works. No, he will never get Rome to agree on the *scriptural* means of *salvation*. Rome will never agree that "a bunch of stuff" like baptism is *not* the means of forgiveness of sins and eternal life or that communion (the "Eucharist") is *not* the *literal* sacrifice of the Lord Jesus Christ for redemption and forgiveness of sins!

Throughout its history, the Roman Catholic Church has been adept at twisting Scripture into a lie. And, grievously, Rome is now being *embraced* by professing Christians even though it has never deviated from teaching *the same false gospel of works* which the Lord Jesus Christ's tortured, faithful martyrs rejected and thereby suffered gruesome deaths by Rome's hand. How times have changed among those who call themselves followers of Christ!

At the Pew Forum's Conference Rick Warren was asked, "How much engagement with Catholics are you really experiencing?" He replied:

"I think it's just getting started . . . I think it's the beginning of a new movement. I've had a number of Catholic people, like Kathleen Kennedy Townsend, came out, and others have kind of made a *pilgrimage* to Saddleback . . . And I just think the word is getting out. *There have been movements that have come along that have broken the denominational barriers* in Christianity, things *like the conferences we do* . . .

"And, you know, growing up as a Protestant boy, I knew nothing about Catholics, but I started watching ETWN, the Catholic channel, and I said, '**Well, I'm not as far apart from these guys as I thought I was**, you know?"—Rick Warren (Emphasis added)[5]

The *Catechism of the Catholic Church*[6] contains a multitude of false doctrines that oppose the Gospel of Christ and deny or ignore what God said in His Holy Scriptures. It was completed at the request of Pope John Paul II who gave the task to a commission chaired by Cardinal Joseph Ratzinger,[7] who is now Pope Benedict XVI. When completed, this very *current* Catechism was approved by Pope John Paul II who "offered [it] to every individual who . . . wants to know what the Catholic Church believes." He declared it to "be a sure and authentic reference text for teaching catholic doctrine," which "is meant to support *ecumenical* efforts" (emphasis added).[8]

Keeping in mind Rick Warren's declaration that "I'm not as far apart from these guys as I thought I was," here is a relatively small sample of Rome's false teachings taken from this Catechism:

Salvation, the work of redemption, and forgiveness of all sins are through Rome and her sacraments, administered by her exalted "divinized" priests—

- "'Sacred Tradition *and* Sacred Scripture make up a single sacred deposit of the Word of God . . .'" (#97; p. 29; emphasis added)
- "'. . . all Christian churches everywhere have held and hold the great Church that is here [at Rome] to be their only basis and foundation . . .'" (#834; p. 221; brackets in the original)
- "The Church is the mother of all believers. 'No one can have God as Father who does not have the Church as Mother.'" (#181; p. 48)
- "The Church is catholic: she proclaims the fullness of the faith. She bears in herself and administers the *totality* of the means of salvation." (#868; p. 230; emphasis added)
- "One who desires to obtain reconciliation with God and with the Church, must confess to a priest all the unconfessed grave sins he remembers . . ." (#1493; p. 374)
- "Indeed bishops and priests, by virtue of the sacrament of Holy Orders, have the power to forgive all sins . . ." (#1461; p. 367)
- "[Who then is the priest? He is] the defender of truth, who stands with angels, gives glory with archangels, causes sacrifices to rise to the altar on high, shares Christ's priesthood, refashions creation, restores it in God's image, recreates it for the world on high and, even greater, is divinized and divinizes." [!] (#1589; p. 397; brackets in the original)
- "The Church affirms that for believers the sacraments of the New Covenant are *necessary for salvation*." (#1129; p. 292)

- "Baptism is necessary for salvation.... The Church does not know of any means other than Baptism that assures entry into eternal beatitude..." (#1257; p. 320)
- "By Baptism *all sins* are forgiven, original sin and all personal sins, as well as all punishment for sin." (#1263; p. 321)
- "The Gospel is the revelation in Jesus Christ of God's mercy to sinners.... The same is true of *the Eucharist*, the sacrament of redemption: '*This* is my blood of the covenant, which is poured out for many for the forgiveness of sins.'" (#1846; p. 452; emphasis added)
- "For it is in the liturgy, especially in the divine sacrifice of the Eucharist, that 'the work of our redemption is accomplished'...." (#1068; p. 278)
- "In the most blessed sacrament of **the Eucharist** 'the body and blood, together with the soul and divinity**, of our Lord Jesus Christ and, therefore, **the whole Christ** is truly, really, and substantially contained.'" (#1374; p. 346; bold added)
- "... the Church ... presents to the Father the offering of his Son which reconciles us with him." [!] (#1354; p. 341)
- "*Holy Communion separates us from sin* .... cleansing us from past sins and preserving us from future sins ..." (#1393; p. 351)
- "*Worship of the Eucharist* .... 'The Catholic Church has always offered and still offers to the sacrament of the Eucharist the cult of adoration, not only during Mass, but also outside of it, reserving the consecrated hosts with the utmost care, exposing them to the solemn veneration of the faithful ....'" (#1378; p. 347)

Salvation through Rome does not require faith in the Gospel of Christ and can occur after death—

- "Those who, through no fault of their own, do not know the Gospel of Christ or his Church ... those too may achieve eternal salvation." (#847; p. 224)
- "Within the unity of the People of God, a multiplicity of peoples and cultures is gathered together .... 'Holding a rightful place in the communion of the Church there are also particular Churches that retain their own traditions.'" (#814; p. 215)
- "... Noah, like Enoch before him, 'walks with God.' This kind of prayer is lived by *many righteous people in all religions*." (#2569; p. 617; emphasis added)

- "To be sure, there are as many paths of prayer as there are persons who pray, but it is the same Spirit acting in all and with all." (#2672; p. 642)
- "All who die in God's grace and friendship, but still imperfectly purified, are indeed assured of their eternal salvation; but after death they undergo purification, so as to *achieve* the holiness necessary to enter the joy of heaven." (#1030; p. 268; emphasis added)

Salvation and deliverance from eternal death are through the saving work of Rome's completely sinless "All-Holy One" who bodily ascended into heaven and was exalted by God over all things. This person is *not* the *Son* of God -- the sinless, all-holy Lord and Saviour Jesus Christ, Who bodily ascended into heaven, was exalted by God over all things, sits at His right hand as the *only* Mediator between God and man, and through Whom is life that ends the death by Adam. No, in Rome the sinless giver of life and salvation is none other than the "*Mother* of God," Mary, "Queen over all things" —

- "As St. Irenaeus says, 'Being obedient **she** became the cause of salvation for herself and for the whole human race.' . . . 'The knot of Eve's disobedience was untied by **Mary's** obedience . . .' Comparing her with Eve, they ['the early Fathers'] call Mary 'the Mother of the living' and frequently claim: '**Death through Eve, *life through Mary*.**'" (#494; p. 125; emphasis added)
- "Mary . . . was preserved from all stain of original sin and by a special grace of God committed *no sin of any kind* during her whole earthly life." (#411; p. 104; emphasis added)
- "'Finally the Immaculate Virgin, preserved free from *all* stain of original sin, when the course of her earthly life was finished, was *taken up body and soul* into heavenly glory, and *exalted* by the Lord as Queen *over all things* . . .'" (#966; p. 252; emphasis added)
- "By asking **Mary** to pray for us, we acknowledge ourselves to be poor sinners and we address ourselves to the 'Mother of Mercy,' **the All-Holy One**. We give ourselves over to **her** now, in the Today of our lives." (#2677; p. 644; emphasis added)
- "**You** ['O Mother of God'] . . . by your prayers, will deliver our souls from death." (#966; p. 252; emphasis added)
- "'Taken up to heaven **she** did not lay aside this **saving** office but by **her** manifold intercession continues to bring us the gifts of eternal salvation . . . . Therefore the Blessed Virgin is invoked in the Church under the titles of

Advocate, Helper, Benefactress, and **Mediatrix**.'" (#969; p. 252; ellipsis dots in the original; emphasis added)

- "In Mary, the Holy Spirit *manifests* the Son of the Father, now become **the Son of the Virgin. She is the burning bush** of the definitive theophany. Filled with the Holy Spirit **she makes the Word visible** in the humility of his flesh. It is to the poor and the first representatives of the gentiles that **she makes him known**." (#724; p. 191; bold added)

The path of Rome leads to becoming "other 'Christs,'" which continues their denial of the uniqueness of the Lord Jesus Christ—

- ". . . by Baptism, he ['the Father'] incorporates us into the Body of his Christ; through the anointing of his Spirit who flows from the head to the members, he makes us **other 'Christs.'** . . . 'So then you who have become sharers in Christ are *appropriately* called '**Christs.**'" (#2782; p. 667; emphasis added)
- "Christ and his Church thus together make up **the 'whole Christ'** (*Christus totus*). The Church is one with Christ. The saints are acutely aware of this unity: 'Let us rejoice then and give thanks that **we have become** not only Christians, but **Christ himself** . . . . Marvel and rejoice: **we have become Christ**.'" (#795; p. 210; parentheses in the original; bold added)
- "The Eucharist is our daily bread. The power belonging to this *divine* food makes it a bond of union. Its effect is then understood as unity, so that, gathered into his Body and made members of him, **we may become what we receive** . . . ." (#2837; p. 681; ellipsis dots in the original; emphasis added)
- ". . . to receive in faith the gift of his Eucharist **is to receive the Lord himself**." (#1336; p. 337; emphasis added)

The path of Rome leads to 'godhood,' which is the ultimate defiance against the Lord God—

- "[Who then is the priest? He is] . . . *divinized and divinizes*." (#1589; p. 397; brackets in the original; emphasis added)
- "Created in a state of holiness, man was destined to be fully '*divinized*' by God in glory." (#398; p. 100; emphasis added)
- "The Church is essentially both human *and divine* . . ." (#771; p. 203; emphasis added)

- "The grace of Christ . . . is the *sanctifying* or **deifying** grace received in Baptism." (#1999; p. 484; bold added)
- "'For the Son of God became man **so that we might become God.**' 'The only-begotten Son of God, wanting to make us *sharers in his divinity*, assumed our nature, so that he, made man, might **make men gods**.'" (#460; p. 116; emphasis added)

What exactly was Rick Warren referring to when he said, "I'm not as far apart from these guys as I thought I was, you know?" Purpose? Unity? Not *God's* purposes or unity of *the* faith!

Putting the label of "Christian" on false religions (faiths), such as Roman Catholicism and Mormonism, is merely the deceptive work of the Angel of light. A label doesn't change false doctrines and gospels into truth. In addition, referring to those who are lost as "brothers and sisters in Christ" is anything but loving toward them. True love does not deceive people into thinking they are saved when they are ensnared in false beliefs that cannot save their souls. This is nothing less than the utmost cruelty. To join in unity with false religions does nothing for furthering the Gospel of Christ. But it does do a great deal for propagating the Angel of light's false gospel that "we are all one."

The Lord God, Who *alone* is God and divine, is the One Who set forth His means of salvation. Mankind can't change the truth just because it wants to be positive, tolerant, and inclusive of those in other religions (faiths). Absolute truth is what it is, regardless of whether or not people choose to believe it or try to change it or choose to broaden the definition of what is considered "Christian."

Rome does say we are saved by grace. But Rome's "grace" is "*deifying*"! Furthermore, the Word of God declares that *faith* gives us access into God's grace—which gives us eternal life not *godhood*! That we are saved by grace *through faith* was the basis of the first Reformation and the subsequent division of the church, which Rick Warren's New Reformation seeks to purposefully undo. If *faith* is not the key that gives us access into the grace of God, then either everyone is or will be saved or works become the key. Both of these things completely contradict God's Holy Scriptures.

"Therefore being justified <u>by faith</u>, we have peace with God through our Lord Jesus Christ: by whom also <u>we have access by faith into this grace</u> wherein we stand, and rejoice in hope of the glory of God." (Romans 5:1-2)

"For by grace are ye saved <u>through faith</u>; and that not of yourselves: it is the gift of God: <u>not of works</u>, lest any man should boast." (Ephesians 2:8-9)

"<u>Knowing that a man is not justified by the works of the law, but by the faith of Jesus Christ</u>, even we have believed in Jesus Christ, that we might be justified by the faith of Christ, and not by the works of the law: for by the works of the law shall no flesh be justified . . . . <u>I do not frustrate the grace of God: for if righteousness come by the law, then Christ is dead in vain</u>." (Galatians 2:16, 21)

Although good works are the *result* of salvation, as *the means to* salvation grace and works render each other null and void by taking from each other the very essence of what they are:

"And if by grace, then is it no more of works: otherwise grace is no more grace. But if it be of works, then is it no more grace: otherwise work is no more work." (Romans 11:6)

"Now to him that worketh is the reward not reckoned of grace, but of debt. But to him that worketh not, but believeth on him that justifieth the ungodly, his faith is counted for righteousness . . . . <u>For if they which are of the law be heirs, faith is made void, and the promise made of none effect</u> . . . Therefore it is of faith, that it might be by grace . . ." (Romans 4:4-6, 14, 16)

"<u>Christ is become of no effect</u> unto you, whosoever of you are justified by the law; <u>ye are fallen from grace</u>. For we through the Spirit wait for the hope of righteousness by faith." (Galatians 5:4-5)

"Consider the work of God: for who can make that straight, which he hath made crooked?" (Ecclesiastes 7:13)

There's a reason Scripture exhorts us to contend for *the faith* not for *the unity of faiths*:

"Beloved, when I gave all diligence to write unto you of the common salvation, it was needful for me to write unto you, and exhort you that ye

> *should earnestly contend for <u>the faith</u> which was once delivered unto the saints." (Jude 1:3)*

> *"But I fear, lest by any means, as the serpent beguiled Eve through his subtilty, so your minds should be corrupted from the simplicity that is in Christ. For if he that cometh preacheth <u>another Jesus</u>, whom we have not preached, or if ye receive <u>another spirit</u>, which ye have not received, or <u>another gospel</u>, which ye have not accepted, <u>ye might well bear with him</u>." (2 Corinthians 11:3-4)*

> "Yet Warren's pastor-training programs welcome Catholics . . . **'I'm not going to get into a debate over the non-essentials.** I won't try to change other denominations. **Why be divisive?'** he [Rick Warren] asks . . ." (Emphasis added)[9]

At the Pew Forum's Conference, Rick Warren was asked, "So are you saying doctrine won't be important or is not important if you bring together all these –." He replied:

> "No, no. I think, though, it's what Augustine said: 'In the essentials, unity; **in the non-essentials, liberty**; and in all things, charity.' And I think **that's how evangelicals and Catholics can get together**." (Emphasis added)[10]

Clearly, the essentials of true Christianity and the essentials of Roman Catholicism are mutually exclusive.[11] In order to "get together" with Rome, the Gospel of Christ (not to mention the truth in general) would have to become *non*-essential in order to bridge the divide between the narrow way and the broad way.

The first Reformation divided *Christ*ianity from *Church*ianity. Yet today it is no longer a problem if not everyone agrees on the Gospel of Christ because religious (doctrinal) distinctions are being bypassed for the sake of uniting together in the name of purpose.

> "There are Purpose Driven churches in over 200 different denominations and associations. We work with denominations to strengthen their churches. **We encourage every church to maintain its own heritage and doctrinal convictions while we cooperate together** on what every church is called to **do** -- the five biblical purposes of worship, fellowship, discipleship, ministry, and evangelism. **Everybody agrees on that!**"—Rick Warren (Emphasis added)[12]

On November 4-6, 2004, the American Society for Church Growth held its 2004 annual conference at Fuller Theological Seminary. This conference was to "learn, interact, and grow with the leading voices of the Emerging Church."[13] Pastor Dennis Costella, Editor of FOUNDATION Magazine, attended this conference "to better understand the latest thinking of the church growth leaders."[14] In the November-December 2004 issue of his magazine, he reported that Rick Warren made the following statements at this conference:

> "We now have 'purpose-driven' churches in 122 countries. And if I were to ask every 'purpose-driven' church in America to raise their hand, it would shock America because we don't tell them to change their label. On the front it says, 'Lutheran, Second Methodist, Holy Power Episcopal,' you name it; 'Four-Peas-in-the-Pod Four Square'—it's got everything! Every name you can imagine. And **we have Catholic 'purpose-driven' churches** . . .
>
> "And I don't make any apology in saying to you that the 'purpose-driven' paradigm is the operating system of a 21st century church. I believe that because we now have 36,000 case studies, and it's in every country.
>
> "And so **it doesn't demand that they change** from being Lutheran or Methodist or Nazarene or Assembly of God or Baptist *or whatever.* **I don't really care what your doctrine is**. What I care about is, do you have a process by which you bring people into membership, build them up to maturity, train them for ministry, send them out on a mission, for the glory of God?"—Rick Warren (Emphasis added)[15]

It was inevitable for doctrine to be bypassed in the purpose-driven Reformation. In Rick Warren's "final exam," "God won't ask about your *religious background or doctrinal views*" (*PDL*; p. 34; emphasis added).

The narrow way's unity of the faith and the Holy Spirit through the truth are too exclusive for the unity-driven world. Instead, the commonality of purpose and values is allowed to transcend doctrinal and religious barriers and advance the broad way's "unity in diversity." "Non-essentials" are put aside for what is deemed the higher value -- unity.

> "God deeply desires that we experience *oneness* and harmony with each other.

"Unity is the soul of fellowship. Destroy it, and you rip the heart out of Christ's Body. It is the essence, the core, of how God intends for us to experience life together in his church." (PDL; p. 160)

"Now, you're never going to get Christians, of all their stripes and varieties, to agree on all of the different doctrinal disputes and things like that, but what I am seeing them agree on are the purposes of the church. And I find great uniformity in the fact that I see this happening all the time."—Rick Warren (Emphasis added)[16]

In "The Essence of Separation," Charles Spurgeon warned against this very thing:

"'To remain divided is sinful! Did not our Lord pray, 'that they may be one, even as we are one'? (John 17:22).' **A chorus of ecumenical voices keep harping the unity tune. What they are saying is, 'Christians of all doctrinal shades and beliefs must come together** in one visible organization, regardless . . . . Unite, unite!'

"Such teaching is false, reckless and dangerous. *Truth alone must determine our alignments. Truth comes before unity.* Unity without truth is hazardous. *Our Lord's prayer in John 17 must be read in its full context.* Look at verse 17: 'Sanctify them through thy truth: thy word is truth.' Only those sanctified through the Word can be one in Christ. *To teach otherwise is to betray the Gospel."* (Emphasis added)[17]

The rampant destructive errors spreading throughout Christianity need to be addressed and corrected according to the light of God's Holy Scriptures. But little if any scriptural addressing and correcting of the destructive errors is allowed to occur with the following taking place:

- Unscriptural covenants are being signed to categorically uphold the unity of purpose-driven churches.
- People are falling for the propaganda that everything's fine and they shouldn't listen to the so-called "gossip" of "divisive" people who say otherwise.
- Contenders of the faith are being encouraged to leave the churches and become "blessed subtractions."
- "Every church" is being encouraged to maintain their own doctrines without regard for their adherence to Scripture's truth.

The Angel of light must be very pleased with the extent of his success in neutralizing Christianity. And his success in achieving non-doctrinal unity within today's Christianity and with Rome is only the beginning.

Interfaith "Spiritual Care" -- "Whatever it Takes!"

"You boldly held up your 'WHATEVER IT TAKES!' sign when I challenged you with the PEACE plan and the vision for the next 25 years."—Rick Warren[18]

"Pastors and church leaders from 49 countries and 200 denominations ended last week's Purpose Driven Church Conference [May 17-20, 2005] with a commitment to do whatever it takes to topple the global giants of spiritual lostness, egocentric leadership, poverty, sickness and illiteracy.

"Conference attendees made the commitment by holding up red and yellow signs as they agreed to do their part in a new worldwide reformation that Purpose Driven Ministries founder Pastor Rick Warren says will focus on what the church does."[19]

There is no difference between "whatever it takes" and "no matter what it costs," and these phrases already have a broad meaning. But the masses in the Purpose-Driven Paradigm are willing to follow this path to a New Reformation that is turning the first Reformation upside down. But it doesn't end there. Their purpose-driven leader "intend[s] to use the Purpose Driven movement *to fulfill PEACE in a new reformation*" (emphasis added).[20]

Rick Warren's global P.E.A.C.E. Plan was publicly launched in 2005. Basically, it consists of fighting the five "global giants":

- spiritual lostness or blindness or, most commonly, emptiness
- egocentric or self-centered leadership
- poverty
- sickness or disease
- illiteracy

The five solutions to these giants, respectively, are:

- **P**lant or Partner with a church or congregation
- **E**quip leaders

- **A**ssist the poor
- **C**are for the sick
- **E**ducate the next generation

Trustfully following a leader into the hazy and open-ended area of "whatever it takes" is risky. Especially when the leader is undiscerning and deceived, as evidenced in his teachings and actions. Over and over and over it is brought up that this P.E.A.C.E. Plan was "quietly" tested for two years. And according to Mike Constantz, Saddleback's pastor of missions, "Rick has tried to keep the PEACE Plan under wraps for two years."[21]

Over the last year, the P.E.A.C.E. Plan has gradually been unveiled in conferences and events. And the extent to which this Plan intends to involve interfaith unity in "whatever it takes" continues to be less and less under wraps. About his P.E.A.C.E. Plan, Rick Warren has said:

> "Now this is the strategy behind the P.E.A.C.E. plan. It's a strategy to mobilize millions of small groups in millions of churches to attack the 5 global giants with a 5 point strategy . . . . P-E-A-C-E is the P.E.A.C.E. plan. Now where does that come from? It comes from Luke 10."—Rick Warren[22]

> "When Jesus sent the disciples . . . into a village he said, '**Find the man of peace.**' And he said, 'When you find the man of peace you start working with that person, and if they respond to you, you work with them. If they don't, you dust the dust off your shoes; you go to the next village.' Who's the man of peace in any village – or it might be a woman of peace – who has the most respect, they're open and they're influential? ***They don't have to be a Christian.*** In fact, **they could be a Muslim**, but they're open and they're influential and **you work with them to attack the five giants. And *that's* going to bring the second Reformation.**"—Rick Warren (Emphasis added)[23]

> "I am working toward a second Reformation of the church which could create a Third Great Awakening in our nation or world . . ."—Rick Warren[24]

> "**Find the man of peace.** Bless him. He blesses you back. Who is the man of peace? He's influential and he's open. He doesn't have to be a Christian. ***Find a non-Christian*** who's influential and open—**a Muslim or an atheist.**"—Rick Warren (Emphasis added)[25]

"... you go in and you deal with gatekeepers, for instance, like pastors, **priests, rabbis, imams**, whoever you would call, **we call them the man of peace** . . ."—Rick Warren (Emphasis added)[26]

"**What do you do once you find the man of peace?** You do the P.E.A.C.E. Plan. **You Partner or Plant with a church**, Equip a leader, Assist the poor, you Care for the sick, you Educate the next generation."—Rick Warren (Emphasis added)[27]

"Planting churches is *the* way to fulfill the Great Commission."—Rick Warren[28]

"The first Reformation divided the church. We need a new one that unites it. And then **I believe that this new Reformation will be *the evangelization of the world*.**"—Rick Warren (Emphasis added)[29]

According to Rick Warren, working with unbelievers in *different faiths* is going to bring in the new Reformation that is to *evangelize* the world! And this P.E.A.C.E. strategy of his even includes working with these non-Christian "men of peace" in *partnering with or planting a church*. What kind of "church" is an atheist or an imam or any other Muslim or unbeliever going to want to plant or partner with?! How is this the solution to spiritual *lostness/blindness/emptiness*? Nevertheless, "planting churches is *the* way to fulfill the Great Commission"!

Even in regards to working with these unbelievers on the solutions to the other giants, what beliefs are they going to equip leaders and educate the next generation with? What "spiritual care" will they offer the poor, sick, and dying?! This is *not* about *God* or *His purposes* or *the Gospel of Christ* or *God's peace* or *eternity*.

An article on Pastors.com reported that Rick Warren made the following statements at his May 2005 Purpose Driven Church Conference about his "new worldwide reformation":

> "'It's time to stop debating and start doing,' said Warren . . . 'It's time to stop criticizing and start cooperating. It's time for the church to be known for love and not legalism. It's time for the church to be known for what we are for not what we are against. It's time for the church to act on what we believe. It's time for the church to be a doer of the Word and not just a hearer.'"[30]

In light of his pursuit of interfaith unity in his New Reformation and P.E.A.C.E. Plan, those statements have quite an impact.

Rick Warren does rightly say, "It's time for the church to act on what we believe," and, "It's time for the church to be a doer of the Word and not just a hearer." However, when churches are believing and propagating error, interfaith unity, and corrupt per-versions of the Word, acting on what they believe and being a doer of "the Word" doesn't mean what it should. (Incidentally, neither does the term "Christian;" according to today's use of the term, even the devil would qualify as one!)

Under the guise of "a new worldwide reformation" of purpose, *the* faith of Christianity is being globally transformed into the unified *faiths* of Churchianity. This interfaith cooperation in the P.E.A.C.E. Plan goes beyond enlisting merely the individuals and leaders who are in other religions (faiths). The Plan seeks to involve even the churches ("houses of worship") of "all the different religions."

> "Now these 5 problems ['global Goliaths'] are so big no government can solve them. The United Nations can't even solve these problems. They're so big. The only thing big enough to solve these problems is the network of millions and millions and millions and millions and millions and millions and millions of churches all around the world. Catholic churches, Protestant churches, Pentecostal churches, Evangelical churches, **and every other kind of church**. I can take you into a thousand villages that don't have a school, don't have a clinic, don't have a fire department, don't have a grocery store, don't have any government, don't even have any business, but they got a church. And what, I began to dream, would happen if we could mobilize millions of small groups, tens of millions of small groups in millions of churches from village to village around the world to begin to address the 5 global giants?"—Rick Warren (Emphasis added)[31]

> "These are problems so big that no government can solve them. The only thing big enough are millions and millions of **local churches of every kind**."—Rick Warren (Emphasis added)[32]

When Rick Warren said "**every** other kind of church," he meant "**every** kind" of church or congregation. He has clarified this in different conferences and events. The following quote is from his Keynote Address to the interfaith, Annual Conference of the Religion Newswriters Association (RNA) in September 2005.

"There's only one thing big enough in the entire world to solve them [the five global giants]. Only one thing. The millions and millions and millions and millions and millions and millions of congregations that are spread out all around the world. I could take you today to a million villages that don't have a school, don't have a clinic, don't have a post office, don't have a fire department, don't have a business, **but they got a church. Or they got a synagogue. They got *something*. They got a house of worship** . . . . All the Wal-Marts and Starbucks and every other franchise put together couldn't compete to the amount of churches that are in the world . . . .

"So I began to think, what is the key to this? And I came up with a thing called the P.E.A.C.E. Plan. When Jesus sent the disciples out, he said, 'When you go into a village, you find the man of peace.' Now this person doesn't have to be a Christian . . . . You find the person of peace, and then you begin to do the P.E.A.C.E. Plan, P-E-A-C-E. It stands for **Partner with congregations, partner with congregations. You start with them because they're already there** . . . . They're in the village. Partner with a congregation. Or you plant a congregation if there's not one there . . . .

"Now why am I telling this to you? Because we're going public with it this next year in 2006 . . . . [W]e're now learning the lessons of the two-year prototype . . . we're going to release it to those 400,000 congregations that we've trained. And I believe it will change the world."—Rick Warren (Emphasis added)[33]

These 400,000 congregations that are to "change the world" aren't even necessarily *Christian*, as pointed out in this same Keynote Address:

"In the 1990s I trained about a quarter of a million pastors. It's now gone, as I said, to over 400,000 . . . **and we're talking about all kinds of different groups**, including priests in the Catholic church, and including rabbis . . . . So anyway, then in the 21st century I said that *now we're going global*."—Rick Warren (Emphasis added)[34]

Regardless of Rick Warren's additional statement at this Conference that "P-E-A-C-E is just what Jesus did when he was here on earth,"[35] his P.E.A.C.E. Plan is about serving the world's physical needs through *interfaith unity*, which *opposes* what Jesus did while He was here on earth. The Lord Jesus Christ met physical needs in the course of *His work of saving souls*. And He *never* partnered with people or congregations in the different religions to do His work!

That interfaith unity underlies the various strategies of Rick Warren's P.E.A.C.E. Plan contradicts all rhetoric that his *Purpose*-Driven Plan is about the *truth*, the *work of Jesus*, the *Gospel, God's purposes*, and the *Great Commandment* and the *"Great Commission."* This is further evidenced in the following, which gets even worse.

Rick Warren spoke at the TIME Global Health Summit on November 1, 2005—a summit which among many other speakers also featured U.N. Secretary-General Kofi Annan, Chairman of the U.N. Foundation Ted Turner, and former U.S. President Bill Clinton.[36]

First, in the initial press conference that day, Rick Warren made the following comment:

> "My personal position is I will use whatever works."[37]

This position obviously refers to much more than the specifics of fighting AIDS, which this statement was in reference to. In his speech later that day, he discussed the world's failure at addressing the five giants listed in his global P.E.A.C.E. Plan. Then Rick Warren actually called for partnering with congregations of "all the different religions" not just for physical care but for *spiritual* care!:

> "Well, as I said, I could take you to villages that don't have a clinic, don't have . . . But they've got a church. In fact, in many countries the only infrastructure that is there is *religion* . . . . What if in this 21st century we were able to *network these churches providing the* . . . *manpower in local congregations*. Let's just take my religion by itself. Christianity . . . . The church is bigger than any government in the world. **Then you add in Muslims, you add in Hindus, you add in *all the different religions*, and you *use those houses of worship*** as distribution centers, not just *for spiritual care* but health care. What could be done? . . .
>
> "Government has a role and business has a role and *churches, houses of worship have a role*. I think it's time to go to the moon, and I invite you to go with us."—Rick Warren (Emphasis added)[38]

To positively refer to all the religions' idolatrous houses of false gods as "houses of *worship*" that should help give "spiritual *care*" to the world is an abomination. To say that this is *not* about reaching or saving "one more for Jesus" is a tremendous understatement! Besides, "worship" is Rick Warren's first purpose, which he defines as "bringing pleasure to God" (*PDL*; p. 64). Since when does faith *in false gods* bring *pleasure* to God, Whose name is Jealous? And believing in a generic "God" of interfaith unity is not faith *in God*.

In the name of purpose, truth continues to be sacrificed on the altar of unity. And it isn't "the moon" this path is heading toward.

> "<u>**Take heed to thyself, lest thou make a covenant with the inhabitants of the land whither thou goest, lest it be for a snare in the midst of thee**</u>: **But ye shall destroy their altars, break their images, and cut down their groves: For thou shalt worship no other god: for the Lord, whose name is Jealous, is a jealous God: <u>Lest thou make a covenant with the inhabitants of the land, and they go a-whoring after their gods</u> . . ." (Exodus 34:12-15)**

This is the purpose of the darkness of the broad way. It is a denial of the Gospel of Christ and of the Word of God and does not care one iota for the souls of people who will be given "spiritual care" by those on the "spiritual journey" (path) to eternal destruction. This is a prime example of how professing Christians who participate in interfaith unity are presenting the Lord Jesus Christ as "merely another way" along with Buddha, Mohammed, and all the false gods represented by the many "houses of worship" of "all the different religions."

Rick Warren says over and over at various conferences and events that partnering with "men of peace" and "houses of worship" in other religions is to be part of his P.E.A.C.E. Plan. The repetitiveness shows that his interfaith statements are not involuntary remarks. He is *purposefully* calling for the religions of the world to work together on his P.E.A.C.E. Plan.

In July 2005, Rick Warren along with "100 of today's most profound and provocative thinkers, writers, artists, corporate heads, policy officials, scholars and other leaders," gathered for the inaugural Aspen Ideas Festival. This Festival was "a public celebration and exploration of the most compelling and thought-provoking ideas of our time."[39]

At the end of Rick Warren's discussion on "Religion and Leadership" with David Gergen, a Muslim man from the audience thanked Rick Warren "for giving so many people such deep and fulfilled lives." He then asked for his advice on involving the evangelical community "in healing the chasm between faith communities" to promote interfaith cooperation in serving the world. Rick Warren's answer to this Muslim reiterated the interfaith aspects of his P.E.A.C.E. Plan:

> "In the global P.E.A.C.E. Plan, which is P-E-A-C-E, . . . **Partner with other houses of worship**, Partner with churches, Equip leaders, . . .
>
> "In the Bible when Jesus sent his followers out, he said, 'When you go into a village, you find the man of peace.' And this is where you and I can work together. Find the man of peace . . . . He does not necessarily have to be a quote Christian, could be Muslim, could be Jewish, could be a nothing. But he's open and influential. And when you find that man of peace then you work together . . . .
>
> "There are millions and millions and millions and millions and millions and millions and millions of churches spread out . . . . And if we could take houses of worship . . . **Together we can make a difference**. You and me, we'll work on that." (Emphasis added)[40]

Working together in interfaith unity with "men of peace" and "houses of worship" in "all the different religions" is not about the eternal peace and purposes of God. This is about the temporal peace and purposes of the world. This is not what the Lord Jesus Christ sent His followers out to do!

The first giant of Rick Warren's P.E.A.C.E. Plan is spiritual lostness/blindness/emptiness. Interfaith unity will *exacerbate* this giant, not solve it! Neither will this giant be solved by working in interfaith unity on the other four giants. Even his P.E.A.C.E. Plan acknowledges that all five giants are "intertwined." Yet ignoring this giant even more is the purpose-driven "strategy" in which "the effort would be on healing, *not proselytizing*." The Gospel of faith has been transformed into a gospel of service.

> "And what's currently on the agenda for Pastor Rick Warren is nothing less than changing the world."—*The Orange County Register*, 11/6/05[41]
>
> "**P.E.A.C.E. is a grassroots church-to-church strategy, which links congregations around the world** to make a difference together. It is also a small group strategy that utilizes group dynamics for support and accountability.
>
> "Moreover, the strategy is comprehensive, attacking all five problems, because *they are all intertwined* . . . . It is also a church-based strategy that makes local congregations the heroes . . . .

"Finally, P.E.A.C.E. is a global strategy. '**Our goal is to mobilize *every church in every nation*,**' he concluded. . . .

"He asked the conference attendees, '**Are you willing to do *whatever it takes?***'"—PurposeDriven, reporting on Saddleback's Nov. 29 - Dec. 1, 2005 Disturbing Voices HIV/AIDS Conference (Emphasis added)[42]

"'**It will take a whole new paradigm between faith communities**, and the private and public sectors,' Warren said. . . .

"There is a new way to address problems we have been unable to solve alone, he said.

"'Just imagine,' he says with a smile, 'what could happen with a new paradigm of increased cooperation.'"—PurposeDriven News, reporting on the Nov. 1-3, 2005 Time Global Health Summit (Emphasis added)[43]

"Pastor Rick Warren, author of the smash best-seller 'The Purpose-Driven Life,' said at the briefing that he has rallied thousands in his church to begin *missionary-style work* in foreign countries. **The effort would be on healing, not proselytizing, he said**."—ABC News, 11/2/05, reporting on the Time Global Health Summit (Emphasis added)[44]

"The bottom line is that we intend to reinvent mission strategy in the 21st century. This will be a new Reformation."—Rick Warren[45]

"The P.E.A.C.E. Plan is a revolutionary missions strategy . . . Purpose Driven Ministries will be sharing the P.E.A.C.E. Plan model with churches throughout the world."—Pastors.com[46]

"The Peace Plan, its a relationship for the global glory of God."—Rick Warren[47]

A Peace Plan that calls for Christians to put their effort on healing, not evangelism (proselytizing), and calls for all faiths to work together despite their differences is about the 'glory' of man, not God.

This New Reformation is definitely a "revolutionary missions strategy" that puts greater effort into sharing the P.E.A.C.E. Plan with the world than it does the

Gospel of Christ. But remember, the solution to the giant of spiritual lostness is to plant *a* church, and, as previously mentioned, Rick Warren has said, "There is one thing you could do *greater than share Jesus Christ* with somebody, and it is help start *a* church" (emphasis added). Even in starting his own church, he told active members "of any kind of religion," "'Great, God bless you, *keep going.*'"

The interfaith direction of his P.E.A.C.E. Plan and its desire to utilize non-Christians from other religions to help plant churches and give "spiritual care" was to be expected. Interfaith unity is more important than the fact that it won't be the *Christian* faith that all the different religions (faiths) will be spreading in their attempt to meet "broad and varied spiritual needs":

> **"He [Rick Warren] said that God uses many churches and traditions to meet broad and varied spiritual needs.**
>
> "'Now I don't agree with everything in everybody's denomination, including my own. I don't agree with everything that Catholics do or Pentecostals do, but what binds us together is so much stronger than what divides us,' he said."
> —*Pittsburgh Post-Gazette*, 11/12/05, reporting on the Anglican Communion Network's Hope and A Future conference (Emphasis added)[48]

It isn't the truth and the Gospel of Christ that binds Catholics with the churches embracing this religion. So exactly *what* is "so much stronger than" *the truth* which is "what divides us"? Creeds are being benched in favor of deeds in this New Reformation that has gone way beyond turning the first Reformation upside down.

The *Pittsburgh Post-Gazette* follows the previous quote with:

> "I really do feel that these people are brothers and sisters in God's family. **I am looking to build bridges** with the Orthodox Church, looking to build bridges with the Catholic Church, with the Anglican Church, and say 'What can we do together that we have been unable to do by ourselves?'"—Rick Warren (Emphasis added)[49]

One's feelings are completely irrelevant in determining truth. And given that he is building bridges with other religions (faiths), his feelings are leading him astray. "What could be done?" was also Rick Warren's question when he called for "all the different religions" to participate in "spiritual care." "What could be done" isn't the issue; ***Thy will be done*** is.

Rick Warren says his P.E.A.C.E. Plan is "a Purpose-Driven strategy, built on the five purposes – worship, evangelism, discipleship, ministry, and fellowship."[50] Indeed, his interfaith Plan continues the man-centered path of his purpose-driven "manifesto." "Religious background or doctrinal views" don't matter in either one. In addition, John 15:5 has essentially been rewritten in both the "manifesto" and P.E.A.C.E. Plan to say, "for without community ye can do nothing." This again elevates community (relationships) above God and His truth. And so does the following:

> "We won't let anybody do the PEACE plan by themselves. You have to do it in a team, in community."—Rick Warren[51]

"Spiritual awakening" appears to be the new term for *blindness* in this upside-down world. What this world is "awakening" to is Oneness on the broad way. Christianity's new message is no different than that of the interfaith world: "Together as ONE we can change the world." And remember, the effort will be on "healing, not proselytizing." Christianity's new message has supplanted the Gospel of Christ.

Along with the world, Christians today are seeking the power of all working together as ONE rather than the power of the one Lord God. This is upside down to the Kingdom of God.

> *"And when he had called the people unto him with his disciples also, he said unto them, Whosoever will come after me, let him deny himself, and take up his cross, and follow me. For whosoever will save his life shall lose it; but whosoever shall lose his life for my sake and the gospel's, the same shall save it. For what shall it profit a man, if he shall gain the whole world, and lose his own soul? Or what shall a man give in exchange for his soul? Whosoever therefore shall be ashamed of me and of my words in this adulterous and sinful generation; of him also shall the Son of man be ashamed, when he cometh in the glory of his Father with the holy angels." (Mark 8:34-38)*

> *"They profess that they know God; but in works they deny him, being abominable, and disobedient, and unto every good work reprobate." (Titus 1:16)*

♦ *Chapter Thirteen* ♦

"Except the LORD Build the House, They Labour in Vain That Build it"

The Kingdom of *God* Is the *Narrow* Way

"You want to know what God cares about most? He wants his lost children found! That's why he went through *that whole thing about the cross*. Legend tells us that Nero fiddled while Rome burned, and yet Christians are fiddling around debating things while the world goes to hell. Friends, it's time to stop debating and start doing. Stop debating the Bible, and start doing it. It's time to stop criticizing and start cooperating."—Rick Warren (Emphasis added)[1]

First, God's Word clearly says that we are only the children of God through faith in the Lord Jesus Christ; the lost are not God's "children." Contending for the faith ("debating things") is a necessary and compelling aspect of true love for the lost. True love does not want to see them go to hell while today's Christianity fiddles around in cooperation with religions, associations, and beliefs on the broad way that can only give the lost a false gospel and a false "Jesus," if any at all.

If the lost are truly cared about, then time will be taken to ensure that they are not led astray by a false religion (faith) and god. Any concern for the lost is undermined when churches are changed or "birthed" to accommodate the unbelieving and pagan perspective of the world and when other religions (faiths) are brought into the "solution" for spiritual lostness and emptiness. This is not compassionate service but a matter of the blind leading the blind.

The Kingdom of God *is* the narrow way. It is neither participated in nor served nor entered in by those on the broad way. Nor is it built through man's interfaith efforts of world service.

> *"Now this I say, brethren, that flesh and blood cannot inherit the kingdom of God; neither doth corruption inherit incorruption." (I Corinthians 15:50)*

"For the kingdom of God is not meat and drink; but righteousness, and peace, and joy <u>in the Holy Ghost</u>." (Romans 14:17)

"Jesus answered and said unto him, Verily, verily, I say unto thee, Except a man be born again, he <u>cannot see</u> the kingdom of God . . . . Jesus answered, Verily, verily, I say unto thee, Except a man be born of water and of the Spirit, he <u>cannot enter</u> into the kingdom of God. That which is born of the flesh is flesh; and <u>that which is born of the Spirit is spirit</u>." (John 3:3, 5-6)

"And when he was demanded of the Pharisees, when the kingdom of God should come, he answered them and said, The kingdom of God cometh not with observation: Neither shall they say, Lo here! or, lo there! for, behold, the kingdom of God is within you." (Luke 17:20-21)

"Marvel not that I said unto thee, Ye <u>must</u> be born again." (John 3:7)

". . . Jesus came into Galilee, <u>preaching the gospel of the kingdom of God</u>, and saying, The time is fulfilled, and the kingdom of God is at hand: <u>repent ye, and believe the gospel</u>." (Mark 1:14-15)

The Gospel of the Kingdom of God is the Gospel of Christ. Believing the Gospel of Christ provides God's salvation through which one is born again of the Spirit. This is the *only* entrance into God's Kingdom. Thus, the true Kingdom of God is built through the power of the Gospel of Christ working within the hearts of repentant people who believe and receive Jesus Christ as their Lord and Saviour, and who are thus born again into newness of spirit and life through the power of the Holy Spirit.

On the other hand, a kingdom built in cooperative unity with the broad way of the world is not founded in the truth or righteousness or peace of *God*, all of which are only found on the narrow way. This is not the Kingdom of the Lord Jesus Christ, which only exists within His true believers who have been called *out of* the world.

"Enter ye in at the strait gate: for wide is the gate, and broad is the way, that leadeth to destruction, and many there be which go in thereat: Because strait is the gate, and narrow is the way, which leadeth unto life, and few there be that find it." (Matthew 7:13-14)

"Then said one unto him, Lord, are there few that be saved? And he said unto them, Strive to enter in at the strait gate: for many, I say unto you, will seek to enter in, and shall not be able." (Luke 13:23-24)

Is Rick Warren's P.E.A.C.E. Plan the Kingdom of God?

Rick Warren's purpose-driven, interfaith P.E.A.C.E. Plan places a far greater emphasis on temporal P.E.A.C.E. than it does on God's eternal peace through faith in *the Lord* Jesus Christ. Nevertheless, according to him, the five aspects of his P.E.A.C.E. Plan are "called the kingdom of God" and are what Jesus "modeled" in His "example" of how to "live the kingdom of God."

"Jesus *modeled* the solution. He *modeled* the kingdom of God."—Rick Warren (Emphasis added)[2]

"The kingdom of God is wherever God is king in your life. That's what it is. So how can I become involved? *Well, fortunately we have a great example in Jesus* . . . . While he was here on earth, Jesus did five things."—Rick Warren (Emphasis added)[3]

"Now what is the solution to these [five giants]? Well, I could get into that in real detail, but let me just tell you in one phrase – it's the kingdom of God . . . . You gotta ask yourself first what is the kingdom and how do I seek it . . . . The Bible tells us that the kingdom of God is what God wants to do on earth. It is God's people doing God's purposes on God's planet for God's glory. And **Jesus modeled how to live the kingdom of God. He did five things**. He shared the Good News and started a church, which by the way we're all a part of. He equipped leaders . . . he helped the poor, he cared for the sick, and he educated the next generation. He taught the truth. He said the truth will set you free. These are the five solutions to the global giants. For the last two years I've had 4,500 of my members overseas in 47 countries working on what we call the P.E.A.C.E. Plan. **The P.E.A.C.E. Plan is to Plant churches, Equip leaders, Assist the poor, Care for the sick, and Educate the next generation.** *It's called the kingdom of God!*"—Rick Warren (Emphasis added)[4]

"You need to understand that at the heart of the P.E.A.C.E. plan is this theme: the kingdom of God. *The P.E.A.C.E. plan is just doing the 5 things Jesus did while he was here on earth . . . It's just doing the 5 things Jesus did. And it is a strategy of global expansion because Jesus cares about the whole world."*—Rick Warren (Emphasis added)[5]

"Not only does God want you to see the world as he sees it and love it the way he loves it, but *he wants you to do the Son's plan, the Son's pattern."*—Rick Warren (Emphasis added)[6]

"Now these five elements of Jesus' ministry are **the practical expression of the kingdom of God. We call it the P.E.A.C.E. Plan**."—Rick Warren (Emphasis added)[7]

An interfaith P.E.A.C.E. Plan that enlists "men of peace" and "houses of worship" in "all the different religions" is not doing the Son's plan or pattern! The Lord Jesus Christ never "modeled" a Kingdom that non-Christians (non-followers of Christ) could work in without being saved. And He never "modeled" interfaith unity, which is excluded from *His* Kingdom.

This is not about *the truth*, which non-Christians do not have and therefore cannot uphold in the P.E.A.C.E. Plan. This is about *relationships* between those on the narrow way and those on the broad way. Relationships, the same dialectical "glue" holding purpose-driven churches together, are to be the uniting force in reaching the P.E.A.C.E. Plan's global "target."

"The Peace Plan, *its a relationship* for the global glory of God."—Rick Warren (Emphasis added)[8]

"In every village, in every home, in every business, in every government there is a man of peace, or a woman of peace. Somebody who's willing to work. By the way they don't necessarily have to be Christian, either."—Rick Warren[9]

In the Purpose-Driven Paradigm, not only does a person not have to be a Christian to live a purpose-driven life of "God's purposes," but they do not even have to be a Christian to "live the kingdom of God." They simply need to be a man or woman "of peace" who is willing to participate in working for peace in Rick Warren's P.E.A.C.E. Plan.

To say that "in *every* village, in *every* home, in *every* business, in *every* government there is a man of peace" is to even further twist the Lord Jesus Christ's words in Luke 10. This global Plan has gone way beyond a Reformation that unites "the church."

> "God invites you to *participate* in the greatest, largest, most diverse, and most significant *cause* in history—his kingdom." (*PDL*; p. 298; emphasis added)

Yet the Lord Jesus Christ, after pointing out that His Kingdom ***"is not of this world"*** (John 18:36), said, ***"for this cause came I into the world, that I should bear witness unto the truth"*** (John 18:37). Interfaith unity is not about *the truth* so is not about *God's* cause or Kingdom.

Rick Warren's article in the December 2005 issue of the *Ladies' Home Journal* was titled, "A PLAN FOR PEACE: Easing suffering around the world *can* be accomplished, one person at a time." Although in this article he quotes Romans 10:14 regarding believing in the Lord, "the Lord" is never said to be the Lord Jesus Christ. In fact, in this entire article on peace, the only time that Jesus (Who is the Prince of Peace) is mentioned is in a statement on "following the example of Jesus."

He also tells the readers of this secular Journal:

> "God is a God of hope, and it's a hope that will not disappoint. We cannot always see the hand of God, but we can trust in the love of God."—Rick Warren[10]

Only those who *believe* in *the Lord* Jesus Christ can trust in the eternal hope and love of God and will not be disappointed. They alone have been saved from the eternal judgment of God's wrath. God says in His Word that He showed the world His love on the cross (e.g., see Romans 5:8 and 1 John 4:9-10); the *eternal* love of God ***"is in Christ Jesus our Lord"*** (see Romans 8:39).

> *"The word which God sent unto the children of Israel, <u>preaching peace by Jesus Christ</u>: (he is Lord of all:) . . . how God anointed Jesus of Nazareth with the Holy Ghost and with power: who went about doing good, and healing all that were oppressed of the devil; for God was with him . . . . <u>And he commanded us to preach unto the people</u>, and to testify that it is he which was ordained of God to be the Judge of quick and dead. To him give all the prophets witness, that through his name whosoever believeth in him shall receive remission of sins." (Acts 10:36, 38, 42-43)*

> "Who <u>by him</u> do believe in God, that raised him up from the dead, and gave him glory; <u>that your faith and hope might be in God</u>." *(1 Peter 1:21)*

Yet more often than not, the world is not being told about Jesus Christ *the Lord and Saviour* Who requires true faith *in Him*. Along with the message of Purpose, the world is being told about Jesus the "model" who wants His "example" followed in works; specifically, the works of Rick Warren's P.E.A.C.E. Plan. Consistent with his belief that "living on purpose is the path to peace" (*PDL*; p. 35), this article presents his P.E.A.C.E. Plan as the solution toward improving people's temporal life and hope on earth. His secular readers, who have a variety of understandings of "the power and presence of God," are told:

> "The Bible teaches that we will never experience a lasting peace on earth apart from the power and presence of God, but it also teaches that **we can offer *a taste* of God's peace to those who've lost all hope. We do this *by following the example* of Jesus**. We see in Scripture that He shared God's love, trained leaders, helped the poor, cared for the sick and taught the children . . . .
>
> "**It [this PEACE plan] calls for *people of faith to work together* to help those with no hope** . . . What would happen if we could mobilize congregations to adopt villages where spiritual emptiness, selfish leadership, poverty, disease and ignorance keep people from experiencing the kind of life God meant for them to have?
>
> ". . . we need everyone doing his or her part . . . . I know God uses ordinary people, just like you, to make significant contributions toward peace on earth.
>
> "I think it all starts with God's family.
>
> "**P stands for plant *faith communities***. If we're going to share the love of God with billions of people, we must help start new faith communities around the world."
>
> "My prayer is that we can mobilize the health-care professionals in faith communities across our country. These professionals have knowledge, expertise

and experience that can make life better for millions of people around our world....

"[T]here are so many in our world who have no hope as they face disease and death .... they cannot get the medical help that's desperately needed....

"These problems are gigantic, but **ordinary people of faith, working together,** can chip away at the chaos and bring hope back to the hopeless."—Rick Warren (Emphasis added)[11]

First, "God's family" doesn't mean what it used to. Second, interfaith unity, by its very nature, automatically changes the focus from people of *the* faith to "people of faith." As previously mentioned, Rick Warren has called for "houses of worship" "in all the different religions" to minister health care *and* "spiritual care," which gives people temporal hope at the expense of eternal hope. And what he admitted at the 2005 Aspen Ideas Festival further shows that it would be irrelevant to him *which* "faith communities" the other religions and their "men of peace" choose to plant:

"I did a demographics study in the summer of '79, and I discovered that the Saddleback Valley, where I live and have lived for 25 years, was the fastest growing area in Orange County, and Orange County was the fastest growing county in America in the 70's.... It caught my attention. **I thought, you know where people are moving in they probably need new houses of worships, temples, and synagogues, and churches, and stuff like that.**"—Rick Warren (Emphasis added)[12]

No wonder he told active members "of any kind of religion," "'Great, God bless you, *keep going*'"!

In "Pragmatism Goes to Church," A.W. Tozer describes today's Christianity well:

"**For the pragmatist there are no absolutes ... Truth and morality float on a sea of human experience** ....

"The truth of any idea is its ability to produce desirable results ....

"The proof is that it succeeds; no one wants to argue with success.

"It is useless to plead for the human soul, to insist that what a man can do is less important than what he is . . . .

"It ['pragmatic philosophy'] asks no embarrassing questions about the wisdom of what we are doing or even about the morality of it . . . . When it discovers something that works it soon finds a text to justify it, 'consecrates' it to the Lord and plunges ahead. Next a magazine article is written about it, then a book, and finally the inventor is granted an honorary degree. After that any question about the scripturalness of things or even the moral validity of them is completely swept away. You cannot argue with success. The method works; *ergo*, it must be good.

"The weakness of all this is its tragic shortsightedness . . . . It is satisfied with present success and shakes off any suggestion that its works may go up in smoke in the day of Christ."—A.W. Tozer (Emphasis added)[13]

Saving Bodies at the Expense of Souls --
A Revolution for Global Christianity

"**The P.E.A.C.E. Plan will be a 'revolution'** for global Christianity, Warren told the congregation.

"'I stand before you confidently right now and say to you that God is going to use you to change the world,' Warren said . . . . 'I'm looking at a stadium full of **people who are telling God they will do *whatever it takes* to establish God's kingdom 'on earth as it is in heaven.'**

"'What will happen if the followers of Jesus say to him, 'We are yours'?' Warren asked. 'What kind of spiritual awakening will occur?'"—PurposeDriven News (Emphasis added)[14]

*F*irst, the answer to his question, "What kind of spiritual awakening will occur?" depends on *which* Jesus is followed: the Lord Jesus Christ Who is hated by the world because of His absolute truth, or a counterfeit "Jesus" who is embraced by the world because of his relativism. The basis of interfaith unity is relativism, not absolute truth.

Second, "whatever it takes" will never establish God's Kingdom for Him. It is the prideful absurdity of man that actually believes *man* has the power and holiness to change the world and establish *God's* Kingdom on earth for Him *as it is in heaven*! Yet even more absurd is man's belief that "whatever it takes" includes *interfaith* unity!

Almighty God is establishing His holy Kingdom *Himself* after His Day of the Lord judgment on a world that has shunned to do His will. Incidentally, did you notice in the previous quote what was missing from the phrase Rick Warren took from the Lord's Prayer?

> *"Thy kingdom come. <u>Thy will be done</u> in earth, as it is in heaven." (Matthew 6:10)*

This phrase is in Luke's recording of it as well:

> *". . . Thy kingdom come. <u>Thy will be done</u>, as in heaven, so in earth." (Luke 11:2)*

"Whatever it takes" in the P.E.A.C.E. Plan includes conforming to the world and diluting, even deleting, the Gospel of Christ in order to unite with the world in the name of purpose. This is not about either God's will or God's Kingdom.

> **"Until recently, Warren said he assumed spreading the Gospel was the most important Christian calling.** When his wife, Kay, began showing him pictures of African AIDS orphans and demanding that he use Saddleback's heft to help them, he realized he had neglected Jesus' command to serve the poor, he said."—*The Orange County Register.* 11/2/03 (Emphasis added)[15]

Setting the Gospel of Christ aside does not serve the poor and sick who even more urgently need *the Saviour*! Again, sharing "the message of Purpose" is more important than telling others about the Lord and Saviour Jesus Christ:

> "Kay and I, and our Saddleback team, have committed to spending the rest of our lives *sharing the message of Purpose and the strategy of the PEACE Plan* with every corner of the world . . . .

"It will be a holy movement, involving all kinds of churches sharing the same purposes together, and I invite you to join us! Will you hear and obey the call of God?"—Rick Warren (Emphasis added)[16]

A *holy* movement would never put physical needs *above* eternal needs. This is not hearing and obeying the call of God. Upside down to *God's* purpose, *man's* purpose is to save bodies at the expense of souls.

"Jesus answered them and said, Verily, verily, I say unto you, Ye seek me, not because ye saw the miracles, but because ye did eat of the loaves, and were filled. <u>Labour not for the meat which perisheth, but for that meat which endureth unto everlasting life</u>, which the Son of man shall give unto you: for him hath God the Father sealed. Then said they unto him, What shall we do, that we might work the works of God? Jesus answered and said unto them, This is the work of God, that ye believe on him whom he hath sent." (John 6:26-29)

"For this is good and acceptable in the sight of God our Saviour; who will have all men to be <u>saved</u>, and to come unto the knowledge of <u>the truth</u>." (I Timothy 2:3-4)

"No man can serve two masters: for either he will hate the one, and love the other; or else he will hold to the one, and despise the other. Ye cannot serve God and mammon. Therefore I say unto you, Take no thought for your life, what ye shall eat, or what ye shall drink; nor yet for your body, what ye shall put on. Is not the life more than meat, and the body than raiment? . . . (For after all these things do the Gentiles seek:) for your heavenly Father knoweth that ye have need of all these things. But seek ye <u>first</u> the kingdom of God, and his righteousness; and all these things shall be added unto you." (Matthew 6:24-25, 32-33)

The Lord Jesus Christ tells us to seek *first* the true Kingdom of God and His righteousness because receiving His righteousness imputed to us through faith is the only way to enter His Kingdom. Then God becomes our Father and meets our physical needs (see Matthew 6:25-33). Yet this, too, has been turned upside down. Today's Christianity has rewritten Matthew 6:33 to say, "But seek ye first to serve the world, and its temporal needs; and the kingdom of God shall be added unto them."

Nothing is more important than giving people the Gospel of Christ with their physical care. If they believe, they can then have the Lord Jesus Christ Himself. He alone has the power to give them God's saving love (salvation) and meet all their physical needs as well. The Saviour Himself said:

> *"And Jesus answered him, saying, It is written, That man shall not live by bread alone, <u>but by every word of God</u>." (Luke 4:4)*

> *"<u>The Spirit of the Lord is upon me, because he hath anointed me to preach the gospel to the poor</u>; he hath sent me to heal the brokenhearted, to preach deliverance to the captives, and recovering of sight to the blind, to set at liberty them that are bruised." (Luke 4:18)*

> *"Jesus answered and said unto them, Go and shew John again those things which ye do hear and see: The blind receive their sight, and the lame walk, the lepers are cleansed, and the deaf hear, the dead are raised up, <u>and the poor have the gospel preached to them</u>." (Matthew 11:4-5)*

Through interfaith unity, people may get physical care that improves the quality of their life on earth. But they will only be given "spiritual care" that will result in far worse suffering than poverty and AIDS -- an eternity of weeping and wailing and gnashing of teeth in the lake of fire (e.g., see Matthew 13:49-50 and Revelation 20:10, 14-15). This is not showing *compassion* on the sick and dying!

> *"There is a way that seemeth right unto a man, but the end thereof are the ways of death." (Proverbs 16:25 & 14:12)*

> *"In the way of righteousness is life; and in the pathway thereof there is no death." (Proverbs 12:28)*

In spite of interfaith efforts, people are still going to die. Perhaps happier and healthier, but they will still die. It is very important to feed and help the poor and sick, but food and medicine will do no good whatsoever in an eternity of fire. Interfaith unity is not the answer in striving for mercy and peace in the world. It is destructive and only seemingly "works," temporarily. With God, neither mercy and truth nor righteousness and peace are separated from each other, and they, in turn, are not found apart from the Lord Jesus Christ.

"Mercy and truth are met together; righteousness and peace have kissed each other." (Psalm 85:10)

People are so focused on this temporal life that even in Jesus' day they didn't want to see that physical needs are secondary to the primary spiritual need of salvation. Those who had their physical needs met first wanted to make Jesus King by force. But when He tried to meet their spiritual need, they weren't interested and walked away from Him. They only wanted what He could do for them physically; they didn't care about His words, which *are life*. (See John 6.) When these people departed from walking with Him and being His disciples (John 6:66), Jesus asked His faithful twelve if they were going to leave, too. Peter answered Him:

"Lord, to whom shall we go? thou hast the <u>words</u> of eternal life. And we believe and are sure that thou art that Christ, the Son of the living God." (John 6:68-69)

Peter responded with strong conviction because he believed what Jesus had told him:

"It is the spirit that quickeneth; <u>the flesh profiteth nothing</u>: <u>the words that I speak unto you</u>, they are spirit, and they <u>are life</u>." (John 6:63)

As truth continues to be sacrificed on the altar of unity, the broad way's relativism and pragmatism have inevitably become the prevailing "new way of thinking and acting." In the name of purpose, today's Christianity is transforming into the image of the world. This is indeed "a 'revolution' for global Christianity."

"We've had a Reformation; what we need now is a transformation."—Rick Warren[17]

"And be not conformed to this world: but be ye transformed by the renewing of your mind, that ye may prove what is that good, and acceptable, and perfect, will of God." (Romans 12:2)

Part 5

The Fulfillment of PEACE on Earth in the Name of Purpose

♦ *Chapter Fourteen* ♦

Declaring the End from the Beginning

"The Global Peace Plan IS GOING TO HAPPEN"

"Among other principles, the plan is built on what Warren calls 'exponential thinking.'"[1]

With the globe as the target, anything that brings less than exponential progress would naturally be deemed undesirable. Since the *narrow* way isn't "exponential," pragmatic unity with the *broad* way is preferred in saving the world from its global giants. James 1:27 has been quoted to rally people into joining the purpose-driven cause. Yet it is often and conveniently quoted with the last phrase deleted, which should be obvious as to why. It doesn't fit with either "exponential thinking" or "whatever it takes":

> *"Pure religion and undefiled before God and the Father is this, To visit the fatherless and widows in their affliction, <u>and to keep himself unspotted from the world.</u>"*

On November 3, 2005, Rick Warren talked with Lisa Mullins of The World about his P.E.A.C.E. Plan. In the course of their discussion, he said:

> "Instead of me going directly, for instance, me taking Americans that go in and work directly to say the people in the villages who are sick, well *that is an addition model that is not reproducible, it's not exponential in growth. But on the other hand, if you go in and you deal with gatekeepers, for instance, like pastors, priests, rabbis, imams,* whoever you would call, we call them the man of peace, or the woman of peace – the difference between this Plan and a lot of others, is that I trust the local leaders. I think they know more about their own people than either nongovernment organizations that send in staff or government organizations that send in diplomats." (Emphasis added)[2]

His goal is an "addition model" that is "reproducible" and "exponential in growth." Hence, his P.E.A.C.E. Plan involves going into countries and also training the "gatekeepers" of different religions (faiths) to "do the PEACE Plan in their own church and context."

> "'We believe average people can train and equip other believers to do the PEACE Plan in their own church and context,' said Warren.
>
> "Among other principles, the plan is built on what Warren calls 'exponential thinking.'
>
> "'We only do what can be reproduced by normal folks in normal churches. That way the plan will keep multiplying and never stop. **Once PEACE is released through other local churches, it will continue to reproduce around the world in an exponential fashion** . . . .' Warren said."—*ASSIST News Service*, 5/14/05 (Emphasis added)[3]
>
> "'We come into this Peace Plan with great humility,' Warren said. 'We will be like a giant mushroom expanding and exploding around the world. Whatever it takes, it will be a holy moment.'"—*Christian Examiner*, May 2005[4]

God's peace is only by Jesus Christ. It is not "released" or "reproduced" through unholy, interfaith efforts. Yet with supreme confidence in his global P.E.A.C.E. Plan and that he is the mouthpiece of God, Rick Warren has further proclaimed:

> "'**I intend** to use the Purpose Driven movement **to fulfill PEACE** in a new reformation.'" (Emphasis added)[5]
>
> ". . . the PEACE Plan we're developing . . . . is a local church-based paradigm for missions in the 21st century, and we believe **God will use it to bring worldwide revival** . . . .
>
> "Kay and I, and our Saddleback team, have committed to spending the rest of our lives sharing the message of Purpose and the strategy of the PEACE Plan with every corner of the world . . . .

"And the Church is the most widely distributed network in the world. It covers the globe and has more people and more power than any government will ever have. Together we will make a difference!

"Today I feel just as confident about **this new vision God has given me** as I did about the first vision he gave me 25 years ago to start Saddleback Church. **God will** raise up tens of thousands of purpose driven churches to fulfill his purposes in their own communities and **use the PEACE plan to help fulfill the Great Commission in our generation**. It will be a holy movement, involving all kinds of churches sharing the same purposes together, and I invite you to join us! Will you hear and obey the call of God?"—Rick Warren (Emphasis added)[6]

"There are three different entities in the world. There is the public sector, which is government, there's the private sector, which is business, and **there is the faith sector, which is religion** . . . . [T]he faith section has something that neither public nor private has . . . **they're in every village in the world** . . . The P.E.A.C.E. Plan is a plan where all three work together, and they each play a different role. And *together* I believe it can be done.

"You know, when I was 25 years old and I started Saddleback . . . and I announced that one day we'd have 20,000 members, everybody laughed. But it happened because it wasn't my idea. It was something I really felt inspired by God to do. I feel more confident about the P.E.A.C.E. Plan then I do about the day I started Saddleback Church, because I believe it is something that *must* be done. And the government will never solve it on its own, and business will never solve it. But **if they add in the third element, the faith sector, it will happen**."—Rick Warren (Bold added)[7]

"**The Global Peace Plan IS GOING TO HAPPEN**."—Rick Warren in his e-mail titled, "GOD'S DREAM FOR YOU - AND THE WORLD!" (Emphasis added; caps in the original)[8]

"I am humbled to be asked to share the vision of fighting the 5 global giants and lead Christians around the world in prayer [at the Global Day of Prayer, 5/15/05].

> This will be a significant step forward for **the PEACE plan. IT IS GOING TO HAPPEN!**"—Rick Warren (Emphasis added; caps in the original)[9]

His global P.E.A.C.E. Plan seeks unholy unity with other religions (faiths), including using "all the different religions" to give "spiritual care" in its involvement of "all kinds of churches sharing the same purposes together." Again, this is neither "a holy movement" nor hearing and obeying "the call of God." Yet Rick Warren is so convinced that his Purpose-Driven Paradigm is of God that a Pastors.com article reporting on the May 2005 Purpose Driven Church Conference said:

> "Through this reformation, Warren *expects* to see:
>
> - a *complete* mobilization of ordinary believers.
> - a rapid multiplication of churches.
> - *the complete eradication* of the five global giants . . .
> - a new cooperation between churches around the world.
> - *the complete evangelization* of the planet." (Emphasis added)[10]

No matter how purposeful *man's* works are (especially those of interfaith unity!), they are not going to bring in the global Kingdom of God in which all physical and spiritual problems have been eradicated. *God's judgment* is. God's Holy Scriptures repeatedly and abundantly make this clear.

Furthermore, it is the Antichrist's kingdom, for which the groundwork is already feverishly being laid, that will eventually control the three segments of the world—religion, government, and business (e.g., see Revelation 13, 17, and 18). Albeit for some noble causes such as helping the poor and sick, Rick Warren is working hard to advance the alignment of these three segments.

> "And these [five] issues are so big that there has to be an alignment of three segments to solve them: the church, government, and business."—Rick Warren[11]

> "A stool needs three legs to stand, and it will take all three sectors working together—public (governments), private (businesses), and faith (churches). Together we can make a difference."—Rick Warren (Parentheses in the original)[12]

> "There's the private sector, there's the public sector, and there's the faith sector. There is government, there's business, and there's religion. I'm absolutely convinced that you cannot do it with one sector or even two. I believe that each has a role . . . .
>
> "Then you add in Muslims, you add in Hindus, you add in all the different religions, and you use those houses of worship . . .
>
> "Government has a role and business has a role and churches, houses of worship have a role."—Rick Warren[13]

An article on Saddleback's website, subtitled "P.E.A.C.E. plan a worldwide revolution," reported the following:

> "Pastor Rick's 'Purpose Driven' movement is an ideal vehicle for launching such an effort . . . .
>
> "Saddleback's network of 2,600 small groups is starting the movement as each one adopts a village where it will seek to implement the P.E.A.C.E. Plan. The congregation has been testing the plan over the past 18 months . . .
>
> "The official rollout of The P.E.A.C.E. Plan will begin this October, when Pastor Rick will mobilize the Saddleback's small groups to focus upon 85 countries around the world . . . . A recent visit to the country convinced Warren that Rwanda had the right qualities for what he called 'the first model of national cooperation' between churches, the government, and major businesses."[14]

The "fall 2005 PEACE Launch," referred to here, was only to be open to select churches. Their goal is to have the PEACE Plan fully operational "for the big fall 2006 launch of the PEACE Plan open to the rest of the purpose driven community."[15] According to their "North America PEACE Pastor" in the PEACE Pilot Briefing 2005:

> "Rick has said repeatedly, *'This is why God made me. Everything else I have done was simply preparation for the PEACE Plan.'* If you choose to lead your Church to participate in the PEACE Plan it will be a wild ride . . ."[16]

No doubt.

> "On Saturday [April 16, 2005], as he prepared for Saddleback Church's 25th Anniversary Celebration today at Angel Stadium, he [Rick Warren] took time to answer a few questions about . . . *why he believes the time is right for him to take his place on the world stage.*"—*The Orange County Register*, 4/17/05 (Emphasis added)[17]

In these answers on going global with his P.E.A.C.E. Plan, Rick Warren made the following comment:

> "I think there is a much deeper spirituality in America than a lot of people realize. So, we will lay all this out for our people. **Purpose. Community. World.**" (Emphasis added)[18]

The fall 2005 PEACE launch and its "40 Days of PEACE" were covered by *The Orange County Register*. It reported that Rick Warren stated the following during his "impassioned appeal to his flock to be part of a global spiritual and humanitarian transformation":

> "'Why are you here? I'll tell you why you are here,' said Warren . . . '*Because you were marked by God to be part of a revolution.*'"—*The Orange County Register*, 9/18/05 (Emphasis added)[19]

Actually, we are *sealed* by God for the day of *redemption* (see Ephesians 4:30). It is the Antichrist who is going to *mark* people for the *revolution* that will bring global spiritual transformation when he comes. People are already being conditioned for this ultimate visible identification with what his kingdom will stand for -- unity and Oneness.

Remember the spies? Not every transformation that occurs in life is a good thing. The spies were transformed by God's judgment because they tried to *thwart* God's purposes after walking by sight rather than by faith. The spies had seen **"the giants"** in the land and were afraid, so they went against God's word (see Numbers 13).

Although the P.E.A.C.E. Plan is attempting to fight the giants it sees in the world, it is afraid of the giants' destructiveness. In its walking by sight rather than by faith and calling for interfaith unity (covenants), it, too, is going against God's Word and thwarting God's ultimate purpose.

> *"But this thing commanded I them, saying, Obey my voice, and I will be your God, and ye shall be my people: and walk ye in all the ways that I have commanded you, that it may be well unto you. But they hearkened not, nor inclined their ear, but walked in the counsels and in the imagination of their evil heart, <u>and went backward, and not forward</u>." (Jeremiah 7:23-24)*

Interfaith participation in his P.E.A.C.E. Plan might give the outward appearance that those on the broad way are merging onto the narrow way. Yet in actuality, Christians today are undiscerningly merging onto the broad way of counterfeit light and counterfeit peace. This is *not* "GOD'S DREAM"! Nor is this a "spiritual awakening." The masses are being led into a unity of spiritual blindness.

Incidentally, God doesn't "dream;" He *knows*. Yet when futurists who contradict God's Word are preferred over God's unchanging warnings, God's sure word of prophecy is replaced with man's vision and God's warnings go unheeded.

> *"<u>We have also a more sure word of prophecy; whereunto ye do well that ye take heed</u>, as unto a light that shineth in a dark place, until the day dawn, and the day star arise in your hearts: Knowing this first, that no prophecy of the scripture is of any private interpretation. <u>For the prophecy came not in old time by the will of man</u>: but holy men of God spake as they were moved by the Holy Ghost." (2 Peter 1:19-21)*

God's Global Judgment *Precedes* God's Global Peace

*W*e are told that Rick Warren "expects to see" "the complete evangelization of the planet" and "the complete eradication of the five global giants." This would indeed be wonderful. Yet his pronouncements of his fulfilled P.E.A.C.E. Plan that "IS GOING TO HAPPEN" do not line up with what God says in His eternal Word.

> "'I have a dream,' he [Rick Warren] said, 'for the global expansion of God's kingdom.'"—*Philadelphia Inquirer*, 6/26/05[20]

> "The first way to start thinking globally is to begin praying for specific countries. World-class Christians pray for the world. **Get a globe or map and pray for nations by name. The Bible says, 'If you ask me, I will give you the nations; all the people on earth will be yours.'** [endnote: Psalm 2:8 (NCV)] . . .

"People may refuse our love or reject our message, but they are defenseless against our prayers." (*PDL*; p. 300; bold added)

    This quote is from a chapter largely about working toward fulfilling the "Great Commission." This verse has been taken *completely* out of context in his continued Scripture twisting. This passage has nothing whatsoever to do with praying Christians being given "the nations" for the "Great Commission" or for anything else. The truth is that people who reject the message of the Gospel of Christ are defenseless against the Lord Jesus Christ's coming wrathful judgment. Twisting Scripture may change a person's beliefs away from the truth, but it does not change the truth Scripture sets forth when rightly divided in context.

    This Scripture is actually a prophecy about the Son of God, the Lord Jesus Christ (see also Acts 13:33), being given the nations in *wrathful judgment*. This will occur with the harvest of the tares in Matthew 13 (see also Revelation 14:14-20). (This harvest of the tares is the parable Rick Warren twisted to avoid maintaining purity in the churches; discussed earlier in chapter 11.) Here is Psalm 2:8 in context:

> *"I will declare the decree: the* Lord *hath said unto me,* **Thou art my Son***; this day have I begotten thee.* **Ask of me, and I shall give thee the heathen for thine inheritance, and the uttermost parts of the earth for thy possession. Thou shalt break them with a rod of iron; thou shalt dash them in pieces like a potter's vessel.** *Be wise now therefore, O ye kings: be instructed, ye judges of the earth. Serve the* Lord *with fear, and rejoice with trembling.* **Kiss the Son, lest he be angry, and ye perish from the way, when his wrath is kindled but a little.** *Blessed are all they that put their trust in him." (Psalm 2:7-12)*

> *"And I saw heaven opened, and behold a white horse; and he that sat upon him was called Faithful and True, and in righteousness he doth judge and make war . . . . And he was clothed with a vesture dipped in blood: and his name is called The Word of God . . . .* **And out of his mouth goeth a sharp sword, that with it he should smite the nations: and he shall rule them with a rod of iron: and he treadeth the winepress of the fierceness and wrath of Almighty God.** *And he hath on his vesture and on his thigh a name written, KING OF KINGS, AND LORD OF LORDS." (Revelation 19:11, 13, 15-16)*

> *"For the Father judgeth no man, but* **hath committed all judgment unto the Son***: That all men should honour the Son, even as they honour the Father.*

He that honoureth not the Son honoureth not the Father which hath sent him." (John 5:22-23)

Despite any truth brought up in his Paradigm regarding God's coming judgment, what Rick Warren "expects to see" and believes "IS GOING TO HAPPEN" is a denial of what God says in His Word. The Lord Jesus Christ *Himself* is personally going to bring global peace *after* He pours out His judgment on a rebellious world.

Rather than enjoying Rick Warren's fulfilled PEACE on earth, this world will be in global turmoil (e.g., see Matthew 24; Mark 13; Luke 21; I Timothy 4:1; 2 Timothy 3; 4:1-4; and 2 Thessalonians 2:1-12). Furthermore, the Lord Jesus Christ is coming to judge the whole world that **"lieth in wickedness"** (I John 5:19). He is not coming in wrath to a completely evangelized planet that had fulfilled "GOD'S DREAM FOR YOU - AND THE WORLD!" To the contrary, this unrepentant world will be filled with the *many* who have rejected His narrow way (see Matthew 7:13-23).

Rick Warren's global P.E.A.C.E. Plan is not the means by which God is going to bring peace to the planet. To believe his proclamation that his "Global Peace Plan IS GOING TO HAPPEN," one would have to take unholy scissors to practically the entire book of Revelation, not to mention to numerous other Scriptures and prophecy passages.

The infinite and omniscient Lord God has perfectly seen and known the end of time from the beginning of time:

> *"Remember the former things of old: for I am God, and there is none else; I am God, and there is none like me, declaring the end from the beginning, and from ancient times the things that are not yet done, saying, My counsel shall stand, and I will do all my pleasure: . . . yea, I have spoken it, I will also bring it to pass; I have purposed it, I will also do it." (Isaiah 46:9-11)*

God's Holy Scripture's clearly and repeatedly declare that the manifestation of God's Kingdom of peace is coming on the heels of God's global judgment, not united mankind's global peace. *This* is what is going to happen. It is *God's* Word, not Rick Warren's or anyone else's metaphysical "vision casting," that speaks the future.

> *"Knowing this first, that there shall come in the last days scoffers, walking after their own lusts, and saying, Where is the promise of his coming? for since the fathers fell asleep, all things continue as they were from the beginning of the creation. For this they <u>willingly</u> are <u>ignorant</u> of, that by*

the word of God the heavens were of old, and the earth standing out of the water and in the water: whereby the world that then was, being overflowed with water, perished: <u>But the heavens and the earth, which are now, by the same word are kept in store, reserved unto fire against the day of judgment and perdition of ungodly men</u> . . . . But the day of the Lord will come as a thief in the night; in the which the heavens shall pass away with a great noise, and the elements shall melt with fervent heat, the earth also and <u>the works that are therein shall be burned up</u>." (2 Peter 3:3-7, 10)

As one might expect, the willing ignorance of God's coming judgment coincides with the willing ignorance of God's desire for *us* to exercise judgment. People today see judging right and wrong and truth and error according to the light of God's Holy Scriptures as too divisive. So contrary to Scripture, they willingly prefer to accept and validate virtually everyone and everything.

"The way of peace they know not; and there is no judgment in their goings: they have made them crooked paths: whosoever goeth therein shall not know peace . . . . And judgment is turned away backward, and justice standeth afar off: for truth is fallen in the street, and equity cannot enter. Yea, truth faileth; and he that departeth from evil maketh himself a prey: and the LORD saw it, and it displeased him that there was no judgment." (Isaiah 59:8, 14-15)

"For my people is foolish, they have not known me; they are sottish children, and they have none understanding: they are wise to do evil, but to do good they have no knowledge." (Jeremiah 4:22)

"<u>Prove</u> all things; hold fast that which is good. Abstain from all appearance of evil." (I Thessalonians 5:21-22)

"(For the fruit of the Spirit is in all goodness and righteousness and truth;) <u>proving</u> what is acceptable unto the Lord. And have no fellowship with the unfruitful works of darkness, but rather reprove them." (Ephesians 5:9-11)

"Do ye not know that the saints shall judge the world? and if the world shall be judged by you, are ye unworthy to judge the smallest matters? Know ye

not that we shall judge angels? how much more things that pertain to this life?" (1 Corinthians 6:2-3)

"But he that is spiritual judgeth all things, yet he himself is judged of no man." (1 Corinthians 2:15)

Those who refuse to **"prove all things"** may find themselves on the receiving end of God's coming judgment. His judgment is coming, willful ignorance of today's futurists notwithstanding.

"For yourselves know perfectly that the day of the Lord so cometh as a thief in the night. For when they shall say, Peace and safety; then sudden destruction cometh upon them, as travail upon a woman with child; and they shall not escape." (1 Thessalonians 5:2-3)

"Therefore wait ye upon me, saith the Lord, until the day that I rise up to the prey: for my determination is to gather the nations, that I may assemble the kingdoms, to pour upon them mine indignation, even all my fierce anger: for all the earth shall be devoured with the fire of my jealousy." (Zephaniah 3:8)

"And to you who are troubled rest with us, when the Lord Jesus shall be revealed from heaven with his mighty angels, in flaming fire taking vengeance on them that know not God, and that obey not the gospel of our Lord Jesus Christ: who shall be punished with everlasting destruction from the presence of the Lord, and from the glory of his power; when he shall come to be glorified in his saints, and to be admired in all them that believe (because our testimony among you was believed) in that day." (2 Thessalonians 1:7-10)

"And shall not God avenge his own elect, which cry day and night unto him, though he bear long with them? I tell you that he will avenge them speedily. Nevertheless when the Son of man cometh, shall he find faith on the earth?" (Luke 18:7-8)

Sadly, the falling away from the faith will be of such great magnitude that the Lord Jesus Christ asks us to consider whether He will actually find faith on the earth when He returns. Given this tragic reality, God has already made provision to use an *angel* to preach His Gospel throughout the earth. To fulfill the prophecy in Matthew 24:14, God is not going to use faithless mankind which has already watered down His saving Gospel to the point of presenting a false gospel. He is going to send one of His own holy, faithful messengers:

> *"And this gospel of the kingdom shall be preached in all the world for a witness unto all nations; and then shall the end come." (Matthew 24:14)*

> *"And I saw another <u>angel</u> fly in the midst of heaven, having the everlasting gospel to preach unto them that dwell on the earth, and to every nation, and kindred, and tongue, and people." (Revelation 14:6)*

The kingdom that will be established on earth seemingly in "peace" when God's global judgment comes will be the Antichrist's global kingdom. Wickedness, unrighteousness, and deception will wax worse and worse until it all climaxes in the Wicked one himself ruling the world for 3½ years (e.g., see 2 Timothy 3:1, 12-13; Daniel 7:25; and Revelation 13:4-9).

Christianity's leaders today are making the same grave error the leaders made in Old Testament times. God warned the people of their wickedness and of His coming judgment, but the false prophets preferred to contradict God's Word by declaring instead that God was going to give them peace:

> *"Thus saith the L*ord *unto this people, Thus have they loved to wander, they have not refrained their feet, therefore the L*ord *doth not accept them; he will now remember their iniquity, and visit their sins. Then said the L*ord *unto me, Pray not for this people for their good. When they fast, I will not hear their cry; and when they offer burnt offering and an oblation, I will not accept them: but I will consume them by the sword, and by the famine, and by the pestilence. <u>Then said I, Ah, Lord G*od*! behold, the prophets say unto them</u>, Ye shall not see the sword, neither shall ye have famine; but <u>I will give you assured peace in this place. Then the L*ord *said unto me, The prophets prophesy lies in my name:</u> I sent them not, neither have I commanded them, neither spake unto them: they prophesy unto you a false vision and divination, and a thing of nought, and the deceit of their heart." (Jeremiah 14:10-14)*

> *"Thus saith the L*ORD *of hosts, Hearken not unto the words of the prophets that prophesy unto you: they make you vain: <u>they speak a vision of their own heart, and not out of the mouth of the L</u>*<u>ORD</u>*. <u>They say still unto them that despise me, The L</u>*<u>ORD</u> <u>*hath said, Ye shall have peace*</u>*; and they say unto every one that walketh after the imagination of his own heart, No evil shall come upon you. For who hath stood in the counsel of the L*ORD*, and hath perceived and heard his word? who hath marked his word, and heard it? Behold, a whirlwind of the L*ORD *is gone forth in fury, even a grievous whirlwind: it shall fall grievously upon the head of the wicked . . . . But if they had stood in my counsel, and had caused my people to hear my words, then they should have turned them from their evil way, and from the evil of their doings." (Jeremiah 23:16-19, 22)*

Teaching a coming global peace and prosperity is "positive" and heartening compared to the truth of God's coming global judgment. But the true good news is that the Lord Jesus Christ died to deliver all who believe in Him from His coming wrath. When Jesus Christ Himself sets up His visible Kingdom after He judges the world *with His truth,* then there will be true peace and prosperity for all who believe His truth and receive His salvation before it's too late.

> *"Before the L*ORD*: for he cometh, for he cometh to judge the earth: he shall judge the world with righteousness, and the people <u>with his truth</u>." (Psalm 96:13)*

> *"Open ye the gates, that the <u>righteous</u> nation <u>which keepeth the truth</u> may enter in." (Isaiah 26:2)*

> *"And the work <u>of righteousness</u> shall be peace; and the effect of righteousness quietness and assurance for ever." (Isaiah 32:17)*

The true Kingdom of God, and its fulfillment of true peace on earth, cannot be seen, served, or entered apart from *the* truth of God. But there is a growing inclusive, interfaith kingdom that is focused on bringing peace to the world through the transcendent purpose of serving the world. The Angel of light's realm is feverishly building this global counterfeit kingdom of "World Servers."

◆ *Chapter Fifteen* ◆

The Angel of Light's "Plan" for World Peace

An Interfaith Kingdom of World Servers Working Together as ONE

Our enemies in the Angel of light's realm have been working long and hard at fulfilling his Plan. They are achieving marked success in enticing the world into his counterfeit kingdom and its (New Age) New Spirituality that appears as "light" and "peace." As mentioned earlier (see chapter six), Alice Bailey (A.A.B.) was approached by the spirit world to detail "the Plan" in writing. These writings are the basis for the descriptions of this counterfeit kingdom "of God" and its Plan to use world service to bring interfaith unity and "peace" to the world. As is to be expected, these enemies commonly twist Scripture after the pattern of the father of lies, who has been twisting God's Word since the Garden of Eden. Also not surprisingly, their deceptions twist the nature and work of the Lord Jesus Christ and reveal an ongoing hatred for His true followers and Word.

> "I [Djwhal Khul] . . . have a vision of the Plan . . . Through the cooperation of A.A.B. I put this plan - as far as was possible - before you, calling your attention to the New Group of World Servers . . . .
>
> "[T]he vision is a vision of group work, of group relationships, of group objectives, and of the group fusion to the larger Whole."—Alice Bailey & Djwhal Khul[1]
>
> "[T]here is a group of human beings, integrating now . . . upon whom is laid the burden of leading humanity. They are starting movements that have in them the new vibration, they are saying things that are universal in their tone, they are enunciating principles that are cosmic, they are inclusive and not exclusive, they do not care what terminology a man uses; they insist that a man shall

keep his own inner structure of truth to himself and not impose it on any one else . . . they demonstrate the universal light, they are servers . . .

"[T]hey are tied by no dogmas or doctrines because they have the word which has come to them in the dark, which they have wrought out for themselves in the strife and stress of their own souls. They meet the need of their fellow men, and theirs is the message of Christ, 'A new commandment I give you that you love one another.' . . .

"'A new commandment I give you' can be summed up in **'inclusiveness', the hallmark of the New Age**, the universal spirit, identification, oneness with all your fellowmen . . . .

"How shall we fit ourselves to meet that requirement, to possess those characteristics which automatically put us into the group of world servers? You will never get there by talking about it . . . You will get there by doing the next thing correctly."—Alice Bailey & Djwhal Khul (Emphasis added)[2]

The desire for people to stop talking and debating and just start doing and cooperating facilitates interfaith unity among all beliefs and religions. This is exactly what the spirit world has been working toward. In the name of purpose, people are being lured away from doctrine to focus on relationships.

"He ['Christ'] emphasized the necessity for cooperation, indicating that if we truly follow the Way, **we shall put an end to competition, and substitute for it cooperation** . . . .

"Love, brotherhood, cooperation, service, self-sacrifice, **inclusiveness, freedom from doctrine**, recognition of divinity - these are the characteristics of the citizen of the kingdom, and these still remain our ideals."—Alice Bailey (Emphasis added)[3]

"As the Members of the Hierarchy [spirit realm] approach closer to us, the dream of brotherhood, of fellowship, of **world cooperation and of a peace (based upon right human relations)** becomes clearer in our minds. As They draw nearer we vision a new and vital world religion, a universal faith, at-one in its basic idealism with the past but different in its mode of expression."—Alice Bailey & Djwhal Khul (Parentheses in the original; emphasis added)[4]

"It is time that the church woke up to its true mission, which is to materialize the kingdom of God on earth, today, here and now . . . . People are no longer interested in a possible heavenly state or a probable hell. They need to learn that **the kingdom is here, and must express itself on earth** . . . **The way into that kingdom is the way that Christ trod. It involves the sacrifice of the personal self for the good of the world, and the service of humanity** . . ."—Alice Bailey (Emphasis added)[5]

"Christ died in order to bring to our notice that **the way into the kingdom of God was the way of love and of service**. He served and loved and wrought miracles, and gathered together the poor and the hungry."—Alice Bailey (Emphasis added)[6]

"True religion will come to be interpreted in terms of the will-to-good and its practical expression, goodwill."—Alice Bailey & Djwhal Khul[7]

Goodwill in world service, not belief and obedience of the doctrine of the faith, is this kingdom's definition of "true religion." It naturally follows that this kingdom has also altered Christ into a counterfeit that all religions (faiths) can follow as their "example."

"**Christ stood as a symbol and also as an example** . . . **and showed us the pattern upon which we should mould our lives.**

"The kingdom and the service! . . .

"We must grasp this; we must realize that we shall find release only in the service of the kingdom. We have been held too long by the dogmas of the past, and there is today a natural revolt against the idea of individual salvation through the blood sacrifice of Christ . . . . *It is essential that today we face the problem of the relation of Christ to the modern world, and dare to see the truth, without any theological bias* . . . . It is quite possible that *Christ is far more inclusive than we have been led to believe* . . . We have preached a God of love and have spread *a doctrine of hate*. We have taught that Christ died to save

the world and have endeavored to show that *only believers could be saved* . . .
But Christ founded a kingdom on earth, wherein all God's children would have
equal opportunity of expressing themselves as sons of the Father. This, many
Christians find impossible to accept . . .

"*Individual salvation is surely selfish* in its interest and its origin. **We must
serve in order to be saved**, and only can we serve intelligently if we believe
in the divinity of all men and also in Christ's outstanding service to the race.
**The kingdom is a kingdom of servers, for every saved soul must without
compromise join the ranks of those who ceaselessly serve their fellow
men.**"—Alice Bailey (Emphasis added)[8]

"Our need today is to see **the hidden thread of purpose** . . . This ['spiritual']
awakening is already here, and the will to good is present. *The teaching of
Christ . . . needs only to be rescued from the interpretations of the theologies
of the past*, and taken at its simple face value, which is an expression of the
divinity of man, of **his participation in the kingdom which is in process of
being brought into recognition**, and of his immortality as a citizen of that
kingdom. What we are in reality passing through is 'a religious initiation into
the mysteries of Being,' . . . and from that **we shall emerge with a deepened
sense of God immanent in ourselves and in all humanity** . . . .

"The vital need is to return to the simple fundamental instruction which Christ
gave, and to learn to love our brother . . . . It is a love which realizes that the
world needs love, and that *a spirit of love (which is a spirit of inclusiveness, of
tolerance, of wise judgment and farsighted vision) can draw all men together into
that outward unity which is based upon a recognized inner relationship.*"—Alice
Bailey (Emphasis added)[9]

"**When the consciousness which is Christ's has been awakened in all men,
then we shall have peace on earth and goodwill among men** . . . . The
expression of our divinity will bring to an end the hatred rampant upon earth
and break down all the separating walls which divide man from man, group
from group, nation from nation, religion from religion. Where there is goodwill
there must be peace; there must be organized activity and a recognition of the
Plan of God, **for that Plan is synthesis; that Plan is fusion; that Plan is
unity and at-one-ment** . . . .

"The realization of this is needed today. Christ in God. God in Christ. Christ in you and Christ in me. This is what will bring into being **that one religion which will be the religion of love, of peace on earth, of universal goodwill,** of divine understanding, and of the deep recognition of God."—Alice Bailey (Bold added)[10]

In the Angel of light's upside-down realm, the belief that God is immanent within All is the basis for the Oneness of All. "Awakening" to this Oneness is this kingdom's so-called At-one-ment, and it is what makes a person "holy" (a complete mockery of the Lord Jesus Christ's atonement):

"What is this holiness to which He calls us, when we take the first step toward the new birth? What is a holy man?

"Wholeness, unity, at-one-ment, completeness - this is the hall mark of a perfect man. Having once seen and with open eyes beheld the vision of divinity, what can we do? . . .

"It means listening for and obeying the insistent demand of the soul for a nearer approach to God and a fuller expression of divinity . . .

"This, Christ taught, and for this He prayed the Father.

"'. . . I in them, and thou in me, that they may be made perfect in one.' (St. John, XVII, 20-23.)

"**This is the doctrine of the At-one-ment; God, immanent in the universe - the cosmic Christ. God, immanent in humanity, revealed through the historical Christ. God, immanent in the individual, the indwelling Christ, the soul.**"—Alice Bailey (Emphasis added)[11]

This Oneness is foundational to the (New Age) New Spirituality—a counterfeit Spirituality which is an intrinsic part of this counterfeit kingdom. The belief that God is immanent within everyone and everything also leads to the belief that God is ONE God of many names and manifestations in the many religions (faiths). This makes it easier to entice all religions together into this interfaith kingdom of "spiritual Oneness" and world service.

On the other hand, this kingdom sees those who refuse to become "holy" through its Oneness as guilty of "separateness" and "hatred." They will be excluded from its otherwise all-inclusiveness:

> "The true Church is the kingdom of God on earth . . . **composed of all, regardless of** race or **creed**, who live by the light within, who have discovered the fact of the mystical Christ in their hearts . . . . The members of the coming kingdom will think in terms of humanity as a whole; and as long as they are separative or nationalistic, or religiously bigoted, or commercially selfish, they have no place in that kingdom. The word *spiritual* will be given a far wider connotation than that which has been given in the old age . . . and we shall no longer regard one activity as spiritual and another as not. The question of motive, **purpose** and group usefulness **will determine the spiritual nature of an activity**."—Alice Bailey (Bold added)[12]

> "Love is unity, at-one-ment and synthesis. Separateness is hatred, aloneness and division. But man, being divine in nature, has to love . . .

> "Each one of us has to tread the way of the cross alone, and enter God's kingdom by right of achievement. But **the way is found in service to our fellow men** . . .

> "It is through supreme service and sacrifice that we become followers of Christ and **earn** the right to enter into His kingdom, because we do not enter alone . . . .

> "He ['Christ'] knew no separateness . . . . and the 'great heresy of separateness' was completely overcome by His all-inclusive spirit."—Alice Bailey (Emphasis added)[13]

> "I. **Countless men and women in every land will form themselves into groups for the promotion of goodwill and for the production of right human relations**. So great will be their numbers that from being a small and relatively unimportant minority, **they will be the largest and the most influential force in the world**. Through them, the New Group of World Servers will be able to work successfully.

> "2. This active energy of loving understanding will mobilize *a tremendous reaction* against the potency of hate. To hate, to be separate, and to be exclusive

will come to be regarded as the only sin . . ."—Alice Bailey & Djwhal Khul (Emphasis added)[14]

Warren Smith has also written the eye-opening book, *Reinventing Jesus Christ: The New Gospel*. He discusses the spirit realm's goal for Oneness and warns about its final solution for those who do not comply.[15] The spirit realm will indeed "mobilize a tremendous reaction" against those who stand firm against ("hate") its Oneness. Its Plan includes a "selection process" to purge all these so-called "cancer cells" from the planet. "Self-centered" separation is supposedly preventing the planet's state of "health" necessary for humanity's ultimate "spiritual evolution" toward its "divine potential"—i.e., the "new birth" of its "Christ consciousness" or "divinity." At least this is the "positive" spin given by the spirit realm to explain their coming war against the saints under the Antichrist's reign (e.g., see Revelation 13:7).

Today's blinded world and Christianity are oblivious to Scripture's prophecies and the underlying diabolical, global Plan of the spirit world. Consequently, they are easily being lured together as ONE, seemingly for the sake of "the common good," "world service," and "global peace" through "love," "goodwill," and "right relations." The Angel of light's counterfeit kingdom and ministers of 'righteousness' epitomize how the road to hell is paved with good works, piety, and spirituality.

> *"For such are false apostles, deceitful workers, transforming themselves into the apostles of Christ. And no marvel; for Satan himself is transformed into an angel of light. Therefore it is no great thing if his ministers also be transformed as the ministers of righteousness; whose end shall be according to their works." (2 Corinthians 11:13-15)*

The Angel of light is very effective in his deceptions. But then, our Adversary no longer has to work very hard to deceive given today's plague of scriptural illiteracy.

Having ears to hear only what is "positive," today's Christianity is falling hook, line, and sinker for the Angel of light's counterfeit kingdom of World Servers. This kingdom seeks to "put an end to competition, and substitute for it cooperation." This kingdom makes it clear that its "Plan is synthesis . . . fusion . . . unity and at-one-ment" and its "love is unity, at-one-ment and synthesis." Even its "peace is unity and synthesis."[16] The Angel of light seeks to "usher in the new era of joy and of peace and *spiritual synthesis* - that synthesis which we call brotherhood" (emphasis added)[17] because the bottom line of his Plan is unity on his broad way.

This has been greatly facilitated by his kingdom's success in presenting its own "Christ" to the world. The "Christ" of this kingdom is the "Christ" of the (New Age) New Spirituality. He is a universal "Christ" who is an interfaith "model" or "example" but not *the Lord* and *Saviour*. He welcomes "all men of peace" from "every world religion" who are being gathered into this "embodiment of the emerging Kingdom of God on earth." This emerging interfaith kingdom will eventually be ruled by the Antichrist, the ultimate "man of peace." This ruler will **"come in peaceably"** but **"by peace shall destroy many,"** and he **"shall destroy wonderfully"** (Daniel 11:21, and 8:24-25). Initially, the destruction will appear wonderful and as peace and not as the destruction it is. **"There is a way that seemeth right . . ."**

> "VATICAN CITY, NOV. 30, 2005 (Zenit.org).- **Whoever seeks peace** and the good of the community with a pure conscience, and keeps alive the desire for the transcendent, **will be saved even if he lacks biblical faith, says Benedict XVI**." (Emphasis added)[18]

> "We are concerned with only one subject, the ushering in of **the new world order** . . . . We are occupied with the formation of that new party which **will gather into its ranks all men of peace** and good will, without interfering with their specific loyalties . . . This new party can be regarded **as the embodiment of the emerging Kingdom of God on earth** . . . It is a grouping of all those who - **belonging as they do to every world religion** and every nation and type of political party - are free from the spirit of hatred and separativeness, and who seek to see right conditions established on earth through mutual good will."—Alice Bailey & Djwhal Khul (Emphasis added)[19]

> "**In every village, in every home, in every business, in every government there is a man of peace**, or a woman of peace. Somebody who's willing to work. By the way **they don't necessarily have to be Christian . . . They could be something else or nothing**. But they're willing to work with you."—Rick Warren (Emphasis added)[20]

> ". . . you go in and you deal with **gatekeepers, for instance, like pastors, priests, rabbis, imams, whoever you would call, we call them the man of peace**, or the woman of peace . . ."—Rick Warren (Emphasis added)[21]

"And then when **you add in all the different peoples of faith who would be people of peace** – you know, when you talk about poverty and disease and illiteracy, these are not *Christian* issues, they're *human* issues. **And I'll work with anybody who wants to work on them. You know?** . . . We just need to get people moving, mobilized."—Rick Warren (Bold added)[22]

"**This kingdom, through its major power (a quality of synthesis, could you but realize it), is gathering together into itself men and women out of every nation and out of all parts of the Earth.** It is absorbing them into itself not because they are orthodox or religious in the generally accepted sense of the term, but because of their *quality* . . . . They, therefore, are demonstrating oneness and synthesis in such a simple way that men everywhere can grasp it. **The New Group of World Servers is the vanguard of the kingdom** of God, the living proof of the existence of the world of spiritual Oneness."—Alice Bailey & Djwhal Khul (Parentheses in the original; emphasis added)[23]

"Saddleback Church is now but one among thousands of **purpose driven churches -- the vanguard of a new reformation**."—PD Staff (Emphasis added)[24]

". . . *the goal for thousands everywhere* is the demonstration of the Christ spirit, and the exemplification of a life conditioned by love and *modeled* upon that of Christ . . .

"This makes possible, therefore, the next great human unfoldment which grows out of the Christ consciousness . . .

"Eventually the truths thus grasped change the consciousness of humanity as a whole . . ."—Alice Bailey & Djwhal Khul (Emphasis added)[25]

The Angel of light is achieving marked success in his Plan to unite the world in "oneness of purpose" and "change the consciousness of humanity as a whole." According to his minions, it is "divine purpose which will foster the coming religious synthesis."[26] In other words, it is the work of world service that is to *automatically overcome religious differences* so that "all religions [will] be regarded as emanating from one great spiritual source"[27]:

"Not as yet is the vision seen with a sufficient clarity by the many servers, to make them work with perfect unanimity of purpose and objective, of technique and method, or complete understanding and oneness of approach. That fluid, perfect cooperation lies as yet in the future. The establishing of an inner contact and relationship, **based on a realized oneness of purpose** and soul love, is magnificently possible, and for this all disciples must struggle and strive . . . . [T]he inner relationships and cooperation *Must* be established and developed, in spite of the outer divergences of opinion. When the inner link is held in love, and **when disciples . . . stand shoulder to shoulder in the One Work, then the differences, the divergences, and the points of disagreement will automatically be overcome** . . . .

"The principle of work is love for all men and service to the race, preserving at the same time a deeper inner love for those with whom you are destined to work. Each soul grows into the way of light through service rendered, through experience gained, through mistakes made, and through lessons learnt. That necessarily must be personal and individual. **But the work itself is one. The Path is one. The love is one. The goal is one. These are the points that matter** . . . .

"**Relinquish the pride of mind which sees its way and its interpretations to be correct and true, and others' false and wrong. This is the way of separation. Adhere to the way of integration which is of the soul and not of the mind** . . . .

"**It is essential that the disciples shall learn to sacrifice the non-essential in order that the work may go forward.** Little as one may realize it, the many techniques and methods and ways are secondary to the major world need . . . . When this Law of Sacrifice governs the mind, it will inevitably lead all disciples to relinquish the personal in favor of the universal and of the soul, that knows no separation, no difference. Then no pride, nor a short and myopic perspective, nor love of interference (so dear to many people), nor misunderstanding of motive will hinder their cooperation with each other as disciples, nor their service to the world."—Alice Bailey & Djwhal Khul (Parentheses in the original; bold added)[28]

 The world is indeed sacrificing "non-essential" religious differences so "the work" of serving the world can take precedence. We are seeing the emergence of the counterfeit kingdom's "new world religion which will emphasize unity but bar out uniformity"[29]:

> "The true values . . . are to be summed up in the one word Service. They are expressed through inclusiveness and non-separateness. It is here that the Church, as usually understood, meets its major challenge. Is it spiritual enough to **let go of theology** and become truly human? Is it interested enough to **widen its horizon and recognize as truly Christian all who demonstrate the Christ spirit, whether they be Hindu, Mohammedan, or Buddhist, whether they are labeled by any name other than that of orthodox Christian?**"—Alice Bailey (Emphasis added)[30]

> "**This religious will is in expression now, not turned to theology or to the formation of doctrines and occupied with their enforcement, but to love and service**, forgetting self, giving the uttermost that is possible for the helping of the world. **This will breaks down all barriers** . . . its quality that of universality, and its technique that of loving service . . . .

> "The time has come when **service must expand and express itself on broader and more inclusive lines**, and we must learn to serve as Christ served, to love all men as He loved them and, by the potency of our spiritual vitality and the quality of our service, stimulate all we meet so that they too can serve and love and become members of the kingdom . . . . The call is for sane and normal men and women who can comprehend the situation, face what must be done, and then give their lives to expressing for the world the qualities of the citizens of the kingdom of Souls: love, wisdom, silence, non-separativeness and freedom from hatreds and partisan, creedal beliefs. **When such men can be gathered together in large numbers (and they are gathering rapidly) we shall have the fulfilment of the angels' song at Bethlehem, 'On earth peace**, *good will toward men.*'"—Alice Bailey (Parentheses in the original; bold added)[31]

Remember the tower of Babel? The world tried to become ONE then, too (see Genesis 11:1-9). God didn't let that succeed, either. However, this time He won't be so lenient when He puts a permanent stop to it. Fulfilled peace on earth *follows* God's global judgment. The rebellious world is sacrificing His truth on the altar of unity.

Chapter Fifteen

"And the Lord said, Behold, the people is one, and they have all one language; and this they begin to do: and now nothing will be restrained from them, which they have imagined to do. Go to, let us go down, and there confound their language, that they may not understand one another's speech. So the Lord scattered them abroad from thence upon the face of all the earth: and they left off to build the city." (Genesis 11:6-8)

Until now . . .

◆ *Chapter Sixteen* ◆

"The Power of ONE"

"Together as ONE We Can Change the World"

On June 3, 2005, Rick Warren announced his support of "The ONE Campaign: To Make Poverty History" in an e-mail titled, "Will You Join Me?" In it, he acknowledged that this Campaign has been "endorsed by a wide coalition of folks from *all across the faith* and political spectrum" (emphasis added). He also explained how he was joining with "U.S. Faith Leaders" in sending a letter to President Bush to lobby him to fight global poverty at the G8 Summit this past July. He and the other Faith Leaders included the following statements in their letter to Bush:

> "Americans are uniting as ONE across political and religious divides to support action to overcome the emergency of global AIDS and extreme poverty."

> "Together as ONE, we can Make Poverty History this July."[1]

Rick Warren also encouraged his readers to visit the website of The ONE Campaign, which has boldly declared:

> "Together as ONE we can change the world."[2]

In support of The ONE Campaign, on July 2, 2005 Rick Warren attended the Live 8 Concert in Philadelphia, of which he was reportedly made "official pastor."[3] In covering this event, *Forbes* reported:

> "Prior to the concert, Warren joined One organizers in a rally on the steps behind the Philadelphia Art Museum to encourage young volunteers.

> "'Because you are involved in the One Campaign, you are interested in change,' he said. 'If you are serious about change, you need to do two things. First, focus

on vision, not need; call out the greatness in people, not their guilt. Secondly, *don't tell it like it is*, but rather like it could be, should be, and may be.

"'We don't want people to die of poverty or diseases for which we already have cures, because God loves them.' Warren continued. I believe with all my heart we can do this - and I believe you are the generation to do it.' Pastor Warren was joined on the platform by Pastor Herb Lusk, with whom he is partnering on the Purpose Driven 'Stand for Africa' campaign.

"'I was in Memphis, Tennessee in 1968 when the voice of Martin Luther King was silenced - it was the darkest day of my life.' Pastor Lusk said. 'But I look at Bono, Rick Warren, the One movement, and I realize that voice is still alive.'

"'I don't know all the statistics -- I'm just a country preacher - but I do know **there is one Lord, one faith, one baptism, one God, and one Father who is in us and above us all - and there is the One campaign.**'" [!] (Emphasis added)[4]

The U.N.'s Goals: Uniting the World as ONE

*T*he ONE Campaign consists of a growing number of partners that either directly or indirectly support strengthening the United Nations and fulfilling its goals. In fact, the following is the Campaign's answer to the question, "How does ONE link to international agreements to fight poverty?":

> "ONE links directly to the international effort to achieve the Millennium Development Goals. 1% more of the US federal budget would help save millions of lives and be a major commitment towards achieving the internationally agreed upon United Nations Millennium Development Goals." (Emphasis added)[5]

In their letter to President Bush, Rick Warren and the U.S. Faith Leaders, in accordance with this purpose of The ONE Campaign, asked him to give "just ONE percent more of the US budget."[6] They did so seemingly without any regard for the far-reaching ramifications of strengthening the United Nations and its goals.

The U.N.'s Millennium Development Goals (MDGs) are uniting the world and its religions (faiths) in transcendent common purpose. These goals are the international development goals in the U.N.'s Millennium Declaration, a Resolution adopted by the General Assembly on September 8, 2000. This Resolution declares the United

Nations and its Charter to be "indispensable foundations of a more peaceful, prosperous and just world." This Resolution also explicitly upholds Agenda 21, the Kyoto Protocol, the Universal Declaration of Human Rights, and the Convention on the Rights of the Child, among other destructive U.N. agendas.[7] This Resolution has been adopted by *all* United Nations Member States,[8] and now it is also being supported by today's Christianity and other religions via its MDGs.

The framework is all coming together for the U.N.'s ultimate goal of uniting the world as ONE under its control. Its comprehensive Resolution, which the world has embraced, also contains the following statements (emphasis added):

> "We are determined to establish a just and lasting peace all over the world *in accordance with the purposes and principles of the Charter.*"

> "As the most universal and most representative organization in the world, *the United Nations must play the central role.*"

> "We will spare no effort to make the United Nations a more effective instrument for pursuing all of these priorities . . ."

> "We solemnly reaffirm, on this historic occasion, that *the United Nations is the indispensable common house of the entire human family, through which we will seek to realize our universal aspirations for peace, cooperation* and development. We therefore pledge our unstinting support for these common objectives and our determination to achieve them."[9]

On the U.N.'s website directly underneath the heading, "Charter of the United Nations," the belief is upheld that unity can change the world:

> "We the Peoples of the United Nations . . . United for a Better World." (Ellipsis dots in the original)[10]

Only on the very surface do the U.N.'s goals appear noble and compassionate. These eight MDGs have much in common with the giants of Rick Warren's Global PEACE Plan, such as fighting poverty, hunger, disease, and lack of education.[11] Yet underlying the seemingly compassionate surface is a massive networking of purposes, principles, and control interweaving throughout every aspect of society that seeks to draw *all* into the new world order.

This new world order will culminate in Satan's global government—a Beast that will fulfill Satan's Dream, Vision, and Plan in its devouring of the whole world (e.g., see Revelation 13 and Daniel 7:7-8, 21, 23-25). It will succeed by using the Angel of light's message and works of counterfeit "light" and "peace" to deceive, assimilate, and unite those who refuse to love God's absolute truth. Those who refuse to compromise the truth and cooperate with its works of darkness will be purged from the planet.

At this time, the U.N. is the most prominent organization behind Satan's Plan for a global government. Skeptics have pointed out that the U.N. has no teeth—i.e., no power to enforce its laws. Satan himself is going to be the teeth in his global government through his coming Antichrist, regarding whom Scripture says **"the dragon gave him his power, and his seat, and great authority"** (Revelation 13:2).

Incidentally, the U.N. has even been referred to as "the body of Christ" by the world-renowned, U.N.-adored Robert Muller, who personifies the (New Age) New Spirituality beliefs and goals of the U.N.[12] When fully implemented, the U.N.'s agendas will hold dire consequences for true believers in the Lord Jesus Christ.

Regarding the comprehensiveness of its Resolution that has already been adopted by the world, even U.N. Secretary-General Kofi Annan has admitted:

> "The Adoption of the Millennium Development Goals, drawn from the United Nations Millennium Declaration, was **a seminal event in the history of the United Nations**. It constituted an unprecedented promise by world leaders **to address, *as a single package*, peace, security, development, human rights and fundamental freedoms**." (Emphasis added)[13]

Nevertheless, a growing number of Christian organizations have blindly joined the world in backing the U.N. and its goals, such as directly or through The ONE Campaign. Likewise, Rick Warren's P.E.A.C.E. Plan "coordinated its early efforts with United Nations and other relief agencies," according to *The Philadelphia Inquirer*.[14] Support for the U.N. is global.

Interfaith "Bread for the World" Feeds the Hungry

> "ONE is students and ministers, punk rockers and NASCAR moms, **Americans of all beliefs and every walk of life, united as ONE** to help make poverty history."—The ONE Campaign (Emphasis added)[15]

One of the founders of The ONE Campaign is the professing Christian organization, Bread for the World.[16] In Bread for the World's "The Power of ONE" handbook on The ONE Campaign, the following statements are found (emphasis added):

> "It is time for each of us to be ONE."—Rev. David Beckmann, President of Bread for the World

> "This is a new effort to rally people in the United States – ONE by ONE. **Together, we stand as God's living presence** to help others help themselves in a historic compact for compassion and justice for the most vulnerable people in our world. This campaign is joined by similar initiatives in several countries around the globe to work to achieve the Millennium Development Goals . . ."

> "'**The ONE Campaign and the Millennium Development Goals embody God's passionate desire for reconciliation and reordering of our broken world**. In an age when inequity and inequality among God's children threaten to destabilize nations and destroy generations . . . I am pleased to endorse the work of the ONE Campaign . . .'"—Most Rev. Frank T. Griswold, Presiding Bishop and Primate, The Episcopal Church, USA

> "When we as individuals take action, we strengthen **the community God seeks to form**. ONE by ONE we can join them to help God's children afflicted with AIDS, extreme poverty and hunger."

> "'One' also affirms that the world's people who are poor and hungry are **each uniquely children of God** . . ."

> "**One by one, each of us stands as God's living presence** in the world that often seeks to divide, alienate and exclude, offering instead the vision of a world redeemed, reconciled and united. **That's the power of one** . . . .

> "**God calls individuals into community: to come together, find common ground and work with singleness of purpose, to be one**."

> "Bind us together in singleness of purpose . . . . Help us to become one with You and your whole human family." (From a prayer)[17]

First, the anti-God goals of the U.N. do not even remotely fit in with God's "reconciliation and reordering of our broken world." Neither is standing together in interfaith unity standing "as God's living presence"! Rather than "the community God seeks to form," this is actually the Angel of light's emerging counterfeit kingdom of World Servers.

Second, as mentioned earlier, God makes it clear in His Holy Scriptures that only true believers in His Son, the Lord Jesus Christ, have been adopted into His family and become God's children. It is universalism that denies this essential scriptural truth. God does not save people (make them His children) according to how poor or rich they are. This would be a denial of His Gospel of Christ which requires *faith* not *circumstances* for salvation.

> ***"But the scripture hath concluded all under sin, <u>that the promise by faith of Jesus Christ might be given to them that believe</u> . . . . For ye are all the children of God <u>by faith in Christ Jesus</u>." (Galatians 3:22, 26)***

> ***"Hearken, my beloved brethren, Hath not God chosen the poor of this world <u>rich in faith</u>, and heirs of the kingdom which he hath promised <u>to them that love him</u>?" (James 2:5)***

Yet loving God has a broad meaning today that encompasses love for false gods. "The Power of ONE" handbook also contains bulletin inserts for churches who wish to become involved in The ONE Campaign. In deference to religious tolerance and inclusiveness, these inserts refer to Jesus as "God's true One" and say the following:

> "As Christians, we know that ONE is a very powerful number. **Though called by different names, there is one God**." (Emphasis added)[18]

This is not referring to the different names of God in the Holy Scriptures. This is referring to the (New Age) New Spirituality's Oneness, the basis of interfaith unity (the new world religion) in which "unity in diversity" reigns. This New Spirituality teaches that God's unity exists in the diverse expressions the many religions (faiths) have given God. Therefore, the false gods in different religions are actually only "different names" for the ONE God.

In other words, the growing belief is that God has revealed Himself in different ways to different religions. Therefore no religion (faith) is without the truth, and in the unity of all the "fullness of truth" will be revealed. This is the epitome of relativism. No matter how strongly those in rebellion to God and His Word believe the opposite, God always has been and always will be Who He says He is in His true Word. And no one can approach Him apart from feeding on the true Bread of Life, the Lord Jesus Christ.

> ***"And Jesus said unto them, I am the bread of life: he that cometh to me shall never hunger; and he that believeth on me shall never thirst." (John 6:35)***

Nevertheless, the power of ONE continues to be preferred over the power of the one Lord God.

Bread for the World, which published "The Power of ONE" handbook, "is playing *a leadership role* in this new [ONE] campaign" (emphasis added).[19] Despite its claims to be a Christian organization, it is on an interfaith path. On June 6, 2005, it sponsored "the first-ever Interfaith Convocation on Hunger."[20]

This Convocation featured "a joint prayer service at the Washington National Cathedral," and was to be "one of the broadest efforts among U.S. faith leaders."[21] Scheduled to attend were 45 Jewish, Catholic, Buddhist, Muslim, mainline Protestant, and Evangelical leaders, including from the National Council of Churches.[22] Among the Evangelicals scheduled to attend were Richard Cizik, of the National Association of Evangelicals, and Brian McLaren, a leader in the anti-scriptural Emerging Church movement.[23]

This Interfaith Convocation is a prime example of how today's "Christianity" is sacrificing truth on the altar of unity in the name of purpose. Interfaith services greatly promote the belief that all religions in attendance are praying to and worshipping the same "God." Thus all in attendance are part of the "family" of God, united as ONE in diversity.

The following quotes are from the Program of this *Interfaith* service (emphasis added)[24]:

> "The living God, the moving Spirit of God, the Breath of life itself *has called us together* in celebration and struggle to reach out toward each other as *our God* reaches out toward us. Arise, sisters and brothers and let us worship God."
>
> "We stand together as leaders of *faith communities* across the United States and *we echo the words of the sacred texts of our various faiths.*"

This latter Response by the faith leaders was followed by "Readings from Sacred Texts"—Sikh, Hebrew, Christian, Muslim, and Buddhist. Later, the Congregational Response included committing "in the presence of the Holy One" to also *"bring others in our synagogues and churches, our mosques, temples and communities into a movement* that works to end hunger, poverty and disease in our world" (emphasis added). A South African Hymn then repeated its only phrases of the entire song -- "You hold the key," "Open the door," and "Walk through." This was then followed by a "Prayer of Thanksgiving for Gifts":

> ". . . we know that **your Spirit is moving when people of many faiths stand in one accord** to feed as we have been fed." (Emphasis added)

God's Word explicitly declares that ***"the world cannot receive" "the Spirit of truth"*** (John 14:17). It isn't the *Holy* Spirit who is working in *interfaith* oneness.

> **"Wherein in time past ye walked according to the course of this world, according to <u>the prince of the power of the air, the spirit that now worketh in the children of disobedience.</u>" (Ephesians 2:2)**

This spirit, the god of this world and Angel of light, is luring the world into an interfaith pursuit of his counterfeit peace and light. In spite of the fact that those attending the Interfaith Convocation belong to religions (faiths) that deny the Lord Jesus Christ, the different religions who attended joined with one voice in singing, "The Peace of the Earth":

> *The peace of the earth be with you,*
> *the peace of the heavens too;*
> *the peace of the rivers be with you,*
> *the peace of the oceans too.*
> *Deep peace falling over you;*
> ***God's peace*** *growing in you.* (Bold added)[25]

Then again with one voice the religions sang the Recessional Hymn which repeated its only words over and over and over, "We are marching *in the light of God*" (emphasis added).

No matter how many times something is stated, it does not make it true. The peace and light of the true God is found *only* through the Lord Jesus Christ on the narrow way of His absolute truth. No matter how many people join together as ONE, the broad way will never see the peace and light of God. There is an eternal difference between being "people of faith" and people of *the* faith.

God has been warning His people for thousands of years through His true prophets and Scriptures against much of what is occurring today. His Word contains a multitude of instances where His people are to remain separate. There is no communion between light and darkness and the narrow way and the broad way. God told Isaiah:

> *"Associate yourselves, O ye people, and ye shall be broken in pieces . . . Take counsel together and it shall come to nought . . . For the* L<small>ORD</small> *spake thus to me with a strong hand, and instructed me that I should not walk in the way of this people, saying, Say ye not, A confederacy, to all them to whom this people shall say, A confederacy; neither fear ye their fear, nor be afraid. Sanctify the* L<small>ORD</small> *of hosts himself; and let him be your fear, and let him be your dread. And he shall be for a sanctuary; but for a stone of stumbling and for a rock of offence . . . And many among them shall stumble, and fall, and be broken, and be snared, and be taken . . . . To the law and to the testimony: if they speak not according to this word, it is because there is no light in them. And they shall pass through it, hardly bestead and hungry: and it shall come to pass, that <u>when they shall be hungry, they shall fret themselves, and curse their king and their God, and look upward</u>. And they shall look unto the earth; and behold trouble and darkness, dimness of anguish; <u>and they shall be driven to darkness</u>." (Isaiah 8:9-15, 20-22)*

Yet instead of heeding the warnings of the loving Lord God, the world prefers to heed the lies of the diabolical Master Deceiver:

> ". . . recognition of the true brotherhood of man, *based on the one divine life, working through the one soul and expressing itself through the one humanity;* recognition, therefore, of relationship both to the divine life throughout the world and to mankind itself. It is this developing spiritual attitude which will lead to right human relations and eventual world peace."—Alice Bailey & Djwhal Khul[26]

Doctrine and faith are being replaced with experiences and service because people assume that what they do is more important than what they believe. They have been deceived into believing that God will accept their ***"filthy rags"*** as righteous service (see Isaiah 64:6). No matter how good or loving they may seem in man's view, the holy Lord God views the good works of *every* "man of peace" and "World Server" as ***"filthy rags"*** apart from the righteousness of the Lord Jesus Christ imputed to us by *faith*.

The truth is, no matter how many hands join together as ONE, they will be powerless to stop God's coming judgment:

> ***"The LORD hath made all things for himself: yea, even the wicked for the day of evil. Every one that is proud in heart is an abomination to the LORD: <u>though hand join in hand, he shall not be unpunished.</u>" (Proverbs 16:4-5)***

Yet the drive toward interfaith unity and its darkness continues. On June 22, 2005, Rick Warren sent a follow up e-mail of gratitude regarding The ONE Campaign and announced:

> "Tens of thousands of pastors and church leaders signed on! In fact, names are still coming in everyday."[27]

Note the following comment Rick Warren also made in his PS to this e-mail. He is referring to an article from Reuters that he included at the bottom of his e-mail which contained the second quote:

> "PS. I had to smile at the terminology used below by the Foreign Ministers. It sounded like **purpose-driven relief** to me!"—Rick Warren

> "*We're being driven forward* by the urgent need to act. We've found ourselves *united with a shared purpose*."—British finance minister Gordon Brown (Italics added)[28]

In the name of purpose, the world is being driven forward into the Angel of light's emerging interfaith kingdom where truth is irrelevant.

"Unity Comes from Purpose, Not from Anything Else"

> "Now let me tell you something. We've been talking a lot about unity out of diversity this week. **We will never have unity over all of our doctrines**

because I can't even get my family to agree on it, much less my church and your church. And we're never going to get everybody to agree on all of the worship styles . . . . We're never gonna agree on all of our styles and all of our methods, so let me tell you what we can agree on: the Great Commandment and the Great Commission. **Unity comes from purpose, *not from anything else*. It comes from purpose** . . . .

"Friends, it's time to stop debating and start doing. Stop debating the Bible, and start doing it. It's time to stop criticizing and start cooperating. It's time for the church to be known for love not legalism, to be known for what we're for not just what we're against. It's time for the church to be the church. That is the new Reformation that I'm praying for . . . . The critical question of this night is this, 'Will we accept the challenge?'"—Rick Warren (Emphasis added)[29]

*R*ick Warren gave this challenge at the Baptist World Centenary Congress -- the 100th birthday celebration of the Baptist World Alliance (BWA). It was held in Birmingham, England on July 27-31, 2005 and featured a variety of speakers, including former U.S. President Jimmy Carter.

"When Warren was asked what was hoped to be gained from the four-day event, he answered: 'This is a celebration of diversity and unity at the same time . . . . If we all have to agree to make a fellowship then the fellowship would remain very small. So celebrating both unity and diversity is what this congress is about.'"—*Christian Today*, 7/28/05[30]

This Centenary Congress, which covered topics such as "poverty, prostitution and the Purpose-Driven Church,"[31] included a drive for unity with other religions (faiths) in its celebration of unity and diversity. The following comments of Jimmy Carter were noted in the article, "Carter: global 'hunger' for healing outweighs beliefs that divide faiths"[32]:

"There is an 'intense hunger' among Christians worldwide -- and among people of all faiths -- to work for justice and oppose terrorism, despite serious differences of faith, Jimmy Carter said July 30.

"'There is an intense hunger among Christians around the world for a healing of the differences that now separate us from one another,' Carter . . . told reporters gathered for the July 27-31 Baptist World Centenary Congress in Birmingham, England."

"Differences of belief -- even among Muslims, Jews and Christians -- are outweighed by a common commitment 'to truth, to justice, to benevolence, to compassion, to generosity and to love,' Carter told a roomful of reporters from around the world. Those commonalities 'make it easy for us to stand united without dissention [sic] and for a common purpose.'

"'We need to come back together,' he said emphatically."

"'I think the main impediment is not knowing each other, not understanding each other, not recognizing that basic truth . . . that *every religion emphasizes truth* and justice and benevolence and compassion and generosity and love.'" (Ellipsis dots in the original; emphasis added)

"The tough work of interfaith dialog is not pointless but well worth the risk and investment of time, he said."

Continuing the challenge for pragmatic unity of purpose, the "closing charge to delegates" at its *Freedom* conference was given by Baptist minister Dr. Michael Taylor. It was reported in the July 27 Press Release for the Baptist World Congress:

> "**Christians must unite with those of other faiths** to tackle oppression around the globe . . . .
>
> "'The only potentially realistic way to get western governments to tackle these issues is to build the strongest, most proactive networks of activists around the world. This will mean linking with other Christians and with people of other faiths, working together in different ways for the common good.'" (Emphasis added)[33]

Rick Warren, whose own P.E.A.C.E. Plan calls for an interfaith network of "men of peace" and "houses of worship" working together in world service, boldly challenged this Congress with, "We will never have unity over all of our doctrines" so "unity comes from purpose, not from anything else." Clearly, in today's pragmatic Christianity which is striving for a purpose-driven unity of faiths, this challenge to relegate doctrinal differences to the list of non-essentials refers to more than just doctrinal differences between *Christians*.

It used to be obvious that the primary issue between religions and true Christianity is that the former worship a different *god*. Yet this isn't the perceived problem today. When interfaith unity of purpose is the goal, these doctrinal/theological differences become "non-essential" and religious differences are reduced to a mere difference in worship "styles." Anyone who believes otherwise is guilty of "misunderstanding" religious differences and becomes the new problem.

In a strange comment, which among other things shows a lack of understanding of *God's* rejection of Cain's "worship practice" (offering), Rick Warren's challenge to this Congress also included the following:

> "We've been talking a lot about unity out of diversity this week . . . . And **we're never going to get everybody to agree on all of the worship styles**. It's not by accident that Spurgeon called his music department the war department. I want to remind you that **the first murder was over a worship practice** when Cain killed Abel, and **brothers have been killing brothers ever since over the worship styles**." (Emphasis added)[34]

Carter similarly reduced religious differences to worship styles, as reported in the article "Carter: global 'hunger' for healing outweighs beliefs that divide faiths:"

> "The common cause of stopping terrorism provides **people of faith a platform for unprecedented cooperation**, he [Carter] said, but added that *finding that one voice is hampered by* **misunderstandings**. 'One thing we lack, in this time, is an understanding of each other when **we worship in different ways**.'
>
> "Carter, who negotiated the Camp David Peace Accords while president, said that historic agreement between predominantly Jewish Israel and predominantly Muslim Egypt was built on the belief that 'the elements of life that we shared could **overcome the differences that we recognize in the way we worship God**.'" (Emphasis added)[35]

As is the Master Deceiver's Plan, bringing the religions together in "oneness of purpose" to "stand shoulder to shoulder in the One Work" is automatically overcoming "the differences, the divergences, and the points of disagreement" between them.

It isn't just professing Christians who have reduced religious differences to intolerance of the worship practices in other religions. In *Deceived On Purpose*, Warren Smith calls attention to a challenge given by (New Age) New Spirituality leader Neale Donald Walsch to every religious leader to preach the new gospel of Oneness. This challenge was given in Walsch's contributing essay to the book *From the Ashes: A Spiritual Response to the Attack on America*, which was published after 9/11. It contains an interfaith collection of essays contributed by New Age and professing Christian leaders, including Rick Warren. As discussed in *Deceived On Purpose*, Christian leaders have responded in virtual silence to this challenge instead of taking the opportunity to contend for the faith.[36]

Walsch's challenge includes the following, which he has taken from his conversations with his false "God":

> "The message of God is clear. No matter what the religion, no matter what the culture, no matter what the spiritual or indigenous tradition, the bottom line is identical: We are all one . . . .
>
> ". . . I hope that each of us will have our own conversation with God, for only the grandest wisdom and the grandest truth can address the greatest problems, and we are now facing the greatest problems and the greatest challenges in the history of our species . . . .
>
> "**We must preach a new gospel**, its healing message summarized in two sentences:
>
> "***We are all one***.
> "***Ours is not a better way, ours is merely another way*** . . . .
>
> "I challenge every priest, every minister, every rabbi and religious clerk to preach this." (Bold added)[37]

Christianity's leaders haven't stood up against Neale Donald Walsch's call to preach the false gospel of Oneness because they are too busy issuing the same call. Attempting to "fulfill God's purposes" through unity or Oneness with those on the broad way actually agrees with rather than repudiates the false gospel that "ours is not a better way, ours is merely another way."

This pragmatic unity says that it doesn't matter which way we follow as long as the desired end or purpose is accomplished. And this pragmatic unity has given temporal manmade "peace" a far greater value than God's eternal peace. Thus both the world and today's Christianity are calling for all religions to drop their differences to work together in unity of purpose.

The Angel of light has been so successful in this endeavor that even today's Christianity is cooperating in the work of finishing his interfaith kingdom. His new universal religion is now emerging in plain view with incredible speed.

Part 6

"Then There Will Emerge the Universal Religion, the One Church, and that Unified Though Not Uniform Approach to God"

(Alice Bailey & Djwhal Khul)

• *Chapter Seventeen* •

"One Truth," Many Theologies

"A Portion of Truth, Great or Small, Is Found in Every Religious and Philosophical System"

The Angel of light knows doctrine will never unite the world. Therefore, his emerging universal religion is founded in the (New Age) New *Spirituality* which teaches there is "One Truth" underlying all religions and theologies. In this universal religion, "humility" seeks "truth" out *wherever* it can be found and is eager to learn from other religions. "Humility" also recognizes that certainty in one truth is "religious bigotry," whereas "pride" fails to recognize that your truth is only one part of the greater mystery of the "fullness of truth." Everything continues to get turned upside down. "Humility" in this counterfeit kingdom is actually human *pride* rebelling against God's narrow way of the truth.

> "In every race and nation, in every climate and part of the world . . . men have found the Path to God . . . The testimony to the existence of this Path is the priceless treasure of *all* the great religions and its witnesses are those who have transcended *all* forms and *all* theologies, and have penetrated into the world of meaning which *all* symbols veil.

> "These truths are part of all that the past gives to man . . . . They are the inner structure of **the One Truth** upon which **all** the world theologies have been built . . ."—Alice Bailey & Djwhal Khul (Emphasis added)[1]

> "Another point which should be remembered is that in the new generation lies hope - . . . hope because of the promptness with which **they recognize truth wherever it is to be found** . . .

> "The churches in the West need to realize that basically there is only one church, but it is not necessarily only the orthodox Christian institution; *God*

*works in many ways, through many faiths and religious agencies; in their union will **the fullness of truth** be revealed."*—Alice Bailey & Djwhal Khul (Emphasis added)²

In his biography of Rick Warren, Richard Abanes has a chapter titled, "A New Spirituality?" in which he tries to show that Rick Warren is against it. In this chapter, he defends Rick Warren's tendency to quote *"many* non-Christians and people of other religious traditions." Abanes points out that Rick Warren does this, not "because he agrees with them on everything," and not "because he is promoting them as examples of sound Christians," but because "**he is showing that all 'truth'**—*wherever it may be found*—**is God's truth**" (emphasis added)!³

This defense even challenges what Abanes had said in the beginning of his book: "Rick Warren's mega-bestseller seems to be helping a lot of people find Jesus and focus on God as the only source of truth."⁴

If "all 'truth' is God's truth," then these other sources of "truth" found in other religions (faiths) and perspectives must be given equal authority with God's Word. Indeed, this is increasingly evident in those that believe this. Contrarily, the Lord God, Who is *not* on the broad way and *is* the truth and light, definitely *is* the only source of truth (light). Therefore, the truth can only be found *in God* and *not* "wherever it may be found" on the broad way of darkness, which is where "non-Christians" and "other religious traditions" are that Rick Warren is supposedly quoting "God's truth" from!

This lack of discernment is prevalent in Christianity today, which is why the (New Age) New Spirituality is making such broad inroads into it. Yet God's Word and warnings go unheeded when people only want to hear what is "positive" rather than the *whole* counsel of God, which includes a great deal of what is deemed "negative."

The Spirit of truth, Who *cannot* be received by the world, is the One Who guides us into **"*all truth*"** when we *believe* in the Lord Jesus Christ (see John 8:31-32, 16:13, and 14:17). He guides us into **"*all truth*"** through the Word of the Lord Jesus Christ, *not* through the teachings of different religions (faiths) as is believed today.

> "We believe we can learn truth -- I've learned a lot of truth from **different religions**. Because **they all have a portion of the truth**."—Rick Warren (Emphasis added)⁵

It isn't *both* God's truth *and* the broad way; it is *either* God's truth *or* the broad way. Yet the former is exactly what the Angel of light, Lucifer, wants mankind to believe and has been teaching through his various channelers for a long time. In the 1888 issue of the theosophical magazine Lucifer, the popular occultist H. P. Blavatsky wrote an article titled, "To the Readers of 'Lucifer,'" in which she expounded this doctrine of devils, which according to Lucifer's devices has twisted and changed the meaning of "absolute truth":

> "Our motto was from the first, and ever shall be: 'THERE IS NO RELIGION HIGHER THAN--TRUTH.' Truth we -search for, and, once found, we bring it forward before the world, **whencesoever it comes** . . . .
>
> "There is, and can be, but one absolute truth in Kosmos. And . . . if it is absolute it must also be omnipresent and universal; and that in such case, *it must be underlying every world-religion* -- the product of the thought and knowledge of numberless generations of thinking men. Therefore, that **a portion of truth, great or small, is found in every religious and philosophical system**, and that if we would find it, we have to search for it at the origin and source of every such system, at its roots and first growth, not in its later overgrowth of sects and dogmatism. *Our object is not to destroy any religion but rather to help to filter each*, thus ridding them of their respective impurities. In this we are opposed by all those who maintain, against evidence, that their particular pitcher alone contains the whole ocean."—H. P. Blavatsky (Emphasis added; caps in the original)[6]

The emerging universal religion (the "New" Spirituality) does not seek to remove all religious divisions. This would actually oppose its purpose of getting people to believe there are many paths to God. Instead, it seeks to draw people into the belief that all religions (faiths) have drawn "a portion of truth" from the same source, the "ocean" of the "fullness of truth." Then they can be lured deeper into deception. Those who believe that "the One Truth" underlies all religions (theologies) can easily be led into believing that all gods are simply diverse manifestations of "the one God" and that all religions are just a different path to God.

Chapter Eighteen

"One God," Many Paths

"The Religions are the Tributaries of One Great River"

"This concept [of unification] . . . does involve the development of a universal public consciousness which realizes the unity of the whole . . . **It requires simply the recognition that all formulations of truth and of belief are only partial** in time and space, and are temporarily suited to the temperaments and conditions of the age and race. Those who favor some particular approach to the truth will nevertheless achieve the realization **that other approaches and other modes of expression and terminologies, and other ways of defining deity can be equally correct and in themselves constitute aspects of a truth which is greater and vaster** than man's present equipment can grasp and express."—Alice Bailey & Djwhal Khul (Emphasis added)[1]

One thing leads to another in the (New Age) New Spirituality's larger understanding of "truth." Since "the One Truth" is believed to underlie every religion, they are all considered to be on different but equally valid paths (approaches) to God. This "unity in diversity" allows for everyone to keep their own theology and doctrinal convictions and worship "styles" as their own *portion* and *expression* of the "fullness of truth." This is the New Spirituality's false gospel of Oneness: "We are all one. Ours is not a better way, ours is merely another way."

This Oneness is found in Theosophy (part of the "Ancient Wisdom") taught by both Alice Bailey and H. P. Blavatsky. It includes the following widespread principles listed by the Blavatsky Net Foundation:

- "Brotherhood is a fact in nature. We are ONE at the highest spiritual component of our nature. We are sparks from one flame."
- "**The religions of the world are branches on the tree whose trunk is the one ancient - once universal - wisdom religion**. The religions are the tributaries of one great river."

- "Humanity's potential is infinite and every being has a contribution to make toward a grander world. We are all in it together. We are one." (Emphasis added)[2]

It isn't the message and Kingdom of God that are growing in popularity, but rather of the god of this world—the same god that enticed all to come together as ONE to build the tower of Babel.

> "**The day is dawning when all religions win [sic] be regarded as emanating from one great spiritual source**; all will be seen as unitedly providing the one root out of which **the universal world religion will inevitably emerge**. Then there will be neither Christian nor heathen, neither Jew nor Gentile, but **simply one great body of believers, gathered out of all the current religions**. They will accept the same truths, not as theological concepts but as essential to spiritual living; they will stand together on the same platform of brotherhood and of human relations; they will recognize divine sonship and will seek unitedly to cooperate with the divine Plan . . . Such a *world religion* is no idle dream but something which is definitely forming today."—Alice Bailey & Djwhal Khul (Bold added)[3]

The Master Deceiver's Plan is indeed forming today. He is achieving tremendous success in neutralizing today's Christianity. A poll conducted in early August 2005 for *Newsweek* and Beliefnet asked the question, "Can a good person who isn't of your religious faith go to heaven or attain salvation, or not?" And 68% of *Evangelical* Protestants and 83% of Non-Evangelical Protestants answered, "YES"! There was virtually no difference between Evangelicals and Non-Christians of whom 73% answered, "Yes."[4]

This is clearly indicative of the current *departure from <u>the</u> faith* (not a "spiritual awakening") in the new *broad*-minded "Christianity." This new "Christianity" that believes the world does not need to change its ways also believes that the world doesn't even need to change its religion (faith). The world can stay in whatever religious faith—whatever path to God—it wants and just add a "relationship" with God to it.

> "I'm not talking about a religion this morning. Okay? **You may be Catholic or Protestant or Buddhist or Baptist or Muslim or Mormon or Jewish or Jain, or you have no religion at all. I'm not interested in your religious**

background. Because God did not create the universe for us to have religion. He came for us to have a relationship with him."—Rick Warren (Emphasis added)[5]

"One day we're gonna stand before God and he is going to ask two questions. The first question is, 'What did you do with my Son Jesus Christ?' **Not 'What religion were you?'** Not what denomination, **not what background**, where did you go to church. We were created for a relationship, not a religion - not rituals, not rules, not regulations."—Rick Warren (Emphasis added)[6]

"I have known **many people who believe in the Messiah of Jesus, regardless of what religion they are**, because they believe in him. It's about a relationship, not a religion. You've heard this many times."—Rick Warren (Emphasis added)[7]

In both the (New Age) New *Spirituality* and the *Purpose*-Driven Paradigm, *doctrinal views* (theological creeds) and the *faith* of *Christianity* are irrelevant:

"One day you will stand before God, and he will do an audit of your life, a final exam, before you enter eternity . . . . **God won't ask about your religious background or doctrinal views**." (*PDL*; p. 34; emphasis added)

"What is this church of Christ? It is constituted of the sumtotal of all those in whom the life of Christ or the Christ-consciousness is to be found or is in process of finding expression; it is the aggregation of all who love their fellowmen, because to love one's fellowmen is the divine faculty which makes us full members of Christ's community. **It is not the accepting of any historical fact or theological creed which places us en rapport with Christ**."—Alice Bailey & Djwhal Khul (Emphasis added)[8]

"**The Christ has no religious barriers** in His consciousness. **It matters not to Him of what faith a man may call himself**."—Alice Bailey & Djwhal Khul (Emphasis added)[9]

"I happen to know **people who are followers of Christ in other religions**." —Rick Warren (Emphasis added)[10]

Clearly, the message has changed! Rick Warren's various statements render one's religion irrelevant, even though he has acknowledged that all religions "have a different way to get to God":

> "I would say I am more interested in having a relationship with God than a religion. To me, I define religion as man's attempt to get to God. And I have studied **all the major religions** . . . and **they all just have a different way to get to God**. Now, they are – anybody who has studied religions knows that they are mutually exclusive."—Rick Warren (Emphasis added)[11]

Incidentally, Rick Warren has said, "Because I had been raised in a Christian home, I rejected it all, and I decided to study the religions of the world. I actually moved to Japan, and I studied Buddhism, Shintoism, Hinduism. I studied all the religions of the world."[12] Then he should know that religions aren't just a "different way to get to God," they follow different *gods*!

At the BWA's Centenary Congress, where the recurrent theme was "unity, unity, unity,"[13] the following statements were made by Jimmy Carter and Rick Warren:

> "One of the world's most prominent Baptists, former U.S. President Jimmy Carter, said **the desire for oneness is a powerful force** for global good. **Differences of belief** -- even among Muslims, Jews and Christians -- **are outweighed** by a common commitment 'to truth . . .' Carter said." (Emphasis added)[14]

> "Many people are 'too glib' in claiming the label of 'Christian.' If instead people **define a 'Christian' as 'a little Christ,'** it would have more meaning and produce more Christ-like behavior, he [Carter] said." (Emphasis added)[15]

> "I don't see many people interested in Christendom. But I see a lot of people interested in God."—Rick Warren[16]

First, as is increasingly evidenced, not even professing Christians are still interested in Christendom. They and the world prefer Oneness because its relativism allows them to follow the path of their choice on the "label" (religion) of their choice. "The desire for oneness" clearly shows the world is not interested in the true and living God or in *the Lordship* of Jesus Christ. Incidentally, it is the reducing of Christ to a universal "example" that leads to the anti-Christ belief that people can become "little Christs." The definition of "Christian" is broadening, true to the Master Deceiver's Plan:

> "It is here that the Church, as usually understood, meets its major challenge. Is it spiritual enough to *let go of theology* and . . . widen its horizon and **recognize as truly Christian all who demonstrate the Christ spirit, whether they be Hindu, Mohammedan, or Buddhist**, whether they are labeled by any name other than that of orthodox Christian?"—Alice Bailey (Emphasis added)[17]

Second, for all intents and purposes, when the beliefs and doctrines (which include theology) of all the different religions are bypassed as irrelevant, the following occurs:

- All gods become "one God" with different names and manifestations.
- Christianity is reduced to "merely another way" to Christ, or God.

The new gospel of Oneness is spreading, regardless of whether it is recognized as such, and regardless of whether it is deliberate. It is the (New Age) New Spirituality's relativism that says there are many paths to Christ so it doesn't matter *which* faith a person is in. God's absolute truth makes it clear that believing and obeying *the faith* is nonnegotiable.

> *"Concerning his Son Jesus Christ our Lord, which was made of the seed of David according to the flesh; and declared to be the Son of God with power, according to the spirit of holiness, by the resurrection from the dead: By whom we have received grace and apostleship, for obedience to <u>the faith</u> among <u>all nations</u>, for his name." (Romans 1:3-5)*

Furthermore, it is the Master Deceiver who is behind the lie that Jesus Christ is known by different names in the different religions (faiths). Contrarily, Jesus Christ is the *only* name given among men that saves. He does not appear as anyone else in any other religion.

> *"Be it known unto you all, and to all the people of Israel, that by <u>the name of Jesus Christ</u> of Nazareth, whom ye crucified, whom God raised from the*

> dead, even by him doth this man stand here before you whole. This is the stone which was set at nought of you builders, which is become the head of the corner. Neither is there salvation in any other: for <u>there is none other name under heaven given among men, whereby we must be saved</u>." (Acts 4:10-12)

> "But if our gospel be hid, it is hid to them that are lost: In whom the god of this world hath blinded the minds of them which believe not, lest the light of the glorious gospel of Christ, who is the image of God, should shine unto them." (2 Corinthians 4:3-4)

There is no other way, no other truth, no other life, and no other name by which we can approach God. The Lord Jesus Christ is neither "a better way" nor "another way;" He is the <u>only</u> way.

> "Which he wrought in Christ, when he raised him from the dead, and set him at his own right hand in the heavenly places, <u>far above all principality, and power, and might, and dominion, and every name that is named</u>, not only in this world, but also in that which is to come." (Ephesians 1:20-21)

It really speaks to the lateness of the hour that professing Christians actually believe that *people on a false way in a false religion with false theology and false doctrines about false gods can still be a follower and believer of the Lord Jesus Christ, can still have a relationship with God, and can still go to heaven and attain salvation!* If that doesn't reveal the dire state of Christianity's scriptural illiteracy today, then what does?

The dire consequences of today's "whole new way of thinking and acting" are already clearly seen in the next generation.

> "For the leaders of this people cause them to err; and they that are led of them are destroyed." (Isaiah 9:16)

> "My people are destroyed for lack of knowledge: because thou hast rejected knowledge, I will also reject thee, that thou shalt be no priest to me: seeing thou hast forgotten the law of thy God, I will also forget <u>thy children</u>." (Hosea 4:6)

"The new world religion is nearer than many think, and this is due to two things: first, the theological quarrels are mainly over non-essentials, and secondly, **the younger generation is basically spiritual but quite uninterested in theology.**"—Alice Bailey & Djwhal Khul (Emphasis added)[18]

"In his book, *Third Millennium Teens*, Barna revealed this stunning fact: 63 percent of church-going, supposedly Christian teens said they believed 'Muslims, Buddhists, Christians, Jews and all other people pray to the same God, even though they use different names for their god.'

"In other critical areas of Christian doctrine – e.g., the divinity of Christ, the resurrection, the reality of absolute truth – **the majority of church-going teenagers simply do not hold to views that are orthodox** . . . .

"Unless Christian leaders want to contemplate a future – much like that unfolding in Europe – in which **their youth abandon Christianity in droves**, there must be a brutally honest re-examination of how we do church." (Bold added)[19]

"We need a new Reformation . . . . But this Reformation will be different . . . . It's not about creeds, it's about deeds . . . . **You see, we know all the right things. We don't need a Reformation of belief** . . . . So we need a Reformation of not creeds but deeds, not beliefs but behavior, to be doers of the word. **It's not about our message. We know what our message is.** It's about our mission, and will we be the church."—Rick Warren (Emphasis added)[20]

Exactly *what* is that message?!

Uniting All Gods into ONE Through Interfaith Prayer Services

On September 13, 2005, Rick Warren took his message to the United Nations. An "interfaith prayer breakfast" was held for its dignitaries and delegates who had gathered for the United Nations 60th Anniversary World Summit 2005.

According to *The Christian Post*, Rick Warren assured "the hundred or so world leaders who gathered to hear the famed preacher" that "I'm not here to talk about religion. I'm here to talk about a relationship with God." He "comforted" the delegates "who represented various faith traditions" "by telling them to trust God."²¹

Which God?! When no clear dichotomy is made between their religion (faith) and the truth, each religion hears "relationship with God" and "trust God" and "God is love," and even "love God" and "love your neighbor," according to the dictates of their own religion's false doctrines and false god. Comforting people in their false religions is the purpose of interfaith services. This doesn't lead to conviction of sin, repentance, or belief, apart from which they can never receive the *eternal* comfort and love of God which are *in Christ Jesus our Lord* (e.g., see Romans 8:39; John 16:27; 14:21-23).

Yet in a Paradigm that is much more about what you *do* than what you *believe*, different religious backgrounds are irrelevant. As a result, it matters less and less *which* God or *which* Jesus or *which* Christ (Jesus and Christ are typically separated by the world), if any, a person believes in.

Rick Warren did tell them that Jesus is God,²² but what he said in lieu of the Gospel of Christ boggles the mind to even know where to begin in addressing it. What message did "America's pastor" take to the U.N. delegates and world leaders?:

> "He [God] came to earth, why? Well, as a human being, me trying to understand God would be like an ant trying to understand the Internet. An ant doesn't have the brain capacity to understand the Internet. ***If God had wanted to communicate to cows he could have become a cow. If he wanted to communicate to birds he could have become a bird. If he wanted to communicate to monkeys he could have become a monkey.*** But God wanted to *communicate* to us human beings so he became one of us. Now, I look at Jesus Christ and go, 'Oh, that's what God is like.'" [!]—Rick Warren (Emphasis added)²³

Cutting holes that are large enough for the world to slip through into the message of why God came to earth does not leave the message unchanged! Regardless of what Rick Warren himself believes, not only does his statement to this interfaith group of world leaders defy just plain sense, it defies scriptural knowledge and the true reason our *Saviour*, the Lord Jesus Christ, came to earth, which is the core of the true Gospel of Christ.

God did not come to earth because He wanted to "communicate" with man. God has been communicating with man ever since man was created in the Garden of

Eden, thousands of years before the Lord Jesus Christ came to earth! God's faithful followers have even described "what God is like" in His Holy Scriptures for thousands of years, and the Lord God says He does not change (e.g., see Malachi 3:6). And given God's all-powerful, all-knowing nature, He sure doesn't need to come to earth as a monkey or any other creature in order to "communicate" with animals!

The Lord Jesus Christ came to earth in the flesh of *man* specifically to become the *Saviour* of the world by shedding His blood for the sins of *mankind* because without the shedding of blood there is no remission of sins:

"This is a faithful saying, and worthy of all acceptation, that <u>Christ Jesus came into the world to save sinners</u> . . ." (1 Timothy 1:15)

"And we have seen and do testify that <u>the Father sent the Son to be the Saviour of the world</u>." (1 John 4:14)

"For all have sinned, and come short of the glory of God." (Romans 3:23)

"For the wages of sin is death; but the gift of God is eternal life through Jesus Christ our Lord." (Romans 6:23)

"And ye know that <u>he was manifested to take away our sins</u>; and in him is no sin." (1 John 3:5)

"But we see Jesus, who was made a little lower than the angels <u>for the suffering of death</u>, crowned with glory and honour; that he by the grace of God should taste death for every man." (Hebrews 2:9)

"For the life of the flesh is in the blood: and I have given it to you upon the altar to make an atonement for your souls: <u>for it is the blood that maketh an atonement for the soul</u>." (Leviticus 17:11)

"And almost all things are by the law purged with blood; and without shedding of blood is no remission." (Hebrews 9:22)

"And from Jesus Christ, who is the faithful witness, and the first begotten of the dead, and the prince of the kings of the earth. Unto him that loved us, and <u>washed us from our sins in his own blood</u>." (Revelation 1:5)

Under God's first covenant He required the sacrifice of animals, including of the "cow" family, for forgiveness of sins. But their sacrifice only provided *temporary* remission so needed to be repeated (e.g., see Hebrews 10:1-3). Yet the blood of the perfect and eternal Lord Jesus Christ, in the flesh of *man*, *eternally finished* the work of the atonement. Believers in Him have been set free from their sins and its penalty of death.

> *"For it is not possible that the blood of bulls and of goats should take away sins. Wherefore <u>when he cometh into the world</u>, he saith, Sacrifice and offering thou wouldest not, but <u>a body hast thou prepared me</u>: In burnt offerings and sacrifices for sin thou hast had no pleasure. . . . Then said he, Lo, I come to do thy will O God. He taketh away the first, that he may establish the second. By the which will <u>we are sanctified through the offering of the body of Jesus Christ once for all</u>." (Hebrews 10:4-6, 9-10)*

> *"Forasmuch as ye know that <u>ye were not redeemed with corruptible things</u> . . . <u>but with the precious blood of Christ, as of a lamb without blemish and without spot</u>: Who verily was foreordained before the foundation of the world, but was manifest in these last times for you, who by him do believe in God, that raised him up from the dead, and gave him glory; that your faith and hope might be in God." (1 Peter 1:18-21)*

To be the perfect, sinless sacrifice without blemish and spot that qualified as an eternal payment for the sins of *mankind*, the perfect and eternal Lord God had to manifest in the flesh as a *man* and live a *sinless* life as a *man*. Given the true reason for His coming, there was never any option about God coming as anything but a *man*! The "cow" family and other animals were already *insufficient sacrifices*. Besides, what kind of savior or lord would a cow or monkey be?! Yet at the same time, what seeds of unity might Rick Warren's statement have sown with those in religions (faiths) whose god *has* taken the form of an animal, and even a cow?

This whole quote is stunning and reveals the lengths today's leaders will go in "whatever it takes" to fulfill their own purposes. All-important interfaith unity unravels when the true message is given regarding Who the Lord Jesus Christ is and why He came to earth. Consequently, for the sake of unity the new definition of the "Great Commission" appears to be, "Go ye into all the world, but avoid preaching the gospel at all costs, or every creature will be offended . . ."

Although Rick Warren mentioned John 14:6 to the interfaith gathering, presenting Jesus as God Who merely came to "communicate" with man shows little to no difference between Him and the false gods who are in "communication" with their own religious devotees. Nothing was said about *why* Jesus is the only way or about the necessity of believing in *the Lord* Jesus Christ in order to even have a "relationship with God." Besides, it no longer matters in today's "Christianity" which religion—which pathway—people take to their "relationship" with God. It was to these interfaith delegates that Rick Warren said:

> "I'm not talking about a religion this morning. Okay? You may be Catholic or Protestant or Buddhist or Baptist or Muslim or Mormon or Jewish or Jain, or you have no religion at all. I'm not interested in your religious background. Because God did not create the universe for us to have religion. He came for us to have a relationship with him."—Rick Warren[24]

Remember, in the purpose-driven "final exam" "God won't ask about your religious background or doctrinal views" (*PDL*; p. 34).

The Lord Jesus Christ is ours as the way and the truth and the life *through faith* in *the truth*. Apart from *the doctrine of Christ* given to us in **"the faith which was once delivered unto the saints"** (Jude 1:3) we don't have God, let alone any relationship with Him (see 2 John 1:9).

The irreconcilable difference between religions and true Christianity is that the other faiths (which have no commitment to the *truth*) worship a different *god*. The divide between the narrow way and the broad way is eternal. It can only *seemingly* be bridged at the cost of betraying the truth.

No, this isn't about *religion* and what a person *believes*. It is about relationships through *purpose* and what a person *does*. In his closing prayer for the United Nations attendees of different religious backgrounds, Rick Warren prayed:

> "And Father, I know that there are some here today who have been living a good life, not realizing that *there's even a far better life, a life of purpose* – a life of purpose and peace and power . . . . I pray that today many will *step across the line to a better life*, a life of purpose and power and peace." (Emphasis added)[25]

Knowing the Lord Jesus Christ is not of primary importance in this *Purpose-Driven Paradigm* which says, "The greatest tragedy is . . . life without purpose" (*PDL*;

p. 30). Who *you* are and what *you* do is given greater importance than the doctrine of Christ which tells us Who *He* is and what *He* did and does. Religion (theology/doctrine) doesn't matter anymore to a world in which interfaith unity is presenting all religions (faiths) as equally valid paths to God, purpose, and peace.

The United Nations, which is very plainly ruled by the god of this world, is working very diligently toward bringing about global interfaith unity in the pursuit of its own *purpose* and *power* and manmade *peace*. Its underlying principles and purposes coincide with Satan's Plan for the world.[26]

If anything, the United Nations needs to be addressed by a mighty man of God, like the prophets of old, not with comfort and gratitude! Yet, *The Christian Post* reported in its article titled, "Rick Warren Speaks about Purpose at United Nations" that "he thanked them for the work they do."[27] In addition, Rick Warren's closing prayer also included the following:

> "First of all, I pray for every person here involved in the activities in the week ahead, that you give them – bless them, I pray with physical strength and emotional strength and spiritual strength to handle the rigors of the mission that you've called them to."—Rick Warren[28]

In essence, prayers for the United Nations to be successful in its work are asking God to bless the devil's work, which is never a mission God calls people to! Ingrid Schlueter, producer and co-host of VCY America's Crosstalk Radio Talk Show, talked with a representative from the Christian Embassy ("an offshoot of Campus Crusade for Christ"), which sponsored this interfaith prayer breakfast for U.N. delegates. He told her that this organization "exists at the UN, not to proselytize, but to 'serve those at the UN and help them be successful'"![29]

This is all way beyond bidding them God speed, which results in partaking of its evil deeds (see 2 John 1:11). Yet support of the United Nations and its goals was the reason for this interfaith prayer breakfast. This is the result when Purpose is elevated above the Lord God. *The Christian Post* reported:

> "Days before the largest gathering of world leaders in history, U.N. ambassadors were struggling to overcome deep divisions on how to tackle extreme poverty, enhance human rights and *approach global security* in the 21st century.
>
> "Meanwhile, Christians were asking, 'Are we missing the bigger picture?'

> "'That's why a prayer breakfast to call on the Almighty God is a good idea,' said the Executive Director of Christian Embassy, John Austin. 'Is there a perspective that we're missing?'
>
> "For Austin, successful anti-poverty measures must involve a perspective that teaches the intrinsic value and worth of each person.
>
> "'Unless you approach the problem of poverty holistically and **allow for the spiritual perspective that flows out of *your view* of God**, creation, and human dignity, you just stand a much poorer chance of success,' he said." (Emphasis added)[30]

Speaking to people in different religions (faiths) as if all worship and trust the same "God" is not about the Lord God or *His* purposes. In fact, this perspective impedes calling on the Almighty God *of truth*. In reality, an unholy interfaith prayer breakfast prays to the false gods of the different religions (whether out loud or silently).

Furthermore, allowing different religions (faiths) to keep their own spiritual perspective of their own view of "God" does not bring *success*, unless success is defined as keeping people *off* the narrow way of life! It does, however, achieve further success for the Master Deceiver and his Plan:

> "There is today in the world a very large number of those who fundamentally believe in the brotherhood of religions. Though the unintelligent masses everywhere have little or no idea of things spiritual, **they can be more easily brought to believe in *the one God* and to the idea of *a universal faith* than to any other idea** . . . .
>
> "Soon we shall have the inner structure of a world-faith so clearly defined in the minds of many thousands . . ."—Alice Bailey & Djwhal Khul (Emphasis added)[31]

The masses are being driven to darkness. To say that Christians are "missing the bigger picture" is a *tremendous understatement!*

◆ *Chapter Nineteen* ◆

"One Church," Many Expressions

"The Religion of the Future"

*T*he *Portugal News* reported the following on the annual interfaith congress "The Future of God," which was inspired by the Vatican and U.N. and held in Fátima during October 2003. Clearly, the religion of the future is no longer "future," even in today's "Christianity":

"One of the principle speakers, the Jesuit theologian Father Jacques Dupuis, was insistent that the religions of the world must unite. '**The religion of the future will be a general converging of religions in *a universal Christ that will satisfy all*,**' he said.

"The Belgium-born theologian argued: 'The other religious traditions in the world are part of God's plan for humanity, and the Holy Spirit is operating and present in Buddhist, Hindu, and other sacred writings of Christian and non-Christian faiths as well.' In an impassioned plea he said: 'The universality of God's kingdom permits this, and this is nothing more than a diversified form of sharing in the same **mystery of salvation**. In the end, it is hoped that the Christian will become a better Christian and each Hindu a better Hindu.'

"An official statement put out by the Congress called for *a non-proselytising approach* by all religions. 'What is needed is that each religion be true to its faith integrally and treat each religion on the same footing of equality with no inferior or superiority complexes.' **It emphasized that the secret to peace amongst all religions is admitting that contradictions exist between creeds but to concentrate on what unites them, as opposed to what separates them**." (Emphasis added)[1]

Sound familiar?

All religions are being gathered into the emerging universal religion: "One Truth" and "one God," yet many theologies and paths—"One Church," yet many expressions. It is no coincidence that the religious harlot of Satan's counterfeit kingdom has **"MYSTERY"** written on her forehead (see Revelation 17:5).

It is this counterfeit kingdom and its universal "Christ" that accept people regardless of what religion (faith) they are in. The Lord Jesus Christ only accepts those on His narrow way.

The Body of Christ Transcends the Borders of *the* Faith of Christianity?

> "*A* church family identifies you as a genuine believer. I can't claim to be **following Christ** if I'm not committed to *any* specific group of disciples."
> (*PDL*; p. 133; emphasis added)

> "I happen to know people who are **followers of Christ *in other religions***."
> —Rick Warren (Emphasis added)²

*T*he "whole new way of thinking" in today's Christianity lines up more with "the religion of the future" than with the Word of God. In this new Paradigm, the "genuine" believers who are following Christ are those who commit to a local church, and, obviously, the specific "church family" one commits to does not even need to be of the Christian faith!

Believing in either a universal "Christ" or a "relationship with God" that transcends religious (theological/doctrinal) barriers is the teaching of the emerging counterfeit kingdom, not the Kingdom of God. To claim that there are followers or believers of the Lord Jesus Christ in other religions (faiths) is to attempt to unite the religions and darkness of the broad way with the Lord and light of the narrow way. This preference to strive for *both/and* rather than *either/or* is found in the (New Age) New Spirituality, as pointed out by one of Satan's minions:

> "That is a sign of maturity, and most human beings . . . begin to see that they do not live in a black-and-white world, that there are multiple shades of gray, and that standing firm in an 'either/or' position rarely serves anyone—least of all, Life.

> "You do not live in an 'either/or' reality. The reality is 'both/and.' . . .

"This will be one of the dramatic shifts to occur in the future, for **your religions *will* adopt this larger understanding in the days of the New Spirituality**."—Neale Donald Walsch's "God" (Bold added)³

They are indeed. Given its own adoption of this "larger understanding," how long until today's Christianity blatantly verbalizes inclusion of the local churches, congregations, and "houses of worship" of other religions in "the Church" or "the Body of Christ"? Regardless of the religion, they have already been included along with "the church" as having the distribution needed to accomplish the P.E.A.C.E. Plan's ministry in the world.

"PEACE is our plan to attack the world's five biggest problems . . .

"There's only one thing that is big enough to handle this: that is **the global church** . . . .

"In the PEACE plan, the P stands for **partnering with other congregations**. You have to start locally . . . There are a lot of places in the world where the only social structure is religion."—Rick Warren (final ellipsis dots in the original; emphasis added)⁴

"I could take you today to a million villages that don't have a school, . . . but **they got a church. Or they got a synagogue. They got *something*. They got a house of worship** . . . .

"**Partner with congregations**, partner with congregations. You start with them because they're already there . . . . They're in the village."—Rick Warren (Emphasis added)⁵

"[C]hurches have two things the [sic] neither government nor business will ever have. Number one, we have universal distribution. **There's a church in every village of the world.** I mean **the church was global** 200 years before anybody started thinking of globalization. I can take you to millions of places that don't have anything but a church."—Rick Warren (Emphasis added)⁶

"**Partner with other houses of worship**, Partner with churches . . ."—Rick Warren (Emphasis added)⁷

> "**'You are part of the only group in the world capable of handling this task**,' he [Rick Warren] told them. 'There's only one organization big enough, and that's **the local church in all of its expressions in places all around the world**."—*The Orange County Register*, 11/6/05 (Emphasis added)[8]

> "**The local church is the Body of Christ, and is the best instrument to accomplish Christ's ministry in the world**."—Rick & Kay Warren (Emphasis added)[9]

In the biography of Rick Warren, he and Richard Abanes engaged in a frivolous interview that contained repeated responses of noted "laughter" and a disregard for warnings being sounded, as well as a sidestepping of many main issues.

Abanes asked, "When you talk a lot about being 'global' and reaching out to the world, are you talking about any kind of spiritual globalism—a New Spirituality—wherein all religious divisions are removed?"

Rick Warren answered, "Not at all. **It is simply a call for *local churches to be the church in all of its expressions***" (emphasis added).[10]

The lack of discernment regarding the (New Age) New Spirituality continues, as does the transformation of today's Christianity.

Incidentally, this biography and its interview were published in 2005. Rick Warren knew that he intended for his P.E.A.C.E. Plan to include local churches of *other religions (faiths)* in villages around the world when he answered this question. In fact, Rick Warren had already admitted earlier in this same interview with Abanes:

> "[My peace plan] is not globalism, **it's church-ism. The P.E.A.C.E. Plan is built on local churches**—built on the idea that these problems are so big they cannot be solved by anybody except **the church**. *That's* the P.E.A.C.E. Plan. Nothing else is big enough—no businesses, no education, no governments. The UN isn't big enough. **It is only the millions of local churches spread around the world [that are big enough]**. You can go into **any village** without a clinic, or school, or store, or post office [around the world]—but **they've got a church**. And *that* church can become the center of the community if it is properly trained to do so." (All brackets in the original; bold added)[11]

Then in his call "for local churches to *be* the church in all of its expressions," Rick Warren went on to say:

"I believe the twenty-first century is the era of **the local church**. And it should be the goal of parachurches to support the churches, not vice versa, because Jesus said, 'I will build **my church**.'" (Emphasis added)[12]

Richard Abanes then commented, "So there is, in your opinion, *no way* to be saved outside of a personal faith in the historic, orthodox Jesus of the Bible."

To which Rick Warren replied, "Absolutely not. John 14:6. Very clear. I'm betting my life on John 14:6."[13]

And yet Rick Warren has said:

> "I have known **many people who believe in the Messiah of Jesus**, *regardless of what religion they are*, because they believe in him. It's about a relationship, not a religion." (Emphasis added)[14]

> "I happen to know **people who are followers of Christ** *in other religions*." (Emphasis added)[15]

Clearly, definitions have changed!

Regardless of his stand on John 14:6, the truth of this Scripture is being denied by his various interfaith actions, such as:

- his reaction of "great, God bless you, keep going," to people who say they are "an active member of a local church – of any kind of religion – synagogue, mosque, whatever;"[16]
- his belief that growing communities "need new houses of worships, temples, and synagogues, and churches, and stuff like that;"[17]
- the various interfaith aspects of his P.E.A.C.E. Plan, including his call for "spiritual care" to be distributed by the "houses of worship" in "all the different religions;"
- his interfaith prayer with those of many religions (faiths) who are either praying to their own false god or seeking to approach God apart from the Lord Jesus Christ;
- his inclusion of other religions (faiths) as paths to a "relationship with God;"
- his belief that Christ can be followed "in other religions;" and so on and so forth.

Even if he affirms the fundamental doctrines for himself and his church, disaffirming their essentiality for every other person and church does not leave the message unchanged. This changes the message from one of absolutism to relativism. And relativism is replacing fundamentalism in today's Christianity.

Fundamentalism: An Enemy of the Universal Religion

The Master Deceiver's Plan continues to achieve obvious success in its neutralization of today's Christianity:

> "[W]ill the churches have the vision and the courage to let the bad old ways go and turn to the people with the message that God is Love, proving the existence of that love by their own lives of simple loving service? Will they tell the people that Christ forever lives and bid them turn their eyes away from the old doctrines of death and blood and divine appeasement and center them upon the Source of all life . . . ? Will they teach that the destruction of the old forms was needed and that their disappearance is the guarantee that a new and fuller unlimited spiritual life is now possible? Will they remind the people that Christ Himself said that it is not possible to put new wine into old bottles? . . . Can churchmen of all faiths in both hemispheres attain that inner spiritual light which will make them light bearers and which will evoke that greater light which the new and anticipated revelation will surely bring? . . .
>
> "Within the churches today there are men responding to the new spiritual idealism, to the urgency of the opportunity and to **the need for change** . . . .
>
> "Men want the conviction that Christ lives; that the Coming One - for Whom all men wait - will come and that **He will not be Christian, Hindu or Buddhist but will belong to all men everywhere** . . . .
>
> "What is the solution of this intricate and difficult relationship throughout the world? **A new presentation of truth, because God is not a fundamentalist** . . . a new mode of interpreting the ancient spiritual teaching . . . These are imperative changes.
>
> "**Nothing can prevent the new world religion from eventually emerging** . . . . **It will be hindered by the fundamentalists**, the narrow-

minded and the theologians in all the world religions, by those **who refuse to let go the old interpretations and methods, who love the old doctrines . . ."**—Alice Bailey & Djwhal Khul (Bold added)[18]

Not surprisingly, the Angel of light doesn't think much of *narrow*-minded Christians who believe in the fundamentals of *the* faith of the *narrow* way. No matter what, true Christian fundamentalism holds to the fundamentals of **"the faith which was once delivered unto the saints"** (Jude 1:3). Thus in reverence and fear of God it does not waver in the belief that God never changes and He said what He meant and meant what He said in His Holy Scriptures. And what He said will always be at odds with the universal religion and its "One Church" of many faiths.

Accordingly, true Christian fundamentalists pose a hindrance to the Master Deceiver's Plan because they contend for **"the faith"** instead of cooperating with his neutralization of today's Christianity. Thus he will complete the neutralization of these "enemies" through his "selection process" when his Antichrist takes power.

> *"Yea, and all that will live godly in Christ Jesus shall suffer persecution. But evil men and seducers shall wax worse and worse, deceiving, and being deceived. But continue thou in the things which thou hast learned and hast been assured of, knowing of whom thou hast learned them." (2 Timothy 3:12-14)*

According to **"the faith,"** a true fundamentalist Christian believes the narrow way of the Lord Jesus Christ is the *only* way to God and His Kingdom. Therefore other religions (faiths) cannot participate in the Kingdom of God or offer "spiritual care," and do not have the salvation of souls as their end. They can only offer the spiritual *destruction* of the broad way they're on.

It would be non-fundamentalists who believe that specific beliefs and *the* faith of the narrow way are irrelevant, and that a relationship with God (salvation) can be achieved regardless of *which* religion (faith) a person is still in.

> *"Consider the work of God: for who can make that straight, which he hath made crooked?" (Ecclesiastes 7:13)*

Yet this is exactly what today's Christianity is trying to do. The fundamentals of *the* faith have become too narrow and exclusive for today's broad-minded

Christianity. Consequently, the Angel of light isn't the only one who sees fundamentalism as an enemy.

> "Warren said he sees religious institutions as more powerful forces than governments for solving the world's problems.
>
> "'I would trust any imam or priest or rabbi to know what is going on in a community before I would any government agency.'
>
> "But, powerful as churches can be in working for the powerless, they can't succeed without governments and nongovernmental organizations, Warren said.
>
> **"Warren predicts that fundamentalism, of all varieties, will be 'one of the big enemies of the 21st century.'**
>
> "'Muslim fundamentalism, Christian fundamentalism, Jewish fundamentalism, secular fundamentalism - they're all motivated by fear. Fear of each other.'"
> —*The Philadelphia Inquirer*, 1/8/06 (Emphasis added)[19]

Regardless of what the Purpose-Driven Paradigm's intentions are, the three segments of the world—government, business, and now "faith communities" (i.e., "the One Church")—are all being fused together into "the larger Whole" to ultimately serve the purpose of the Master Deceiver and his Antichrist.

> "[T]he vision is a vision of group work, of group relationships, of group objectives, and of the group fusion to the larger Whole."—Alice Bailey & Djwhal Khul[20]
>
> "The vision of the giving of the individual in sacrifice and service, within the group and to the group ideal, will be the goal of the masses of advanced thinkers in the New Age, whilst for the rest of humanity, brotherhood will be the keynote of their endeavor. *These words have a wider connotation and significance than the thinkers of today can know and understand."*—Alice Bailey & Djwhal Khul (Emphasis added)[21]

This "group fusion" is taking place willingly now by the masses who want to help the world, but it will become mandatory when the Antichrist assumes power. Oneness is ultimately all about assimilating individualism into the global community and global mind, with nonconformity to be punishable by death under the iron fist of Satan's Beast.

The (New Age) New Spirituality teaches that those who refuse to become ONE with the many and who remain separate in their beliefs that there is no other way to God are full of "fear" of Oneness with God and each other.[22] Thus, as mentioned earlier, these so-called "enemies" ("cancer cells") will be selected for removal from the planet so the purged world can then finally achieve its sought after "health" and "peace."

As relationships continue to be elevated above the truth, the conditioning for this "selection process" against "fearful" fundamentalists continues. The following is from Rick Warren's interview with Larry King on December 2, 2005:

> Larry King: "Before we talk about Rick Warren's peace plan are you a fundamentalist?
>
> Rick Warren: "No . . . . a fundamentalist is not an evangelical. **There are all kinds of fundamentalists**, Larry, **and they're *all* based on fear**. There are Christian fundamentalists." (Emphasis added)[23]

For those who are true *Christian* fundamentalists, it's called the fear of God!

Regardless of what Rick Warren's definition of fundamentalism is, in both of his two previous quotes he lumps "*all* varieties" and "*all* kinds" together and critically says "they're *all*" based on and motivated by "fear." When interfaith unity is desired it is inevitable that true Christian fundamentalism will eventually be deemed an "enemy" because the fundamentals of the faith oppose interfaith unity.

At the Aspen Ideas Festival last July, Rick Warren made the following comments in contrasting fundamentalists with evangelicals:

> "*I could count the number of true fundamentalists on a couple hands today. There really aren't that many left. It's a term that's pushed around, but they happen to be on the media, okay. They happen to be on the media a lot. But* **evangelicals simply are those who would say we believe in a personal relationship to God**. *And it's not a denomination.* **There are Catholic evangelicals**, *which surprises people . . . . There are evangelicals in every denomination. It is not a denomination. But it is a –* **the focus is more on relationship than religion**." (Emphasis added)

> "**Fundamentalism is an angry religion. It is a reactionary religion. It is an exclusive religion.** It is an inclusive and primarily it is an isolationist view of religion that says in order to protect ourselves we will build walls around us and we will fight culture . . . . [Y]ou know the word evangelical, I don't know if you know it, it comes from the Greek word 'good news.' That's all it means . . . . I think as a whole **evangelicals are far more positive, and they're far more engaged in culture, okay**. A fundamentalist wouldn't go see Star Wars. I've seen it three times." (Emphasis added)[24]

The actual message that comprises the "good news" of today's "evangelicals" has obviously changed, as evidenced in Rick Warren's own belief that people can be "followers of Christ in other religions." The magnitude of the changes to the evangelical's new message is summarized in the previously mentioned poll conducted for *Newsweek* and Beliefnet: 68% of *evangelicals* believe that "a good person who isn't of your religious faith [can] go to heaven or attain salvation." One thing leads to another in relativism which has replaced fundamentalism. First the world is given back its own ways ("styles"), and then its own religions and "truth," and finally its own "salvation."

These "evangelicals" are separating themselves from the fundamentals of the faith in their "whole new way of thinking." In addition, their new beliefs are consistent with the (New Age) New Spirituality belief that the religions (faiths) of the world are drawn from the same source and that mankind is "ONE at the highest *spiritual* component of our nature." Rick Warren is clearly right when he says there aren't many fundamentalists left.

The world is allowed to stay on its own dead-end path to God by those in today's Christianity who are far more interested in what is "positive" and inclusive than what is holy and true and who view obediently contending for the faith as reactionary.

Keep in mind Rick Warren's repeated clarifications that he is *not* a "fundamentalist" and that "Fundamentalism is an angry . . . reactionary . . . exclusive religion" when you consider his definition of "the word 'fundamentalist.'" In addition, given the inclusive beliefs of today's evangelicals, watered-down definitions are obviously behind his description of "evangelical" (e.g., what happened to saved by grace *through faith?*):

> "[S]o what's an evangelical? Let's just review. An evangelical believes the Bible is God's Word, Jesus is who he claimed to be, salvation is only by grace – in

other words, you can't earn your way to heaven – and everybody needs to hear the good news; information, not coercion . . . .

"There is a difference between 'evangelicalism' and 'fundamentalism' and 'the religious right.' . . . – they are very, very different. I am an evangelical . . . . I'm not a fundamentalist."—Rick Warren[25]

". . . I'm just tired of having other people represent me and represent the hundreds of thousands of churches where the pastors I've trained would nowhere, no way, relate to some of the supposed spokesmen of a previous generation.

"Now the word '**fundamentalist**' actually comes from a document in the 1920s called the Five Fundamentals of the Faith. And **it is a very legalistic, narrow view of Christianity** . . ."—Rick Warren (Emphasis added)[26]

The list of five essential doctrines of faith—which also became known as "The Five Points of Fundamentalism"—was first adopted in 1910 as a basic list of beliefs that candidates for ordination must affirm. This list was reaffirmed in 1916 and 1923, but it was strongly opposed in 1924. The opposition came from a large group of preachers who viewed the following five so-called "theories" as too narrow and legalistic. In seeking unity and liberty, these preachers preferred more latitude in even their basic beliefs.[27] Some things never change.

The document makes it clear that these five doctrines are not the *only* essential doctrines but that they must be the starting place or foundation of a pastor's beliefs. And, yes, this starting place is "narrow" because *"narrow is the way, which leadeth unto life"* (Matthew 7:14). It is *not* unreasonable or *"very legalistic"* to require pastors to believe these fundamentals of the faith! On the other hand, these five doctrines could seem "very legalistic" to those who prefer interfaith unity of purpose and who encourage churches to maintain their own "doctrinal convictions":

The inerrancy and inspiration of the Holy Scriptures (without which we would only have relativism and no standard for life or faith)—

"1. It is an essential doctrine of the Word of God and our Standards, that the Holy Spirit did so inspire, guide and move the writers of the Holy Scriptures as to keep them from error."[28]

The virgin birth (without which the Lord Jesus Christ would not be God manifest in the flesh, so He would be nothing more than a sinful man)—

> "2. It is an essential doctrine of the Word of God and our Standards, that our Lord Jesus Christ was born of the Virgin Mary."[29]

The Lord Jesus Christ's atonement for our sins (without which we would all be going to hell)—

> "3. It is an essential doctrine of the Word of God and our Standards, that Christ offered up 'himself a sacrifice to satisfy divine justice, and to reconcile us to God.'"[30]

The Lord Jesus Christ's bodily resurrection (without which our faith would be in vain and there would be no forgiveness of sins)—

> "4. It is an essential doctrine of the Word of God and our Standards, concerning our Lord Jesus, that 'on the third day he arose form [sic] the dead, with the same body in which he suffered; with which also he ascended into heaven, and there sitteth at the right hand of his Father, making intercession.'"[31]

The miracles of the Lord Jesus Christ (without which He would have given no evidentiary manifestation of His claim to be God)—

> "5. It is an essential doctrine of the Word of God as the supreme Standard of our faith, that the Lord Jesus showed his power and love by working mighty miracles . . . . These great wonders were signs of the divine power of our Lord, making changes in the order of nature."[32]

These five fundamentals of the faith are "a very legalistic, narrow view of Christianity"?

> "What is the solution of this intricate and difficult relationship throughout the world? **A new presentation of truth, because God is not a fundamentalist** . . . a new mode of interpreting the ancient spiritual teaching . . . **These are imperative changes**."—Alice Bailey & Djwhal Khul (Emphasis added)[33]

The subtle switch from religion to relationship is a key aspect of the "new presentation of truth." Believers in the Lord Jesus Christ do indeed have a personal relationship with the Lord God, *but* it stems from believing the doctrines of *the faith (religion) of true Christianity*. Yet in the switch, relationship transcends religion so that a "relationship with God" can be attained in any religion. The subtilty of this switch lies in its replacement of *believing the doctrines* of Christ in *the* faith with *experiences* of Christ in *any* faith (religion).

> *"To the law and to the testimony: if they speak not according to this word, it is because there is no light in them." (Isaiah 8:20)*

> *"Now we know that what things soever the law saith, it saith to them who are under the law: that every mouth may be stopped, and all the world may become guilty before God." (Romans 3:19)*

> *"But the scripture hath concluded all under sin, that the promise by faith of Jesus Christ might be given to them that believe." (Galatians 3:22)*

Regardless of how convinced people in other religions are that they follow Christ and have a relationship with God, the Lord Jesus Christ warns:

> *"He that rejecteth me, and <u>receiveth not my words</u>, hath one that judgeth him: <u>the word that I have spoken, the same shall judge him in the last day</u>." (John 12:48)*

This passage also says the Lord Jesus Christ didn't come to judge the world, but to save it (see verse 47). The Lord Jesus Christ came to **"bear witness unto <u>the truth</u>"** (John 18:37), and His Word—the truth—will do the judging.

> *"There remaineth therefore a rest to the people of God . . . . Let us labour therefore to enter into that rest, lest any man fall after the same example of unbelief. <u>For the word of God is quick, and powerful, and sharper than any twoedged sword, piercing even to the dividing asunder of soul and spirit, and of the joints and marrow, and is a discerner of the thoughts and intents of the heart.</u> Neither is there any creature that is not manifest in his sight: but all things are naked and opened unto the eyes of him with whom we have to do." (Hebrews 4:9, 11-13)*

The last thing many evangelicals need is another "worship" *experience* that furthers their passionate zeal for God that is *not* according to knowledge. What they need are Bible Studies that actually study the Word of God rather than the books of men, where they can thoroughly *learn* the fundamentals of the faith, study to show themselves approved, and then go out and preach the true Gospel of Christ to a lost and dying world. (Saddleback's *Foundations* curriculum which has spread to other churches is clearly ineffectual, perhaps because it is "*A Purpose-Driven Discipleship Resource*"?)

If people would shed half as many tears because people are hell-bound as they do because people are in poverty or have AIDS then maybe they would care enough to help people God's way.

> *"And this I pray, that your love may abound yet more and more in knowledge and in all judgment; that ye may approve things that are excellent; that ye may be sincere and without offence till the day of Christ; being filled with the fruits of righteousness, which are by Jesus Christ, unto the glory and praise of God." (Philippians 1:9-11)*

This isn't just for the sake of those in the world. It is also for the sake of the many in today's Christianity who no longer know or believe the fundamentals of the faith so are uniting with the post-truth world in more ways than one. Regarding the *Newsweek* and Beliefnet poll, the Editor-in-Chief and co-founder of Beliefnet wrote an article titled, "The Pearly Gates are Wide Open," in which he comments:

> "How could so many Americans be tossing aside such a central element of theology? I think the Newsweek cover story that grew in part out of this poll has the best theory. **Americans have become so focused on a very personal style of worship—forging a direct relationship with God—that spiritual experience has begun to supplant dogma.**" (Emphasis added)[34]

It appears the world is more aware of what's going on than are Christians today who have fallen for the propaganda that "the message hasn't changed." The *Newsweek* article "In Search of the Spiritual" includes the following astute observation in its discussion of this poll:

> "'**Rather than being about a god who commands you, it's about finding a religion that empowers you.**'" (Emphasis added)[35]

Finding One's Own Self-Empowering Religious Expression

"There is no 'one-size-fits-all' approach to worship and friendship with God. One thing is certain: You don't bring glory to God by trying to be someone he never intended you to be. God wants you to be yourself. *'That's the kind of people the Father is out looking for: those who are **simply and honestly themselves** before him in their worship.'* [endnote: John 4:23 (Msg)]" (*PDL*; p. 103; bold added)

According to God's Holy Scriptures, neither approaching God nor worship of God nor friendship with God is about our *unique expression* in being "simply and honestly" ourselves before God. We can only approach the Lord God on *His* terms, which the world has rejected in its search for self-empowerment. Contrary to the man-centered *Message*, Scripture actually says in John 4:23:

> *"But the hour cometh, and now is, when the true worshippers shall worship the Father **in spirit and in truth:** for the Father seeketh such to worship him."*

"In spirit and in truth" are obviously being sacrificed (deleted and redefined) in today's inclusive "Christianity." This narrow, exclusive, *one-size-fits-all* approach to worship and friendship with God requires everyone to first receive *a new spirit*, born of the Holy Spirit through belief in *the truth*. It is not about finding our own religious expression.

> *"Then said Jesus to those Jews which believed on him, If ye continue in my word, then are ye my disciples indeed; and ye shall know the truth, and the truth shall make you free."* (John 8:31-32)

> *"<u>Being born again</u>, not of corruptible seed, but of incorruptible, <u>by the word of God</u>, which liveth and abideth for ever."* (1 Peter 1:23)

The world has rejected truth, rejected being born again in the spirit, and rejected any relationship or friendship with the Lord God by rejecting the Lord God of truth, His Word of truth, and His narrow way of truth.

> *"Can two walk together, except they be agreed?"* (Amos 3:3)

> *"Whosoever transgresseth, and abideth not in the doctrine of Christ, hath not God. He that abideth in the doctrine of Christ, he hath both the Father and the Son." (2 John 1:9)*

The world's religions have their own doctrines and their own sacred texts that oppose God's Word of truth and thereby oppose God's means by which we are *born again*. Contrary to the teachings of the (New Age) New Spirituality, there isn't one river or one ocean or one tree from which every religion and perspective draws their portion of "wisdom" and "truth," through their own "well" or "branch." There are *two ways*, one *narrow* and one *broad*:

- The narrow way is the absolute truth of the Lord God found only in true Christianity -- **"the faith which was once delivered unto the saints."**
- The broad way is the counterfeit and relative "truths" of the god of this world and his various religions (faiths).

- The narrow way of absolutism is believing and doing what is right in *the Lord's* eyes.
- The broad way of relativism is believing and doing what is right in *man's* eyes.

- The narrow way leads to life and only a few are on it.
- The broad way leads to destruction and many are on it.

These two ways are *eternally separate* and cannot be synthesized. The broad way will *never* lead to *life*, or to a relationship with the Lord Jesus Christ or God.

The true Body of Christ, which *is* the true Church, does not transcend the narrow way. Those in other religions must *exit* the broad way, where their religion and false gods are, to come to the true Lord God. There is *no bridge* or unity of light and darkness that allows people to be on *both* the broad *and* narrow ways. There are only *seeming* bridges put up by the Angel of light to deceive people into thinking they are eternally safe and spiritually ONE.

> *"**This then is the message** which we have heard of him, and declare unto you, that God is light, and in him is no darkness at all. If we say that we have fellowship with him, and walk in darkness, we lie, and do not the truth." (1 John 1:5-6)*

Contrary to the propagandistic claims, the message is *definitely* being *changed*. The new broad-minded "Christianity" prefers to see the world as the victim of a narrow-minded and so-called "outdated" and "religiously bigoted" Christianity. So instead of telling the world that the holy Lord God is the One Who determines how we can approach Him, worship Him, and find friendship with Him, it is leading the world to believe that all religions (faiths) are valid paths to God. This isn't about the Lord God; it is about empowering mankind to be itself and find its own religious expression.

> *"Not every one that saith unto me, Lord, Lord, shall enter into the kingdom of heaven; but he that doeth the will of my Father which is in heaven. Many will say to me in that day, Lord, Lord, have we not prophesied in thy name? and in thy name have cast out devils? and in thy name done many wonderful works? And then will I profess unto them, <u>I never knew you: depart from me, ye that work iniquity</u>." (Matthew 7:21-23)*

> *"Nevertheless the foundation of God standeth sure, having this seal, <u>The Lord knoweth them that are his</u>. And, Let every one that nameth the name of Christ <u>depart from iniquity</u>." (2 Timothy 2:19)*

The Lord God only knows those as His who depart from iniquity according to *His* definition. The choice is simple -- either we will depart from iniquity or we will depart from God. A seeming "relationship" with the Lord Jesus Christ that is apart from believing and obeying His truth on the narrow way will not get anyone into heaven.

Many people who do many wonderful works *in Jesus' name* and call Him "Lord" obviously believe they have a relationship with Jesus. Yet the Lord Jesus Christ is going to tell even them that *He* never knew *them*. It is a one-sided "relationship" because of disobedience to the essential will of God. (Obedience is *not* legalism!) Sadly, as a result, He is "Lord" in lip service only to many who clearly have purpose and faith, but not *the* faith (believing *and* obeying *the truth*).

> *"And if the righteous scarcely be saved, where shall the ungodly and the sinner appear?" (1 Peter 4:18)*

> *"Then said one unto him, Lord, are there few that be saved? And he said unto them, Strive to enter in at the strait gate: for many, I say unto you, will seek to enter in, and shall not be able." (Luke 13:23-24)*

> *"Take heed therefore that the light which is in thee be not darkness."* (Luke 11:35)

Perhaps those who keep insisting that the message hasn't changed have incrementally or dialectically lost sight of what the true message is. This is, after all, the purpose behind the Angel of light's transformational process.

What we are seeing is not a spiritual "awakening" *to* the truth but, rather, *away from* the truth. The masses are being driven into the universal religion—the "One Church" where theology is irrelevant. Toward this aim, some of the successful devices of the Angel of light and his minions include:

- redefining "truth" and its message;
- redirecting the focus from beliefs to works;
- replacing the Lordship of Christ with the "example" of Christ;
- replacing the absolute authority of *God* with the relative authority of *self* and its experiences.

The following quote of Alice Bailey and Djwhal Khul provides a summary of the transformational process of the Angel of light's emerging kingdom of Oneness:

> "Out of the darkness of time there have emerged the great religions. These religions *though diverse in their theologies and forms of worship* . . . and though differing in their methods of application of truth, are united in three basic aspects:
>
> 1. In their teaching as to *the nature of God* and of man.
> 2. In their symbolism.
> 3. In certain fundamental doctrines.
>
> "When men recognize this and succeed in isolating that inner significant structure of truth which is the same in all climes and in all races, **then there will emerge the universal religion, the One Church, and that unified though not uniform approach to God . . . Theologies will disappear into the knowledge of God; doctrines and dogmas will no longer be regarded as necessary, for faith will be based on experience**, and authority will give place to personal appreciation of Reality . . . . Man will enter into his divine heritage and know himself as the Son of the Father, with all the divine characteristics,

powers and capacities which are his because of his divine endowment. But in the meantime what have we? A breaking away from old established tradition, a revolt from authority, whether of the Church, of dogma, doctrine or theology; a tendency towards self-determination and an overthrowing of the old standards, and of old barriers of thought and the divisions existing between races and faiths."—Alice Bailey & Djwhal Khul (Emphasis added)[36]

Since the Garden of Eden, the Master Deceiver has been incrementally leading mankind toward "his divine heritage," the ultimate transformation and Self-empowerment -- man's recognition of his own "divinity."

♦ Chapter Twenty ♦

"One Divine Life," Many 'Little Christs'

"That Which Will Eventually Reorganize Our Human Life Is the Presence in the World of Those Who Know Christ as Their Example, and Recognize That They Possess the Same Divine Life"

*A*s mentioned earlier, the counterfeit kingdom of World Servers presents Christ as an "example" or "model" to be followed in any religion. It is an effective deception:

- It lures people into believing there is a compatibility between Christ and "the One Truth" and "the One Church."
- It lures Christians onto the way that *seems* Christian.
- It lures people into thinking they are following Christ Himself rather than just His example.
- It lures people into encroaching upon that which belongs to the Lord alone, including His divinity.

In essence, this subtle switch from the Lordship of Jesus Christ to the 'modelship' of Christ deceptively exchanges *the truth* of Who He is and what He did for the *principles* that He lived. Thus the Gospel of *faith* is effectively transformed into a false gospel of *works*, and the Lord Jesus Christ is replaced with the universal "Christ" or "Jesus" of the counterfeit kingdom:

> "Christ, in His high place, cares not whether men accept the theological interpretations of scholars and churchmen, **but He does care whether the keynote of His life of sacrifice and service is *reproduced* among men**; it is immaterial to Him whether the emphasis laid upon the detail and the veracity of the Gospel story is recognized and accepted, for He is more interested that the search for truth and for subjective spiritual experience should persist; He knows that within each human heart is found that which

responds instinctively to God, and that the hope of ultimate glory lies hid in the Christ-consciousness.

"Therefore, **in the new world order, spirituality will supersede theology**; living experience will take the place of theological acceptances."—Alice Bailey & Djwhal Khul (Emphasis added)[1]

"We have fought over the doctrines whereby men shall be saved.... We have regarded half the world as lost and only the Christian believer as saved, yet all the time Christ has told us that love is the way into the kingdom, and that the fact of the presence of divinity in each of us makes us eligible for that kingdom.... *Men are not saved by belief in the formulation of a theological dogma, but by the fact of His living Presence, of the living immediate Christ*.... **That which will eventually reorganize our human life is the presence in the world of those who know Christ as their example, and recognize that they possess the same divine life**, just as the affirmation of the basic law of the kingdom of God, the Law of Love, will finally save the world."—Alice Bailey (Bold added)[2]

"Our task in life is to express divinity. **And that divinity manifests itself in the same way that the divinity of Christ expressed itself**; in harmless living and ceaseless service to our fellow men ... in the sharing with Christ of the urgency which he felt *to meet the world's need and to **act the part** of a savior to men*."—Alice Bailey (Emphasis added)[3]

"The work of pouring out the principle of love (which is the Christ principle) and of lifting the masses in their consciousness to the pitch where they can understand and welcome **that love-principle is the main work of the new age, and it will inaugurate the age of brotherhood and mould humanity into the likeness of the Christ**. That the oriental peoples may call this great Official by another name than that of 'The Christ' has no bearing on reality and alters not the fact of His influence and His esoteric coming."—Alice Bailey & Djwhal Khul (Parentheses in the original; emphasis added)[4]

"... **the goal for thousands everywhere is the demonstration of the Christ spirit, and the exemplification of a life conditioned by love and modeled upon that of Christ** ...

"This makes possible, therefore, the next great human unfoldment which grows out of the Christ consciousness . . ."—Alice Bailey & Djwhal Khul (Emphasis added)[5]

"A Leadership Model That Can Transform Your Life"

*T*he new message which replaces Lord with "model" has given today's movements new impetus. It is much easier to get the masses to follow the example of a "model" than it is to get them to bend the knee to *the Lord*. And these *principles* of "love and service" transcend religious beliefs and facilitate interfaith unity, whereas *the truth* does not.

As discussed earlier, according to the Purpose-Driven Paradigm Jesus "modeled a purpose-driven life"[6] and "modeled the kingdom of God"—a.k.a. "the P.E.A.C.E. Plan."[7] Both of these are inclusive of other religions.

The Lead Like Jesus Movement is another inclusive, popular movement. According to this Movement, Jesus "modeled implementing servant leadership with everyone He met,"[8] providing "a leadership model" which those in any religion or culture can follow.

The co-founders of this movement, Ken Blanchard and Phil Hodges, released their new book, *Lead Like Jesus: Lessons from the Greatest Leadership Role Model of All Time*, in January 2006. The first page of this book contains an endorsement by Rick Warren that links this Movement with the "E" of his P.E.A.C.E. Plan, which aims to fight the giant of ego-centric leadership:

> "One of our world's great problems is ego-centric, self-serving leadership—leaders who think people exist for their benefit, instead of vice versa. In stark contrast, **Jesus modeled servant leadership, leading by example**. He said, 'I came to serve, not to be served.' Now, two thousand years later, Jesus has over 2.1 billion followers, *which makes Him* the undisputed greatest leader of all time. No one else comes close! *This is why* you need to know how to lead like Jesus. He is the only flawless example. That's why you should read this book!"—Rick Warren (Emphasis added)[9]

First, Jesus Christ is the Almighty Lord even if *no one* on earth was following Him. In the name of purpose, the belittling of the uniqueness and preeminence of Who the eternal Lord actually is continues. Second, Rick Warren had announced the relationship between his P.E.A.C.E. Plan and Ken Blanchard and his Lead Like Jesus Movement at a Saddleback Church service on November 2, 2003:

> "The Bible tells us in Hebrews 2 that God made Jesus a perfect leader. *That means we all need to learn to lead like Jesus because there is a leadership shortage in the world.* That's why on November 20, on a Thursday, in a couple weeks, Ken Blanchard and I are gonna teach a national, nationwide, simulcast called, 'Learning to Lead Like Jesus.' We'll be broadcasting it from Birmingham . . . and I'm hoping you'll be able to take the day off and come for a full day of leadership training . . . . **Now Ken has signed on to help with the P.E.A.C.E. Plan, and he is going to be helping train us in leadership and in how to train others to be leaders all around the world.**"—Rick Warren (Emphasis added)[10]

At the November 20, 2003 Lead Like Jesus simulcast announced here, in referring to Blanchard Rick Warren again stated:

> "[T]here is a dramatic shortage of servant leadership in the world . . . .
>
> **"So, we've come up with a little plan called the peace plan. You and I are working together on this** . . . . It is my goal and vision and your goal and vision to be used of God to *raise up millions and millions of local churches* and businesses and everybody else to plant churches, equip leaders, assist the poor, care for the sick, and educate the next generation. *That can only be done when we get the right* **model of leadership**."—Rick Warren (Emphasis added)[11]

Since this P.E.A.C.E. Plan consists of an interfaith network of "men of peace" and "local churches," their "right model of leadership" enables all barriers to be transcended in their equipping of "all leaders" of *all* "aspirations" to follow this "model." The message has definitely changed -- they are presenting Jesus as a "*style*" that transcends culture and religion!:

> "Number two – this one surprises people but it is the source of all of our other problems – egocentric leadership. That is the second global giant: self-centered, self-serving, instead of leadership like Jesus . . .

"'E' is 'Equip leaders.' And we're equipping leaders in a way that is *culturally relevant*—not Western-style leadership but **Jesus-*style* leadership**."—Rick Warren (Emphasis added)[12]

"Today's leadership crisis *transcends cultures, religions* and vocations. **Jesus' servant-leader *style* provides a perfect role model for *all* leaders**. Lead Like Jesus exist [sic] to help leaders of all shapes, ages, and aspirations explore and express the leadership *principles* that Jesus lived."—Lead Like Jesus website (Emphasis added)[13]

"Ken Blanchard and Phil Hodges . . . have developed a unique interactive program to help leaders find new fulfillment and effectiveness in **following leadership behaviors as modeled by Jesus** . . . . A two-day transformational encounter with **Jesus as a role model** . . . Leadership Encounter will challenge *people of faith and anyone else* searching for **a relevant and effective model** for their own day-to-day leadership, to look at Jesus in a *new* and life changing way."—Lead Like Jesus website (Emphasis added)[14]

"Where can you find **a LEADERSHIP MODEL that can TRANSFORM your LIFE**? . . .

"Since today is a day that will never come again, why not start today with the best leader—Jesus! It is the journey of a lifetime and it's for you—whether you are a CEO or a parent, a teacher or a Scout leader, a pastor or an electrician, **leading like Jesus is for you! Choose Jesus today as your role model!**"
—*Lead Like Jesus*, back cover (Bold added)[15]

The "LEADERSHIP MODEL" of this movement has submitted to its own "vision and values" as its preferred "boss":

"'You can't talk about servant leadership without talking about Jesus,' Blanchard explained. '. . . *We are fortunate we have Jesus as a model.*'

"Noting that some managers have avoided the servant leader mentality because they are afraid it is an 'inmates-running-the-prison' type of concept, Blanchard said this is not true. 'It is a new style of leadership with two words. **Leadership is about going somewhere—What is the vision? Servant is to *serve the***

> ***vision** and the direction. **The vision and values become the boss**. You turn the traditional hierarchy upside down.' . . .
>
> "Believing that 'the whole nation is ready for *this model*,' Blanchard is co-hosting—with Rick Warren . . . —a 'Lead Like Jesus' celebration Nov. 20 in Birmingham . . . .
>
> "Blanchard said everyone can benefit from this conference . . . 'For a follower of Jesus, being a servant leader isn't just an option, *it's a mandate*.'"—*The Alabama Baptist*, 10/30/03 (Emphasis added)[16]

It's amazing how leaders believe their own movement based on their own understanding and vision is a *mandate* from God. Announcing the April 29, 2004 Lead Like Jesus celebration, which was hosted by Ken Blanchard and Bill Hybels with Rick Warren speaking on video, Rick Warren's Pastors.com repeated Blanchard's mandate almost verbatim:

> "For a follower of Jesus, servant leadership isn't an option . . . *it's a mandate!* Lead Like Jesus will inspire and equip you, your congregation, and your community to experience Jesus in a powerfully *different way* - as the perfect leader for all time."—Pastors.com (Ellipsis dots in the original; emphasis added)[17]

Servant leadership is about serving "the vision and the direction." It therefore becomes a *mandate* to serve both the vision and the direction of this Movement in which the vision and values are "the boss." This is not the same thing as serving and following Jesus Christ as one's Lord, especially when the vision and values transcend religious barriers and have included the avoidance of "trying to evangelize":

> "According to Blanchard, **'We really just want to say to people, 'Jesus is the greatest leadership role model.'** We want to celebrate that . . . .
>
> "'We hope, at the end of the day, to have people come forward to say, 'I commit to try to lead like Jesus and behave in a different way,'" says Blanchard. 'I think the next big movement in Christianity is going to be demonstration *not proclamation*. **We want to make sure that people understand *we are not trying to evangelize*.** If all Christians would behave like Jesus, everybody would want to be a Christian.'" (Emphasis added)[18]

> "It's the vision—the purpose, the picture of the future, and the values—that everyone should serve. To do that requires leaders to have a servant heart and a strategy to develop and empower others to live according the [sic] established vision, values, and goals."—*Lead Like Jesus* (Emphasis added)[19]

Replacing evangelism with "leading like Jesus" denies the Lord Jesus Christ's commands to preach *His Gospel*, which is **"the power of God unto salvation,"** to the world. It also denies the reason He gave as to why people do *not* want to come to Him and His true light. "Leading like Jesus" is not going to change this, especially when they seek to get "all leaders" to relativistically "lead like Jesus" in their own religion and culture! Yet this self-empowering movement also claims to be "not about you" but "about Jesus."

> "The [Lead Like Jesus] program will celebrate the leadership model of Jesus, and will train and encourage all leaders to follow His model."[20]

> "It's not about us, it's not about you, it's about Jesus. If you can get Him into your heart *as the greatest leadership role model* of all time, you can make an incredible difference in the lives of all the people around you including yourself."—Ken Blanchard (Emphasis added)[21]

Although "it's not about you," the Lord Jesus Christ continues to be reduced to the position of "model" so that mankind, which has become so desperate for *significance*, can seek to usurp *His* work in an increasing number of areas. This has escalated to the point that the latest Lead Like Jesus Celebration, scheduled for February 3-4, 2006 in Virginia and hosted by Ken Blanchard, was to include the following five tracks of "learning experiences":

> "You and your church leaders can come for a morning and talk with others who are interested in learning how to Reach Like Jesus . . . **Redeem Like Jesus** . . . Serve Like Jesus . . . Call Like Jesus . . . Empower Like Jesus." (Ellipsis dots in the original; emphasis added)[22]

Anyone who thinks that human works can even come close to *redeeming* "like Jesus" needs to know what the redemption of *the* Lord and Saviour Jesus Christ actually is (not to mention *His* call and empowerment of us, etcetera). The Almighty Lord God does not just sit back and watch mankind do His work for Him in trying to *be* Jesus Christ through following His Son as a *model*! *He* redeems and calls *us* and commands us to obey Him as *Lord*.

> "We have degenerated into the place where we put God on charity and make Him to be a foreman who can't find help. He stands at the wayside asking, 'How many helpers will come to My rescue and come and do My work?' If we could only remember that God doesn't need anybody here . . ."—A.W. Tozer[23]

> ***"God that made the world and all things therein, seeing that he is Lord of heaven and earth, dwelleth not in temples made with hands; neither is worshipped with men's hands, <u>as though he needed any thing, seeing he giveth to all life, and breath, and all things</u>." (Acts 17:24-25)***

> ***"I know that, whatsoever God doeth, it shall be for ever: nothing can be put to it, nor anything taken from it: and God doeth it, that men should fear before him." (Ecclesiastes 3:14)***

> ***"Look unto <u>me</u>, and be ye saved, all the ends of the earth: for I am God, and there is none else." (Isaiah 45:22)***

The many aspects of *God's* work that belong to Him alone are being usurped and redefined by man. Even if the term "divinity" is not widely used, a growing number of people within Christianity are treating mankind as if it is divine, claims to the contrary notwithstanding. This is only one small example in an overabundance of them. The behavior is there, even if the language isn't. They display it through their man-centered "whole new way of thinking and acting."

Obviously, the message has changed for these learning tracks to even be considered for leadership training. We cannot *be* Jesus Christ to the world, regardless of how successful we are in works of love and service. We are not "little Christs"! The truth and uniqueness of *the Lord and Saviour* Jesus Christ continue to get shoved aside in both the New Age and today's Christianity in man's exaltation of himself first to Jesus Christ's work and then ultimately to His divinity. This is the direction the Master Deceiver and his workers envisioned.

Giving Heed to "the Fundamental Doctrines of the Ageless Wisdom"

"Now the Spirit speaketh expressly, that in the latter times some shall depart from the faith, giving heed to seducing spirits, and <u>doctrines of devils</u>." (1 Timothy 4:1)

The exaltation of spiritual *experience* at the expense of scriptural knowledge, along with the "positive only" attitude, have led to a failure to keep watch and to heed the warnings. The destructive tidal wave of relativism is sweeping people away from *the* faith and into the (New Age) New Spirituality, which is based on the Ancient (Ageless) Wisdom and its Oneness. The depth of deception in today's Christianity is staggering.

> *"But I fear, lest by any means, as the serpent beguiled Eve through his subtilty, so your minds should be corrupted from the simplicity that is in Christ. For if he that cometh preacheth another Jesus, whom we have not preached, or if ye receive another spirit, which ye have not received, or another gospel, which ye have not accepted, ye might well bear with him." (2 Corinthians 11:3-4)*

The deception is of such great magnitude that the Ancient Wisdom has even become a selling point. The Newbury Park First Christian Church, through its Via Vita program, held its first "Ancient Spiritual Wisdom: Principles and Practices for Life" conference, on February 25, 2006.[24] Not surprisingly, the speakers at this conference included popular leaders of the Emerging Church and Spiritual Formation movements, both of which are also steeped in the "New" Spirituality. Dallas Willard, John Ortberg, John Burke, and Tony Jones were scheduled to speak at this conference,[25] right after they were to speak at the 2006 National Pastors Convention on February 22-25, 2006.

Incidentally, this year's Pastors Convention, which again featured the labyrinth, also promoted the Emerging Church.[26] This emerging counterfeit church is aptly described in the promotion for the speakers of the Ancient Spiritual Wisdom conference:

> "John Burke asks the question, 'What do a Buddhist, a biker couple, a gay rights activist, a transient, a high-tech engineer, a Muslim, a twenty-something single mom, a Jew, an unmarried couple living together, and an atheist all have

in common?' and then answers it, *'They are the future church in America!'* . . . He says **the emerging church is an indigenous church, rising up out of the surrounding community and culture to form the Body of Christ.**" (Emphasis added)[27]

Believing and obeying the Lord Jesus Christ is irrelevant in the emerging interfaith church. Via the (New Age) New Spirituality, the many are becoming ONE in the "One Church" of the counterfeit kingdom. Contrary to the deceptive claims, these principles and practices were not "actually taught by Jesus." The ancient principles of Oneness and practices of occultic mysticism come from the Master Deceiver.

The following is from one of Via Vita's announcements of its conference:

> "Two thousand years ago, Christian spirituality was new to the world. This was a time before churches as we know them. **A time before religious dogma and creeds.** A time when a small group of ordinary people began to follow the teachings of a young Jewish carpenter . . . .
>
> "This conference will be about spiritual transformation, spiritual principles and practices as they were <u>actually taught</u> by Jesus and his early followers. We will explore questions and ideas – and beliefs and doubts – about this ancient spirituality . . . .
>
> **"We're hoping to have a vibrant dialogue between people who have a wide range of beliefs.** We'll explore life's most profound and hardest questions – <u>together</u>. With open minds, new ideas and fresh thinking . . . .
>
> "Few people are familiar with spirituality as Jesus actually taught it. What do we actually know about it? *How can we use this knowledge today?*
>
> "Ancient spiritual principles have been in place since the beginning of time. *What are they? Why are they important?* . . .
>
> "Your spirit was created 'imago dei', in the image of God. *What is the nature of this spirit?* . . .
>
> "How can you find **a spiritual path** that will lead to the fullest realization of your potential?

> **"The spiritual realm can be accessed through the ancient practices** of Via Contemplativa (bodily quiet and stillness) and Via Activa (bodily engagement). *What are these practices? How can you use them?"*—Via Vita (Parentheses in the original; bold added)[28]

The Master Deceiver wants everyone to bypass the narrow way to find their own unique "spiritual path," with the "fullest realization" of their potential being the "awakening" to the *"divine"* nature of their own spirit. And with the ever-increasing popularity of ancient occult practices deceptively designed for this very purpose, today's Christianity is right on the verge of this "awakening" becoming widespread.

Everything the Lord Jesus Christ taught which He wants us to know has been included in His Holy Scriptures, which remarkably enough do *not* include accessing the spiritual realm through ancient mystical practices of the "New" Spirituality! Putting a Christian veneer on worldly and occultic beliefs and practices is what the Angel of light does to seduce people into believing his broad way of deception is actually the narrow way of the truth. In Christianity today, the growing number of seekers of the Ancient Wisdom and its inner path "to God" are being seduced by the same deceptions as were Catholicism's early mystics.

Included in this group is Ken Blanchard, who "signed on to help with the P.E.A.C.E. Plan." Despite the fact that the "New" Spirituality has his ongoing assent, he and his Lead Like Jesus Movement remain popular. Rick Warren is a member of the Lead Like Jesus National Board, as are those who espouse the ways and teachings of the (New Age) New Spirituality.[29]

Although Blanchard claims to be equipping leaders to "lead like Jesus," he continues to endorse explicitly Eastern religion (inherent to the New Spirituality) books and teachings as well as the Hoffman Quadrinity Process.[30] In fact, he has credited the occultic Hoffman Process for "bring[ing] forth *spiritual leadership* in a person" and for making his "spirituality come alive" (emphasis added). This endorsement still remains in various places on the Hoffman Institute's website.[31] Blanchard also remains a member of the Hoffman Advisory Board, along with other members who overtly follow the ways and teachings of the Eastern religions.[32]

This occultic Process that Blanchard continues to support utilizes the same principles and practices of the Ancient Wisdom that are enticing many of today's Christians. Bob Hoffman was a self-proclaimed "spiritual intuitive" (typically used by the world as more acceptable terminology for "psychic," or the practitioner of forbidden divination). He said that he "found a path to recovering our innate ability to love," and through 'intuition' came up with his Quadrinity Process. Referring to his Process, he said, "This will be the beginning of understanding, in an *experiential way*, of **your own** emotional and **spiritual truth**" (bold added).³³

Hoffman's panentheistic path to one's own 'divinity' utilizes the occult practice of going deep within to "awaken" to one's "essential nature"/"true self" of "pure Light":

> "For thousands of years, human beings have attempted to understand and come to terms with the mystery of life and of creation itself. One enduring notion maintains that the 'source' of everything is a nonphysical, intelligent, loving spirit, or being and that *we are connected to that spirit* . . . .
>
> "People have searched for ways to connect and have communion with this presence . . . . I came to understand that because we are of this Light, we should be able to communicate and make contact with it directly and at will, without intermediaries. To facilitate this, I developed *the 'Light Journey Visualization,' through which anyone can enter the Light of peace and compassion* . . . . If desired, *virtually anyone* can experience being in the Light, and their Spiritual Self as being of the Light.
>
> "**In the Light we know that our essence is perfect** and that we are not negative . . . The experience of being in the Light brings our Spiritual Selves to the forefront . . . .
>
> "As we begin to experience our Spiritual Self, (in our spiritual dimension), **we recognize our fundamental goodness** and begin the journey toward Integral Being."—Bob Hoffman (Parentheses in the original; emphasis added)³⁴
>
> "Isn't it time to **uncover your true self** and allow its brilliance to shine? . . .
>
> "**Love is the essence** of life and of the Universe itself . . . .
>
> "**Nothing is lacking in any of us**; our positive integral self is always there, always available. You can rediscover and consistently live from **your own wonderous perfection**, lovability, dignity and authenticity."—Bob Hoffman (Emphasis added)³⁵

Raz Ingrasci, the President of the Hoffman Institute, further describes this Process:

> "For 35 years people from all walks of life have been using the Hoffman Quadrinity Process to produce the positive and lasting life changes that they want. Through this work, **participants awaken to their essential natures** . . . Through the HQP it is possible to know and give voice to **your miraculous spirit** . . ." (Emphasis added)[36]
>
> "And then, there is **the Light, which we experience as unconditional love**. Through working intensely with thousands of people, **Bob [Hoffman] learned that when you remove the patterns** [within yourself] **and go down as far as you can go, you run into pure Light.** *The Process is shaped by this fundamental knowledge.* Discovering this Light for yourself, within and beyond, brings enormous depth of meaning, connection, and belonging to life . . . .
>
> "Bob Hoffman always said his mission was peace." (Emphasis added)[37]

The Angel of light brings *seeming* peace to those on his path of Ancient Wisdom. But, ultimately, those who remain on this path will only find the opposite of God's true peace.

The way of the Lord Jesus Christ—the true Light of the world—cannot be accessed by the occult way of darkness. The Angel of light's seeming "light" denies that the essence of man is full of sin and we are all in desperate need of the Saviour. It denies that the Lord God alone *is* good and love and perfect and divine. At the same time, in total denial of the truth and yet true to his own Dream, the Angel of light's way deceives mankind into believing it *"will be like the most High."* His way teaches that to accomplish this, the "one divine Life" just needs to be brought to "birth" (or "awakened") within mankind:

> "[T]here is only one divine Life, expressing itself through the multiplicity of forms in all the kingdoms of nature, and that the sons of men are, therefore, *One* . . . .
>
> "**[W]ithin each human being is a point of light, a spark of the one Flame.** This, we believe, is the soul, the second aspect of divinity and that of which Paul spoke when he referred to 'Christ in you, the hope of glory.' **It is the *demonstration***

of the divine livingness in each person which is our goal . . ."—Alice Bailey ("Fundamental Doctrines of the Ageless Wisdom;" bold added)³⁸

"The immortal destiny of each and all of us is to *attain the consciousness of the higher self*, and subsequently that of the Divine Spirit . . . . **One can have a perfect image or picture, but it lacks life. The life can be modeled on the divine as far as may be; it may be an excellent copy but lacks the indwelling Christ principle**. The germ has been there, but it has lain dormant. *Now it is fostered and brought to the birth* and the first initiation is attained."—Alice Bailey & Djwhal Khul (Emphasis added)³⁹

This is the Angel of light's occult counterfeit for the new birth and life of the spirit which only those who believe in *the Lord* Jesus Christ receive. Those who only want Jesus Christ as a "model" or "example" cannot be born again through God's power and truth so must look to counterfeits to "birth" their spiritual "life."

Given the occult nature of this counterfeit "birth," contacting one's spirit guide through visualization is key. The following is a testimonial of the Hoffman Process, reprinted by the Hoffman Institute:

"People may have encountered some of the Gestalt, NLP bioenergetic, visualisation, *and shamanic techniques* before in some form, but the transformative and magical way that they are *woven together in this process* awed me . . . .

"I felt it to be a great testimony to the Process that **everyone on the course appeared able to embrace their spiritual self and their spirit guide without fear** . . ." (Emphasis added)⁴⁰

Joan Borysenko, the Chair of the Hoffman Advisory Board, on which Ken Blanchard still sits, had this to say in her own testimonial of going through the Hoffman Process:

"In this powerful visualization we were brought into the presence of the Light (God or however you understand the Source of your being) and our won [sic] wise, compassionate, loving, spiritual self . . . .

"*All of my classmates experienced the Light Journey as a spiritual homecoming, a reawakening to their own true nature. The desire to live in the peace of core

> self . . . infused us all with a sense of higher purpose as we went into the anger work. And we didn't go into it alone. **During the Light Journey we also met our spirit guides, or guardian angels . . . . with whom I have had a lively relationship since completing the Hoffman Process** . . . .
>
> "The Tibetan Buddhists compare our spiritual self, what they call our own true nature, or rigpa, to a mirror. It reflects the drama, but is itself changeless. *Healing is about parting the clouds that obscure the mirror-like perfection that we are.* In the process, we become alchemists who transmute woundedness into wisdom." (Emphasis added)[41]

The spirit realm is feverishly working under their Master's Plan to lead the seduced masses into "godhood."

> *". . . If therefore the light that is in thee be darkness, how great is that darkness!" (Matthew 6:23)*

Incidentally, evil spirits can and do appear as beings of "light," and even call themselves "Jesus" or "Christ" or "the Holy Spirit" or "God the Father"—all counterfeits of course. The true and living Lord God does not leave His throne to become subject to the imaginations of mankind. Yet professing Christians think they have "Christianized" occult visualization techniques so refuse to scripturally **"try the spirits whether they are of God"** (1 John 4: 1). Consequently, they are easily bewitched into believing their own visualized spirit guide is the Lord Jesus Christ. The Angel of light and his minions are adept at masterfully deceiving the masses who hunger and thirst for the way of *experience* to their own "spiritual truth."

> "The Hoffman Process brings forth spiritual leadership in a person. **It made my spirituality come alive.**"—Ken Blanchard (Emphasis added)[42]

Showing that Ken Blanchard still accepts these ways and teachings, he has also endorsed *In the Sphere of Silence* by Vijay Eswaran (published in June 2005). This is an Eastern religion book that espouses beliefs similar to the Hoffman Process:

> "Effective leadership is more than what we do; it starts on the inside. Great Leaders are able to tap inner wisdom and strength by cultivating the habit of

solitude. This book is a wonderful guide on how to enter the realm of silence and draw closer to God."—Ken Blanchard[43]

This book promotes "the way of silence," another occultic tool which today's deceived Christianity thinks it has "Christianized." Eswaran's website for *In the Sphere of Silence* states the following:

"This website is dedicated to the way of silence and to the souls interested in knowing the creative force it unleashes, to know it and to master it . . . .

"To learn and to understand how to achieve this exalted state of listening to ourselves . . . .

"Explore, learn, think and discover your inner self."[44]

"It ['this practice'] stems from the ancient Hindu concept, especially from yogic traditions, of practicing mouna (silence), a concept that finds resonance in *all religions and philosophies of the world*." (Emphasis added)[45]

"The process of being in the Sphere of Silence leads us to the silence within us. This is a process that goes all the way back to ancient times . . . .

"The Sphere of Silence, if it is practiced properly, is a very powerful tool. *It is not just oriented to any one religion, it is universally accepted and practiced by almost all faiths on the planet. It is through silence that you find your inner being.*

"This book will help you find the silence within so that you may find peace and harmony without . . . .

"The Sphere of Silence to the Mind is like the Lotus flower opens [sic] up its petals to sunlight, **the mind in the Sphere of Silence, opens to receive the knowledge that leads us to wisdom**."—Vijay Eswaran (Emphasis added)[46]

The Hoffman Process and the way of silence open the mind to the Ancient Wisdom and lead man toward his own "divinity." Yet Ken Blanchard, sought after by today's undiscerning Christianity to teach it how to "lead like Jesus," has praised these counterfeit ways to "God" for eliciting effective spiritual leadership in a person.

Even as recently as January 2006, Blanchard continues to endorse additional anti-Christ books that explicitly follow the path of the "New" Spirituality.[47] And in teaching Christians to "lead like Jesus," he even enlists the help of those who follow this same path.

New Age author Mark Victor Hansen sits on the Lead Like Jesus National Board,[48] despite the fact that he has referred to Christ as "one of the master teachers."[49] The "Christ" who is "one of the master teachers" is a member of the Spiritual Hierarchy and is the universal "Christ" of the counterfeit kingdom. This "Christ" is *not* the Lord Jesus Christ. Apparently, it doesn't matter *which* Jesus those in this "Lead Like Jesus Movement" are trying to teach others to lead like!

Along with Blanchard, Hansen also endorses the Hoffman Process and has said that the Process is able to fill one's "spiritual hole" and that "one of the places I'm encouraging absolutely everyone to go is The Hoffman Process."[50] The occult has its own proselytizers, whether they are aware of it or not, who have infiltrated Christianity's organizations and movements.

Ken Blanchard has also included co-host John Ortberg[51] (who also spoke at the Ancient Spiritual Wisdom conference) and speaker Laurie Beth Jones at his Lead Like Jesus leadership training events. Jones touted walking the labyrinth as "an incredible experience"[52] during her time to train leaders to "lead like Jesus" at the 2003 event that Rick Warren co-hosted.

The Lord Jesus Christ *never* leads people into the occult. And it isn't the leading of the Lord Jesus Christ that is prompting Christianity today to choose the leadership and instruction of those who are unable to discern the difference between His ways and teachings and those of the (New Age) New Spirituality "Jesus."

True to this "New" Spirituality and its new gospel that "we are all one," Laurie Beth Jones says that her "personal mission is to recognize, promote, and inspire *divine connection* in myself and others" (emphasis added).[53] Her Jesus CEO website elaborates:

> "**First, we must remember what unites us rather than what divides us, and *cast aside* doctrines and tribal beliefs** -- the we're-better-than-you stuff. We don't need to lose our traditions, but we do need to gain the understanding that Jesus did not come to set up a new religion, but to teach us about the individual connections we *each* have with God."—Laurie Beth Jones (Emphasis added)[54]

> "Members of the Jesus CEO Foundation embrace and support compassionate Christianity, which **emphasizes relationship over religion**. We refuse to be

divided by doctrinal differences, and respect each individual's *unique connection to God, which may or may not yet be fully realized."* (Emphasis added)[55]

Further denying Who the Lord Jesus Christ is, and among other atrocities, Jones has written in her national bestseller, *Jesus CEO:* **Using Ancient Wisdom** *for Visionary Leadership*:

> "**The words *I AM*** therefore **reflect all the creative power** in the Universe."

> "**Words have power**. And Jesus always spoke loving, powerful, and confident words about himself . . . .

> "**His 'I am' statements were what he *became*.**" (Emphasis added)[56]

Keep in mind that Jones sits on the Lead Like Jesus National Board (along with Rick Warren),[57] and carefully compare her above quotes to the following "Affirmations for Leaders" from this same book:

> "***My*** **word** goes out and **accomplishes that which *I* send it to do**."

> "I proudly say *I AM*, . . .

> "**What I believe, I *become*.**" (Emphasis added)[58]

In their search for Self-empowerment, today's professing Christians are following the lead of the New Age "Jesus" and the Ancient Wisdom straight into the delusion of their own "divinity." Regardless of the intention, creating anything by speaking it into existence can *only* be done by the Lord God, the eternal I AM, not by mere humans! (See also Exodus 3:14 and John 8:58.)

> *"So shall my word be that goeth forth out of my mouth: it shall not return unto me void, but it shall accomplish that which I please, and it shall prosper in the thing whereto I sent it."* (Isaiah 55:11)

> *"To whom will ye liken me, and make me equal, and compare me, that we may be like? . . . Remember the former things of old: for I am God, and there is none else; I am God, and there is <u>none</u> like me."* (Isaiah 46:5, 9)

It is clear which doctrines and beliefs are being "cast aside" by today's leaders, as well as by their followers. It wasn't too long ago when the subtitle of her book would have been a dead give-away to the anti-Christ content of the book. But no longer. The transformation is nearing completion in today's bewitched "Christianity."

"When you borrow methods from Eastern religion, you get their understanding of God."—Ray Yungen[59]

"There is a way that seemeth right unto a man, but the end thereof are the ways of death." (Proverbs 16:25 & 14:12)

It is the emerging universal religion that would have the world believe that "whosoever shall follow Christ as their Example shall be saved," and "that if thou shalt confess with thy mouth the Model Jesus, and shalt follow the principles that he lived, thou shalt be saved." The resulting 'salvation' this counterfeit kingdom offers is Satan's lying word to mankind in the Garden of Eden -- ***"Ye shall not surely die . . . your eyes shall be opened, and ye shall be as gods"*** (Genesis 3:4-5).

"When, therefore, **sight** has been attained and the light streams forth, **revelation of the oneness of all life** is a simple and immediate occurrence . . .

"This kingdom, through its major power (a quality of synthesis, could you but realize it), is gathering together into itself men and women out of every nation and out of all parts of the Earth . . . .

"To all applicants the call has gone out to *see* the Christ as He is, . . . that 'as He is, so should we be in the world.' To disciples and initiates the call goes out to reveal to the world . . . the nature of the Christ consciousness which knows no separation, which recognizes, all men everywhere as Sons of God in process of expression. This is all desired because of the need to emphasize the all-inclusive approach of divinity to humanity. These working disciples and initiates regard all as essentially one and as brothers, which . . . says to all men everywhere: **'We are all the children of God; we are all equally divine; we are all on our way to the revelation of divinity** . . .'"—Alice Bailey & Djwhal Khul (Parentheses in the original; bold added)[60]

Part 7

"The Last Gasp of Christendom"

♦ *Chapter Twenty-One* ♦

Letting the Old Faith Crumble Away

The Spiritual Transformation of Today's Christianity

On June 16, 2005, Rick Warren spoke to the Synagogue 3000 Leadership Network regarding "the challenges and strategies of building a compelling spiritual community."[1] He was explaining to them how to transition a church to the new when the congregation is hanging on to the old, and he gave the following illustration:

> "Be a proponent of the new, not an opponent of the old. This is very important. Don't be a reactionary. It's not *but* or *or*, it's *and*; yes *and* this, yes *and* this . . . .
>
> "If you go down to the New Orleans, they build these houses up on stilts, so that when the Mississippi River comes and it floods, it doesn't flood the homes . . . About every six or seven years those stilts go bad from the floods coming down, okay. Well they don't just come in and knock out all the stilts. What they do is they come in and they just build up new ones underneath and leave the others. And they eventually just crumble, okay. And that's what I teach pastors to do. I say, you know, don't go in and say well we shouldn't do this anymore, that's out of date . . . . **Just go in there and build the new thing and let the other stuff kind of crumble away. It saves you a lot of war**."—Rick Warren (Emphasis added)[2]

Please carefully read that again, and keep in mind that although he reportedly is referring to traditions rather than theology, this is clearly happening to theology as well.

This same craftiness and subtilty saves the Angel of light a lot of war in the transition from *the faith* to his (New Age) New Spirituality and its global interfaith unity. No wonder *both/and* is his methodology of choice.

"It is surely easier to swing the masses into step and give them the newer light of truth if that light is poured on to familiar ground."—Alice Bailey & Djwhal Khul[3]

The Angel of light's (New Age) New Spirituality has been built up underneath the old way of thinking and acting—*"the faith which was once delivered unto the saints."* As the old doctrines and faith are allowed to crumble away, the new counterfeit "Christianity" is departing from the faith and emerging with a new foundation -- the New Spirituality of the universal religion.

The Master Deceiver's very effective transformational process has allowed him to turn the thinking of many Christians upside down:

- They think they are still believing and obeying God and His truth while they are increasingly following and serving the god of this world and his deceptive lies.
- They think they are still believing and preaching the *same* faith and the *same* Gospel of Christ while they are increasingly believing and preaching *another* gospel of *another* "Christ" of *a* faith, not *the* faith.
- They think they are not trying to take the place of God or become god while they are increasingly believing and following the Angel of light's devices designed to do just that.

In *A Time of Departing*, Ray Yungen makes the following astute observations in his section titled, "The New Age Christian—An Accepted Oxymoron":

"All this popularity with meditative mysticism presents a very new and perplexing challenge for evangelical Christianity. We are beginning to encounter the *New Age or Aquarian Christian*. This new term describes someone who remains in his or her home church and professes the Christian faith but has also incorporated various aspects of the New Age or Aquarian mindset into his or her life. New Age author David Spangler was very optimistic about the possibility of this integration when he wrote, 'The point is that **the New Age is here . . . it builds itself and forms itself in the midst of the old.'**

"What has fueled the momentum of this trend is the buffet-style dining approach that has become a hallmark of American religious sensibilities in the last twenty years—you take what you want and leave the rest. **Americans are picking and** blending religions as if they were ordering espressos: pick your espresso blend, but you still get coffee—pick your spiritual path, but you still get God. Whatever suits your spiritual tastes, you bring together. The result is hybrid New Age spirituality." (Ellipsis dots in the original; bold added)[4]

Little by little, Christians have been purposefully lured into this (New Age) New Spirituality. This new foundation of today's Christianity is succinctly summarized in the observation of *Newsweek* regarding the poll it conducted with Beliefnet:

> "'**Rather than being about a god who commands you, it's about finding a religion that empowers you**.'" (Emphasis added)[5]

Today's double-minded "Christianity" is succumbing to its epidemic of the blind leading and endorsing the blind. God repeatedly warned in His Holy Scriptures about false teachers that would arise *among* believers and that *many* would follow them.

> "But there were false prophets also among the people, even as there <u>shall be</u> false teachers <u>among you</u>, who privily shall bring in damnable heresies, even <u>denying the Lord</u> that bought them, and bring upon themselves swift destruction. And <u>many</u> shall follow their pernicious ways; by reason of whom the way of truth shall be evil spoken of." (2 Peter 2:1-2)

Yet exercising scriptural *judgment* in discerning between right and wrong, and truth and error, has been cast aside in favor of pragmatic unity and relativism. God's Holy Scriptures have been replaced with the teachings of today's leaders who want us to believe that:

- we shouldn't judge anything because it isn't "loving;"
- we shouldn't judge our pastor's teachings in light of Scripture because that doesn't protect the all-important unity of our local church;
- we shouldn't listen to anyone who tries to warn us that we might be listening to false teachers because that's "self-righteous" "gossip."

Although God is displeased when scriptural judgment is not exercised (e.g., see Isaiah 59:15), many still refuse to judge truth from error. Instead, in their effort to assuage their itching ears the masses are heaping to themselves false teachers to lead them in their preferred way.

"For the time will come when they will not endure sound doctrine; but after their own lusts shall they heap to themselves teachers, having itching ears; and they shall turn away their ears from the truth, and shall be turned unto fables." (2 Timothy 4:3-4)

In condemning the departure from doctrine in his day, A.W. Tozer admonished in "The Importance of Sound Doctrine":

"It would be impossible to overemphasize the importance of sound doctrine in the life of a Christian . . . . [S]ound character does not grow out of unsound teaching . . . .

"It is the sacred task of all Christians, first as believers and then as teachers of religious beliefs, to be certain that these beliefs correspond exactly to truth. A precise agreement between belief and fact constitutes soundness in doctrine. We cannot afford to have less.

"The apostles not only taught truth but contended for its purity against any who would corrupt it . . . .

"While truth itself is unchanging, the minds of men are porous vessels out of which truth can leak and into which error may seep to dilute the truth they contain . . . .

"**Only in religious thought is faithfulness to truth looked upon as a fault**. When men deal with things earthly and temporal they demand truth; when they come to the consideration of things heavenly and eternal they hedge and hesitate as if truth either could not be discovered or didn't matter anyway . . . .

"The teacher of spiritual things only is required to be unsure in his beliefs, ambiguous in his remarks and tolerant of every religious opinion expressed by anyone, even by the man least qualified to hold an opinion . . . .

"These ['liberal churches'] will not quite give up the Bible, neither will they quite believe it; the result is an unclear body of beliefs more like a fog . . . where anything *may* be true but nothing may be trusted as being *certainly* true . . . .

"Certain of our evangelical brethren appear to be laboring under the impression that they are advanced thinkers . . . but so far are they from being advanced thinkers that they are merely timid followers of modernism—fifty years behind the parade.

"Little by little evangelical Christians these days are being brainwashed. One evidence is that increasing numbers of them are becoming ashamed to be found unequivocally on the side of truth. They say they believe but . . ."—A.W. Tozer (Bold added)[6]

There is nothing more fundamental to salvation than the Lordship of Jesus Christ (e.g., see Romans 10:9). And the Lordship of Jesus Christ is inseparable from His absolute *truth*. It is through believing and obeying the truth that Jesus Christ is truly our *Lord*.

The ***"many"*** who are obviously doing the works and following the 'modelship' of Jesus -- they ***"prophesied," "cast out devils,"*** and did ***"many wonderful works,"*** all in the name of Jesus -- will never be accepted by the Lord Jesus Christ because they didn't believe and obey *the truth* (see Matthew 7:21-27). To drop *the truth* of Jesus Christ is to drop *the Lordship* of Jesus Christ, lip service notwithstanding.

They say they believe, but they are allowing the faith and the Lordship of Jesus Christ to crumble away, even in their new "Bibles." One such example is Eugene Peterson's book, *The Message*, which is referred to as a "Bible" by its publisher and the masses and leaders in Christianity who have embraced it as God's Word. Yet his counterfeit *Message* only contains the word *Lord* (or *Lord's*) in a paltry 23 *verses* in its supposedly unchanged "New Testament"![7] To show the magnitude of this change, the New Testament in the King James Bible contains *632 verses* with *Lord* (670 if one also counts those with *lord*, many of which are also clearly referring to the Lord Jesus Christ).

Yet as galling as this change is, an even more significant and appalling change in this "fresh" so-called "Bible" is that *the following terms are in Peterson's changed "Message" ZERO times!*:[8]

- *Lord Jesus*
- *Lord Jesus Christ*
- *Christ Jesus my Lord*
- *Christ Jesus our Lord*
- *Christ Jesus the Lord*

- *Lord and Saviour Jesus Christ*
- *Jesus Christ our Lord*
- *Jesus Christ is Lord*

But this deletion will no doubt be viewed as trifling by those who have already replaced *Lord* with "model." *The Message: The Bible in <u>Contemporary Language</u>* is popular for a reason.

> *"Beloved, when I gave all diligence to write unto you of the common salvation, it was needful for me to write unto you, and exhort you that ye should <u>earnestly contend for the faith</u> which was once delivered unto the saints. <u>For there are certain men crept in unawares</u>, who were before of old ordained to this condemnation, ungodly men, turning the grace of our God into lasciviousness, and <u>denying</u> the only <u>Lord</u> God, and <u>our Lord Jesus Christ</u>." (Jude 1:3-4)*

Simply marketing a book as another "translated" or "paraphrased" version of God's Word does not mean that it actually is God's Word. With the Lordship of Jesus Christ absolutely indispensable to salvation, God would never delete the references to this from His true Word and then deceive people into believing that the only change made is that it has been rewritten in "contemporary language."

The truth is, today's Christianity claims that—along with "outdated" "preaching styles"—an "old-fashioned" Bible also prevents the world from hearing God's Word. So it has taken upon itself to repeatedly rewrite God's Word for Him into language that matches the world's itching ears.

Yet the *purity* of the Word is the issue, not how well it matches the people. God's Word and message and ways and worship and faith are all being conformed to the image of man. This is clearly *all about you*, or mankind, not the truth and purposes of the Lord God.

The Master Deceiver's Vision is coming to pass. The new has been built up underneath the old, leaving the old faith to crumble virtually without notice. It saves our Adversary a lot of war this way.

♦ Chapter Twenty-Two ♦

"A Radically Different Kind of Church" for "the New Age"

"A Whole New Species of Church Is Emerging"

*T*here is a "Christian" book that epitomizes the current path of the counterfeit Christianity, which is emerging as the old faith crumbles away. Although there are many such books published now, *Growing Spiritual Redwoods* by William Easum and Thomas Bandy[1] provides a clear illustration of the "new way of thinking," and has been acclaimed as "perhaps the best book about church transformation in this century."[2]

Bill Easum is "one of the pioneering pastors of the church growth movement," and is "one of the most highly respected church consultants and Christian futurists in North America."[3] Tom Bandy "consults with congregations for church growth and transformation," and "congregational and denominational leaders regard Tom as one of the leading thinkers and writers today."[4] The two joined forces to form Easum, Bandy and Associates, which consults "with churches of every size and culture" and links "countless" leaders through "one of the largest religious interactive websites in North America."[5]

In spite of the blatant (New Age) New Spirituality in their book, *Growing Spiritual Redwoods* has received high praises by men who are popular leaders themselves in today's Christianity. Rick Warren, Lyle Schaller, and Leonard Sweet—whose own books are self-evident that he has fallen for the (New Age) New Spirituality[6]—have given this book the following endorsements:

> "This may be the most significant study book for congregational leaders published in this century."—Lyle Schaller (*Growing Spiritual Redwoods* – GSR; front cover)

> "An epoch-marking—if not epoch-making—book. For a church living off of checks that reality won't cash, this book is like an acid bath accounting from

the bank examiners. There is no better audit of the collapse of the Christendom era, and no better audition for how to do ministry in the new world, than this one."—Leonard Sweet (*GSR*; back cover)

"***Every* passage of this book contains spiritual nuggets of *truth*** that can help your church to grow healthy and strong."—Rick Warren (*GSR*; back cover; emphasis added)

In addition to this glowing endorsement, after he wrote *The Purpose Driven Life*, *Growing Spiritual Redwoods* was given five stars in one of Rick Warren's Ministry Toolbox™ newsletters for 2003.[7] And on Easum and Bandy's website under, "What Christian leaders have to say about Tom Bandy," the following praise by Rick Warren is still posted (more praise by Leonard Sweet and also by Brian McLaren is included there as well):

"'I try to read *everything* Tom Bandy writes. He is *always* thought-provoking and helpful.'"—Rick Warren (Emphasis added)[8]

According to Tom Bandy, "a whole new species of church is emerging." This emerging church is "not a *machine*"—"preoccupied with theological purity, ideological correctness, and behavioral conformity"—but "an *organism*." This "organism" "worships differently, thinks differently, and depends on an entirely different kind of leadership."[9] This "new species of church" is the "Spiritual Redwood" growing in the midst of the diverse, cultural "forest" (*GSR*; p. 21).

"Some call it a 'permission-giving', 'seeker sensitive', 'mall', or 'mega' church, but it is in reality a 'Tree of Life' for the spiritually yearning public of the post-Christendom period . . . .

"They are churches designed *to grow in a riot of diversity*, rather than in repetitive sameness of polity or doctrine. They are designed *to grow in constant, creative chaos* . . ."—Thomas Bandy ("Growing Spiritual Redwoods (Summary)")[10]

"Just finding your way through the forest, in order to discover the Spiritual Redwoods, can be a challenging prospect. Yet church leaders and spiritual seekers are setting out as never before to explore new territory, and **grow a**

twenty-first-century version of the 'Body of Christ.' Before you even start, you need to equip yourself with a different map . . . .

"In *Sacred Cows Make Gourmet Burgers*, Bill [Easum] began to explore the 'coastline' of this new age by describing the 'quantum world.' It is a world of fluid processes and changing relationships, rather than fixed forms and enduring structures. In *Kicking Habits: Welcome Relief for Addicted Churches*, Tom [Bandy] began to explore the 'coastline' of this new age by describing systems of constant change, surrounded by energy fields of core visions, values, and beliefs. Together we have been further inspired by George Hunter's description of the new age as a 'pre-Christian' world of religious and cultural ferment, and deep and **diverse spiritual yearning**." (*GSR*; p. 22; bold added)

No doubt this would adamantly be denied, but Easum and Bandy's various descriptions of this "new age" have remarkable similarities to the New Spirituality of *the* New Age. The following pages of nuggets from their teachings in *Growing Spiritual Redwoods* speak clearly for themselves in this regard.

Their highly acclaimed book includes the following changes taking place "that are changing the map for Christians"—

♦ from "Ultimate Truths" to "Dialogical Truths;"
♦ from "Either-Or Choices" to "Both-And Choices;"
♦ from "Male vs. Female Genders" to "Unique Personhoods;"
♦ from "Formal Boundaries" to "Changing Patterns;"
♦ from "Religion" to "Spirituality;"
♦ from "Prophetic Confrontation" to "Visionary Direction;"
♦ from "Authoritative Voices" to "Spiritual Coaches;"
♦ from "Guardians of Truth" to "Motivators for Mission."
(*GSR*; pp. 23-24)

This new post-truth age has been embraced by those who welcome the demise of traditional Christianity. Their "changing patterns" have abandoned the "formal boundaries" of God's truth to explore man's "visionary direction" for attempting to unite *both* God *and* the broad way.

Although religion (theology/doctrine) divides, God and spirituality are viewed as universal and uniting. And this "spirituality" that people want to talk about in the emerging "new species of church" is no different than the "new religion" (faith) that the Angel of light and his fallen minions have been working toward:

> ". . . people do not want to talk about religion; *they do want to talk about spirituality!* . . . The religion 'Church Folks' want to discuss is a body of correct information and acceptable behavior with which they want others to agree and conform. The **'spirituality'** about which people want to talk is **an attitude or orientation to daily living**, and perspective from anyone is equally welcome." (GSR; p. 37; bold added)

> "**The new religion** is on the way, and it is one for which all previous religions have prepared us. It differs only in that it will no longer be distinguished by dogmas and doctrines, but it will be essentially **an attitude of mind, an orientation to life**, to man and to God. It will also be a living service . . . . Individualism and separatedness will disappear as that kingdom comes into being. The collective consciousness is its major expression and quality . . . . This is the challenge which today confronts the Christian Church. The need is for vision, wisdom and that wide tolerance which will see divinity on every hand and *recognize the Christ in every human being.*"—Alice Bailey (Emphasis added)[11]

> "They [Spiritual Redwoods] empower people . . . *to find their own incarnation of Jesus in the lives of people who have not yet experienced the gospel.*" (GSR; p. 209; emphasis added)

This inclusive New Spirituality/new religion has been further described by Neale Donald Walsch's "God":

> "[A]ll people do not hold the same religious beliefs. And, in fact, not all people even participate in religion or church, in any form.
>
> "Spirituality, on the other hand, is universal. All people participate in it. All people agree with it . . . .
>
> "This is because **'spirituality' is nothing more than life itself**, as it is . . . .
>
> "The only discussion left then is whether life and God are the same things. And I tell you, they are." (Emphasis added)[12]

This (New Age) New *Spirituality*, common to both the counterfeit kingdom and the emerging false church, is all-inclusive and presents Jesus as a way of relativism.

". . . culture itself, in *all* its complexities and nuances, can become *a vehicle for eternal truth.*" (*GSR*; pp. 199-200; emphasis added)

"***Anyone and anything*** can be a vehicle for the expression of God—but never contain the fullness of God. Therefore, the church recognizes that *God will simultaneously employ and shatter* . . . *all doctrines*, all ideologies . . . even within the church itself." (*GSR*; p. 36; emphasis added)

"Even the Term 'Christ' Carries Little Meaning"

*T*he broad way of relativism follows the universal, false "Jesus"/"Christ" of the counterfeit kingdom. The Lord Jesus Christ is too narrow and authoritative for the broad-minded many who prefer to believe and do what's right in their own eyes.

"Fewer and fewer people are interested in stories about 'the Creator God . . . Such a God is too distant . . . For Christians, this means the conversation must be about Jesus . . . .

"One might say that there is a resurgent interest in 'Christology' amid the cultural conversation about spirituality and personal change. However, institutional 'Church Folks' have difficulty perceiving it, understanding it, or participating in it, because **this conversation about Jesus has rejected the accumulated christological terminology of the institutional church. Indeed, *even the term 'Christ' carries little meaning.***" (*GSR*; p. 38; emphasis added)

"**The term 'Christ'** carries an enormous weight of complex dogma, and invites seekers into an arena of religious disagreement and institutional obligation that is (to them) frightening in its *irrelevance*. In the same way, terms like '**Lord**,' '**Messiah**,' '**King**,' '**Son of God**,' and even '**Savior**' have become so laden with underlying nuances that seekers are too nervous to consider them. The use of such terms requires a greater theological knowledge than most people possess, and a deeper commitment to institutional church tradition than most people want. **Such terms have become *relics of a Christendom that has passed away*.**" [!] (*GSR*; p. 39; parentheses in the original; emphasis added)

"*Every* passage of this book contains spiritual nuggets of *truth* that can help your church to grow *healthy* and strong."—Rick Warren (*GSR*; back cover; emphasis added)

First, although Easum and Bandy repeatedly claim that "the gospel" is all that really matters, they are clearly not referring to the Gospel of *Christ*! The Word of God, which is absolute truth not metaphor, repeatedly makes it clear how essential these so-called "relics" of "irrelevance" are (e.g., see 1 John 2:22-26; 5:5, 10-12; 2 Peter 2:20-22; John 3:18; Philippians 2:11; and Revelation 17:14; 19:11, 15-16).

"And we have seen and do testify that the Father sent <u>the Son</u> to be <u>the Saviour</u> of the world. Whosoever shall confess that Jesus is <u>the Son of God</u>, God dwelleth in him, and he in God." (1 John 4:14-15)

"But these are written, that ye might believe that Jesus is <u>the Christ, the Son of God</u>; and that believing ye might have life through his name." (John 20:31)

"That if thou shalt confess with thy mouth <u>the Lord</u> Jesus, and shalt believe in thine heart that God hath raised him from the dead, thou shalt be saved. . . . For whosoever shall call upon the name of <u>the Lord</u> shall be saved." (Romans 10:9, 13)

"If any man love not <u>the Lord</u> Jesus <u>Christ</u>, let him be Anathema Maranatha." (1 Corinthians 16:22)

". . . for if ye believe not that I am he, ye shall die in your sins." (John 8:24)

Along with these "relics" of a dead Christendom (!), Easum and Bandy write that the image of "The Ecclesiastical Christ and the Dream of a Doctrinally Consistent Christology" is "disappearing" (pp. 40, 41), and is even "tragic idolatry"!:

"**The Christ who would critique every individual's experience of the Holy**, and reign supreme over a consistent orthodoxy of public agreement, has been revealed to be *mere heritage* at best . . . and **tragic idolatry** at worst." (*GSR*; p. 42; ellipsis dots in the original; bold added)

They prefer to emphasize truth through *experience* rather than doctrine. In their discussion of the North Americans' "important discovery about Christian doctrine," they declare:

> "They do not understand it ['Christian doctrine']. They do not want to understand it. But most important—and here is the key discovery at the end of the twentieth century—***they do not need to understand it!*** . . .
>
> "**The equation between 'Truth' and 'Doctrinal Competence' has broken down**. 'Truth' for the twenty-first century is a power that changes the heart . . . .
>
> "It means that the experience of grace precedes the understanding of grace, and that integrity of interpretation is no longer measured by continuity with the historical record." (*GSR*; p. 41; bold added)

Easum and Bandy then move their discussion to the "disappearing" image of "The Magical Christ and the Dream of Eternal, Personal Safety," in which they unbelievably refer to the Saviour as a *"mere human neurosis"*!:

> "[T]he promise of **eternal, personal security *in heaven*** is also being greeted by growing public indifference . . . . Our relationships are everything . . . . The promise of personal, eternal security has become empty, so long as the relationships we cherish cannot be included . . . .
>
> "**The Christ who would guarantee personal security has been revealed to be a *mere human neurosis*.**" (*GSR*; pp. 42-43; bold added)

In their continued discussion, they distinguish these disappearing understandings of Christ from "authentic faith":

> "In the emerging pre-Christian era, these ['christological images'] have more to do with ideology and ecclesiology than authentic faith.

"The *real, authentic,* and *vibrant* conversation about the fullness of Christ is happening not inside the church, but beyond the church." (*GSR*; p. 43)

This "real, authentic" new conversation about Jesus for the new age is not to be about "historical trivialities" (p. 43) but, rather, is to be a new "Christological consensus" regarding Jesus. According to Bandy, "this conversation about Jesus is *the experiential glue that holds everything together*" in their "reorientation of Christological thinking" (emphasis added).[13] True faith is founded in God's absolute truth, not the vain imaginings and consensus of man's relativism.

Yet as has already been evidenced, today's "Christianity" emphasizes relationship over religion (doctrinal/theological beliefs). It prefers the false "gospel" of relativism and its universal "Jesus" who does not require faith in the truth to have a relationship with him:

> "It is becoming ever more clear that those churches emerging as 'Spiritual Redwoods' in the forest of North American culture emphasize Jesus, and one's relationship with Jesus, as the fundamental issue of faith and purposeful living. **At the same time, however, these churches celebrate enormous diversity of perspective about Jesus, and enormous variety in the manner in which people find themselves 'in relationship' with Jesus.**" (*GSR*; p. 50; bold added)

> "Jesus is 'the fullness of God' in purposeful and timely connection with *every* creature great or small . . . .

> "Churches that aspire to be Spiritual Redwoods are **centered on Jesus, and yet their roots are not entwined around a single rational explanation of the meaning of Jesus**. Their root systems *span many perspectives,* and draw sustenance from *many symbols* . . . . The Christology of the church is *more 'collage' than 'snapshot,'* because it continually points to a *mystery* beyond itself.

> "The extraordinary combination of the absolute centrality of Jesus, with **enormous variety of perspective about Jesus, makes the Spiritual Redwoods of *the new age* a radically different kind of church.**" (*GSR*; p. 51; emphasis added)

Obviously! This is because their preferred "Jesus" is the radically different "Jesus" of the New Age, which twists and deletes the true Gospel for the sake of all-inclusive unity.

"Finally, the Council of Chalcedon of A.D. 451 sought to end the intolerance and bickering by identifying **this single, essential truth**:

> "**that Jesus was at once both fully God and fully Human**, and that this unique paradox, irrational though it might be, is **the only essential mystery of faith necessary for salvation**.

"In a sense, the Council resolved conflict **about the person and work of Jesus** by declaring that **every perspective was both right and wrong**. The truth of Jesus could be described with many metaphors, and the benefits of relationship with Jesus could be experienced in many forms . . .

"**The cross and resurrection of Jesus do not necessarily imply any particular theory or explanation of atonement**, but simply guarantee that this central mystery of Jesus that *was* true, also *remains true for eternity*. Like the branch grafted onto the True Vine, **what is crucial is that an individual 'participate in' or 'be in relationship with' this mysterious Jesus**. Spiritual Redwoods of our pre-Christian era are not primarily an 'Easter People.' They are primarily a 'Christmas People'!

"This mystery, this paradox, is all that really matters. **Everything else is metaphor**. Everything else is valuable perspective, but always discussable, **debatable, and changeable**. This paradox of incarnation is **the thread of continuity between all representations of Jesus** . . . for it is the mystery that lies behind life itself." (*GSR*; pp. 52-53; bold added)

"*Every* passage of this book contains spiritual nuggets of *truth* that can help your church to grow *healthy* and strong."—Rick Warren (*GSR*; back cover; emphasis added)

First, *to throw out the Crucifixion and Resurrection as "debatable" and "changeable" "metaphor" throws out the Gospel of Christ as "debatable" and "changeable" "metaphor"!* This changes the Gospel of absolute truth into a false gospel of relativism. But this does explain why the cross and resurrection are rarely mentioned anymore when "the gospel" or "altar calls" are given today. A relativistic "relationship" is the new message.

> **"For the preaching of the cross is to them that perish foolishness; but unto us which are saved it is the power of God . . . . For after that in the wisdom of God the world by wisdom knew not God, it pleased God by the foolishness of preaching to save them that believe . . . . But we preach Christ crucified . . ."** *(1 Corinthians 1:18, 21, 23; see also Romans 10:8-9)*

Second, *there is no thread of continuity that validates all representations of "Jesus"!* Jesus is *the truth,* not *relativism!*

> **"Jesus Christ the same yesterday, and today, and for ever. Be not carried about with divers and strange doctrines . . . ."** *(Hebrews 13:8-9)*

Third, even the (New Age) New Spirituality believes that its own false "Jesus" was both fully God and fully human; it teaches this about *every* person! To claim this is the *only* belief necessary for salvation is to deny the Gospel of Jesus Christ and declares everyone saved who idolatrously believes in *any* false "Jesus." Changing the Gospel of Christ to be more inclusive inevitably leads to changing "the Body of Christ" in the same way.

> "[C]hurch leaders and spiritual seekers are setting out as never before to explore new territory, and grow *a twenty-first-century version of the 'Body of Christ.'* Before you even start, you need to equip yourself with a different map." *(GSR; p. 22; emphasis added)*

> "That Body of Christ which grows in your immediate environment may not resemble *in any detail* the Body of Christ which grows in Bill's environment, or in Tom's environment." *(GSR; p. 110; emphasis added)*

> "Spiritual Redwoods do *not* gather the 'family' of God, but rather *the 'peoples' of God.* The Body of Christ is made up of *many, many parts." (GSR;* p. 69; emphasis added)

"The Point of Interfaith Conversation Is Not to Decide Which Religious Propositions Are Right or Wrong"

*A*s the truth of *the* faith is allowed to crumble away, today's counterfeit "Christianity" continues to further unveil the relativistic New Spirituality of the universal religion as its new foundation. Unlike the truth, this foundation allows, and even encourages, the pursuit of interfaith unity.

After sharing an illustration of Bandy's "religious tolerance" toward Islam, they declare:

> "It is an illustration of **profound interfaith conversation that is in fact encouraged** by the central paradox of Christian faith celebrated by Spiritual Redwoods of the new era.
>
> "Only the mysterious paradox of incarnation is essential to Christian faith. All else is metaphor . . . . The mystery of incarnation inspires a veritable riot of definition, description, and perspective. It proves to be **a celebration of diversity** in the cultural forest of our times.
>
> "The same mystery that is the thread of continuity between experience and description, also guides the Spiritual Redwood to **avoid dogmatism, intolerance, and religious bigotry** . . . .
>
> "The paradox of Jesus as fully God and fully Human is an authentic paradox . . . . Such a paradox invites diversity—indeed, welcomes diversity!—both within and beyond the church . . . .
>
> "**[R]elationship with Jesus is experiential**. The experience of the transforming power of God precedes any rational statement of faith, and acceptance of some stated dogma does not function as a gate through which one must pass to gain access to that grace. Relationship with Jesus is a matter not of intellectual conversion and agreement with correct propositional statements, but of personal transformation and evidence of a change in behavior. Wherever personal transformation occurs, in whatever form and in whatever context, there is an opportunity to discern Jesus. **Therefore, the point of interfaith conversation is not to decide which religious propositions are right or wrong, but to**

build connections between one's own experience of the divine and the experiences of others." (GSR; pp. 54-55; bold added)

The emerging counterfeit church clearly prefers the relativism of the broad way over the absolute truth of the narrow way. The scriptural illiteracy among professing Christians is at a dangerous level.

God's Word makes the essentiality of "conversion" clear (e.g., see Acts 3:19). It even details the character of those who don't want to be converted:

"For this people's heart is waxed gross, and their ears are dull of hearing, and their eyes they have closed; lest at any time they should see with their eyes, and hear with their ears, and should understand with their heart, and should be <u>converted</u>, and I should heal them." (Matthew 13:15)

God's Word also makes it clear that *faith precedes* God's transforming power and grace; it is *not* the other way around:

"And what is <u>the exceeding greatness of his power to us-ward who believe</u>, according to the working of his mighty power." (Ephesians 1:19)

"Therefore being justified by faith, we have peace with God through our Lord Jesus Christ: By whom also we have access <u>by faith</u> into this grace wherein we stand, and rejoice in hope of the glory of God." (Romans 5:1-2)

God's transforming power is ours through the power of the Holy Spirit indwelling *believers* of the Lord Jesus Christ. Personal transformation or behavioral change that occurs before faith cannot be taken as evidence in itself of a relationship with Jesus.

Despite all the teachings and warnings in God's Holy Scriptures, scriptural illiteracy continues.

"**One does not take direction from Jesus**, but one walks with Jesus into the unknown. **One does not learn from Jesus**, but one grows in Jesus in unexpected ways. Such humility shuns self-righteousness and confrontation . . ." (GSR; p. 55; emphasis added)

"Spiritual Redwoods of our pre-Christian era can **avoid religious bigotry, and build positive interfaith conversation**, by relying on the central paradox of

Jesus. As long as the absolute centrality of Jesus for the church *is a paradox*, opportunity for dialogue and mutual respect abounds. Only when the centrality of Jesus for the church ceases to be a paradox, becoming instead a complex, but ultimately **understandable certainty, will the specter of religious bigotry become harsh reality** . . . .

"Religion that is founded on dogmatic certainties and reasonable propositions works only when culture is broadly homogeneous. When the forest breaks in upon civilization, and culture becomes a tapestry of race, lifestyle, and perspective, consensus over creeds and catechisms becomes impossible—and **undesirable!** . . .

"These vain attempts to police the spiritual lives and theological reflections of others represent **the last gasp of Christendom**. The global village is not homogeneous . . . .

"Spiritual Redwoods seeking to represent Jesus in the pre-Christian era . . . must not ask: *How can this church educate the public about Christ?* This suggests that the church possesses an understandable truth, to which others can and should be persuaded to give assent . . . Such a mission invites religious bigotry. Instead, Spiritual Redwoods ask: *How can this church live in relationship with Jesus?* This celebrates the fact that the church acknowledges **a central mystery, which others can and may already experience**, the sign of which is renewed hope and personal transformation." (*GSR*; pp. 56-57; bold added)

    First, being unwilling to "take direction from Jesus" supports their contention that *Lord* is a "relic" of "irrelevance." Second, they contend here that *representing Jesus <u>excludes</u> educating people about Christ!* In other words, obedience to the Lord's command to preach the Gospel *of Christ* is to them an unwanted mission that "invites religious bigotry" because it suggests possession of "an understandable truth"! Itching ears have turned everything upside down.
    To deny the *certainty* of God's Word is to deny that it is the Word of *God* and *the truth*. This denial is the opposite of faith and cannot lead to God.

> *"This I say therefore, and testify in the Lord, that ye henceforth walk not as other Gentiles walk, in the vanity of their mind, <u>having the understanding darkened</u>, being alienated from the life of God through the ignorance that*

is in them, <u>because of the blindness of their heart</u>." (Ephesians 4:17-18; see also Daniel 9:13)

"Through thy precepts I get <u>understanding</u>: therefore I hate every false way." (Psalm 119:104)

"And we know that the Son of God is come, and <u>hath given us an understanding, that we may know him</u> that is true, and we are in him that is true, even in his Son Jesus Christ. This is the true God, and eternal life." (1 John 5:20)

"Have not I written to thee excellent things in counsels and knowledge, that I might make thee <u>know the certainty of the words of truth</u>; that thou mightest <u>answer the words of truth</u> to them that send unto thee?" (Proverbs 22:20-21; see also Luke 1:1-4)

Nevertheless, instead of answering the words of truth to people:

"They ['Spiritual Redwoods'] focus all their energies to respond to **the spiritual yearnings of the public**: . . .

"to be free, rather than to be rooted;
"to be mentored, rather than to be lectured;
"to be **vindicated**, rather than to be corrected;
"to be destined, **rather than to be saved**." (GSR; pp. 57-58; emphasis added)

"And yet Christendom is dead." (GSR; p. 64)

Its demise is no wonder, given that the understandable certainty of God's Word has been thrown out to cater to the truth-rejecting world that seeks interfaith unity. God warns in his Word that in the last days rebellious mankind will avidly pursue learning, but they will be:

"Ever learning, and never able to come to the knowledge of the truth." (2 Timothy 3:7)

"Salvation is far from the wicked: for they seek not <u>thy</u> statutes." (Psalm 119:155)

"The Most Important Factor Is Vision!"

*M*an prefers to seek his own vision rather than the knowledge of God and His Word. Consequently, believing and doing what is right in *God's* eyes have been replaced with believing and doing what is right in *man's* eyes.

> "The vision speaks to the heart, rather than to the mind . . . .
>
> "**The vision is *true north for the soul*.** It is a permanent, intuitive compass direction for a human being. Every person inevitably strays from the path. Life is an endless experiment and course correction. **The vision brings one back to the true path.**" (*GSR*; p. 117; bold added)
>
> "The most important factor is *vision!*" (*GSR*; p. 101)

The vision that man prefers deliberately changes the truth of God into a new 'reality'—a "paradigm shift":

> "Unfortunately, *the church will wither away* in the 21st century unless we make three paradigm shifts that *abandon the past*, and embrace the future. A 'paradigm' is like a filter or lens with which you sort out or focus the realities of God and world. **A 'paradigm shift' happens when you change the filter or lens to sort out the realities of God and world *differently*.**"—Thomas Bandy (Emphasis added)[14]

In this changed way of thinking, calling for *repentance* is seen as an "*attack.*" Thus, according to Bandy, the church "must surrender the old paradigm," which he criticizes as follows:

- "society is assumed to be a godless morass"
- "only God can do something about it"
- "self-sacrifice and the *penitent* response of absolute *obedience to divine will* is their only hope"
- "the whole mission of the church is to **attack society with the prophetic call to repent**" (Emphasis added)[15]

According to Bandy, this "old paradigm" is to be replaced with "the paradigm of the 21st century," which he praises as follows:

- "society is not assumed to be a godless, materialistic morass"
- society is "literally seething with the passionate desire for reunion with God"
- "the spiritual response will no longer be obedience to dogmatic and ideologic agendas, but searching and self-discovery"
- "the context of meaning will no longer be a mix of dogma . . . but the world itself permeated by God"
- "the mission of the church **will no longer be to issue calls to repentance, but to proclaim visions of unity** and meaning so rich that they can never be contained in a single symbol"
- "visionary, motivating leadership . . . will proclaim persuasively and dramatically from the 'watchtower' *the vision* that awaits its time"
- "it will not try to set people straight, but let God set people straight, and accept the resulting diversity"
- "Pastor Bob in the 21st century will be spending most of his time proclaiming the vision, sharing the vision, and building ownership for the vision"
- "he's spending all his time among the unchurched, learning new futures for the vision" (Emphasis added)[16]

> "'I try to read *everything* Tom Bandy writes. He is *always* thought-provoking and *helpful*.'"—Rick Warren (Emphasis added)[17]

Remember, in the new paradigm, *the vision* "is true north for the soul" and "brings one back to the true path." According to their chosen vision, this makes relativism "true north" and "the true path." Relativism enables the cultural forest to change the rules of determining Who God is and what His Holy Scriptures say so that it can maintain its chosen course on the broad way. The forest prefers to "find its own way" rather than "learn from Jesus."

> "The 'forest' is a metaphor for culture, the public, or people and the environments and yearnings in which they live. This 'forest' is incredibly diverse, and growing more diverse every minute. **All the rules of the 'forest' are changing** . . . and they are completely different from the supposed 'civilization' of the twentieth-century institutional church." (*GSR*; p. 21; ellipsis dots in the original; emphasis added)

> "**The standards of scriptural interpretation, faith, and behavior** can no longer be established by an institution demanding obedience; they can only

be discerned and owned by the creatures of the forest themselves." (*GSR*; p. 85; emphasis added)

". . . every branch, twig, or leaf, and every root, vine, or tendril, is free to find **its own way**." (*GSR*; p. 145; emphasis added)

"Life only thrives when people **take risks and celebrate mysteries!** Life only thrives when churches **embrace change** and are willing to let go of control and allow that which is newly born to **find its own way!**" (*GSR*; p. 194; emphasis added)

"Spiritual midwives [visionaries, synthesizers, and motivators] . . . are not afraid to get out of the way of new life, because they are convinced that **the fullness of truth** lies ever beyond themselves . . . .

"The spiritual midwife cannot know, and will not control, the future of the mystery that has been born." (*GSR*; p. 186; emphasis added)

"**Each cell is free to discover God, interpret scriptures, define doctrines, and develop ideas as they wish** . . . . They are free to . . . participate in *any* experience that helps them . . . deepen their faith." (*GSR*; pp. 148-149; emphasis added)

"Any profound experience of faith must include:

"a. An experience of the Holy that questions, deepens, changes, and enriches . . . . It needs to . . . open one to mystery . . . . and **allow one to interpret for oneself who this God is** . . ." (*GSR*; p. 150; bold added)

"*Every* passage of this book contains spiritual nuggets of *truth* that can help your church to grow *healthy* and strong."—Rick Warren (*GSR*; back cover; emphasis added)

"[S]eekers of the pre-Christian twenty-first century . . . *seek direct connections with God*. These direct connections may be established through *passive meditation* or active social service, through private self-discovery or intimate sharing and corporate celebration. *However* the connection is made, the immediate **experience** of God **authenticates** religious **experience** by making it highly individual, spontaneous, and creative." (*GSR*; pp. 174-175; emphasis added)

First, nowhere in the Holy Scriptures are we told to "connect" with God. This is a pagan concept rooted in panentheism (i.e., "God is in everything") and attempted through contemplative spirituality. Incidentally, Easum and Bandy refer to the "contemplative movement" as one of "the great spiritual movements" (*GSR*; p. 196).

Second, when the Word of God is thrown out, each person is left to decide for himself who his god is based on his subjective interpretation of his subjective experience. This is the epitome of mankind's rebellious pride.

". . . behold, ye walk every one after the imagination of his evil heart, that they may not hearken unto me." (Jeremiah 16:12)

Neither our subjective experiences nor our imaginings determine Who God is. The true God is not relative. No matter how many have joined the "Flat Earth Society," the earth never has been and never will be flat. Likewise, God always is Who He is regardless of people's beliefs and experiences. No one can recreate God into Who they prefer Him to be. Those who try are thereby removing themselves from the true God to worship a god of their own making.

Despite their statements regarding the authority of the Bible, relativism continues to be the foundation of this emerging "new species of church." Under "Core Beliefs" Easum and Bandy reiterate:

"Spiritual Redwoods allow *enormous* scope for individual interpretations of *doctrine*, contextual perspectives in *theology*, and personal definitions of *faith* . . . .

"In the end, it is not propositional agreement or dogmatic assent that binds the organism together, but the continuing touch of The Holy that is closely linked to their *experience* of the core *vision*." (*GSR*; pp. 120-121; emphasis added)

Subjective *experience* is so crucial to the emerging false church that it is relied on for ultimate acceptance by God, even with these experiences being "irrational" and "positively bizarre!":

"Not only is the immediate experience of God often unexpected; it may well be positively bizarre! The unusual, the different, the odd, the abnormal, the irrational, and the bizarre all emerge powerfully in the pre-Christian era." (GSR; p. 196)

"The continuous possibility of 'being wrong' that is revealed in radical humility, is countered with a profound trust in the immediate *experience* of God. That trust is *not a certainty about being right*, but a confidence about being ultimately accepted by God *even when wrong*." (GSR; p. 198; emphasis added)

First, denying the truth of God's Word is rebellious *pride*, not "radical humility." Second, regardless of what a person's experiences tell them about "who this God is," anyone who does not have the true *doctrine of Christ* does not have God and therefore has no chance of "being ultimately accepted by God" (e.g., see 2 John 1:9; 1 John 5:10-12; and John 14:6).

This reliance on one's own subjectivity is the inevitable result when *Lord, Christ,* and *Saviour* are rejected as "relics" of "irrelevance." Trusting in one's subjective interpretations of experiences that "may well be positively bizarre" is as foolish as trusting the "lifeblood" of a local church filled with pagans, etcetera, to prevent one's spiritual life from ceasing to exist! But if people don't want to be "rooted" in Christ Jesus the Lord (see Colossians 2:6-7) or to even be "saved," then it most likely wouldn't matter to them if their experience of "the Holy" is a counterfeit that leaves them with nothing more than mystery.

Contrasting the "Essence" of "Machines" and "Spiritual Redwoods," Easum and Bandy approvingly acknowledge the following changes in the emerging false church:

- "Historical creeds" have been changed to "Compass Orientation."
- "Obedience to unintelligible deity" has been changed to "Celebration of mysterious love."
- "Fear of either-or judgment" has been changed to "Confidence in unity of acceptance and justice." (GSR; pp. 141-142)

They continue with:

"Ecclesiastical machines leave a community legacy of religious competition . . . and *an adversarial struggle between the sacred and the secular* . . . .

"Ye shall know them by their fruits . . . ." (*GSR*; p. 143; final ellipsis dots in the original; emphasis added)

We shall indeed.

"The distinctions between the 'sacred' and the 'secular' have disappeared." (*GSR*; p. 177; emphasis added)

"*Narrow*-mindedness and mediocrity are systematically eliminated." (*GSR*; p. 149; emphasis added)

"We have set ourselves on a path of continuous learning to sensitively partner with *Christian leaders in other cultures, traditions, and disciplines* so that together we can walk in the way of Christ . . . . and we want to help you give birth to the divine potential that is *already within you*."—Easum & Bandy's website (Emphasis added)[18]

"Have you ever felt as if you were standing at the edge of a wide, deep canyon that seemed too wide to leap across . . . but a still, small voice within you said, '*Go for it!*'? You feel a primal urge to jump. Yet you hesitate, because it's a long way across and a long way down . . . .

"There must be something bigger, broader, wider, higher, and deeper in faith and ministry than what you are currently experiencing.

"You know it's time to take the leap! . . .

"You are standing at the edge of your future." (*GSR*; pp. 210-212; spaced ellipsis dots in the original)

It isn't the voice of God that is being heeded by the many. The narrow way of the Lord Jesus Christ is too narrow for the broad-minded many who seek Oneness. Consequently, the counterfeit kingdom is growing as more and more people who are lured by the Angel of light's vision take the leap of departure from the faith and land on his broad way.

"As one emerges into the clearing . . . one marvels that **the redwood has integrated all the diversity of the forest into a single great purpose** . . . .

"This is more than a tree. This is an event in which *every* creature and organism has been granted asylum in the midst of the forest, and is fed, nurtured, and transformed. One cannot help being challenged and empowered.

"This is a Tree of Life . . . .

"You are in the midst of **a great purpose, a giant synthesis** . . . What does it matter if you fall? There are many branches beneath ready to catch you. The Redwood itself is an assurance that change . . . constant change . . . is good . . . . **You are living a vision!**" (*GSR*; pp. 205-206; spaced ellipsis dots in the original; emphasis added)

"They ['church leaders'] have been captured by a new . . . and an ancient . . . vision of the *Tree of Life*." (*GSR*; p. 209; ellipsis dots in the original)

The inclusive values and vision of the Angel of light's counterfeit kingdom have become the boss.

"**Synthesis dictates the trend** of all the evolutionary processes today; all is working towards larger unified blocs, . . . brotherhood, . . . interdependence, **fellowship of faiths**, movements based upon the welfare of humanity as a whole, and ideological concepts which deal with wholes and which militate against division, separation and isolation . . . .

"It is **the sense of synthesis**, putting it very simply, which will be the goal of all the educational movements, once **the New Age idealism** is firmly established."—Alice Bailey & Djwhal Khul (Emphasis added)[19]

"[T]he vision is a vision of group work, of group relationships, of group objectives, and **of the group fusion to the larger Whole**."—Alice Bailey & Djwhal Khul (Emphasis added)[20]

"... **we vision a new and vital world religion**, a universal faith, at-one in its basic idealism with the past but different in its mode of expression."—Alice Bailey & Djwhal Khul (Emphasis added)[21]

"Today men's minds are recognizing the dawn of freedom; **they are realizing that every man should be free to worship God in his own way** .... His own God-illumined mind will search for truth and **he will interpret it for himself**. The day of theology is over ...

"Men have gone far today in the rejection of dogmas and doctrine and this is good and right and encouraging."—Alice Bailey & Djwhal Khul (Emphasis added)[22]

"Either Everything Is Worship—or Nothing Is Worship"

"Her priests have violated my law, and have profaned mine holy things: <u>they have put no difference between the holy and profane</u>, neither have they shewed difference between the unclean and the clean . . . <u>and I am profaned among them</u>." (Ezekiel 22:26)

*W*hen the world is allowed to interpret for itself who its god is, it naturally follows that it be allowed to use *any* method it chooses in "worship." This relativism is all about man, and lines up with the false gospel, "we are all one." *This* is the message being spread through the mission and methods of the emerging counterfeit "Christianity":

"**The message of God is clear.** No matter what the **religion**, no matter what the **culture**, no matter what the **spiritual** or **indigenous tradition**, the bottom line is identical: **We are all one.**"—Neale Donald Walsch (Emphasis added)[23]

"**[W]orship must be indigenous**. The gospel must be communicated in the language, **cultural forms**, and technology of the people you are trying to reach." (*GSR*; p. 66; bold added)

"Worship for Spiritual Redwoods designs multiple options of worship to **target the tastes, lifestyles, and *diverse spiritual* needs of the public.**"—Thomas Bandy ("Growing Spiritual Redwoods (Summary);" emphasis added)[24]

True to this Oneness gospel of the (New Age) New Spirituality, Easum and Bandy *want* indigenous worship to break down the theological barriers between religions:

> "Either **everything** is worship—or nothing is worship . . . .
>
> "*Indigenous music is essential.*" (GSR; p. 94; bold added)
>
> "Indigenous worship breaks down stereotypes of *theological*, ideological, and denominational perspective . . . .
>
> "Perhaps the most unexpected *benefit* of indigenous worship, however, is the door of communication that has opened between Spiritual Redwoods and the *religious pluralism of the forest.* **Strip away the *religious competitiveness*,** aesthetic snobbery, and unthinking stereotyping **that surrounds *worship*** at the end of the Christendom era, and you will find new friendships and shared ideals." (GSR; p. 103; emphasis added)
>
> "These first hesitant steps toward **indigenous worship** aimed at thanksgiving for transformation had . . . *forged a new and continuing conversation between two distant faiths,* and **brought Christians and Muslims together in prayer** for the first time in this community . . . .
>
> "*Indigenous worship can be a gateway* into unexpected partnerships . . . . Who knows where these new conversations will lead? One day God will lead us poor humans to *a truer harmony of which our indigenous worship is only a sign.*" (GSR; pp. 104-105; emphasis added)

Replacing unity in *the faith* with interfaith unity is intensifying, as man's word continues to replace God's Word as the preferred source of "truth." In fact, the emerging counterfeit "Christianity" has so transformed its thinking, it even blatantly opposes the truth in its drive for Oneness with the world.

> "*In the worship of Christendom, what mattered was correct information.* People reaffirmed the doctrinally pure or politically correct truths authorized by the denomination." (GSR; p. 63)

"Spiritual Redwoods cannot be grown from the traditional, informational worship of Christendom." (*GSR*; p. 65)

"The worship focus that is increasingly *irrelevant* . . . communicates huge amounts of *theological information* . . . Such services include:

- traditional hymns with abstract theological words . . .
- historical or denominational creeds . . .
- expository preaching designed to provide correct information
- designated children's messages repeating correct information in simpler language . . ." (*GSR*; pp. 79-80; emphasis added)

"*Worship designers target peoples . . . not principles.* Their goal is not to gather all people within a practical expression of systematic theology, but to convey specific facets of a larger mystery to specific human needs. They are wholly pragmatic. **Worship does not need to be proper. It needs to work.**" (*GSR*; p. 68; ellipsis dots in the original; emphasis added)

"Civilized religion has been replaced by the noise of the jungle . . . . **The spoken word has been replaced** by interactive drama . . . . The nice, **reverent**, orderly, down-home, intergenerational, and carefully contained *presentation* of the Holy has been replaced by an unsettling, **irreverent**, unpredictable, out-of-this-world, cross-cultural, and barely contained *experience* of the Holy." (*GSR*; p. 69; bold added)

In this upside-down world, it is the "spiritual giants" who "create an environment of change" and "devote themselves to experiencing God through indigenous worship" (*GSR*; p. 17). These so-called "spiritual giants" have deliberately replaced doctrine, theology, the spoken word, and the reverent in their preference for secular lyrics and MTV behavior in their "worship":

"The music is often secular because this generation does not distinguish secular from religious . . . .

"Kids the world over know Michael Jackson and can sing his songs." (*GSR*; p. 75)

"... melody will be more important than lyrics." (*GSR*; p. 78)

"*The worshipers will choose the music* . . . **It is Pentecost! Each person hears his or her choice of music.**" [!] (*GSR*; p. 91; bold added)

"(*The best way to determine if your worship is on the experiential track is to videotape your worship service and play it on a VCR side-by-side with a television tuned to MTV. The more similarity there is, the more likely it is that your worship is able to share the gospel with people*, especially those born after 1965. Next, count the number of times there is complete silence in your worship for more than five seconds. More than one or two such occurrences mean that the service is not indigenous.)" [!] (*GSR*; p. 96; emphasis added)

I did not make this up! They even provided a clarification:

"*Worship designers use the cultural forms of the people. No single musical taste, dress code, behavioral standard, lifestyle, or sense of propriety is elevated above any other. Use the music to which people really listen, dress the way they dress, dance the way they dance, accept who they are, and **do purposely what they already do naturally**.*" (*GSR*; p. 67; emphasis added)

In addition, they even declare that "establishing an indigenous worship service is one of the most important decisions a church can make" (*GSR*; p. 97), and "the only excuse" churches have that do not want "to attempt indigenous worship is that they just do not want to reach emerging generations and subcultures with the gospel" (*GSR*; p. 102)!

No, it's because heaven and its saving true Gospel are preferred over hell and its damning false gospels, and being led by and walking after the Spirit are preferred over walking after the flesh and following "visionaries" who have changed the truth of God into a lie!

'Shining' the darkness of the world's ways—and of MTV no less (!)—on the Gospel does not enlighten anyone's darkness or get anyone to unplug their ears from hearing the truth **"lest his deeds should be reproved"** (see John 3:20 and also 1 Corinthians 2:14). Regardless of what supposedly does or does not "work" in mankind's "whole new way of thinking," we are to shine the light of the Gospel on the world's ways, not the other way around!

> "We must have a new reformation. There must come a violent break with that irresponsible, amusement-mad, paganized pseudo-religion which passes today for the faith of Christ and which is being spread all over the world by unspiritual men employing unscriptural methods to achieve their ends."—A.W. Tozer[25]

The wolves are not only prowling around the flock, they have infiltrated the flock in sheep's clothing, as God's Holy Scriptures warned they would (e.g., see Matthew 7:15 and Acts 20:29-30). The consequences of Christianity's "whole new way of thinking and acting" are that people are no longer able to tell the difference between the wolves and the sheep of God, let alone discern the unscriptural and harmful aspects of their teachings.

Growing Spiritual Redwoods is steeped in the teachings of the universal religion and its counterfeits (e.g., "One Truth," "One God," and "One Church"). Given that Rick Warren's Purpose-Driven Paradigm is following the same path, his glowing endorsements are to be expected:

> "*Every* passage of this book contains spiritual nuggets of *truth* that can help your church to grow *healthy* and strong."—Rick Warren (GSR; back cover; emphasis added)

> "'I try to read *everything* Tom Bandy writes. He is *always* thought-provoking and *helpful*.'"—Rick Warren (Emphasis added)[26]

The Angel of light's minions have made it clear that his "Plan is synthesis . . . fusion . . . unity and at-one-ment,"[27] and today's "Christianity" is becoming increasingly cooperative:

> "The Redwood may be described as one great, dynamic 'synergy' of life. It is the combined or cooperative action of multiple cells that together increase one another's effectiveness. It is a whole that is greater than the sum of all its parts, because as a dynamic unity it gives birth to new life." (GSR; p. 173)

> "If the Spiritual Redwood is a synergy of life, then leaders who are spiritual giants must be 'synergists' who build synergies for life.

"... spiritual giants who could envision radically new futures, **synthesize extraordinarily different cultures and ideas** . . ." (*GSR*; p. 176; emphasis added)

"Spiritual Redwoods are a different species of church. They are leaving behind . . . the legacies of Christendom, and **creating a fresh synthesis to meet the needs of a new age**." (*GSR*; p. 209; emphasis added)

The gathering of the many into ONE continues. As mentioned earlier, the counterfeit kingdom's Plan also includes the "selection process." It intends to reject, attack, and purge from the planet all so-called "cancer cells" who refuse to become "at-one" with the global community. Far too reminiscent of these New Age goals is the following:

"The machine in the forest is an intrusion. It does not belong. It is irrelevant. The forest relentlessly **attacks and rejects them, like foreign bacteria in a living organism**." (*GSR*; p. 108; emphasis added)

"'Evangelism' to these machines means only *assimilating the raw material of spiritual seekers into our homogeneous practice and perspective*. Culture beyond the church remains an enemy . . .

"Spiritual Redwoods, emerging to flourish in our pre-Christian era, have a completely different inclination. They are not machines. They are **organisms at one with community**." (*GSR*; p. 127; bold added)

In its drive for Oneness, today's emerging counterfeit "Christianity" is embracing the (New Age) New Spirituality of the broad way.

◆ Part 8 ◆
"Take Heed Therefore That the Light Which Is in Thee Be Not Darkness"
(Luke 11:35)

♦ *Chapter Twenty-Three* ♦

Ripe for the Harvest

Unity at All Costs

The universal religion with its spiritual transformation is not coming; it is here. Its false gospel that "we are all one" is being embraced by today's Christianity with open arms. Yes, *change* is the order of the day:

> "The mission of the church will no longer be to issue calls to repentance, but to proclaim visions of unity and meaning so rich that they can never be contained in a single symbol."[1]

There are those who believe that interfaith unity is fine as long as they don't agree with their beliefs. Guilt by association? Yes! The issue is not merely whether we agree with the beliefs of those we unite with but that God clearly sets forth limits for fellowship (associations) throughout His Holy Scriptures.

When we disregard God's Word and do instead what's right in our own eyes, we are *guilty* of sin. Regardless of what the world's logic says, associating (joining together and uniting) with whom or what God tells us to separate (disassociate) from and not fellowship with is direct disobedience to God. This is *guilty* by association rather than *holy* by separation.

"Association" is also defined as "an organization of persons having common . . . purposes."[2] Guilt by association is even more grievous when the association is with organizations and religions (faiths) that are blatant enemies of God and whose common purpose is to destroy everything of God in this world.

Not only is guilty association sinful disobedience, but it is also a lack of discernment. Discernment is the ability to recognize that which is separate and different; therefore, it is also the opposite of Oneness. But in pursuit of this Oneness, even professing Christians are viewing division between "sacred and secular" as "heresy."[3] This actually turns *discernment* into "heresy" in the upside-down new way of thinking.

According to (un)common sense and the dictionaries, "sacred" and "secular" are *opposites*. The unity of opposites is thoroughly based in occult philosophy and opposes God's Word from beginning to end. The Holy Spirit warned that people would choose **"doctrines of devils"** over the faith in the latter days (see 1 Timothy 4:1).

Christian author Craig Hawkins has given a definition of witchcraft in which much of his description actually fits the emerging new "Christianity." His definition has been approvingly posted by a "Dianic Witch" in a Pagan Network forum:

> "Witch. Individual who practices or concurs with the views or experiences of witchcraft. Most witches view **divinity as immanent** in nature, **seeing all life as sacred, thus denying any sacred/secular distinction** . . . .
>
> "Witchcraft. (Also known as wicca, the craft, or the craft of the wise.) An antidogmatic, antiauthoritarian, diverse, decentralized, eclectic, experience-based, nature-oriented religious movement whose followers are polytheists and/or pantheists, and/or panentheists . . ." (Emphasis added)[4]

The underlying purpose in removing the division between sacred and secular is the elimination of all separation, leaving Oneness and relativism. These apostasies are all burgeoning in today's bewitched Christianity through books, music, videos, curricula, worship "styles," spiritual formation and its various mystical prayer practices, contemplative retreats, seminars, conferences, interfaith and intercultural unity, unity in transcendent purpose, and so on and so forth, ad nauseam, ad infinitum.

Christians weren't willing enough, and are now no longer able, to stop itching ears from turning Christianity upside down. Truth becomes the sacrifice when:

- *absolutism* is out, and *relativism* is in;
- *obedience* is out, and *pragmatism* is in;
- *black and white* is out, and *gray* is in;
- *teaching* is out, and *dialogue* is in;
- *thus saith the Lord* is out, and *consensus of opinion* is in;
- *using Scripture to judge right and wrong* is out, and *unity with tolerance at all costs* is in;
- *the faith* is out, and *interfaith unity* is in;
- *the narrow way* is out, and *the broad way* is in.

This is not "for the global glory of God"!

"(For many walk, of whom I have told you often, and now tell you even weeping, that they are the enemies of the cross of Christ: whose end is destruction, whose God is their belly, and whose glory is in their shame, who mind earthly things.)" (Philippians 3:18-19)

"It is time for thee, Lord, to work: for they have made void thy law." (Psalm 119:126)

There is a high cost to preferring man's inclusive, relative word over God's exclusive, absolute Word.

"Hath a nation changed their gods, which are yet no gods? but my people have changed their glory for that which doth not profit. Be astonished, O ye heavens, at this, and be horribly afraid, be ye very desolate, saith the Lord. For my people have committed two evils; they have forsaken me the fountain of living waters, and hewed them out cisterns, broken cisterns, that can hold no water." (Jeremiah 2:11-13)

The tidal wave of relativism sweeping throughout today's sleeping Christianity is leaving widespread spiritual destruction in its wake. As mentioned in the Note to the Reader, warning people in the path of a destructive tidal wave is done by urgently proclaiming the truth, not by offering sugar-coated affirmations designed to help people feel good in their error. The spiritual battle is intensifying as the end draws near, and evil spiritual powers are coming out of the woodwork seeking whom they may devour.

In his book *The Light That Was Dark: From the New Age to Amazing Grace*, Warren Smith wrote:

> "[T]he New Age movement has expanded its reach into almost every aspect of society—including the evangelical Church. Unfortunately, most Christian leaders have not been watchful, and as a result the Church is in the process of being greatly deceived. In my 2004 book, *Deceived on Purpose*, I wrote: . . .
>
>> "Over the last decade, as New Age teachings exploded in popularity, church leaders suddenly became very quiet about the New Age. Perhaps distracted by church growth concerns and tracking what they considered to be the latest 'moves of God,' church leaders seemed to be missing the latest moves of our spiritual Adversary . . . .

"Mysticism and spiritual experience are taking precedence over biblical discernment and truth. **The mystery of iniquity is masquerading as the mystery of godliness, while the Church is being methodically transitioned into the New Age**. A personal saving relationship with the true Jesus Christ is giving way to 'another Jesus,' 'another gospel,' and 'another spirit.' Sadly, hardly anyone seems to notice or care.

"**Today, our spiritual Adversary is purposefully tempting everyone in the world and in the Church to *change* with the times and to accept his *fresh* new approach to spirituality and divinity** . . . . He is promising *world peace* to those who are willing to *enlarge* their beliefs enough to accept the bottom-line teaching of his New Spirituality—that *we are all one* because God is *in* everyone and everything.

"The professing Christian Church does not seem to understand how it is walking right into this most ingeniously contrived spiritual trap. Placing its faith in men and mass movements rather than in properly translated and rightly divided Scripture, the Church is starting to adopt some of *the very same* teachings I renounced when I left the New Age . . . .

"When the New Age teachings of the New Spirituality present themselves as a 'fresh' new approach to traditional biblical Christianity, stand fast against them . . . .

"The Lord Jesus Christ warned that great deception in the world and in the Church would precede His return. Those days are definitely here. Beware of the mystical, New Age teachings that are starting to characterize today's emerging Church. Beware of the New Spirituality that is knocking at your door.

"Beware of the light that is dark." (Bold added)[5]

The final signs and lying wonders that will complete the deception of falling for the counterfeit "Christ" have not even begun, yet professing Christians are already falling for the deception. Christians in their predilection for the world's relativism will soon find out that the emperor has no clothes; no armor that is.

"Finally, my brethren, be strong in the Lord, and in the power of his might. Put on the whole armour of God, that ye may be able to stand against the

> *wiles of the devil. For we wrestle not against flesh and blood, but against principalities, against powers, against the rulers of the darkness of this world, against spiritual wickedness in high places. <u>Wherefore take unto you the whole armour of God, that ye may be able to withstand in the evil day, and having done all, to stand</u>. Stand therefore, having your loins girt about with <u>truth</u>, and having on the breastplate of <u>righteousness</u>; and your feet shod with the preparation of <u>the gospel of peace</u>; above all, taking the shield of <u>faith</u>, wherewith ye shall be able to quench all the fiery darts of the wicked. And take the helmet of <u>salvation</u>, and the sword of the Spirit, which is <u>the word of God</u>: praying always with all prayer and supplication in the Spirit, and watching thereunto with all perseverance and supplication for all saints." (Ephesians 6:10-18)*

The many prophetic details and warnings the Lord Jesus Christ has given throughout His Holy Scriptures clearly indicate that time is running out. But when people are convinced that God is using and blessing something, they aren't interested in hearing "negative" warnings from God's Word that don't cater to ears that are positively itching. It is not possible to obey Scripture's repeated admonishments to *watch* while covering one's eyes and ears to the "negative." This is willful ignorance and leads to easy deception.

> "For myself, I long ago decided that I would rather know the truth than be happy in ignorance. If I cannot have both truth and happiness, give me truth. We'll have a long time to be happy in heaven."—A.W. Tozer[6]

Christianity, a once vocal mouthpiece for God's absolute truth and obstacle to the completion of Satan's Plan, is no longer much of a light to the world nor a threat to his Plan's materialization. Basically, all that's left to finalize the Master Deceiver's Plan is for his counterfeit "Christ" to be revealed in his Antichrist. He, along with the False Prophet, will complete the interfaith unity of all who refuse to abide on the narrow way. Today's Christianity is ripe for his harvest.

> *"Ye are the salt of the earth: but if the salt have lost his savour, wherewith shall it be salted? it is thenceforth good for nothing, but to be cast out, and to be trodden under foot of men." (Matthew 5:13)*

Chapter Twenty-Four

The Coming of the Universal "Christ" for the Many Who Are ONE vs The Coming of the Lord Jesus Christ for the Few Who Are His

The Ultimate "Man of Peace"

*I*n spite of man's efforts to "fulfill the Great Commission," deception is going to wax worse and worse (see 2 Timothy 3:13) until God ultimately tops it off. Those who are not deceived at first but continue to reject God's absolute truth are going to be given strong delusion by God Himself so that they will believe a lie and will have no more opportunity to repent.

> *"I also will choose their delusions, and will bring their fears upon them; because when I called, none did answer; when I spake, they did not hear: but they did evil before mine eyes, and chose that in which I delighted not."* (Isaiah 66:4)

> *"And then shall that Wicked be revealed, whom the Lord shall consume with the spirit of his mouth, and shall destroy with the brightness of his coming: Even him, whose coming is after the working of Satan with all power and signs and lying wonders, and with all deceivableness of unrighteousness in them that perish; because they received not the love of the truth, that they might be saved. And for this cause God shall send them strong delusion, that they should believe a lie: That they all might be damned who believed not the truth, but had pleasure in unrighteousness."* (2 Thessalonians 2:8-12)

The people who will become deluded when the Antichrist comes are those who prefer their **"pleasure in unrighteousness"** over believing the truth. People will reap what they sow. It is not a coincidence that God's Word mentions the Antichrist in this passage of *either* loving the world and its things *or* doing God's will:

> *"Love not the world, neither the things that are in the world. If any man love the world, the love of the Father is not in him. For all that is in the world, the lust of the flesh, and the lust of the eyes, and the pride of life, is not of the Father, but is of the world. And the world passeth away, and the lust thereof: but he that doeth the will of God abideth for ever. Little children, it is the last time: and as ye have heard that antichrist shall come, even now are there many antichrists; whereby we know that it is the last time." (I John 2:15-18)*

Scripture gives many warnings about the coming of this Antichrist. Following the example of Satan he will oppose and exalt himself above the Lord God in his attempt to **"be like the most High"** (see Isaiah 14:12-14; and also Revelation 13:5-6 and Daniel 7:25.)

> *"Now we beseech you, brethren, by the coming of our Lord Jesus Christ, and by our gathering together unto him, that ye be not soon shaken in mind, or be troubled, neither by spirit, nor by word, nor by letter as from us, as that the day of Christ is at hand. Let no man deceive you by any means: for that day shall not come, except there come a falling away first, <u>and that man of sin be revealed, the son of perdition; who opposeth and exalteth himself above all that is called God, or that is worshipped; so that he as God sitteth in the temple of God, shewing himself that he is God.</u>" (2 Thessalonians 2:1-4)*

> *"And the king shall do according to his will; and <u>he shall exalt himself, and magnify himself above every god, and shall speak marvellous things against the God of gods</u>, and shall prosper till the indignation be accomplished: for that that is determined shall be done. Neither shall he regard the God of his fathers, nor the desire of women, nor regard any god: <u>for he shall magnify himself above all.</u>" (Daniel 11:36-37)*

Our Adversary's counterfeit kingdom will become a Beast government that **"shall devour the whole earth, and shall tread it down, and break it in pieces"** (Daniel 7:23). Its two Beast world leaders (the Antichrist and False Prophet) will be given the power **"over all kindreds, and tongues, and nations"** and **"to make** *war with the saints, and to overcome them"* (Revelation 13:7). They will *"cause that as many as would not worship the image of the beast should be killed,"* and will cause *"all, both small and great, rich and poor, free and bond, to receive a mark in their right hand, or in their foreheads: and that no man might buy or sell, save he that had the mark, or the name of the beast, or the number of his name"* (Revelation 13:15-17).

Although all who follow the Antichrist will be allowed to continue to live and buy and sell and succeed in this world, there is an eternal cost.

> *"And the third angel followed them, saying with a loud voice, If any man worship the beast and his image, and receive his mark in his forehead, or in his hand, the same shall drink of the wine of the wrath of God, which is poured out without mixture into the cup of his indignation; and he shall be tormented with fire and brimstone in the presence of the holy angels, and in the presence of the Lamb: and the smoke of their torment ascendeth up for ever and ever: and they have no rest day nor night, who worship the beast and his image, and whosoever receiveth the mark of his name." (Revelation 14:9-11)*

Ultimately, Satan's Plan for a global government is not at all about politics. It's spiritual, it's personal, and it's where today's seduced world and Christianity are being driven by our devouring Adversary. He knows just the bait to use in enticing the world into his spiritual trap -- world peace. Global government, global economy, and global religion: through the lure of false *peace* he shall hook and *destroy many*.

> *"And in the latter time of their kingdom, <u>when the transgressors are come to the full</u>, a king of fierce countenance, and understanding dark sentences, shall stand up. And his power shall be mighty, but not by his own power: and <u>he shall destroy wonderfully</u>, and shall prosper, and practise, and shall destroy the mighty and the holy people. And through his policy also he shall cause craft to prosper in his hand; and he shall magnify himself in his heart, <u>and by peace shall destroy many</u>: he shall also stand up against the Prince of princes; but he shall be broken without hand." (Daniel 8:23-25)*

As mentioned earlier, the Antichrist's kingdom will initially appear wonderful and as peace and not as the destruction it actually is. "Churched" and "unchurched" alike will be in wonder of this ultimate "man of peace" who will embody the universal "Christ" and his seemingly "Christian" ideals.

The Universal "Christ" and "World Teacher"

The Angel of light's counterfeit "Christ" is already followed by the bewitched world. He prefers Mystery to the certainty of God's Word. He is the cosmic "Christ" behind the principles and practices of the (New Age) New Spirituality, the Ancient Wisdom, and Eastern Enlightenment, including the "Christ Principle" and "Christ consciousness." He is the "World Teacher" of every religion:

> "The work and the teaching of the Christ will be hard for the Christian world to accept, though easier of assimilation in the East. Nevertheless, some hard blow or some difficult presentation of the truth is badly needed if the Christian world is to be awakened, and if Christian people are to recognize their place within a worldwide divine revelation and **see Christ as representing all the faiths and taking His rightful place as World Teacher. He is the *World* Teacher and not a Christian teacher . . . . They may not call Him Christ, but they have their own name for Him and follow Him** as truly and faithfully as their Western brethren."—Alice Bailey & Djwhal Khul (Bold added)[1]

This universal "Christ" accepts people from all religions (faiths) regardless of who they believe he is. His counterfeit kingdom is founded on relationships and works, so beliefs and the true doctrine of Christ are irrelevant. His kingdom is already "gather[ing] into its ranks all men of peace and good will, without interfering with their specific loyalties . . . who - belonging as they do to every world religion . . . - are free from the spirit of hatred and separativeness."[2]

The Angel of light's workers have summed up man's required preparation for the coming universal "Christ" in a "prayer." This prayer is also a song that is especially popular in Religious Science and Unity churches.

> "Where there is this unification of purpose, this uniformity of spiritual intention and of realized demand, then there is only one thing which can arrest His reappearance and that is the failure of mankind to prepare the world stage for that stupendous event . . . to familiarize the people everywhere with the idea of His coming, and bring about *the required measure of peace on earth - a peace based upon right relations* . . . .

> "The little prayer which says, 'Lord God Almighty! **Let there be peace on earth and let it begin with me,' sums up all the requirements for those who seek to work in preparation for the coming of the Christ** . . . and the preparation *required* is that of working, with strength and understanding, to *bring about right human relations* - a broader objective."—Alice Bailey & Djwhal Khul (Emphasis added)[3]

The so-called "hatred" and "separativeness" of the Lord Jesus Christ's exclusive narrow way will not be tolerated in this kingdom in which manmade "peace on earth" is the order of the day. True peace on earth begins and ends in *God*—specifically in the Lord Jesus Christ—not *man*. Yet this prayer is being widely circulated now in diverse circles oblivious to its broad ramifications. It even closed Rick Warren's article titled "A PLAN FOR PEACE," in the December 2005 issue of *Ladies' Home Journal* (discussed earlier in chapter 13):

> "'God blesses those who work for peace for they will be called the children of God.' Do you remember the song that begins with 'Let there be peace on earth'? Let it begin with me."—Rick Warren[4]

His statement here was made in an article that is devoid of the Gospel of Christ and is all about his global P.E.A.C.E. Plan. This greatly twists and gives an entirely different meaning to the words of the Lord Jesus Christ Who said, **"Blessed are the peacemakers: for they shall be called the children of God"** (Matthew 5:9). Given how hard Rick Warren is trying to get everyone in any religion to *work together for peace*, the obvious implication is that those who work for peace in his P.E.A.C.E. Plan will be called the children of God.

Yet this statement of the Lord Jesus Christ's is not at all about working for peace according to the world's definition, and especially not manmade peace through interfaith unity. Nor is this work the means to becoming children of God (salvation)! On the contrary, only those who believe in the Lord Jesus Christ are saved and have become the children of God because through faith they have *made peace with God*.

> *"For ye are all the children of God by faith in Christ Jesus." (Galatians 3:26)*

> *"Who <u>by him</u> do believe in God, that raised him up from the dead, and gave him glory; that your faith and hope might be in God." (I Peter 1:21)*

> *"Therefore being justified by faith, we have peace with God through our Lord Jesus Christ." (Romans 5:1)*

Nevertheless, Christians today are increasingly gravitating toward the universal "Christ's" feel-good message of unity and brotherhood -- that all are children of God regardless of what religion (faith) they are in.

> "When the Christ reappears, the non-essentials will surely disappear . . . That new world religion *must* be based upon those truths which have . . . brought assurance and comfort to men everywhere . . . .
>
> "The second truth to which all give allegiance - no matter what the faith - is that of **man's essential relationship to God** . . . . **'We are all the children of God'** . . ."—Alice Bailey & Djwhal Khul (Bold added)[5]

In the counterfeit kingdom of this universal "Christ," relationship transcends "non-essential" religious (doctrinal/theological) barriers. The different religions (faiths) are just another path to a relationship with God or Christ in its popular "new world religion."

> "The Christ Who will return will not be like the Christ Who (apparently) departed. He will not be a 'man of sorrows' . . .
>
> "He has been for two thousand years the supreme Head of the Church Invisible, the Spiritual Hierarchy, composed of **disciples of all faiths**. He recognizes and loves **those who are not Christian but who retain their allegiance to Their Founders - the Buddha, Mohammed and others**. *He cares not what the faith is if the objective is love of God and of humanity.* If men look for the Christ Who left His disciples centuries ago, they will fail to recognize the Christ Who is in process of returning. **The Christ has no religious barriers in His consciousness.** *It matters not to Him of what faith a man may call himself.*"—Alice Bailey & Djwhal Khul (Parentheses in the original; emphasis added)[6]

> "I happen to know people who are **followers of Christ in other religions**."
> —Rick Warren (Emphasis added)[7]

> "He ['the Christ'] inaugurated the new era and . . . **the new world religion began to take form.** *The word 'religion' concerns relationship*, and the era of right human relations and of a right relation to the Kingdom of God began."—Alice Bailey & Djwhal Khul (Emphasis added)[8]

> "I have known **many people who believe in the Messiah of Jesus, regardless of what religion they are**, because they believe in him. *It's about a relationship, not a religion.*"—Rick Warren (Emphasis added)[9]

> "**You may be Catholic or Protestant or Buddhist or Baptist or Muslim or Mormon or Jewish or Jain,** or you have no religion at all. I'm not interested in your religious background. Because God did not create the universe for us to have religion. He came for us to have a relationship with him."—Rick Warren (Emphasis added)[10]

As time grows shorter, the inclusive values of the interfaith "Christ" and his "new world religion" are being widely embraced. These values are ultimately inclusive of all except true fundamentalism, which is his kingdom's big enemy.

"And it Was Given unto Him to Make War with the Saints, and to Overcome Them"

> "The major effect of His ['Christ's'] appearance will surely be to demonstrate in every land the effects of *a spirit of inclusiveness* - an inclusiveness which will be channeled or expressed through Him. All who seek right human relations will be gathered automatically to Him, whether they are in one of the great world religions or not; all who see no true or basic difference between religion and religion or between man and man or nation and nation will rally around Him; **those who embody the spirit of exclusiveness and separativeness will stand automatically and equally revealed** and all men will know them for what they are. **The cleaving sword of the spirit** will - without wounding - bring revelation and indicate the first needed step towards human regeneration."—Alice Bailey & Djwhal Khul (Bold added)[11]

Completely opposite to "without wounding," this false "Christ" is going to brutally judge all true believers in the Lord Jesus Christ who stand separate from a world united in its rebellion against God's absolute truth and the Lordship of Jesus Christ. Yet it is far better to be viewed as the presumed "enemies" of man than to become actual enemies of God.

> "[T]he expressed aims and efforts of the United Nations will be eventually brought to fruition and a new church of God, gathered out of all religions and spiritual groups, **will untidily bring to an end the great heresy of separateness.**"—Alice Bailey & Djwhal Khul (Emphasis added)[12]

> "You will now understand the meaning of the words used by so many of you in the second of the Great Invocations:

> *"The hour of service of the saving force has arrived.*

> "This 'saving force' is the energy which science has released into the world for the destruction, first of all, of those who continue (if they do) to defy the Forces of Light working through the United Nations. Then - as time goes on - this liberated energy will usher in the new civilization, the new and better world and the finer, more spiritual conditions."—Alice Bailey & Djwhal Khul (Parentheses in the original)[13]

> "**[T]he Hierarchy took its stand upon the side of the United Nations and let it be known that it had done so**. In doing this, definite physical steps were taken to aid the Forces of Light; men and leaders were carefully chosen and picked disciples were placed in positions of power and of authority. The leaders of the United Nations and of their armies . . . are able thus to work - consciously or unconsciously - under the inspiration of the Hierarchy. This has been amply demonstrated. **On account of this decision of the Hierarchy, Christ became automatically the Leader of these Forces** . . . .

> "**[A]nd the simple-minded are apt to forget that the Christ said, 'He that is not with me is against me.'**"—Alice Bailey & Djwhal Khul (Emphasis added)[14]

> "'Let light and love and power **and death** fulfil the purpose of the Coming One.'"—Alice Bailey & Djwhal Khul (Emphasis added)[15]

This evil, counterfeit "Christ" has been referred to befittingly as "the christ of Satan."[16]

"... Woe to the inhabiters of the earth and of the sea! for the devil is come down unto you, having great wrath, because he knoweth that he hath but a short time. And when the dragon saw that he was cast unto the earth, he persecuted the woman which brought forth the man child .... And the dragon was wroth with the woman, and went <u>to make war with the remnant of her seed, which keep the commandments of God, and have the testimony of Jesus Christ</u>." *(Revelation 12:12-13, 17)*

"And I stood upon the sand of the sea, and saw a beast rise up out of the sea, having seven heads and ten horns, and upon his horns ten crowns, and upon his heads the name of blasphemy .... and <u>the dragon gave him his power, and his seat, and great authority</u>. And I saw one of his heads as it were wounded to death; and his deadly wound was healed: <u>and all the world wondered after the beast. And they worshipped the dragon which gave power unto the beast: and they worshipped the beast</u>, saying, Who is like unto the beast? who is able to make war with him? And there was given unto him a mouth speaking great things and blasphemies; and power was given unto him to continue forty and two months. And he opened his mouth in blasphemy against God, to blaspheme his name, and his tabernacle, and them that dwell in heaven. <u>And it was given unto him to make war with the saints, and to overcome them</u>: and power was given him over all kindreds, and tongues, and nations. And all that dwell upon the earth shall worship him, whose names are not written in the book of life of the Lamb slain from the foundation of the world. If any man have an ear, let him hear." *(Revelation 13:1-9)*

In the past, people were told to renounce the Lord Jesus Christ if they wanted to live. Like everything else, the coming persecution will be completely upside down. It will try to deceive people into thinking they have already renounced or don't really believe in the Lord Jesus Christ if they don't go along with the counterfeit kingdom's Oneness and world service. This deception will be very great in its attempts to frighten true believers into thinking they really aren't believers. It is essential that we grow in the wisdom and knowledge of the Holy Scriptures, which are a major part of the armor of God.

"Wherefore come out from among them, and <u>be ye separate, saith the Lord</u>, and touch not the unclean thing; <u>and I will receive you, and will be a Father</u>

<u>unto you</u>, *and ye shall be my sons and daughters, saith the Lord Almighty."*
(2 Corinthians 6:17-18)

"Peace I leave with you, <u>my peace I give unto you: not as the world giveth</u>, give I unto you. Let not your heart be troubled, neither let it be afraid."
(John 14:27)

"For <u>he</u> is our peace . . ." (Ephesians 2:14)

"Confirming the souls of the disciples, and exhorting them to continue in the faith, and that <u>we must through much tribulation enter into the kingdom of God</u>." (Acts 14:22)

"The night is far spent, the day is at hand: let us therefore <u>cast off</u> the works of darkness, and let us put on the armour of light." (Romans 13:12)

"And fear not them which kill the body, but are not able to kill the soul: but rather fear him which is able to destroy both soul and body in hell." (Matthew 10:28)

*"<u>And wisdom and knowledge shall be the stability of thy times</u>, and strength of salvation: the fear of the L*ORD *is his treasure." (Isaiah 33:6)*

Yet today's unprepared, sleeping Christianity has de-emphasized growing in the true knowledge of God and His Word. It has chosen to deliberately keep its eyes tightly closed for fear its gaze may behold something "negative" that may distract it from its path of unity and purpose.

"Be sober, be vigilant; because your adversary the devil, as a roaring lion, walketh about, seeking whom he may devour." (1 Peter 5:8)

"How, Where or When He Will Come Is None of Our Concern"

"If men look for the Christ Who left His disciples centuries ago, they will fail to recognize the Christ Who is in process of returning."—Alice Bailey & Djwhal Khul[17]

$\mathcal{F}$or reasons that should be obvious, the Master Deceiver wants people to focus on works at the expense of the knowledge of God's Word. And since prophecy is so important and takes up so much of God's Word, he also prefers that people ignore the details of Christ's return as "none of our concern." This way they will more easily fall for his coming false "Christ" and get on board with his kingdom of World Servers.

> "One thing it is most necessary to have in mind. It is *not* for us to set the date for the appearing of the Christ or to expect any spectacular aid or curious phenomena. If our work is rightly done, He will come at the set and appointed time. **How, where or when He will come is none of our concern**. Our work is to do our utmost and on as large a scale as possible to bring about right human relations, for **His coming depends upon our work**."—Alice Bailey & Djwhal Khul (Bold added)[18]

Similarly, Rick Warren would also have us believe that Christ's return depends on our work, therefore our work is to be our focus. He even would have us believe that it is the true Jesus Who said, "The details of my return are *none of your business*"!:

> "**God's timetable for history's conclusion is connected to the completion of our commission.** Today there's a growing interest in the second coming of Christ and the end of the world. When will it happen? Just before Jesus ascended to heaven the disciples asked him this same question, and his response was quite revealing. He said, '*It is not for you to know the times or dates the Father has set by his own authority. But you will receive power when the Holy Spirit comes on you; and you will be my witnesses in Jerusalem, and in all Judea and Samaria, and to the ends of the earth.*' [endnote: Acts 1:7-8 (NIV)]
>
> "When the disciples wanted to talk about prophecy, Jesus quickly switched the conversation to evangelism. He wanted them to concentrate on their mission in the world. He said in essence, '**The details of my return are none of your business**. What *is* your business is the mission I've given you. Focus on that!'" (*PDL*; p. 285; bold added)

Contrary to Rick Warren's word, the Lord Jesus Christ never said or implied any such thing and gave His disciples and us the *plethora* of prophetic details in *His* Word for a reason. In addition, the disciples did not ask the Lord Jesus Christ "this same question" regarding His return and the end of the world in this passage of Scripture. The answer He gave them in Acts 1:7-8 was to their question, **"Lord, wilt thou at this time restore again the kingdom to Israel?"** (Acts 1:6).

When the disciples actually did ask Him, **"Tell us, when shall these things be? and what shall be the sign of thy coming, and of the end of the world?"** (Matthew 24:3), the Lord Jesus Christ's response was *not* the reprehensible and deceptive claims by Rick Warren. Rather, His clear response was, **"<u>Take heed that no man deceive you</u>. For many shall come in my name, saying, I am Christ; and shall deceive many"** (Matthew 24:4-5). He then followed this with *numerous* prophetic details.

No, we do not know the exact day or hour. But the Lord Jesus Christ has given us an abundance of prophetic details in His Holy Scriptures so that we can avoid deception and not fall for the false "Christs" and false prophets and other deceptions rampant today (e.g., see Matthew 24, Mark 13, Luke 17:20-37, and Luke 21). The Lord Jesus Christ even told His disciples:

> *"<u>Behold, I have told you before</u>. Wherefore if they shall say unto you, Behold, he is in the desert; go not forth: behold, he is in the secret chambers; believe it not. For as the lightning cometh out of the east, and shineth even unto the west; so shall also the coming of the Son of man be." (Matthew 24:25-27)*

> *"<u>And take heed to yourselves</u>, lest at any time your hearts be overcharged with surfeiting, and drunkenness, and cares of this life, and so <u>that day come upon you unawares. For as a snare shall it come</u> on all them that dwell on the face of the whole earth. <u>Watch ye therefore</u>, and pray always, that ye may be accounted worthy to escape all these things that shall come to pass, and to stand before the Son of man." (Luke 21:34-36)*

Even the very passage of Acts 1 that Rick Warren twisted in his previous quote gives *indispensable* prophetic details of the Lord Jesus Christ's return. Right after He ascended into the clouds, the disciples were told by two men in white apparel:

> *". . . Ye men of Galilee, why stand ye gazing up into heaven? <u>this same Jesus</u>, which is taken up from you into heaven, <u>shall so come in like manner</u> as ye have seen him go into heaven." (Acts 1:11)*

Their words reiterated the prophetic details and warnings the Lord Jesus Christ had already given regarding His return. It is not possible to obey the Lord Jesus

Christ's warning to **"take heed"** that no man deceive us regarding His return if the details of His return are "none of [our] business"! This claim in itself is deceitful regarding His return.

The *exact same* Lord Jesus Christ is returning **"in the clouds"** to gather His faithful true believers to meet Him **"in the air"**:

> *"For this we say unto you by the word of the Lord, that we which are alive and remain unto the coming of the Lord shall not prevent them which are asleep. For the Lord himself shall <u>descend from heaven</u> with a shout, with the voice of the archangel, and with the trump of God: and the dead in Christ shall rise first: then we which are alive and remain shall be caught up together with them <u>in the clouds</u>, to meet the Lord <u>in the air</u>: and so shall we ever be with the Lord." (1 Thessalonians 4:15-17)*

On the other hand, it is an unbelieving world in awe of its universal "Christ" that will assemble to welcome its new leader when he appears *on the earth* (e.g., see Revelation 13:3-9). The difference in location is one of the very things the Lord Jesus Christ was warning about in the plethora of prophetic details He has given. Any "Jesus" or "Christ" who appears on this earth before the Day of the Lord judgment is a counterfeit (e.g., see also Acts 3:20-21).

> *"For our conversation is in <u>heaven; from whence also we look for the Saviour, the Lord Jesus Christ</u>: Who shall change our vile body, that it may be fashioned like unto his glorious body, according to the working whereby he is able even to subdue all things unto himself." (Philippians 3:20-21)*

Thankfully, the Lord Jesus Christ's return from heaven does *not depend* on the work or mission of mankind. If God's timetable for His return had to wait for Christians to be faithful enough to finish His work and bring in His Kingdom, we would never see history's conclusion! Contrary to unscriptural Kingdom Dominion teachings,[19] God Himself will establish His Kingdom on earth, and His timetable has already been set in *His own power* and cannot be manipulated or hindered by mankind.

Besides, as mentioned earlier, the falling away from the faith at the end will be so great that the Lord Jesus Christ asks us to consider whether He will actually find faith on the earth when He returns (see Luke 18:8). Given the following, it's no wonder the Lord Jesus Christ asked this!:

- *Christians* are trading in *the* truth of *the* faith for the interfaith unity of the "One Truth," the "One God," and the "One Church."
- *Christians* are trading in the Gospel of Christ for the false gospel of Oneness that says all religions (faiths) are equally valid paths to a relationship with God.
- *Christians* are trading in the Lord Jesus Christ, the Rock of Offence and Stumblingstone, for the universal "Christ" who accepts people in any religion.
- *Christians* are trading in the narrow way for the broad way.

Quite the contrary to "the complete evangelization of the planet," the Angel of light's Vision is being fulfilled. It is later than we think.

> **"Now the Spirit speaketh expressly, that in the latter times some <u>shall depart from the faith</u>, giving heed to seducing spirits, and doctrines of devils." (1 Timothy 4:1)**

Incidentally, there are those who think that prophecy is irrelevant because they also don't believe we will be here to be subjected to the deceptions, etcetera. Aside from the fact that none of *God's* Word is irrelevant, regardless of whether one believes the Lord Jesus Christ is coming back before or after the Antichrist is revealed, He is not coming for anyone who has turned away from loving and obeying the truth.

> *"Whosoever transgresseth, and <u>abideth not in the doctrine of Christ</u>, hath not God . . . ." (2 John 1:9)*

> *"Whosoever therefore shall be ashamed of me <u>and of my words</u> in this adulterous and sinful generation; of him also shall the Son of man be ashamed, when he cometh in the glory of his Father with the holy angels." (Mark 8:38)*

Two Paths, Two Christs, Two Kingdoms, Two Eternities

The Lord Jesus Christ is *the one and only Christ*, the Creator of the universe, the Lord from heaven, God manifest in the flesh, the Saviour of the world. *Christ* is a *Person*, not a "Principle" or "consciousness," and can no more be separated from the true Lord Jesus Christ than Jehovah can be separated from the true God.

There is absolutely no comparison whatsoever between the Lord Jesus Christ Who is light and the universal false "Christ" who is darkness.

- The Lord Jesus Christ is the truth, not relativism.
- The universal "Christ" is relativism, not the truth.

- The Lord Jesus Christ's narrow way is the Kingdom of God.
- The universal "Christ's" broad way is the kingdom of the god of this world, the Angel of light.

- The Lord Jesus Christ's narrow way leads to eternal life.
- The universal "Christ's" broad way leads to eternal destruction.

- The Lord Jesus Christ's narrow way is the way of *the faith*, as set forth in His Holy Scriptures.
- The universal "Christ's" broad way is the way of works in any faith.

- The Lord Jesus Christ's narrow way is the way of repentance and forsaking the world's ways and thoughts.
- The universal "Christ's" broad way is the way of preserving and conforming to the world's ways and thoughts.

- The Lord Jesus Christ's narrow way is the way of believing.
- The universal "Christ's" broad way is the journey of becoming through doing.

- The Lord Jesus Christ unites through faith in the eternal Word of truth.
- The universal "Christ" unites through spiritual experience, purpose, vision, and mystery apart from the truth.

- The Lord Jesus Christ is coming for the few separated from the broad way.
- The universal "Christ" is coming for the many united on the broad way.

- The Lord Jesus Christ is coming for those who are *in* Him by faith and being born again of the Holy Spirit.
- The universal "Christ" is coming for those who have relativistically "centered" around Jesus apart from scriptural doctrine.

- The Lord Jesus Christ is coming for those who yield their lives and selves to Him as *Lord*.
- The universal "Christ" is coming for those who pattern their lives and works after Jesus but do not follow Him as *Lord*.

- The Lord Jesus Christ is coming for those who have an eternal relationship with God on the narrow way.
- The universal "Christ" is coming for those who have a temporal, *seeming* relationship with God on the broad way.

- The Lord Jesus Christ is coming for His faithful believers in true *Christ*ianity who abide in *His* doctrine of *the* faith.
- The universal "Christ" is coming for his followers in the New Spirituality who abide in their own doctrine of any faith (religion).

- The Lord Jesus Christ is coming for the few who are His.
- The universal "Christ" is coming for the many who are ONE.

Which one is coming for you?

♦ *Chapter Twenty-Five* ♦

People of Faith vs People of the Faith

Mindlessly Following the Crowd

One thing Rick Warren has said that should be heeded is:

"People without conviction often mindlessly follow the crowd."[1]

Yes they do, to their own detriment. People would be far better served to heed God's Holy Scriptures rather than to mindlessly follow what the many approve.

> *"Enter ye in at the strait gate: for wide is the gate, and <u>broad</u> is the way, that leadeth to <u>destruction</u>, and <u>many</u> there be which go in thereat: Because strait is the gate, and <u>narrow</u> is the way, which leadeth unto <u>life</u>, and <u>few</u> there be that find it." (Matthew 7:13-14)*

> *"There is a way that seemeth right unto a man, but the end thereof are the ways of death." (Proverbs 16:25 & 14:12)*

The masses are following leaders who are imitating the serpent's subtilty in the Garden of Eden. The serpent enticed Eve to rethink what God had said and meant. She heeded his words and then noticed that contrary to what God had said about needing to abstain from the delicacies of the tree, it was actually **"good for food,"** **"pleasant to the eyes,"** and **"to be desired to make one wise"** (see Genesis 2:17 and 3:1-7).

Now, in essence, the crafty leaders are saying these same things about the delicacies of the world: "Yea, hath God said, **'Be ye separate,'** and, **'Whosoever therefore will be a friend of the world is the enemy of God?'** Look, rather, how unity with the world is *good for food* for the poor. And it is *pleasant to the eyes*: the ways of the world 'work' because they are fun and entertaining and hold people's attention longer, thereby increasing numbers and income. This allows so much more to be accomplished for God. And humbly learning from the world and its different perspectives and religious faiths is *to be desired to make us wise* and better able to accomplish our goals of reaching the world for Jesus."

It used to be that faithfulness to God turned the world upside down (e.g., see Acts 17:6). Now faithfulness to the world is turning Christianity upside down. We are to walk worthy of God, not worthy of the world!

> *"I hearkened and heard, but they spake not aright: no man repented him of his wickedness, saying, What have I done? every one turned to his course, as the horse rusheth into the battle. Yea, the stork in the heaven knoweth her appointed times; and the turtle and the crane and the swallow observe the time of their coming; but my people know not the judgment of the* Lord*. How do ye say, We are wise, and the law of the* Lord *is with us? Lo, certainly in vain made he it; the pen of the scribes is in vain. The wise men are ashamed, they are dismayed and taken: lo, they have rejected the word of the* Lord*; and what wisdom is in them? . . . For they have healed the hurt of the daughter of my people slightly, saying, Peace, peace; when there is no peace . . . . We looked for peace, but no good came; and for a time of health, and behold trouble!"* (Jeremiah 8:6-9, 11, 15)

The uniting masses in today's world and Christianity are being driven into the darkness of the broad way, which rejects that the Lord Jesus Christ came to **"bear witness unto the truth"** (John 18:37) and to call **"sinners to repentance"** (Luke 5:32). This so-called "attack" is how God seeks to *bless* the world.

> *"Unto you first God, having raised up his Son Jesus, sent him <u>to bless you, in turning away every one of you from his iniquities</u>." (Acts 3:26)*

> *"And that repentance and remission of sins should be preached in his name among <u>all</u> nations . . ." (Luke 24:47)*

Although leaders today are doing the opposite of bearing witness unto the truth and calling sinners to repentance, they nevertheless claim to be "leading like Jesus."

The Lord Jesus Christ makes it very clear how futile it is to put works *in His name* above the truth and obedience of His Word (e.g., see Matthew 7:21-27). Naming

God's name or calling oneself a "child of God" or a "*Christ*ian" apart from the faith and obedience of the truth is nothing more than taking the name of God *in vain*. It is to no purpose and for naught because **"the LORD will not hold him guiltless that taketh his name in vain"** (Exodus 20:7). The Lord Jesus Christ warned that He is going to tell many people who have done **"many wonderful works"** in His name to depart from Him eternally, because He **"never knew"** these workers of **"iniquity"** who took His name and called Him Lord *in vain*.

> *"Ye hypocrites, well did Esaias prophesy of you, saying, This people draweth nigh unto me with their mouth, and honoureth me with their lips; but their heart is far from me. But <u>in vain they do worship me</u>, teaching for doctrines the commandments of men." (Matthew 15:7-9)*

> *"All the ways of a man are clean in his own eyes; but the LORD weigheth the spirits . . . . By mercy <u>and truth</u> iniquity is purged: and by the fear of the LORD men depart from evil." (Proverbs 16:2, 6)*

> *"And why call ye me, Lord, Lord, and do not the things which I say?" (Luke 6:46)*

Who we live for determines *how* we will live.

> *"Thou shalt not follow a multitude to do evil; neither shalt thou speak in a cause to decline after many to wrest judgment." (Exodus 23:2)*

Anyone whose feet are more comfortable walking on the *broad* way needs to carefully consider the path they are choosing to walk on. We can only walk with the Lord Jesus Christ on His path of light; He does not walk with us on the world's path of darkness.

> *"<u>Ponder the path of thy feet</u>, and let all thy ways be established. Turn not to the right hand nor to the left: remove thy foot from evil." (Proverbs 4:26-27)*

> *"Peter saith unto him, Thou shalt never wash my feet. Jesus answered him, <u>If I wash thee not, thou hast no part with me</u> . . . . He that is washed needeth not save to <u>wash his feet</u>, but is clean every whit . . ." (John 13:8, 10)*

> *"If we say that we have fellowship with him, and <u>walk in darkness, we lie, and do not the truth</u>. But if we <u>walk in the light, as he is in the light</u>, we have fellowship one with another, and the blood of Jesus Christ his Son cleanseth us from all sin." (1 John 1:6)*

We cannot have it both ways. We need to give serious heed to the warnings of the Lord Jesus Christ, including the one regarding the *many* who deceived themselves into believing they were following in His footsteps:

> *"Not every one that saith unto me, Lord, Lord, shall enter into the kingdom of heaven; but he that doeth the will of my Father which is in heaven." (Matthew 7:21)*

> *"Take heed therefore that the light which is in thee be not darkness." (Luke 11:35)*

> *"The light of the body is the eye: if therefore thine eye be single, thy whole body shall be full of light. But if thine eye be evil, thy whole body shall be full of darkness. If therefore the light that is in thee be darkness, how great is that darkness!" (Matthew 6:22-23)*

The Israelites thought they could use the world's ways and beliefs in serving God, but God did not accept their strange fire and had the harshest of words for them, not to mention judgment. Elijah asked them, **"How long halt ye between two opinions? if the LORD be God, follow him: but if Baal, then follow him"** (1 Kings 18:21). And Joshua declared unto them, ***"And if it seem evil unto you to serve the LORD, choose you this day whom ye will serve . . . but as for me and my house, we will serve the LORD"*** (Joshua 24:15).

Similar admonishments are necessary today, as Christians try to balance with one foot on the narrow way and one foot on the broad way. If the Lord is God and if His Word is the truth, then follow the Lord God and His Holy Scriptures on His narrow way. But if it seems evil to serve the Lord by standing uncompromisingly on the absolutes of God's unchanging truth because the world and the churches will cry, "Outdated!", "Unloving!", "Too negative!", "Intolerant!", "Judgmental!", "Fearful!", "Separative!", and "Divisive!", then choose you this day whom you will serve. Will it be the god of this world who sacrifices truth on the altar of unity, or the Almighty Lord God Who exalts His truth above even His own name?

The line is being drawn, and everyone is making their choice as to which side they will be on. There is no middle way, only the narrow way or the broad way. Trying to balance in the middle is being lukewarm, which is so distasteful to the Lord Jesus Christ that He is going to spit the lukewarm church out of His mouth:

"So then because thou art lukewarm, and neither cold nor hot, I will spew thee out of my mouth. Because thou sayest, I am rich, and increased with goods, and have need of nothing; and knowest not that thou art wretched, and miserable, and poor, and blind, and naked: I counsel thee to buy of me gold tried in the fire, that thou mayest be rich; and white raiment, that thou mayest be clothed, and that the shame of thy nakedness do not appear; and anoint thine eyes with eyesalve, that thou mayest see. As many as I love, I rebuke and chasten: be zealous therefore, and repent." (Revelation 3:16-19)

"For what is a man profited, if he shall gain the whole world, and lose his own soul? or what shall a man give in exchange for his soul?" (Matthew 16:26)

We can mindlessly follow the crowd and its leaders, or we can mindfully follow the Lord and Saviour Jesus Christ, without Whom there is no Christian living or salvation.

"A New Religion Has Been Initiated, Which Is No More Christianity than Chalk Is Cheese"

The apostle Paul was so grieved by God's warning of the coming deception from *"grievous wolves"* and from men who would arise *within* Christianity, that *for three years* he *"ceased not to warn every one night and day with* <u>tears</u>*"* (see Acts 20:29-31). This is a far cry from the leaders today who respond to earnest warnings with laughter, mockery, contempt, and so forth.

These "change agents" can marginalize and censure those refusing to budge from the narrow way all they want. Their transformation of *the* faith of Christianity into *a* faith of the broad way is in plain view for those who have eyes to see and ears to hear. Their responses and marginalization are only exposing themselves.

Today's behavior is similar to that of Old Testament times and is even prophesied in Scripture.

"Thus saith the L<small>ORD</small>*, Stand ye in the ways, and see, and ask for the old paths, where is the good way, and walk therein, and ye shall find rest for*

> *your souls. But they said, We will not walk therein. Also I set watchmen over you, saying, Hearken to the sound of the trumpet. <u>But they said, We will not hearken</u>. Therefore hear, ye nations, and know, O congregation, what is among them. Hear, O earth: behold, I will bring evil upon this people, even the fruit of their thoughts, because they have not hearkened unto my words, nor to my law, but rejected it." (Jeremiah 6:16-19)*

> *"Moreover all the chief of the priests, and the people, <u>transgressed very much after all the abominations of the heathen; and polluted the house of the</u> L<small>ORD</small> which he had hallowed in Jerusalem. And the L<small>ORD</small> God of their fathers sent to them by his messengers, rising up betimes, and sending; because he had compassion on his people, and on his dwelling place: <u>But they mocked the messengers of God, and despised his words, and misused his prophets, until the wrath of the</u> L<small>ORD</small> <u>arose against his people, till there was no remedy</u>." (2 Chronicles 36:14-16)*

> *"But, beloved, remember ye the words which were spoken before of the apostles of our Lord Jesus Christ; how that they told you <u>there should be mockers in the last time</u>, who should walk after their own ungodly lusts." (Jude 1:17-18)*

There is a saying indicative of the times we are living in: "Truth can stand alone and often must."

> *"O earth, earth, earth, hear the word of the L<small>ORD</small>." (Jeremiah 22:29)*

> *"Blessed is the man that walketh not in the counsel of the ungodly, nor standeth in the way of sinners, nor sitteth in the seat of the scornful. But his delight is in the law of the L<small>ORD</small>; and in his law doth he meditate day and night. And he shall be like a tree planted by the rivers of water, that bringeth forth his fruit in his season; his leaf also shall not wither; and whatsoever he doeth shall prosper. The ungodly are not so: but are like the chaff which the wind driveth away. Therefore the ungodly shall not stand in the judgment, nor sinners in the congregation of the righteous. For the L<small>ORD</small> knoweth the way of the righteous: but the way of the ungodly shall perish." (Psalm 1:1-6)*

Today's Christianity may be having a lot of fun in its new way of thinking and behaving, but this isn't a game. Eternal souls are at stake, and the *departure* from the faith is real. Jesus Christ is being presented as a way of relativism rather than as *the* way and *the* truth, and *the* faith is being presented as an ever-changing *method* or *experience* that can be inserted into *any* faith.

The words Charles Spurgeon penned in 1887 might as well have been written today:

> "No lover of the gospel can conceal from himself the fact that the days are evil . . . . our solemn conviction is that things are much worse in many churches than they seem to be, and are rapidly tending downward . . . . How much farther could they go? What doctrine remains to be abandoned? What other truth to be the object of contempt? **A new religion has been initiated, which is no more Christianity than chalk is cheese; and this religion, being destitute of moral honesty, palms itself off as the old faith with slight improvements, and on this plea usurps pulpits which were erected for gospel preaching.** The Atonement is scouted, the inspiration of Scripture is derided, the Holy Spirit is degraded into an influence, the punishment of sin is turned into fiction, and the resurrection into a myth, and yet these enemies of our faith expect us to call them brethren, and maintain a confederacy with them! . . .

> "Is it any wonder that church members forget their vows of consecration, and run with the unholy in the ways of frivolity, when they hear that persons are tolerated in the pastorate who do the same? We doubt not that, for writing these lines we shall incur the charge of prudery and bigotry, and this will but prove how low are the tone and spirit of the churches in many places. The fact is, that many would like to unite church and stage, cards and prayer, dancing and sacraments . . . . When the old faith is gone, and enthusiasm for the gospel is extinct, it is no wonder that people seek something else in the way of delight. Lacking bread, they feed on ashes; rejecting the way of the Lord, they run greedily in the path of folly . . . .

> **"Too many ministers are toying with the deadly cobra of 'another gospel,' in the form of 'modern thought.'** . . .

> "Where the gospel is fully and powerfully preached, with the Holy Ghost sent down from heaven, our churches not only hold their own, but win converts; but when that which constitutes their strength is gone—we mean when the gospel

is concealed, and the life of prayer is slighted—the whole thing becomes a mere form and fiction . . . . Conformity, or nonconformity, *per se* is nothing; but a new creature is everything, and the truth upon which alone that new creature can live is worth dying a thousand deaths to conserve . . . .

"Certain ministers are making infidels. Avowed atheists are not a tenth as dangerous as those preachers who scatter doubt and stab at faith . . . . Germany was made unbelieving by her preachers, and England is following in her track . . . .

"A little plain-speaking would do a world of good just now. These gentlemen desire to be let alone. They want no noise raised. Of course thieves hate watch-dogs, and love darkness. It is time that somebody should spring his rattle, and call attention to the way in which God is being robbed of his glory, and man of his hope.

"It now becomes a serious question how far those who abide by the faith once delivered to the saints should fraternize with those who have turned aside to another gospel . . . . For the present it behoves believers to be cautious, lest they lend their support and countenance to the betrayers of the Lord . . . . Numbers of easy-minded people wink at error so long as it is committed by a clever man and a good-natured brother, who has so many fine points about him. Let each believer judge for himself; but, for our part, we have put on a few fresh bolts to our door, and we have given orders to keep the chain up; for, under color of begging the friendship of the servant, there are those about who aim at robbing THE MASTER . . . .

"If for a while the evangelicals are doomed to go down, let them die fighting, and in the full assurance that their gospel will have a resurrection when the inventions of 'modern thought' shall be burned up with fire unquenchable." (Bold added)[2]

What on Earth Am I Here For? Keep *the* Faith!

*T*here is nothing new under the sun. Even in the apostle Paul's day, the Word of God was being corrupted and deceitfully used and speaking the truth was not well received:

> *"Am I therefore become your enemy, because I tell you the truth?" (Galatians 4:16)*

> *"For we are not as <u>many, which corrupt the word of God</u>: but as of sincerity, but as of God, in the sight of God speak we in Christ." (2 Corinthians 2:17)*

> *"Therefore seeing we have this ministry, as we have received mercy, we faint not; but have renounced the hidden things of dishonesty, not walking in craftiness, nor <u>handling the word of God deceitfully</u>; but by manifestation of the truth commending ourselves to every man's conscience in the sight of God." (2 Corinthians 4:1-2)*

No matter how popular or right anyone or anything seems to be and no matter how well something seems to "work," it is God's Word of absolute truth that determines right and wrong and gives us the saving faith we are to keep. God allows things to come to pass to test our faithfulness.

> *"If there arise among you a prophet, or a dreamer of dreams, and giveth thee a sign or a wonder, and the sign or the wonder come to pass, whereof he spake unto thee, saying, Let us go after other gods, which thou hast not known, and let us serve them; <u>thou shalt not hearken unto the words of that prophet, or that dreamer of dreams: for the</u> Lord <u>your God proveth you, to know whether ye love the</u> Lord <u>your God with all your heart and with all your soul</u>. Ye shall walk after the* Lord *your God, and fear <u>him</u>, and keep <u>his</u> commandments, and obey <u>his</u> voice, and ye shall serve <u>him</u>, and cleave unto <u>him</u>." (Deuteronomy 13:1-4)*

Throughout the true Scriptures, the Lord God Himself is the Means and End of life, including why we are here. For all who know and love Him, whether we live or die, the precious Lord God Himself is the Road of life, the Goal of life, the Blessing of life, and the Prize of life. When *He* is the be-All and end-All of our lives, then scriptural worship, scriptural fellowship, scriptural discipleship, scriptural ministry, scriptural mission, and all the other purposes He gives us in His Holy Scriptures automatically fall into place.

> "Who, when he came, and had seen the grace of God, was glad, <u>and exhorted them all, that with purpose of heart they would cleave unto the Lord</u>." (Acts 11:23)

> "Let us hear the conclusion of the whole matter: Fear God, and keep his commandments: for this is the whole duty of man." (Ecclesiastes 12:13)

> "Jesus saith unto him, I am the way, the truth, and the life: <u>no man</u> cometh unto the Father, but <u>by me</u>." (John 14:6)

The Lord Jesus Christ is neither "a better way" nor "another way;" *He is the <u>only</u> way*. Keeping *the faith* is essential.

> "For it pleased the Father that in him should all fulness dwell; and, having made peace through the blood of his cross, by him to reconcile all things unto himself; by him, I say, whether they be things in earth, or things in heaven. And you, that were sometime alienated and enemies in your mind by wicked works, yet now hath he reconciled in the body of his flesh through death, <u>to present you holy and unblameable and unreproveable in his sight: If ye continue in the faith grounded and settled, and be not moved away from the hope of the gospel</u>, which ye have heard, and which was preached to every creature which is under heaven; whereof I Paul am made a minister." (Colossians 1:19-23)

> "Whosoever denieth the Son, the same hath not the Father: [but] he that acknowledgeth the Son hath the Father also. Let that therefore abide in you, which ye have heard from the beginning. <u>If that which ye have heard from the beginning shall remain in you, ye also shall continue in the Son, and in the Father</u>. And this is the promise that he hath promised us, even eternal life. These things have I written unto you concerning them that seduce you." (1 John 2:23-26; brackets in the original)

> "<u>Look to yourselves, that we lose not those things which we have wrought, but that we receive a full reward. Whosoever transgresseth, and abideth not in the doctrine of Christ, hath not God.</u> He that abideth in the doctrine of Christ, he hath both the Father and the Son." (2 John 1:8-9)

> *"Take heed, brethren, lest there be in any of you an evil heart of unbelief, in <u>departing from the living God</u>. But exhort one another daily, while it is called Today; lest any of you be hardened through the deceitfulness of sin. <u>For we are made partakers of Christ, if we hold the beginning of our confidence stedfast unto the end.</u>" (Hebrews 3:12-14)*

> *". . . I know thy works, that thou hast a name that thou livest, and art dead. <u>Be watchful, and strengthen the things which remain, that are ready to die</u>: for I have not found thy works perfect before God. <u>Remember therefore how thou hast received and heard, and hold fast, and repent.</u> If therefore thou shalt not watch, I will come on thee as a thief, and thou shalt not know what hour I will come upon thee." (Revelation 3:1-3)*

> *"<u>Examine yourselves, whether ye be in the faith</u>; prove your own selves. Know ye not your own selves, how that Jesus Christ is in you, except ye be reprobates?" (2 Corinthians 13:5)*

To depart from the faith is to remove oneself from God. God will deny us and remain faithful to Himself and His truth if we deny Him in order to become ONE with the many, or for any other reason.

> *"Now the just shall live by faith: but <u>if any man draw back</u>, my soul shall have no pleasure in him." (Hebrews 10:38)*

> *"If we suffer, we shall also reign with him: <u>if we deny him, he also will deny us</u>: If we believe not, yet he abideth faithful: <u>he cannot deny himself.</u>" (2 Timothy 2:12-13)*

> *"But whosoever shall deny me before men, <u>him will I also deny before my Father which is in heaven</u>. Think not that I am come to send peace on earth: I came not to send peace, but a sword." (Matthew 10:33-34)*

In "Divisions Are Not Always Bad," A.W. Tozer warned that "unity is no treasure to be purchased at the price of compromise":

> "To divide what should be divided and unite what should be united is the part of wisdom . . . .

"**The first divider was God who at the creation divided the light from the darkness. This division set the direction for all God's dealings in nature and in grace. Light and darkness are incompatible** . . .

"What shall we unite with and from what shall we separate? The question of coexistence does not enter here, but the question of union and fellowship does . . . .

"Unity is so devoutly to be desired that no price is too high to pay for it and nothing is important enough to keep us apart. **Truth is slain to provide a feast to celebrate the marriage of heaven and hell, and all to support a concept of unity which has no basis in the Word of God.**

"The Spirit-illuminated church will have none of this. In a fallen world like ours unity is no treasure to be purchased at the price of compromise. Loyalty to God, faithfulness to truth and the preservation of a good conscience are jewels more precious than gold of Ophir or diamonds from the mine. For these jewels . . . followers of Christ have paid the last full measure of devotion and quietly died, unknown to and unsung by the great world, but known to God and dear to His Father heart . . . .

"'Divide and conquer' is the cynical slogan of Machiavellian political leaders, but **Satan knows also how to *unite* and conquer** . . . . Then follows almost perfect unity indeed, but it is the unity of the stockyards and the concentration camp. We have seen this happen several times in this century, **and the world will see it at least once more when the nations of the earth are united under Antichrist.**

"When confused sheep start over a cliff the individual sheep can save himself only by separating from the flock. Perfect unity at such a time can only mean total destruction for all. **The wise sheep to save his own hide disaffiliates.**

"Power lies in the union of things similar and the division of things dissimilar. Maybe what we need in religious circles today is not more union but some wise and courageous division. Everyone desires peace but it could be that revival will follow the sword." (Bold added)[3]

May the leaders whose eyes have been opened to any deception they promoted come out and *publicly* acknowledge the error of their ways, for the sake of all those who heeded them in their deception. We must take a stand for the Lord God and His Word over man. When the religious leaders tried to silence the apostles from speaking the truth, their response was an acknowledgment of the Lordship of God:

> *"Then Peter and the other apostles answered and said, We ought to obey God rather than men." (Acts 5:29)*

The costs are very high, but the costs are even higher in not doing so. Our loving Lord God is worth it all, and He gave His all for us.

> *"But ye, beloved, building up yourselves on your most holy faith, praying in the Holy Ghost, keep yourselves in the love of God, looking for the mercy of our Lord Jesus Christ unto eternal life. <u>And of some have compassion, making a difference: And others save with fear, pulling them out of the fire;</u> hating even the garment spotted by the flesh." (Jude 1:20-23)*

> *"For do I now persuade men, or God? or do I seek to please men? for if I yet pleased men, I should not be the servant of Christ." (Galatians 1:10)*

> *"But watch thou in all things, endure afflictions, do the work of an evangelist, make full proof of thy ministry." (2 Timothy 4:5)*

We are to contend for and keep the faith and be separated (holy) unto God in our flesh *and spirit*, not united with the world and its darkness, no matter how noble the transcendent purpose seems.

> *"Be ye not unequally yoked together with unbelievers: for what fellowship hath righteousness with unrighteousness? and what communion hath light with darkness? And what concord hath Christ with Belial? or what part hath he that believeth with an infidel? And what agreement hath the temple of God with idols? for ye are the temple of the living God; as God hath said, I will dwell in them, and walk in them; and I will be their God, and they shall be my people. Wherefore come out from among them, and be ye separate, saith the Lord, and touch not the unclean thing; and I will receive you, and will be a Father unto you, and ye shall be my sons and daughters, saith the Lord Almighty. Having therefore these promises, dearly beloved,*

let us cleanse ourselves from all filthiness of the flesh <u>and spirit</u>, perfecting holiness in the fear of God." (2 Corinthians 6:14-7:1)

May we all have the faith and perseverance of Moses and the rest of the great cloud of faithful witnesses who have gone before us:

"Choosing rather to suffer affliction with the people of God, than to enjoy the pleasures of sin for a season; esteeming the reproach of Christ greater riches than the treasures in Egypt: for he had respect unto the recompence of the reward. By faith he forsook Egypt, not fearing the wrath of the king: for he endured, as seeing him who is invisible." (Hebrews 11:25-27)

"Hearken unto me, ye that know righteousness, the people in whose heart is my law; fear ye not the reproach of men, neither be ye afraid of their revilings .... Therefore the redeemed of the Lord *shall return, and come with singing unto Zion; and everlasting joy shall be upon their head: they shall obtain gladness and joy; and sorrow and mourning shall flee away." (Isaiah 51:7, 11)*

"Let us go forth therefore unto him without the camp, bearing his reproach. For here have we no continuing city, but we seek one to come." (Hebrews 13:13-14)

"At my first answer no man stood with me, but all men forsook me ... Notwithstanding the Lord stood with me, and strengthened me; that by me the preaching might be fully known, and that all the Gentiles might hear: and I was delivered out of the mouth of the lion. And the Lord shall deliver me from every evil work, and will preserve me unto his heavenly kingdom: to whom be glory for ever and ever. Amen." (2 Timothy 4:16-18)

"I have fought a good fight, I have finished my course, I have <u>kept the faith</u>: Henceforth there is laid up for me a crown of righteousness, which the Lord, the righteous judge, shall give me at that day: and not to me only, but unto all them also that love his appearing." (2 Timothy 4:7-8)

After all is said and done, for those who in the name of purpose are seeking broad, inclusive unity with the world over narrow, exclusive separation unto God, and for those who have been led to believe they can live a purpose-driven life in other faiths (religions), may this actual CNN transcription error serve as an additional warning before it is too late:

> ". . . finding your religion in the bookstore, meet the Christian authors of the best-selling series '**Left Behind in the Purpose Driven Life**,' part of our special weeklong series 'Keeping the Faith.'" (Emphasis added)[4]

Endnotes

(Website information was current at the time it was written.)

Acknowledgments
1. From the hymn "If I Gained the World, but Lost the Savior" by Anna Ölander, 1904, Trans. Composite, from the Swedish; THE HYMNAL of The Evangelical Mission Covenant Church of America (Chicago, Illinois: Covenant Press, 1950), 397.

Introduction
1. About Rick Warren, RickWarren.com, http://www.rickwarren.com/about.html.

Chapter One
1. Rick Warren, *The Purpose Driven Life: What On Earth Am I Here For?* (Grand Rapids, Michigan: Zondervan, 2002).
2. As quoted in "Purpose-Driven® Life Named Book of the Year" by Jon Walker, Pastors.com, http://www.pastors.com/article.asp?ArtID=4382.
3. As quoted in Discussion "Myths of the Modern Mega-Church," May 23, 2005, the Pew Forum's biannual Faith Angle conference on religion, politics and public life, Event Transcript, http://pewforum.org/events/index.php?EventID=80.
4. Interview with Rick Warren, CNN Larry King Live, Aired November 22, 2004, Transcript, http://transcripts.cnn.com/TRANSCRIPTS/0411/22/lkl.01.html.
5. "This evangelist has a 'Purpose'" by Cathy Lynn Grossman, *USA TODAY*, July 21, 2003, http://www.usatoday.com/life/2003-07-21-rick-warren_x.htm.
6. "A Pastor With a Purpose" by Sonja Steptoe, *TIME* Magazine, April 18, 2005, Special Issue, "The TIME 100: The 2005 list of the world's most influential people . . . ," http://www.time.com/time/subscriber/2005/time100/scientists/100warren.html.
7. As quoted in "The Man With The Purpose" by Sonja Steptoe, *TIME* Magazine, March 29, 2004, http://www.time.com/time/magazine/article/0,9171,1101040329-603246,00.html.
8. Rick Warren, transcribed from the 40 DAYS OF PURPOSE Small Group & Sunday School Video Curriculum, Session One.

Chapter Two

1. See "What Is Transformation?" by Lynn and Sarah Leslie, August 15, 2005, NewsWithViews.com, http://newswithviews.com/Leslie/sarah.htm; "Are you in the throes of Transformation?" posted March 9, 2006 at http://herescope.blogspot.com/2006/03/are-you-in-throes-of-transformation.html.

Chapter Four

1. *Tozer on Worship and Entertainment*, A.W. Tozer, Selected Excerpts Compiled by James L. Snyder, (Camp Hill, Pennsylvania: Christian Publications, 1997), p. 178.
2. Rick Warren, *The Purpose Driven Church: Growth Without Compromising Your Message & Mission* (Grand Rapids, Michigan: Zondervan, 1995), p. 61.
3. "Two Faces Of Faith: 'Purpose Driven' preaching for an MTV world" by Gillian Flaccus, *Associated Press*, *The Modesto Bee*, April 9, 2005, http://www.modbee.com/life/faithvalues/story/10279980p-11088489c.html.
4. "What a purpose driven church is not" by Rick Warren, Rick Warren's Ministry Toolbox™, Issue #208, 5/25/2005, http://www.pastors.com/RWMT/?artid=8275&id=208.
5. "Two Faces Of Faith: 'Purpose Driven' preaching for an MTV world" by Gillian Flaccus, http://www.modbee.com/life/faithvalues/story/10279980p-11088489c.html. (This quote is also in "Putting Christianity on a modern footing" by Gillian Flaccus, *AP*, *Chicago Sun-Times*, March 25, 2005, http://www.suntimes.com/output/religion/cst-nws-purp25.html.)
6. As quoted in "Purpose-Driven Preaching: An Interview with Rick Warren" by Michael Duduit, Editor, *Preaching*, September-October 2001 issue, http://www.preaching.com/preaching/pastissues/rickwarren.htm.
7. "What is PurposeDriven?", PurposeDriven, http://www.purposedriven.com/en-US/AboutUs/WhatIsPD/7+Myths+of+PD.htm.
8. *Morning and Evening*, a Devotional series by Charles H. Spurgeon, Answers in Genesis, http://www.answersingenesis.org/Devotions/devotions.asp?reqDate=7/14/2005&reqDayPer=1.
9. "Why We Are Lukewarm About Christ's Return" by A.W. Tozer, *The Best of A.W. Tozer*, Compiled by Warren W. Wiersbe, (Camp Hill, Pennsylvania: Christian Publications, 1978), p. 57.
10. "Spurgeon and Places of Entertainment," Charles Haddon Spurgeon, *Sword & Trowell*, Issue 1995 No. 2, as reprinted by The Middletown Bible Church, http://www.middletownbiblechurch.org/christia/spurgeon.htm.
11. "Feeding Sheep or Amusing Goats?" by Charles Haddon Spurgeon, http://www.crossroad.to/Quotes/Church/Spurgeon.htm.
12. Rick Warren, as quoted in *Rick Warren and the Purpose that Drives Him: An Insider Looks at the Phenomenal Bestseller* by Richard Abanes, (Eugene Oregon: Harvest House Publishers, 2005), pp. 29-30.
13. Rick Warren, *The Purpose Driven Church: Growth Without Compromising Your Message & Mission*, p. 65.

14. *Tozer on Worship and Entertainment*, A.W. Tozer, Selected Excerpts Compiled by James L. Snyder, pp. 165-166.
15. Ibid., p. 136.
16. Ibid., pp. 136-137.
17. Ibid., p. 185.

Chapter Five

1. Acts of Mercy, http://www.acts-of-mercy.com/.
2. As quoted in "Rick Warren: purpose-driven balance means more than technique" by Staff, An interview with Rick Warren, https://pastors.com/article.asp?ArtID=4212.
3. "Rick Warren: relationships hold your church together" by Rick Warren, http://www.pastors.com/article.asp?ArtID=3917.
4. "Will Your Church Be Closed for Christmas?" by Paul Proctor, NewsWithViews.com, November 27, 2005, http://newswithviews.com/PaulProctor/proctor83.htm. (Note: Although this quote has since been removed from this article, it has been included here with permission of the author. The article is still posted in full at Moriel Ministries, http://www.moriel.org/articles/notice_board/will_your_church_be_closed_for_christmas.htm.)
5. "Transforming the Church Through the Dialectic" by Dean Gotcher, Discernment Newsletter, March/April 2003, http://www.discernment-ministries.org/NLmarchapril_2003.htm.
6. "Turning attendees into a part of the family" by Rick Warren, Rick Warren's Ministry Toolbox™, Issue #225, 9/21/2005, http://www.pastors.com/RWMT/?id=225&artid=4137&expand=1.
7. Rick Warren, General Editor, *Better Together: What on earth are we here for?*, 40 Days of Community Workbook, (Lake Forest, CA: Purpose Driven Publishing, 2004), p. 69.
8. Rick Warren, *The Purpose Driven Church: Growth Without Compromising Your Message & Mission*, p. 310.
9. As quoted in "Rick Warren: purpose-driven balance means more than technique" by Staff, https://pastors.com/article.asp?ArtID=4212.
10. Rick Warren, General Editor, *Better Together*, 40 Days of Community Workbook, p. 97.
11. Ibid., p. 80.

Chapter Six

1. Transcribed from a sermon video clip televised in Josh Mankiewicz' interview of Rick Warren that aired on NBC's Dateline, October 3, 2004.
2. http://www.nationalpastorsconvention.com/programs/gs/sandiego.php and http://www.nationalpastorsconvention.com/sched/sandiego/3.php. (A copy of the schedule has also been posted at http://www.lighthousetrailsresearch.com/nationalpastorsconv2004.htm.)
3. There are many ministry websites that address the spiritual dangers of mysticism/contemplative prayer and the (New Age) New Spirituality, such as those listed in this book and at "'Emerging'

+ 'New Spirituality' = 'Emergent Church'" at http://www.erwm.com/TheNewSpiritualFormation.htm. See also, "Extra Activities," National Pastors Convention 2006, http://www.nationalpastorsconvention.com/content.aspx?sp=extras; and "National Pastor's Convention: Where America's Pastors Meet Contemplative" at http://www.lighthousetrailsresearch.com/nationalpastors.htm.

4. Ray Yungen "For Many Shall Come In My Name": How mainstream America is accepting the 'Ancient Wisdom' teaching and what this foreshadows, Revised Edition, (Woodburn, Oregon: Solid Rock Books, Inc., 1991) and A Time of Departing: How Ancient Mystical Practices are Uniting Christians with the World's Religions, 2nd Edition (Silverton, Oregon: Lighthouse Trails Publishing Company, 2006), (available through http://www.lighthousetrails.com).

5. "'The Purpose-Driven Life': Author Rick Warren," Talk Today: Interact with people in the news, March 25, 2004, USATODAY.com, http://cgi1.usatoday.com/mchat/20040325002/tscript.htm.

6. Spirituality, Introduction, SriChinmoy.org, http://www.srichinmoy.org/spirituality/.

7. "Breathing Exercises," Sri Chinmoy Centre, http://www.srichinmoycentre.org/meditation/meditation_exercises/breathing_exercises.

8. Yogi Ramacharaka, The Hindu-Yogi Science of Breath, Chapter XVI - Yogi Spiritual Breathing, © 1903 (Expired), Online Magical Library, http://www.hermetics.org/pdf/ScienceOfBreath.pdf, see pp. 62-65.

9. Alice Bailey, The Unfinished Autobiography, Appendix - The Arcane School - Its Esoteric Origins and Purposes (Appendix written by Foster Bailey), (Caux, Switzerland: Netnews Association and/or its suppliers, 2002), http://www.netnews.org -- http://laluni.helloyou.ws/netnews/bk/autobiography/auto1103.html. See also this book's Appendix - My Work (Appendix written by the Tibetan), http://laluni.helloyou.ws/netnews/bk/autobiography/auto1084.html.

10. Ray Yungen, A Time of Departing: How Ancient Mystical Practices are Uniting Christians with the World's Religions, 2nd Edition, pp. 28, 112.

11. Alice Bailey & Djwhal Khul, Esoteric Psychology II, Chapter II - The Ray of Personality, The Coordination of the Personality, (Caux, Switzerland: Netnews Association and/or its suppliers, 2002), http://www.netnews.org -- http://laluni.helloyou.ws/netnews/bk/psychology2/psyc2149.html.

12. Alice Bailey, From Intellect to Intuition, Chapter VI - Stages in Meditation, III. The Stage of Contemplation, (Caux, Switzerland: Netnews Association and/or its suppliers, 2002), http://www.netnews.org -- http://laluni.helloyou.ws/netnews/bk/intellect/inte1043.html.

13. Ibid., http://laluni.helloyou.ws/netnews/bk/intellect/inte1042.html.

14. Alice Bailey & Djwhal Khul, Initiation, Human and Solar, Chapter XII - The Two Revelations, (Caux, Switzerland: Netnews Association and/or its suppliers, 2002), http://www.netnews.org -- http://laluni.helloyou.ws/netnews/bk/initiation/init1047.html.

15. Ray Yungen, A Time of Departing, p. 196.

Chapter Seven

1. James Sundquist, *Who's Driving the Purpose Driven Church?: A Documentary on the Teachings of Rick Warren* (Bethany, Oklahoma: Bible Belt Publishers, 2004), (available through Southwest Radio Church Ministries at http://www.swrc.com/offers/internet_0205.htm, various ministries on the Internet, and Amazon.com). See also "The Adulation of Man in *The Purpose Driven Life*" by Richard Bennett, Berean Beacon, http://www.bereanbeacon.org/articles_pdf/rick_warren_purpose_driven.pdf.
2. For information on Psychology and its assimilation into Christianity, see PsychoHeresy Awareness Ministries at http://www.psychoheresy-aware.org/.
3. Interview with Rick Warren, CNN Larry King Live, Aired March 22, 2005, Transcript, http://transcripts.cnn.com/TRANSCRIPTS/0503/22/lkl.01.html.
4. Ibid.
5. *Tozer on Worship and Entertainment*, A.W. Tozer, Selected Excerpts Compiled by James L. Snyder, p. 65.

Chapter Eight

1. "Muslims in our Pulpits" by Dr. Tom White, Executive Director, Voice of the Martyrs, in "Have We Shamed the Face of Jesus?," Editorial by Voice of the Martyrs, sent out with VOM's monthly newsletter in December 2001, http://christianunplugged.com/muslims_in_church.htm. (The editorial is also posted at http://bereanpublishers.com/Cults/Muslims/have_we_shamed_the_face_of_jesus.htm.)
2. Rick Warren, *The Purpose Driven Church: Growth Without Compromising Your Message & Mission*, p. 225.
3. *Tozer on Worship and Entertainment*, A.W. Tozer, Selected Excerpts Compiled by James L. Snyder, p. 138.
4. "purpose driven church conference 2005" brochure, PurposeDriven, http://pddocs.purposedriven.com:8088/docs/pdchurch/2005_PDC_Brochure.pdf, p. 5.

Chapter Nine

1. Rick Warren, Saddleback Church Service, November 2, 2003; transcribed from http://www.saddlebackfamily.com/peace/Services/110203_high.asx.
2. Ibid.
3. "11 characteristics of a PD church" by Rick Warren, Rick Warren's Ministry Toolbox™, Issue #205, 5/4/2005, http://www.pastors.com/rwmt/?id=205&artid=8227&expand=1.
4. "The Cellular Church" by Malcolm Gladwell, *The New Yorker* magazine, September 12, 2005, http://www.gladwell.com/2005/2005_09_12_a_warren.html.
5. "*New Yorker* article on the ministry of Rick Warren" by Malcolm Gladwell, Pastors.com, http://www.pastors.com/article.asp?ArtID=9636.

6. As quoted in "Rick Warren," The Power of Purpose Awards, http://www.powerofpurpose.org/judges_warren.html; (now at http://www.templeton.org/powerofpurpose/judges_warren.html).
7. THE JUDGES, The Power of Purpose Awards, http://www.powerofpurpose.org/judges.html; (now at http://www.templeton.org/powerofpurpose/judges.html).
8. The Quotable Sir John, On Life and Spirituality, John Templeton Foundation, http://www.templeton.org/sir_john_templeton/quotes.asp.
9. "Biography: Sir John Templeton," John Templeton Foundation, http://www.templeton.org/sir_john_templeton/index.asp.
10. John Marks Templeton, *The Humble Approach: Scientists Discover God* (Radnor, Pennsylvania: Templeton Foundation Press, 1995), p. 46.
11. "Biography: Sir John Templeton," http://www.templeton.org/sir_john_templeton/index.asp.
12. Ibid.
13. Ibid.
14. The Quotable Sir John, On Life and Spirituality, http://www.templeton.org/sir_john_templeton/quotes.asp.
15. The Power of Purpose Awards Backgrounder, http://www.powerofpurpose.org/backgrounder.html; (now at http://www.templeton.org/powerofpurpose/backgrounder.html).
16. "Sir John Templeton," The Power of Purpose Awards, http://www.powerofpurpose.org/aboutsjt.html; (now at http://www.templeton.org/powerofpurpose/aboutsjt.html).
17. The Power of Purpose Awards, http://www.powerofpurpose.org; (now at http://www.templeton.org/powerofpurpose/index.html).
18. ABOUT THIS COMPETITION, The Power of Purpose Awards, http://www.powerofpurpose.org/whatispurpose.html; (now at http://www.templeton.org/powerofpurpose/whatispurpose.html).
19. Ibid.
20. "Brother John" by August Turak, The Power of Purpose Awards, http://www.powerofpurpose.org/winners/printer_turak.html; (now at http://www.templeton.org/powerofpurpose/winners/printer_turak.html; and also at http://www.selfknowledge.org/whoweare/templeton_augie.htm).
21. See under the description of the links Rose Publication and The Theosophical Society in America, Self Knowledge Symposium Resources, http://www.selfknowledge.org/resources/resources.htm; and also "Five Years with a Zen Master" by Self Knowledge Symposium founder Augie Turak, http://www.selfknowledge.org/events/fiveyears_TapeInfo.htm.
22. 2004 Essay Winners, August Turak, The Power of Purpose Awards, http://www.powerofpurpose.org/winners/essay_turak.html; (now at http://www.templeton.org/powerofpurpose/winners/essay_turak.html).
23. "Brother John" by August Turak, http://www.powerofpurpose.org/winners/printer_turak.html; (now at http://www.templeton.org/powerofpurpose/winners/printer_turak.html; and also at http://www.selfknowledge.org/whoweare/templeton_augie.htm).

24. Warren Smith, *Deceived on Purpose: The New Age Implications of the Purpose-Driven Church*, Second Edition, (Magalia, California: Mountain Stream Press, 2004), p. 84. (Available through various ministries on the Internet and Amazon.com.)
25. Tom Holladay & Kay Warren, *Foundations: A Purpose-Driven Discipleship Resource*, Participant's Guide, (Grand Rapids, Michigan: Zondervan, 2003), p. 46. See also the section "Immanence: the 'God' Within," pp. 155-159, in the book *Deceived on Purpose*, Second Edition, by Warren Smith.
26. Alice Bailey & Djwhal Khul, *Problems of Humanity*, Chapter V - The Problem of the Churches, I. *The Fact of God, Immanent and Transcendent*, (Caux, Switzerland: Netnews Association and/or its suppliers, 2002), http://www.net news.org -- http://laluni.helloyou.ws/netnews/bk/problems/prob1057.html.
27. Alice Bailey & Djwhal Khul, *The Reappearance of the Christ*, Chapter VI - The New World Religion, (Caux, Switzerland: Netnews Association and/or its suppliers, 2002), http://www.netnews.org -- http://laluni.helloyou.ws/netnews/bk/reappearance/reap1043.html.
28. Richard Abanes, *Harry Potter and the Bible: The Menace behind the Magick* (Camphill, Pennsylvania: Horizon Books, 2001), p. 159; quoting Susan Harwood Kaczmarczik, et al, "Alt. Pagan Frequently Asked Questions," January 25, 1993.
29. Richard Abanes, *Rick Warren and the Purpose that Drives Him*, p. 95.
30. Rick Warren, as quoted in ibid., p. 96.
31. "Of Monks and Mushrooms: Prize-winning Essays on The Power of Purpose" by Bill Newcott, the October 2004 issue of *Milestones*, a publication of the John Templeton Foundation, http://www.templeton.org/milestones/milestones_2004-10.asp.
32. "OVER 7,000 ESSAYS FROM 97 COUNTRIES *and all 50 United States Caps Contest Closing!*", The Power of Purpose Awards e~LETTER, July 2004, #9, http://www.powerofpurpose.org/newsletter/July012004.html; (now at http://www.templeton.org/powerofpurpose/newsletter/july012004.html).
33. As quoted in "Evangelism Gone Entrepreneurial," *BusinessWeek* Online Extra, May 23, 2005, http://www.businessweek.com/magazine/content/05_21/b3934015_mz001.htm.
34. Transcribed from Josh Mankiewicz' televised interview of Rick Warren that aired on NBC's Dateline, October 3, 2004.
35. As quoted in "Of Monks and Mushrooms: Prize-winning Essays on The Power of Purpose" by Bill Newcott, http://www.templeton.org/milestones/milestones_2004-10.asp.

Chapter Ten

1. Interview with Rick Warren, CNN Larry King Live, Aired November 22, 2004, Transcript, http://transcripts.cnn.com/TRANSCRIPTS/0411/22/lkl.01.html.
2. Ibid.

3. Dante Velasco, Reviews, In the Sphere of Silence, http://www.inthesphereofsilence.com/DesktopDefault.aspx?Myurl=p_default&tabindex=8&tabid=11&subtabid=11.
4. Interview with Rick Warren, CNN Larry King Live, Aired December 2, 2005, Transcript, http://transcripts.cnn.com/TRANSCRIPTS/0512/02/lkl.01.html.
5. Interview with Rick Warren, CNN Larry King Live, Aired November 22, 2004, http://transcripts.cnn.com/TRANSCRIPTS/0411/22/lkl.01.html.
6. Alice Bailey & Djwhal Khul, *The Reappearance of the Christ*, Chapter VI - The New World Religion, http://laluni.helloyou.ws/netnews/bk/reappearance/reap1046.html.
7. "This evangelist has a 'Purpose'" by Cathy Lynn Grossman, *USA TODAY*, July 21, 2003, http://www.usatoday.com/life/2003-07-21-rick-warren_x.htm.
8. Richard Abanes, *Rick Warren and the Purpose that Drives Him*, p. 90.
9. See "Purpose Driven Catholics," PurposeDriven, http://www.purposedriven.com/en-US/40DayCampaigns/PurposeDrivenChurches/Catholics/PDCatholics.htm and http://www.purposedriven.com/en-US/40DayCampaigns/PurposeDrivenChurches/Catholics/FromChurchLeaders.htm.
10. Richard Abanes, *Rick Warren and the Purpose that Drives Him*, p. 90.
11. Discussion "Myths of the Modern Mega-Church," May 23, 2005, the Pew Forum's biannual Faith Angle conference on religion, politics and public life, Event Transcript, http://pewforum.org/events/index.php?EventID=80.
12. For information on the Global Day of Prayer, building the Kingdom, and the second Reformation, see "The Global Day of Prayer: Part One" by Sarah Leslie, Discernment Newsletter, May/June 2005, http://www.discernment-ministries.org/NLMayJune_2005.htm; and "The Second Reformation: The Global Day of Prayer - Part Two" by Sarah Leslie; Discernment Newsletter, July/August 2005, http://www.discernment-ministries.org/NLJulyAugust_2005.htm.
13. As quoted in "Pastor found 'purpose' in spreading God's word" by Emily Ramshaw, *The Dallas Morning News*, May 16, 2005, http://www.dallasnews.com/sharedcontent/dws/dn/religion/stories/051605dnccowarrenq&a.b0dfb56a.html; it is also posted at http://www.purposedriven.com/en-US/AboutUs/PdintheNews/Archives/Pastor_found_purpose.htm.
14. "What is Purpose Driven?" by PD Staff, http://www.pastors.com/article.asp?ArtID=8096.
15. "What is PurposeDriven?", PurposeDriven, http://www.purposedriven.com/en-US/AboutUs/WhatIsPD/7+Myths+of+PD.htm.
16. "Purpose Driven in Rwanda" by Timothy C. Morgan, posted 9/23/05, *Christianity Today*, October 2005, http://www.christianitytoday.com/ct/2005/010/17.32.html.
17. "We Must Learn To Think Like Unbelievers" by Rick Warren, Rick Warren's Ministry Toolbox™, Issue #24, 10/17/2001, http://www.pastors.com/RWMT/?artid=742&id=24.
18. As quoted in "Rick Warren Interview," Pastors.com, http://www.pastors.com/portal/news/August/RickInterview.asp.

19. "We Must Learn To Think Like Unbelievers" by Rick Warren, http://www.pastors.com/RWMT/?artid=742&id=24.
20. Rick Warren, Saddleback Church Service, November 2, 2003; transcribed from http://www.saddlebackfamily.com/peace/Services/110203_high.asx.
21. As quoted in Discussion "Myths of the Modern Mega-Church," May 23, 2005, http://pewforum.org/events/index.php?EventID=80.
22. "We Must Learn To Think Like Unbelievers" by Rick Warren, http://www.pastors.com/RWMT/?artid=742&id=24.
23. *"You are invited to the* . . . 25th Anniversary Celebration of Saddleback Church," PurposeDriven, http://www.purposedriven.com/en-US/AboutUs/SaddlebackAnniversary.htm.
24. "Purpose Driven movement continues to gain momentum" by PD Staff, http://www.pastors.com/article.asp?ArtID=8257.
25. "What is Purpose Driven?" by PD Staff, http://www.pastors.com/article.asp?ArtID=8096.

Chapter Eleven

1. "Christians No Different from the World" by Pastor Chuck Baldwin, NewsWithViews.com, June 2, 2005, http://www.newswithviews.com/baldwin/baldwin239.htm.
2. "A Strange Faith -- Are Church-Going Kids Christian?" by Ed Vitagliano, news editor of *AFA Journal*, November/December 2005 issue, reprinted in *AgapePress*, November 15, 2005, http://headlines.agapepress.org/archive/11/152005a.asp.
3. Rick Warren, speaker at the Baptist World Centenary Congress -- "Cleansing Water," July 30, 2005, transcribed from Congress Internet Video Streaming, http://www.bwacongress2005.org.uk/feature.asp?id=832#; (can also be ordered at http://www.bwanet.org/Congress/).
4. "Survey Reveals The Books and Authors That Have Most Influenced Pastors," The Barna Update, May 30, 2005, http://www.barna.org/FlexPage.aspx?Page=BarnaUpdate&BarnaUpdateID=189.
5. As quoted in "POWER PASTOR: Will Success Spoil Rick Warren?" by Marc Gunther, *FORTUNE* Magazine, October 2005, http://www.fortune.com/fortune/print/0,15935,1118645,00.html; (now at http://money.cnn.com/magazines/fortune/fortune_archive/2005/10/31/8359189/index.htm).
6. Sidebar advertisement, "Holiday Sermon Series CD," in "Three things to remember this Christmas" by Rick Warren, Rick Warren's Ministry Toolbox™, Issue #238, 12/21/2005, http://www.pastors.com/RWMT/?id=238&artid=7511&expand=1; and Sidebar advertisement, "Holiday Sermon Series CD," in "Sing along with Handel" by John Fischer, Rick Warren's Ministry Toolbox™, Issue #236, 12/7/2005, http://www.pastors.com/rwmt/?artid=8946&id=236.
7. On the Links, "Holiday sermons," Rick Warren's Ministry Toolbox™, Issue #234, 11/23/2005, http://www.pastors.com/RWMT/?ID=234.

8. Sidebar advertisement, "Holiday Sermon Series CD," in "Three things to remember this Christmas" by Rick Warren, http://www.pastors.com/RWMT/?id=238&artid=7511&expand=1.
9. Holiday Message Transcript Collection CD, http://www.pastors.com/pcom/sermons/holidaysp.asp.
10. "Holiday Sermons and More!", an e-mail Pastors.com sent on December 12, 2005 to its subscribers.
11. About Rick Warren, RickWarren.com, http://www.rickwarren.com/about.html.
12. Ibid.
13. Ibid.
14. Ibid.
15. As quoted in Discussion "Myths of the Modern Mega-Church," May 23, 2005, the Pew Forum's biannual Faith Angle conference on religion, politics and public life, Event Transcript, http://pewforum.org/events/index.php?EventID=80.
16. "'We're Made for More Than Success,'" an interview of Rick Warren by Jennifer Barrett, *Newsweek*, December 15, 2005, MSNBC.com, http://msnbc.msn.com/id/10495711/site/newsweek/.
17. "Purpose Driven in Rwanda" by Timothy C. Morgan, posted 9/23/05, *Christianity Today*, October 2005, http://www.christianitytoday.com/ct/2005/010/17.32.html.
18. "Legislators welcome Rick Warren in session's final week" by James A. Smith Sr., Executive Editor, *Florida Baptist Witness*, May 6, 2004, http://www.floridabaptistwitness.com/2523.article.
19. About Rick Warren, RickWarren.com, http://www.rickwarren.com/about.html.
20. Rick Warren, Keynote Address, 2005 RNA Annual Conference in Miami, Friday, September 30, 2005, Religion Newswriters Association, http://www.rna.org/programschedule.php. Transcribed from the audio available in the RNA conference archives at http://www.rna.org/meetingdates.php; below Friday, Sept. 29 [sic] -- "The Rev. Rick Warren." The audio is also available at Lighthouse Trails Research Project, Rick Warren Transcripts, Audio and Video Clips, Audio Sessions, #6 -- "RW at the Religious Newswriters Association" -- at http://www.lighthousetrailsresearch.com/warrenclips.htm.
21. About Rick Warren, RickWarren.com, http://www.rickwarren.com/about.html.
22. Rick Warren, 2005 RNA Annual Conference in Miami, Friday, September 30, 2005. Transcribed from the audio available at http://www.rna.org/meetingdates.php; below Friday, Sept. 29 [sic] -- "Questions and answers."
23. As quoted in "Rick Warren's Second Reformation," part two of this "exclusive" two-part interview with Rick Warren, by David Kuo, Beliefnet, http://www.beliefnet.com/story/177/story_17718.html.
24. Aspen Ideas Festival, The Aspen Institute, July 6, 2005, "Discussion: Religion and Leadership," with David Gergen and Rick Warren, http://www.aspeninstitute.org/site/c.huLWJeMRKpH/b.901097/k.C0C7/Agenda.htm. Transcribed from the audio available at Lighthouse Trails Research

Project, Coming From the Lighthouse Newsletter, November 2005 -- "Aspen Festival of Ideas Audio (Large File)" -- at http://www.lighthousetrailsresearch.com/newsletternovember05.htm.
25. "Rick Warren tour to mark 2-year point for 'Purpose-Driven Life'" by BP Staff, https://pastors.com/article.asp?ArtID=7292.
26. "Purpose Driven movement continues to gain momentum" by PD Staff, http://www.pastors.com/article.asp?ArtID=8257.
27. Aspen Ideas Festival, The Aspen Institute, July 6, 2005, "Discussion: Religion and Leadership," with David Gergen and Rick Warren. Transcribed from the audio available at http://www.lighthousetrailsresearch.com/newsletternovember05.htm.
28. As quoted in Discussion "Myths of the Modern Mega-Church," May 23, 2005, http://pewforum.org/events/index.php?EventID=80.
29. "Warren of Rwanda" by David Van Biema, *Time* Online Edition, August 22, 2005 (posted 8/15/05), http://www.time.com/time/magazine/article/0,9171,1093746,00.html.
30. "Purpose Driven in Rwanda" by Timothy C. Morgan, http://www.christianitytoday.com/ct/2005/010/17.32.html.
31. As quoted in Discussion "Myths of the Modern Mega-Church," May 23, 2005, http://pewforum.org/events/index.php?EventID=80.
32. Rick Warren's public address, "Election 2004: a New Spiritual Awakening," March 9, 2005, at Harvard's Kennedy School of Government, sponsored by the Kennedy School's Saguaro Seminar, http://www.ksg.harvard.edu/press/press%20releases/2005/warren_030705.htm. Transcribed from the audio available at The Saguaro Seminar: Civic Engagement in America, at http://www.ksg.harvard.edu/saguaro/; below "In The News" -- "Kennedy School Forum in March 2005."
33. As quoted in Discussion "Myths of the Modern Mega-Church," May 23, 2005, http://pewforum.org/events/index.php?EventID=80.
34. "Influential Forum," Council on Foreign Relations brochure, http://www.cfr.org/content/publications/attachments/Council_brochure.pdf, p. 4.
35. Council on Foreign Relations, An Influential Forum, Past Meetings, http://www.cfr.org/about/what_we_do/influential_forum.html?year=2005. (Note: The specific page with Rick Warren's meeting of September 12, 2005 keeps changing as pages of more recent meetings keep getting added before it; as of today it is page 11 on this webpage.)
36. "*Update* Rick Warren at the United Nations" by Ingrid Schlueter, Slice of Laodicea, September 15, 2005, http://www.sliceoflaodicea.com/archives/2005/09/update_rick_war.php.
37. "Peace Plan" by Rick Warren, http://www.saddlebackfamily.com/home/todaystory.asp?id=6213.
38. "POWER PASTOR: Will Success Spoil Rick Warren?" by Marc Gunther, http://www.fortune.com/fortune/print/0,15935,1118645,00.html; (now at http://money.cnn.com/magazines/fortune/fortune_archive/2005/10/31/8359189/index.htm).

39. "'God branding' in films gains religious acceptance" by Ann Pepper, *The Orange County Register*, December 9, 2005, http://www.ocregister.com/ocregister/news/atoz/article_882265.php.
40. "This evangelist has a 'Purpose'" by Cathy Lynn Grossman, *USA TODAY*, July 21, 2003, http://www.usatoday.com/life/2003-07-21-rick-warren_x.htm.
41. About Rick Warren, RickWarren.com, http://www.rickwarren.com/about.html.
42. Aspen Ideas Festival, The Aspen Institute, July 6, 2005, "Discussion: Religion and Leadership," with David Gergen and Rick Warren. Transcribed from the audio available at http://www.lighthousetrailsresearch.com/newsletternovember05.htm.
43. "POWER PASTOR: Will Success Spoil Rick Warren?" by Marc Gunther, http://www.fortune.com/fortune/print/0,15935,1118645,00.html; (now at http://money.cnn.com/magazines/fortune/fortune_archive/2005/10/31/8359189/index.htm).
44. *Tozer on Worship and Entertainment*, A.W. Tozer, Selected Excerpts Compiled by James L. Snyder, pp. 179-180.
45. As quoted in Saddleback Sayings, Rick Warren's Ministry Toolbox™, Issue #89, 2/12/2003, http://www.pastors.com/RWMT/?ID=89.
46. As quoted in "Rick Warren Interview," Pastors.com, http://www.pastors.com/portal/news/August/RickInterview.asp.
47. As quoted in ibid.
48. As quoted in "Rick Warren: purpose-driven balance means more than technique" by Staff, An interview with Rick Warren, Pastors.com, https://pastors.com/article.asp?ArtID=4212.

Chapter Twelve

1. "Peace Plan" by Rick Warren, http://www.saddlebackfamily.com/home/todaystory.asp?id=6213.
2. "Pastors commit to 'new Reformation' at PDC Conference" by Tobin Perry, http://www.pastors.com/article.asp?ArtID=8310.
3. "'Second Reformation' will unify church, Warren tells Dallas GDOP" by Ken Camp, http://www.pastors.com/article.asp?ArtID=8280.
4. As quoted in Discussion "Myths of the Modern Mega-Church," May 23, 2005, the Pew Forum's biannual Faith Angle conference on religion, politics and public life, Event Transcript, http://pewforum.org/events/index.php?EventID=80.
5. Ibid.
6. *Catechism of the Catholic Church* (Washington, D.C.: United States Catholic Conference, 1994), Libreria Editrice Vaticana, *Imprimi Potest* + Joseph Cardinal Ratzinger.
7. Pope John Paul II, Apostolic Constitution *Fidei Depositum* on the Publication of the *Catechism of the Catholic Church*, ibid., p. 3.
8. Pope John Paul II, ibid., pp. 6, 5.

9. "This evangelist has a 'Purpose'" by Cathy Lynn Grossman, *USA TODAY*, July 21, 2003, http://www.usatoday.com/life/2003-07-21-rick-warren_x.htm.
10. As quoted in Discussion "Myths of the Modern Mega-Church," May 23, 2005, http://pewforum.org/events/index.php?EventID=80.
11. For information, see Richard Bennett's website at http://www.bereanbeacon.org; he is a former Roman Catholic Priest who is now saved by the grace of God through faith in the Lord Jesus Christ, and he is working to help those in Catholicism find the true Gospel of Jesus Christ.
12. "What a purpose driven church is not" by Rick Warren, Rick Warren's Ministry Toolbox™, Issue #208, 5/25/2005, http://www.pastors.com/RWMT/?artid=8275&id=208.
13. "American Society for Church Growth Examines the Emerging Church," News and Events, Fuller Theological Seminary, http://www.fuller.edu/news/html/church_growth04.asp.
14. As quoted in "The Church Growth Movement in the 21st Century—Have the Rules Changed?" by Dennis W. Costella, *FOUNDATION* Magazine, Nov-Dec 2004 Issue, http://www.fundamentalbiblechurch.org/Foundation/fbcChurchGrowht21stCentpuryP1.htm [sic].
15. Ibid.
16. As quoted in Discussion "Myths of the Modern Mega-Church," May 23, 2005, http://pewforum.org/events/index.php?EventID=80.
17. As quoted in "Quotable," *The Berean Call*, May 1999 issue; (ellipsis dots in the original).
18. "News From Pastor Rick" by Rick Warren, an e-mail he sent on May 14, 2005 to his Saddleback Family.
19. "Pastors commit to 'new Reformation' at PDC Conference" by Tobin Perry, http://www.pastors.com/article.asp?ArtID=8310.
20. Rick Warren, as quoted in "Legislators welcome Rick Warren in session's final week" by James A. Smith Sr., Executive Editor, *Florida Baptist Witness*, May 6, 2004, http://www.floridabaptistwitness.com/2523.article.
21. As quoted in "Pastor makes PEACE a mission" by Gwendolyn Driscoll, *The Orange County Register*, September 17, 2005, http://www.ocregister.com/ocr/2005/09/17/sections/local/local/article_679625.php.
22. Rick Warren, Saddleback's 25th Anniversary Celebration, April 17th, 2005, transcribed from http://www.saddlebackfamily.com/home/anniversary_celebration.asp.
23. As quoted in Discussion "Myths of the Modern Mega-Church," May 23, 2005, http://pewforum.org/events/index.php?EventID=80.
24. As quoted in ibid.
25. As quoted in "Purpose Driven in Rwanda" by Timothy C. Morgan, posted 9/23/05, *Christianity Today*, October 2005, http://www.christianitytoday.com/ct/2005/010/17.32.html.
26. From the TIME Global Health Summit, Rick Warren talks with Lisa Mullins of The World—a co-production of the BBC World Service, PRI, and WGBH Boston—November 3, 2005. Transcribed

from the audio available at http://www.theworld.org/heardonair/2005/11/index.shtml. The audio is also available at Lighthouse Trails Research Project, Rick Warren Transcripts, Audio and Video Clips, Audio Sessions, #4 -- "November 2005: BBC World News Interview with RW" -- at http://www.lighthousetrailsresearch.com/warrenclips.htm.

27. Rick Warren, speaker at the Baptist World Centenary Congress -- "Cleansing Water," July 30, 2005, transcribed from http://www.bwacongress2005.org.uk/feature.asp?id=832#. Rick Warren had also made a similar statement at Saddleback's 25th Anniversary Celebration, April 17th, 2005, http://www.saddlebackfamily.com/home/anniversary_celebration.asp.

28. Ibid (Congress).

29. Ibid.

30. "Pastors commit to 'new Reformation' at PDC Conference" by Tobin Perry, http://www.pastors.com/article.asp?ArtID=8310.

31. Rick Warren, Saddleback's 25th Anniversary Celebration at Angel Stadium in Anaheim, California, April 17th, 2005, transcribed from http://www.saddlebackfamily.com/home/anniversary_celebration.asp.

32. As quoted in "Pastor lays out a global vision" by Ann Pepper, http://www.ocregister.com/ocr/2005/04/17/sections/local/local/article_484964.php.

33. Rick Warren, Keynote Address, 2005 RNA Annual Conference in Miami, Friday, September 30, 2005, Religion Newswriters Association, http://www.rna.org/programschedule.php. Transcribed from the audio available in the RNA conference archives at http://www.rna.org/meetingdates.php; below Friday, Sept. 29 [sic] -- "The Rev. Rick Warren."

34. Ibid.

35. Ibid., but under the link "Questions and answers."

36. Speakers, TIME Global Health Summit, *TIME* magazine, http://www.time.com/time/2005/globalhealth/speakers.html.

37. TIME Global Health Summit, Press Conference – Rick Warren, November 1, 2005, 2:15pm, Transcript, *TIME* magazine, http://www.time.com/time/2005/globalhealth/transcripts/110105warrenpc.pdf. The webcast can be viewed at http://www.time.com/time/2005/globalhealth/webcasts.html.

38. TIME Global Health Summit, The Case for Optimism, November 1, 2005, 5:30pm, Transcript, *TIME* magazine, http://www.time.com/time/2005/globalhealth/transcripts/110105optimism.pdf. The webcast can be viewed at http://www.time.com/time/2005/globalhealth/webcasts.html.

39. "Aspen Institute Set To Launch Aspen Ideas Festival; Jane Goodall, Colin Powell and Toni Morrison Among the Headliners," 2005 News Releases and Media Alerts, The Aspen Institute, http://www.aspeninstitute.org/site/apps/nl/content2.asp?c=huLWJeMRKpH&b=696077&ct=1132763.

40. Aspen Ideas Festival, The Aspen Institute, July 6, 2005, "Discussion: Religion and Leadership," with David Gergen and Rick Warren, http://www.aspeninstitute.org/site/c.huLWJeMRKpH/

b.901097/k.C0C7/Agenda.htm. Transcribed from the audio available at Lighthouse Trails Research Project, http://www.lighthousetrailsresearch.com/newsletternovember05.htm.
41. "No spectators allowed" by Ann Pepper, *The Orange County Register*, November 6, 2005, http://www.ocregister.com/ocregister/news/article_751553.php.
42. "Attack on AIDS part of global P.E.A.C.E. strategy, Rick Warren says" by Shannon Baker, http://www.purposedriven.com/en-US/AboutUs/PDintheNews/Attack_on_AIDS_part_of_global_PEACE_strategy.htm.
43. "Solution to AIDS, other woes 'right in front of us,' Warren tells NYC summit" by Dorianne Perrucci, PurposeDriven News, http://www.purposedriven.com/en-US/AboutUs/PDintheNews/Archives/Solution_to_AIDS.htm.
44. "Methodist Leaders Pledge to Tackle Malaria Scourge" by Joy Victory, ABC News, November 2, 2005, http://abcnews.go.com/Health/GlobalHealth/story?id=1271450.
45. "Peace Plan" by Rick Warren, http://www.saddlebackfamily.com/home/todaystory.asp?id=6213.
46. Sidebar, "The P.E.A.C.E. Plan," in "Solution to AIDS, other woes 'right in front of us,' Warren tells NYC summit" by Dorianne Perrucci, http://www.pastors.com/article.asp?ArtID=8816.
47. As quoted in "Rick Warren enters 26th year of ministry with new vision: 'Purpose' pastor unveils global Peace Plan" by Christina M. Testa, *Christian Examiner*, May 2005, http://www.christianexaminer.com/Articles/Articles%20May05/Art_May05_02.html.
48. As quoted in "Pastor urges Anglicans to unite and care for poor" by Ann Rodgers, *Pittsburgh Post-Gazette*, November 12, 2005, post-gazette.com, http://www.post-gazette.com/pg/05316/605324.stm.
49. As quoted in ibid.
50. "Attack on AIDS part of global P.E.A.C.E. strategy, Rick Warren says" by Shannon Baker, PurposeDriven, http://www.purposedriven.com/en-US/AboutUs/PDintheNews/Attack_on_AIDS_part_of_global_PEACE_strategy.htm.
51. As quoted in "Rick Warren's Second Reformation," part two of this "exclusive" two-part interview with Rick Warren, by David Kuo, Beliefnet, http://www.beliefnet.com/story/177/story_17718.html.

Chapter Thirteen

1. Rick Warren, speaker at the Baptist World Centenary Congress -- "Cleansing Water," July 30, 2005, transcribed from Congress Internet Video Streaming, http://www.bwacongress2005.org.uk/feature.asp?id=832#.
2. Ibid.
3. Rick Warren, Saddleback's 25th Anniversary Celebration at Angel Stadium in Anaheim, California, April 17th, 2005, transcribed from http://www.saddlebackfamily.com/home/anniversary_celebration.asp.

4. Rick Warren, Global Day of Prayer Dallas, TX, Part 8 of 10, May 15, 2005, transcribed from Global Day of Prayer Streaming & Downloadable Video Resources, American Bible Society, http://www.gdopvideo.com.
5. Rick Warren, Saddleback's 25th Anniversary Celebration, April 17th, 2005, transcribed from http://www.saddlebackfamily.com/home/anniversary_celebration.asp.
6. Rick Warren, speaker at the Baptist World Centenary Congress -- "Cleansing Water," July 30, 2005, transcribed from http://www.bwacongress2005.org.uk/feature.asp?id=832#.
7. Ibid.
8. As quoted in "Rick Warren enters 26th year of ministry with new vision: 'Purpose' pastor unveils global Peace Plan" by Christina M. Testa, *Christian Examiner*, May 2005, http://www.christianexaminer.com/Articles/Articles%20May05/Art_May05_02.html.
9. Rick Warren, Saddleback's 25th Anniversary Celebration, April 17th, 2005, transcribed from http://www.saddlebackfamily.com/home/anniversary_celebration.asp.
10. "A Plan for Peace" by Rick Warren, *Ladies' Home Journal*, December 2005 issue, p. 26.
11. Ibid., pp. 26, 28.
12. Aspen Ideas Festival, The Aspen Institute, July 6, 2005, "Discussion: Religion and Leadership," with David Gergen and Rick Warren, http://www.aspeninstitute.org/site/c.huLWJeMRKpH/b.901097/k.C0C7/Agenda.htm. Transcribed from the audio available at Lighthouse Trails Research Project, http://www.lighthousetrailsresearch.com/newsletternovember05.htm.
13. "Pragmatism Goes to Church" by A.W. Tozer, *The Best of A.W. Tozer*, Book Two, Compiled by Warren W. Wiersbe, (Camp Hill, Pennsylvania: Christian Publications, 1980), pp. 254-256.
14. "P.E.A.C.E. Plan a worldwide revolution, Warren tells Angel Stadium crowd" by Mark Kelly, PurposeDriven News, http://www.purposedriven.com/en-US/AboutUs/PDintheNews/Archives/25th_Celebration.htm.
15. "Pastor: Mission possible // Saddleback Church leader has assignment for his congregation, if they care enough to accept it" by Jim Hinch, *The Orange County Register*, November 2, 2003, (available through the archives of http://www.ocregister.com).
16. "The task before us is enormous, but God is equipping us" by Rick Warren, http://www.pastors.com/RWMT/?id=200&artid=8139&expand=1.
17. As quoted in "Rick Warren: Global Baptists 'are all in this together'" by Trennis Henderson, Western Recorder, Baptist Congress Today, July 30, 2005, http://www.bwanet.org/Congress/congresstoday29f.htm.

Chapter Fourteen

1. "Rick Warren's Plan to mobilize one billion foot soldiers for the gospel" by Michael Ireland, Chief Correspondent, ASSIST News Service, May 14, 2005, http://www.assistnews.net/Stories/s05050056.htm. (This was also reported in "Warren's New PEACE Global Evangelism Vision

Inspired by Purpose Driven Life," Christian Today, May 16, 2005, http://www.christiantoday.com/news/ministries/warrens.new.peace.global.evangelism.vision.inspired.by.purpose.driven.life/265.htm.)

2. From the TIME Global Health Summit, Rick Warren talks with Lisa Mullins of The World, November 3, 2005. Transcribed from the audio available at http://www.theworld.org/heardonair/2005/11/index.shtml.

3. "Rick Warren's Plan to mobilize one billion foot soldiers for the gospel" by Michael Ireland, http://www.assistnews.net/Stories/s05050056.htm. (These statements were also reported in "Warren's New PEACE Global Evangelism Vision Inspired by Purpose Driven Life," http://www.christiantoday.com/news/ministries/warrens.new.peace.global.evangelism.vision.inspired.by.purpose.driven.life/265.htm.)

4. "Rick Warren enters 26th year of ministry with new vision" by Christina M. Testa, *Christian Examiner*, May 2005, http://www.christianexaminer.com/Articles/Articles%20May05/Art_May05_02.html.

5. Rick Warren, as quoted in "Legislators welcome Rick Warren in session's final week" by James A. Smith Sr., Executive Editor, *Florida Baptist Witness*, May 6, 2004, http://www.floridabaptistwitness.com/2523.article.

6. "The task before us is enormous, but God is equipping us" by Rick Warren, http://www.pastors.com/RWMT/?id=200&artid=8139&expand=1.

7. Rick Warren, Keynote Address, 2005 RNA Annual Conference in Miami, Friday, September 30, 2005, Religion Newswriters Association, http://www.rna.org/programschedule.php. Transcribed from the audio available in the RNA conference archives at http://www.rna.org/meetingdates.php; below Friday, Sept. 29 [sic] -- "Questions and answers."

8. "GOD'S DREAM FOR YOU - AND THE WORLD!" by Rick Warren, an e-mail he sent on October 27, 2003 to his Saddleback Family. For information on this, see Chapter 12 - "Rick Warren's P.E.A.C.E. Plan," pp. 131-142, in the book *Deceived on Purpose*, Second Edition, by Warren Smith.

9. "News From Pastor Rick" by Rick Warren, an e-mail he sent on May 14, 2005 to his Saddleback Family.

10. "Pastors commit to 'new Reformation' at PDC Conference" by Tobin Perry, http://www.pastors.com/article.asp?ArtID=8310.

11. As quoted in "Evangelism Gone Entrepreneurial," *BusinessWeek* Online Extra, May 23, 2005, http://www.businessweek.com/magazine/content/05_21/b3934015_mz001.htm.

12. "The P.E.A.C.E. Plan: Attacking The Five Global Goliaths" by Rick Warren, P.E.A.C.E., http://pddocs.purposedriven.com:8088/docs/media/HIV_Media_PEACE_Handout.pdf.

13. TIME Global Health Summit, The Case for Optimism, November 1, 2005, 5:30pm, Transcript, *TIME* magazine, http://www.time.com/time/2005/globalhealth/transcripts/110105optimism.pdf. The webcast can be viewed at http://www.time.com/time/2005/globalhealth/webcasts.html.

14. "Celebrating 25 Years: P.E.A.C.E. plan a worldwide revolution" by Mark Kelly, news editor of Purpose Driven Ministries, http://www.saddlebackfamily.org/home/todaystory.asp?id=7312.
15. Skip Lanfried, North America PEACE Pastor, PEACE Pilot Briefing 2005, http://www.purposedriven.com/en-US/Events/PEACEPilotBriefing2005/PeacePilotBriefing2005/peacebriefingoverview.htm.
16. Ibid.
17. "Pastor lays out a global vision" by Ann Pepper, http://www.ocregister.com/ocr/2005/04/17/sections/local/local/article_484964.php.
18. As quoted in ibid.
19. "Saddleback pastor launches PEACE plan" by Gwendolyn Driscoll, *The Orange County Register*, September 18, 2005, http://www.ocregister.com/ocregister/news/local/article_680667.php.
20. "Burning with a new purpose" by Jim Remsen, *The Philadelphia Inquirer*, June 26, 2005, http://www.philly.com/mld/inquirer/2005/06/26/news/editorial/11985718.htm.

Chapter Fifteen

1. Alice Bailey & Djwhal Khul, *The Externalization of the Hierarchy*, Section II - The General World Picture, (Caux, Switzerland: Netnews Association and/or its suppliers, 2002), http://www.netnews.org -- http://laluni.helloyou.ws/netnews/bk/externalisation/exte1040.html.
2. Alice Bailey & Djwhal Khul, *The Labors of Hercules* - Labor XII, Lecture by A.A.B. - 1936, (Caux, Switzerland: Netnews Association and/or its suppliers, 2002), http://www.netnews.org -- http://laluni.helloyou.ws/netnews/bk/hercules/herc1062.html.
3. Alice Bailey, *From Bethlehem to Calvary*, Chapter Seven - Our Immediate Goal, The Founding of the Kingdom, (Caux, Switzerland: Netnews Association and/or its suppliers, 2002), http://www.netnews.org -- http://laluni.helloyou.ws/netnews/bk/bethlehem/beth1078.html.
4. Alice Bailey & Djwhal Khul, *The Externalization of the Hierarchy*, Section III - Forces behind the Evolutionary Process, http://laluni.helloyou.ws/netnews/bk/externalisation/exte1178.html.
5. Alice Bailey, *From Bethlehem to Calvary*, Chapter Five - The Fourth Initiation, The Crucifixion, http://laluni.helloyou.ws/netnews/bk/bethlehem/beth1063.html.
6. Ibid., http://laluni.helloyou.ws/netnews/bk/bethlehem/beth1064.html.
7. Alice Bailey & Djwhal Khul, *The Externalization of the Hierarchy*, Section III - Forces behind the Evolutionary Process, http://laluni.helloyou.ws/netnews/bk/externalisation/exte1194.html.
8. Alice Bailey, *From Bethlehem to Calvary*, Chapter Five - The Fourth Initiation, The Crucifixion, http://laluni.helloyou.ws/netnews/bk/bethlehem/beth1068.html.
9. Ibid., Chapter Seven - Our Immediate Goal, The Founding of the Kingdom, http://laluni.helloyou.ws/netnews/bk/bethlehem/beth1079.html.
10. Ibid., Chapter Two - The First Initiation, The Birth at Bethlehem, http://laluni.helloyou.ws/netnews/bk/bethlehem/beth1022.html.

11. Ibid., http://laluni.helloyou.ws/netnews/bk/bethlehem/beth1025.html.
12. Ibid., Chapter Seven - Our Immediate Goal, The Founding of the Kingdom, http://laluni.helloyou.ws/netnews/bk/bethlehem/beth1082.html.
13. Ibid., Chapter Five - The Fourth Initiation, The Crucifixion, http://laluni.helloyou.ws/netnews/bk/bethlehem/beth1062.html.
14. Alice Bailey & Djwhal Khul, *The Reappearance of the Christ*, Chapter V - The Teachings of the Christ, The Establishing of Right Human Relations, http://laluni.helloyou.ws/netnews/bk/reappearance/reap1033.html.
15. Warren Smith, *Reinventing Jesus Christ: The New Gospel* (Ravenna, Ohio: Conscience Press, 2002). (Available through http://discernment-ministries.org/Catalog.htm, and it is posted online with Smith's 2006 chapter updates at http://www.reinventingjesuschrist.com.) Also see the section "Persecution Through the 'Selection Process,'" pp. 162-166, in his book *Deceived on Purpose*, Second Edition.
16. Alice Bailey, *From Bethlehem to Calvary*, Chapter One - Introductory Remarks on Initiation, http://laluni.helloyou.ws/netnews/bk/bethlehem/beth1007.html.
17. Alice Bailey & Djwhal Khul, *The Externalization of the Hierarchy*, Section II - The General World Picture, http://laluni.helloyou.ws/netnews/bk/externalisation/exte1110.html.
18. "Nonbelievers Too Can Be Saved, Says Pope," November 30, 2005, ZENIT News Agency - The World Seen From Rome, http://www.zenit.org/english/visualizza.phtml?sid=80888.
19. Alice Bailey & Djwhal Khul, *Esoteric Psychology II*, Chapter III - Humanity Today, The World Situation, http://laluni.helloyou.ws/netnews/bk/psychology2/psyc2250.html.
20. Rick Warren, Saddleback's 25th Anniversary Celebration at Angel Stadium in Anaheim, California, April 17th, 2005, transcribed from http://www.saddlebackfamily.com/home/anniversary_celebration.asp.
21. From the TIME Global Health Summit, Rick Warren talks with Lisa Mullins of The World, November 3, 2005. Transcribed from the audio available at http://www.theworld.org/heardonair/2005/11/index.shtml.
22. Rick Warren, Keynote Address, 2005 RNA Annual Conference in Miami, Friday, September 30, 2005, Religion Newswriters Association, http://www.rna.org/programschedule.php. Transcribed from the audio available in the RNA conference archives at http://www.rna.org/meetingdates.php; below Friday, Sept. 29 [sic] -- "Questions and answers."
23. Alice Bailey & Djwhal Khul, *The Rays and the Initiations*, Part One - Fourteen Rules for Group Initiation, (Caux, Switzerland: Netnews Association and/or its suppliers, 2002), http://www.netnews.org -- http://laluni.helloyou.ws/netnews/bk/rays/rays1111.html.
24. "What is Purpose Driven?" by PD Staff, http://www.pastors.com/article.asp?ArtID=8096.

25. Alice Bailey & Djwhal Khul, *Discipleship in the New Age II*, Teachings on Initiation - Part III, (Caux, Switzerland: Netnews Association and/or its suppliers, 2002), http://www.netnews.org -- http://laluni.helloyou.ws/netnews/bk/discipleship2/disc2087.html.
26. Alice Bailey & Djwhal Khul, *Esoteric Psychology I*, Section Two, III. The Rays and Man, (Caux, Switzerland: Netnews Association and/or its suppliers, 2002), http://www.netnews.org -- http://laluni.helloyou.ws/netnews/bk/psychology1/psyc1111.html.
27. Alice Bailey & Djwhal Khul, *Problems of Humanity*, Chapter V - The Problem of the Churches, III. The Essential Truths, http://laluni.helloyou.ws/netnews/bk/problems/prob1056.html.
28. Alice Bailey & Djwhal Khul, *Esoteric Psychology II*, Chapter I - The Egoic Ray, The Seven Laws of Soul or Group Life, http://laluni.helloyou.ws/netnews/bk/psychology2/psyc2040.html.
29. Alice Bailey & Djwhal Khul, *Esoteric Psychology I*, Section Two, III. The Rays and Man, http://laluni.helloyou.ws/netnews/bk/psychology1/psyc1111.html.
30. Alice Bailey, *From Bethlehem to Calvary*, Chapter Seven - Our Immediate Goal, The Founding of the Kingdom, http://laluni.helloyou.ws/netnews/bk/bethlehem/beth1083.html.
31. Ibid., http://laluni.helloyou.ws/netnews/bk/bethlehem/beth1085.html.

Chapter Sixteen

1. "Will You Join Me?" by Rick Warren, an e-mail dated June 3, 2005 and sent on June 4, 2005. This e-mail contains a copy of the letter sent to President Bush, which is dated June 1, 2005 and signed "U.S. Faith Leaders."
2. The ONE Campaign, http://www.one.org/. (The home page has since been changed.) This quote is also found in the "ONE Volunteer Tool Kit" webpage of Bread for the World, one of the founders of The ONE Campaign, at http://www.bread.org/get-involved/one-campaign/volunteer-tool-kit.html.
3. "POWER PASTOR: Will Success Spoil Rick Warren?" by Marc Gunther, *FORTUNE* Magazine, October 2005, http://www.fortune.com/fortune/print/0,15935,1118645,00.html; (now at http://money.cnn.com/magazines/fortune/fortune_archive/2005/10/31/8359189/index.htm).
4. "Pastors Warren and Lusk Stress Spiritual Purpose to 'Stand For Africa' With One Campaign at Live 8 Concert," *Forbes*, 7/2/05, PR Newswire, http://www.forbes.com/prnewswire/feeds/prnewswire/2005/07/02/prnewswire200507022219PR_NEWS_B_MAT_NY_NYSA014.html.
5. About the Campaign, The ONE Campaign, http://www.one.org/About.html.
6. "Will You Join Me?" by Rick Warren, an e-mail he sent on June 4, 2005.
7. Resolution adopted by the General Assembly, "United Nations Millennium Declaration," 8th plenary meeting September 8, 2000, http://www.un.org/millennium/declaration/ares552e.htm. For information on the MDGs, the goals of this Millennium Declaration, see "Two UN Summits - One Millennium Goal: Conforming Humanity to Socialist Solidarity" by Berit Kjos, November 2000, http://www.crossroad.to/articles2/TwoSummits.htm. And for more information on the

U.N. and its various agendas, check out this website of Berit Kjos (who has done a great deal of research on the subject), including her new 4 part series "Warren's P.E.A.C.E. Plan & UN Goals" that starts on http://www.crossroad.to/articles2/05/peace-un.htm.
8. "Road Map towards the implementation of the United Nations Millennium Declaration," Report of the Secretary-General, United Nations General Assembly, September 6, 2001, http://www.un.org/documents/ga/docs/56/a56326.pdf, p. 7.
9. Resolution adopted by the General Assembly, "United Nations Millennium Declaration," 8th plenary meeting September 8, 2000, http://www.un.org/millennium/declaration/ares552e.htm.
10. "Charter of the United Nations," http://www.un.org/aboutun/charter/.
11. UN Millennium Development Goals, http://www.un.org/millenniumgoals/.
12. "The Millennium Messiah and World Change" by Carl Teichrib, January 2005, http://www.crossroad.to/articles2/05/teichrib/messiah.htm, quoting from *New Genesis: Shaping a Global Spirituality* by Robert Muller, (Anacortes, Washington: World Happiness and Cooperation, 1993/1982), pp. 126-127. See also "Evangelicals and New Agers Together" by Warren Smith, http://www.erwm.com/EvangelicalsandNewAgers.htm.
13. Foreword by Kofi A. Annan, UN Secretary-General, The Millennium Development Goals Report 2005, United Nations, Published by the United Nations Department of Public Information, May 2005, http://millenniumindicators.un.org/unsd/mi/pdf/MDG%20Book.pdf, p. 3.
14. "Burning with a new purpose" by Jim Remsen, *The Philadelphia Inquirer*, June 26, 2005, http://www.philly.com/mld/inquirer/2005/06/26/news/editorial/11985718.htm.
15. About the Campaign, The ONE Campaign, http://www.one.org/About.html.
16. Ibid.
17. "The Power of ONE: THEONECAMPAIGN.ORG," Bread for the World Institute, http://www.bread.org/get-involved/one-campaign/ONE-20handbook-20low-res.pdf, pp. 2, 3, 12, 6, 9, 8, 11.
18. Ibid., p. 15.
19. Ibid.
20. "Religious Leaders to Push Action on Hunger" by Kevin Eckstrom, Religion News Service, March 24, 2005, Bread for the World, http://www.bread.org/media/articles/2005/rns_mar_28.htm. (The article is also posted at http://www.catholicvoiceoakland.org/todaysnewsarchives/todaysnewsMar2505.htm.)
21. Ibid.
22. "Hunger No More: An Interfaith Convocation" – "Faith Leaders Scheduled to Attend," One Table, Many Voices, http://www.onetableconference.org/faith_leaders.html.
23. Ibid.
24. "Hunger No More: An Interfaith Convocation," June 6, 2005, Washington National Cathedral, Program, Bread for the World, http://www.bread.org/about-us/national-gathering/Interfaith-

Convocation-Program.pdf. The webcast of this service is also available at Bread for the World, http://www.bread.org/about-us/national-gathering/page.jsp?itemID=28171393.
25. Ibid.
26. Alice Bailey & Djwhal Khul, *The Reappearance of the Christ*, Chapter III - World Expectancy, http://laluni.helloyou.ws/netnews/bk/reappearance/reap1013.html.
27. "Thank You & Good News!" by Rick Warren, an e-mail he sent on June 22, 2005.
28. Ibid., quoting the article "G8 hammers out debt relief deal for poor nations" by Sumeet Desai and Brian Love, Reuters, June 11, 2005.
29. Rick Warren, speaker at the Baptist World Centenary Congress -- "Cleansing Water," July 30, 2005, transcribed from Congress Internet Video Streaming, http://www.bwacongress2005.org.uk/feature.asp?id=832#.
30. "Rick Warren Celebrates Baptist Congress with Message to UK Churches" by Daniel Blake, *Christian Today*, July 28, 2005, http://www.christiantoday.com/news/church/rick.warren.celebrates.baptist.congress.with.message.to.uk.churches/698.htm.
31. "Focus Group Topics Announced," Baptist World Congress, Media Release 17 June 2005, Baptist World Alliance, http://www.bwanet.org/News/05apr-jun/focusgrouptopicsannounced.htm.
32. "Carter: global 'hunger' for healing outweighs beliefs that divide faiths" by Greg Warner, Associated Baptist Press, Baptist Congress Today, July 31, 2005, Baptist World Alliance, http://www.bwanet.org/Congress/congresstoday31.htm.
33. As quoted in "Baptist World Congress: Christians must unite with those of other faiths to tackle oppression around the globe," July 27, 2005, Baptist World Centenary Congress, http://www.bwacongress2005.org.uk/information.asp?id=837; (also at http://www.bwanet.org/Congress/congresstoday28d.htm).
34. Rick Warren, speaker at the Baptist World Centenary Congress -- "Cleansing Water," July 30, 2005, transcribed from http://www.bwacongress2005.org.uk/feature.asp?id=832#.
35. "Carter: global 'hunger' for healing outweighs beliefs that divide faiths" by Greg Warner, http://www.bwanet.org/Congress/congresstoday31.htm.
36. Warren Smith, *Deceived On Purpose*, pp. 14-17.
37. "What Is the Proper Response to Hatred and Violence?" by Neale Donald Walsch, an essay in *From the Ashes: A Call to Action—The Spiritual Challenge*, Beliefnet Editors, (USA: Rodale Inc., 2001), pp. 19-21.

Chapter Seventeen

1. Alice Bailey & Djwhal Khul, *The Externalization of the Hierarchy*, Section III - Forces behind the Evolutionary Process, http://laluni.helloyou.ws/netnews/bk/externalisation/exte1174.html.
2. Alice Bailey & Djwhal Khul, *Problems of Humanity*, Chapter V - The Problem of the Churches, http://laluni.helloyou.ws/netnews/bk/problems/prob1062.html.

3. Richard Abanes, *Rick Warren and the Purpose that Drives Him*, p. 88.
4. Ibid., p. 11.
5. Interview with Rick Warren, CNN Larry King Live, Aired November 22, 2004, Transcript, http://transcripts.cnn.com/TRANSCRIPTS/0411/22/lkl.01.html.
6. "To the Readers of 'Lucifer'" by H. P. Blavatsky, *Lucifer*, January, 1888, http://www.blavatsky.net/blavatsky/arts/ToTheReadersOfLucifer.htm.

Chapter Eighteen

1. Alice Bailey & Djwhal Khul, *A Treatise on White Magic*, Rule Ten - The New Group of World Servers, (Caux, Switzerland: Netnews Association and/or its suppliers, 2002), http://www.netnews.org -- http://laluni.helloyou.ws/netnews/bk/magic/magi1172.html.
2. "Checklist of Some Principles of Theosophy," Blavatsky Net Foundation, http://www.blavatsky.net/theosophy/theosophy-checklist.htm.
3. Alice Bailey & Djwhal Khul, *Problems of Humanity*, Chapter V - The Problem of the Churches, III. The Essential Truths, http://laluni.helloyou.ws/netnews/bk/problems/prob1056.html.
4. Newsweek/Beliefnet Poll Results, Beliefnet, http://www.beliefnet.com/story/173/story_17353_1.html?rnd=39. The Poll was "conducted for Newsweek/Beliefnet by Princeton Survey Research Associates on August 2-4, 2005."
5. United Nations, Interfaith Prayer Breakfast, September 2005, transcribed from the audio of Rick Warren's message available at Lighthouse Trails Research Project, "The New Missiology—Keep Your Own Religion, Just Add Jesus" at http://www.lighthousetrailsresearch.com/newmissiology.htm; below Rick Warren's quote -- "Listen to entire transcript."
6. As quoted in "Rick Warren: 'God Didn't Need Us, He Wanted Us,'" part one of a two-part interview with Rick Warren, by David Kuo, Beliefnet, http://www.beliefnet.com/story/177/story_17737.html.
7. Interview with Rick Warren, CNN Larry King Live, Aired December 2, 2005, Transcript, http://transcripts.cnn.com/TRANSCRIPTS/0512/02/lkl.01.html.
8. Alice Bailey & Djwhal Khul, *The Reappearance of the Christ*, Chapter IV - The Work of the Christ Today and in the Future, http://laluni.helloyou.ws/netnews/bk/reappearance/reap1020.html.
9. Ibid., Chapter III - World Expectancy, http://laluni.helloyou.ws/netnews/bk/reappearance/reap1018.html.
10. Aspen Ideas Festival, The Aspen Institute, July 6, 2005, "Discussion: Religion and Leadership," with David Gergen and Rick Warren, http://www.aspeninstitute.org/site/c.huLWJeMRKpH/b.901097/k.C0C7/Agenda.htm. Transcribed from the audio available at Lighthouse Trails Research Project, http://www.lighthousetrailsresearch.com/newsletternovember05.htm.
11. Rick Warren's public address, "Election 2004: a New Spiritual Awakening," March 9, 2005, at Harvard's Kennedy School of Government, http://www.ksg.harvard.edu/press/

press%20releases/2005/warren_030705.htm. Transcribed from the audio available at The Saguaro Seminar: Civic Engagement in America, at http://www.ksg.harvard.edu/saguaro/.
12. As quoted in Discussion "Myths of the Modern Mega-Church," May 23, 2005, the Pew Forum's biannual Faith Angle conference on religion, politics and public life, Event Transcript, http://pewforum.org/events/index.php?EventID=80.
13. "A World of Baptists" by Greg Warner, Associated Baptist Press, 8/5/05, The Baptist Standard, http://www.baptiststandard.com/postnuke/index.php?module=htmlpages&func=display&pid=3720; quoting Denton Lotz, BWA General Secretary.
14. Ibid.
15. "Carter: global 'hunger' for healing outweighs beliefs that divide faiths" by Greg Warner, Associated Baptist Press, Baptist Congress Today, July 31, 2005, http://www.bwanet.org/Congress/congresstoday31.htm.
16. As quoted in "Rick Warren: Global Baptists 'are all in this together'" by Trennis Henderson, Western Recorder, Baptist Congress Today, July 30, 2005, http://www.bwanet.org/Congress/congresstoday29f.htm.
17. Alice Bailey, From Bethlehem to Calvary, Chapter Seven - Our Immediate Goal, The Founding of the Kingdom, http://laluni.helloyou.ws/netnews/bk/bethlehem/beth1083.html.
18. Alice Bailey & Djwhal Khul, The Externalization of the Hierarchy, Section II - The General World Picture, http://laluni.helloyou.ws/netnews/bk/externalisation/exte1087.html.
19. "A Strange Faith -- Are Church-Going Kids Christian?" by Ed Vitagliano, news editor of AFA Journal, November/December 2005 issue, reprinted in AgapePress, November 15, 2005, http://headlines.agapepress.org/archive/11/152005a.asp.
20. Rick Warren, speaker at the Baptist World Centenary Congress -- "Cleansing Water," July 30, 2005, transcribed from Congress Internet Video Streaming, http://www.bwacongress2005.org.uk/feature.asp?id=832#.
21. As quoted and reported in "Rick Warren Speaks about Purpose at United Nations" by Rhoda Tse, The Christian Post, September 14, 2005, http://www.christianpost.com/article/society/1835/section/rick.warren.speaks.about.purpose.at.united.nations/1.htm.
22. United Nations, Interfaith Prayer Breakfast, September 2005, transcribed from the audio available at http://www.lighthousetrailsresearch.com/newmissiology.htm.
23. Ibid.
24. Ibid.
25. Ibid.
26. Regarding the underlying beliefs of the United Nations, see http://www.crossroad.to/text/articles.html; and "The New World Religion" by William F. Jasper, The New American, September 23, 2002 issue, http://www.thenewamerican.com/tna/2002/09-23-2002/vo18no19_religion.htm.

See also "Will You Live under 'The Earth Charter'?" by Dennis L. Cuddy, NewsWithViews.com, January 11, 2006, at http://www.newswithviews.com/Cuddy/dennis54.htm; and "The Unholy Blend of Politics and Religion" at http://www.inplainsite.org/html/Page13a_political.html. The websites of the United Nations and the various organizations under its umbrella are very eye-opening themselves.

27. "Rick Warren Speaks about Purpose at United Nations" by Rhoda Tse, http://www.christianpost.com/article/society/1835/section/rick.warren.speaks.about.purpose.at.united.nations/1.htm.
28. United Nations, Interfaith Prayer Breakfast, September 2005, transcribed from the audio available at http://www.lighthousetrailsresearch.com/newmissiology.htm.
29. "*Update* Rick Warren at the United Nations" by Ingrid Schlueter, Slice of Laodicea, September 15, 2005, http://www.sliceoflaodicea.com/archives/2005/09/update_rick_war.php.
30. "Rick Warren Speaks about Purpose at United Nations" by Rhoda Tse, http://www.christianpost.com/article/society/1835/section/rick.warren.speaks.about.purpose.at.united.nations/1.htm.
31. Alice Bailey & Djwhal Khul, *Esoteric Psychology I*, Section Two - I. The Seven Creative Builders, the Seven Rays, http://laluni.helloyou.ws/netnews/bk/psychology1/psyc1053.html.

Chapter Nineteen

1. *The Portugal News*, 11/1/03, as quoted in the News Alert of the December 2003 issue of *The Berean Call*. (This news clip is also posted as "Catholic Fatima Shrine Has Developed Into Centre Where All Religions of World Can Pay Homage To Their Various Gods!" at http://www.cuttingedge.org/news_updates/nz1479.htm.)
2. Aspen Ideas Festival, The Aspen Institute, July 6, 2005, "Discussion: Religion and Leadership," with David Gergen and Rick Warren, http://www.aspeninstitute.org/site/c.huLWJeMRKpH/b.901097/k.C0C7/Agenda.htm. Transcribed from the audio available at Lighthouse Trails Research Project, http://www.lighthousetrailsresearch.com/newsletternovember05.htm.
3. Neale Donald Walsch, *Tomorrow's God: Our Greatest Spiritual Challenge* (New York, New York: Atria Books, 2004) p. 236.
4. As quoted in "'We're Made for More Than Success,'" an interview of Rick Warren by Jennifer Barrett, *Newsweek*, December 15, 2005, http://msnbc.msn.com/id/10495711/site/newsweek/, (pages 2-3).
5. Rick Warren, Keynote Address, 2005 RNA Annual Conference in Miami, Friday, September 30, 2005, Religion Newswriters Association, http://www.rna.org/programschedule.php. Transcribed from the audio available in the RNA conference archives at http://www.rna.org/meetingdates.php; below Friday, Sept. 29 [sic]—"The Rev. Rick Warren."
6. Interview with Rick Warren, CNN Larry King Live, Aired December 2, 2005, Transcript, http://transcripts.cnn.com/TRANSCRIPTS/0512/02/lkl.01.html.

7. Aspen Ideas Festival, The Aspen Institute, July 6, 2005, "Discussion: Religion and Leadership," with David Gergen and Rick Warren. Transcribed from the audio available at http://www.lighthousetrailsresearch.com/newsletternovember05.htm.
8. "No spectators allowed" by Ann Pepper, *The Orange County Register*, November 6, 2005, http://www.ocregister.com/ocregister/news/article_751553.php.
9. http://www.acts-of-mercy.com/.
10. As quoted in *Rick Warren and the Purpose that Drives Him* by Richard Abanes, p. 30.
11. As quoted in ibid., pp. 23-24.
12. As quoted in ibid., p. 30.
13. As quoted in ibid.
14. Interview with Rick Warren, CNN Larry King Live, Aired December 2, 2005, http://transcripts.cnn.com/TRANSCRIPTS/0512/02/lkl.01.html.
15. Aspen Ideas Festival, The Aspen Institute, July 6, 2005, "Discussion: Religion and Leadership," with David Gergen and Rick Warren. Transcribed from the audio available at http://www.lighthousetrailsresearch.com/newsletternovember05.htm.
16. Rick Warren, as quoted in Discussion "Myths of the Modern Mega-Church," May 23, 2005, the Pew Forum's biannual Faith Angle conference on religion, politics and public life, Event Transcript, http://pewforum.org/events/index.php?EventID=80.
17. Rick Warren, Aspen Ideas Festival, The Aspen Institute, July 6, 2005, "Discussion: Religion and Leadership," with David Gergen and Rick Warren, Transcribed from the audio available at http://www.lighthousetrailsresearch.com/newsletternovember05.htm.
18. Alice Bailey & Djwhal Khul, *Problems of Humanity*, Chapter V - The Problem of the Churches, http://laluni.helloyou.ws/netnews/bk/problems/prob1055.html.
19. "The purpose-driven pastor" by Paul Nussbaum, *The Philadelphia Inquirer*, January 8, 2006, http://www.philly.com/mld/inquirer/living/religion/13573441.htm.
20. Alice Bailey & Djwhal Khul, *The Externalization of the Hierarchy*, Section II - The General World Picture, http://laluni.helloyou.ws/netnews/bk/externalisation/exte1040.html.
21. Alice Bailey & Djwhal Khul, *Esoteric Psychology I*, Section Two - III. The Rays and Man, http://laluni.helloyou.ws/netnews/bk/psychologyI/psyc1111.html.
22. For information, see *Reinventing Jesus Christ* by Warren Smith, especially pp. 16, 19, 60-64.
23. Interview with Rick Warren, CNN Larry King Live, Aired December 2, 2005, http://transcripts.cnn.com/TRANSCRIPTS/0512/02/lkl.01.html.
24. Aspen Ideas Festival, The Aspen Institute, July 6, 2005, "Discussion: Religion and Leadership," with David Gergen and Rick Warren. Transcribed from the audio available at http://www.lighthousetrailsresearch.com/newsletternovember05.htm.
25. As quoted in Discussion "Myths of the Modern Mega-Church," May 23, 2005, http://pewforum.org/events/index.php?EventID=80.
26. As quoted in ibid.

27. "The Auburn Affirmation," The American Presbyterian Church, http://www.americanpresbyterianchurch.org/the_affirmation1.htm.
28. "Historic Documents of American Presbyterianism: The Doctrinal Deliverance of 1910," PCA Historical Center, Archive & Manuscript Repository for the Continuing Presbyterian Church, http://www.pcahistory.org/documents/deliverance.html.
29. Ibid.
30. Ibid.
31. Ibid.
32. Ibid.
33. Alice Bailey & Djwhal Khul, *Problems of Humanity*, Chapter V - The Problem of the Churches, http://laluni.helloyou.ws/netnews/bk/problems/prob1055.html.
34. "The Pearly Gates are Wide Open: A new Newsweek/Beliefnet poll shows a stunning level of acceptance of other people's faiths" by Stephen Waldman, Beliefnet, http://www.beliefnet.com/story/173/story_17348.html.
35. "In Search of the Spiritual" by Jerry Adler, *Newsweek*, Aug. 29 - Sept. 5, 2005 issue, http://www.msnbc.msn.com/id/9024914/site/newsweek/, (page 2); quoting Alan Wolfe, director of the Boisi Center for Religion and American Public Life at Boston College.
36. Alice Bailey & Djwhal Khul, *A Treatise on White Magic*, Rule Ten - The Present Age and the Future, http://laluni.helloyou.ws/netnews/bk/magic/magi1139.html.

Chapter Twenty

1. Alice Bailey & Djwhal Khul, *The Externalization of the Hierarchy*, Section II - The General World Picture, http://laluni.helloyou.ws/netnews/bk/externalisation/exte1087.html.
2. Alice Bailey, *From Bethlehem to Calvary*, Chapter Five - The Fourth Initiation, The Crucifixion, http://laluni.helloyou.ws/netnews/bk/bethlehem/beth1064.html.
3. Ibid., http://laluni.helloyou.ws/netnews/bk/bethlehem/beth1062.html.
4. Alice Bailey & Djwhal Khul, *The Externalization of the Hierarchy*, Section IV - Stages in the Externalization of the Hierarchy, The Subjective Basis of the New World Religion, http://laluni.helloyou.ws/netnews/bk/externalisation/exte1215.html.
5. Alice Bailey & Djwhal Khul, *Discipleship in the New Age II*, Teachings on Initiation - Part III, http://laluni.helloyou.ws/netnews/bk/discipleship2/disc2087.html.
6. *PDL*; p. 310.
7. Rick Warren, speaker at the Baptist World Centenary Congress -- "Cleansing Water," July 30, 2005, transcribed from Congress Internet Video Streaming, http://www.bwacongress2005.org.uk/feature.asp?id=832#.
8. Ken Blanchard and Phil Hodges, *Lead Like Jesus: Lessons from the Greatest Leadership Role Model of All Time* (Nashville, Tennessee: W Publishing Group, 2005), p. 114.
9. As quoted in Ibid., the first page of endorsements inside the front cover.

10. Rick Warren, Saddleback Church Service, November 2, 2003; transcribed from http://www.saddlebackfamily.com/peace/Services/110203_high.asx.
11. Lead Like Jesus Celebration, The Church at Brook Hills, Birmingham, Alabama, November 20, 2003, as quoted in the transcript posted at http://www.gprxnow.com/bonuses/BlanchardLeadLikeJesus.pdf, pp. 2-3, and also at http://www.bibleoncassette.com/lead_like_Jesus.html.
12. As quoted in Discussion "Myths of the Modern Mega-Church," May 23, 2005, http://pewforum.org/events/index.php?EventID=80.
13. Who We Are, Lead Like Jesus, http://www.leadlikejesus.com/common/content.asp?PAGE=270.
14. Events & Services, Leadership Encounter, Lead Like Jesus, http://www.leadlikejesus.com/common/content.asp?PAGE=340.
15. Ken Blanchard and Phil Hodges, *Lead Like Jesus*, back cover.
16. "Ken Blanchard co-hosting 'Lead Like Jesus' at Brook Hills" by Jennifer Davis Rash, *The Alabama Baptist*, October 30, 2003, http://www.thealabamabaptist.org/ip_template.asp?upid=1586.
17. On the Links, Lead Like Jesus celebration, Rick Warren's Ministry Toolbox™, Issue #146, 3/17/2004, http://www.pastors.com/RWMT/?ID=146.
18. "Learning to Lead Like Jesus" by Janet Chismar, Senior Editor for Faith, http://www.crosswalk.com/faith/1230643.html.
19. Ken Blanchard and Phil Hodges, *Lead Like Jesus*, p. 114.
20. "Learning to Lead Like Jesus" by Janet Chismar, http://www.crosswalk.com/faith/1230643.html.
21. Lead Like Jesus Celebration, The Church at Brook Hills, Birmingham, Alabama, November 20, 2003, as quoted in the transcript posted at http://www.gprxnow.com/bonuses/BlanchardLeadLikeJesus.pdf, p. 10, and also at http://www.bibleoncassette.com/lead_like_Jesus.html.
22. Lead Like Jesus Celebration at 21-C, http://www.21-c.org/.
23. *Tozer on Worship and Entertainment*, A.W. Tozer, Selected Excerpts Compiled by James L. Snyder, p. 21.
24. Home page, Newbury Park First Christian Church, http://www.npfcc.org. (The home page has since been changed.) See also "What would Jesus teach?" by Kim Lamb Gregory, *Ventura County Star*, March 4, 2006, http://www.venturacountystar.com/vcs/religion_and_ethics/article/0,1375,VCS_151_4513855,00.html.
25. Ancient Spiritual Wisdom Principles and Practices for Life Speakers, Via Vita, http://www.viavita.us/conference_spkrs.htm. See also Conference, Conference Program at http://www.viavita.us/ for their listing of the speakers' topics.
26. National Pastors Convention, http://www.nationalpastorsconvention.com/downloads/npc05brochure.pdf (the labyrinth is on p. 6), and http://www.nationalpastorsconvention.com/content.aspx?sp=emergent.

27. Ancient Spiritual Wisdom Principles and Practices for Life Speakers, http://www.viavita.us/conference_spkrs.htm.
28. Conference, Via Vita, http://www.viavita.us/conference.htm. (Note: After the Conference, they reworded this webpage somewhat and deleted some of the phrases.)
29. National Board Members of Lead Like Jesus, http://www.leadlikejesus.org/templates/cusleadlikejesus/details.asp?id=21633&PID=88945&mast=. (Note: They removed this webpage sometime after late January 2006 when they revamped their website. For a brief overview of some of the Board members, see "Lead Like Jesus: New Agers Mixing with Christians," http://www.lighthousetrailsresearch.com/leadlikejesus.htm.)
30. For examples of Blanchard's endorsement of the Hoffman Process see http://www.hoffmaninstitute.org and http://www.hoffmaninstitute.org/interviews-articles/interviews/career/blanchard.html. Blanchard's endorsement of the Hoffman Process was also included in the book *The Hoffman Process: The World-Famous Technique That Empowers You to Forgive Your Past, Heal Your Present, and Transform Your Future*, by Tim Laurence, a director of Hoffman International, (New York, New York: Bantam Dell: 2004), first page inside the front cover, titled, "Praise for THE HOFFMAN PROCESS."
31. As quoted on the Hoffman Institute home page, http://www.hoffmaninstitute.org.
32. Board of Advisors, Hoffman Institute, http://www.hoffmaninstitute.org/about/directors-advisors/advisors.html; and Blanchard is listed as a current member of the Advisory Board in the Hoffman Institute's Jan/Feb 2006 issue of The LIGHT News, http://www.hoffmaninstitute.org/pdfs/ln_jan-feb-06.pdf, p. 8.
33. "The Negative Love Syndrome and the Quadrinity Model: A Path to Personal Freedom and Love" by Bob Hoffman, Hoffman Institute, http://www.hoffmaninstitute.org/pdfs/nls.pdf, pp. 1, 2. (Also at http://www.hoffmaninstitute.org/process/negative-love/index.html.)
34. Ibid., pp. 2-3.
35. Ibid., p. 18.
36. "A Message from the President" by Raz Ingrasci, Hoffman Institute, http://www.hoffmaninstitute.org/about/directors-advisors/president.html.
37. "The Quadrinity Process, 35 Years of Transformation," an interview with Raz Ingrasci, President, by Light News Staff, Hoffman Institute, http://www.hoffmaninstitute.org/interviews-articles/interviews/spiritual/raz.html.
38. Alice Bailey, *The Unfinished Autobiography*, Appendix - The Principles of the Arcane School - VII. The Arcane School presents the Fundamental Doctrines of the Ageless Wisdom, http://laluni.helloyou.ws/netnews/bk/autobiography/auto1102.html.
39. Alice Bailey & Djwhal Khul, *Initiation, Human and Solar*, Chapter VII - The Probationary Path, http://laluni.helloyou.ws/netnews/bk/initiation/init1025.html.

40. "A Journey to Love and Freedom" by Michelle Pilley, an article in Kindred Magazine 2001, Hoffman Institute International, http://www.quadrinity.com/articles/article2a.htm. For more on the Process and spirit guides, see also "Mend Mom's Mistakes" by Sasha Lessin, Ph.D., School of Tantra, http://www.schooloftantra.com/Education/CertificationProgram/TantraCertification/CertifiedTantraPractitioner/CTA70-79ParentsPastLives/CTA70MendMomsMistakes.htm; and "VISUALIZATION: God-Given Power or New Age Danger? (Part One)" by John Weldon and John Ankerberg, CRI, http://www.equip.org/free/DN388-1.pdf, p. 3.
41. "The Retreat That Changed My Life" by Joan Borysenko, Hoffman Institute, http://www.hoffmaninstitute.org/article_joan.html. (Now posted as "The Therapy That Changed My Life," http://www.hoffmaninstitute.org/pdfs/process_borysenko.pdf, p. 5.)
42. As quoted on the Hoffman Institute home page, http://www.hoffmaninstitute.org.
43. About The Book, Reviews, Kenneth Blanchard, In the Sphere of Silence, http://www.inthesphereofsilence.com/DesktopDefault.aspx?Myurl=p_default&tabindex=8&tabid=11&subtabid=46. Ken Blanchard is also mentioned as having "admired and praised" this book in the January 27, 2006 interview with Vijay Eswaran, in "Holding hands with Silence," http://www.inthesphereofsilence.com/media/interview.pdf, p. 3.
44. About The Site, In the Sphere of Silence, http://www.inthesphereofsilence.com/DesktopDefault.aspx?Myurl=My_pcs&tabindex=0&tabid=10&subtabid=0.
45. "Holding hands with Silence," an interview with Vijay Eswaran, January 27, 2006, http://www.inthesphereofsilence.com/media/interview.pdf, p. 1.
46. Author's Message, "In the Sphere of Silence" by Vijay Eswaran, http://www.inthesphereofsilence.com/DesktopDefault.aspx?Myurl=p_default&tabindex=3&tabid=11&subtabid=5.
47. For additional endorsements, including as recent as January 2006, see "Ken Blanchard Still Endorsing the New Age: Update on Ken Blanchard #3" by Bud Press, Director, Christian Research Service, February 11, 2006, http://www.christianresearchservice.com/KenBlanchard8.htm. See also "Ken Blanchard and the New Age Movement," Lighthouse Trails Research Project, http://www.lighthousetrailsresearch.com/blanchardtable.htm.
48. National Board Members of Lead Like Jesus, http://www.leadlikejesus.org/templates/cusleadlikejesus/details.asp?id=21633&PID=88945&mast=.
49. As quoted in "A Banquet for the Soul," An interview with Mark Victor Hansen, by Raz Ingrasci, President, Hoffman Institute, http://www.hoffmaninstitute.org/interviews-articles/interviews/spiritual/hansen.html.
50. Mark Victor Hansen, as quoted in ibid.
51. Ortberg spoke at the Lead Like Jesus Celebration held at Louisville, Kentucky on November 18, 2004. Lead Like Jesus 3, Church Communication Network, http://www.ccn.tv/programming/event/evt_18nov04.htm. See also, Celebration DVD, http://www.leadlikejesus.cc/llj/item_M101904002.htm.

52. Lead Like Jesus Celebration, The Church at Brook Hills, Birmingham, Alabama, November 20, 2003, as quoted in the transcript posted at http://www.gprxnow.com/bonuses/BlanchardLeadLikeJesus.pdf, p. 38, and also at http://www.bibleoncassette.com/lead_like_Jesus.html.
53. Home page, Laurie Beth Jones, https://www.lauriebethjones.com/.
54. Laurie Beth Jones Biography, Q & A with Laurie Beth Jones, under "What do you see as the major challenges to the Christian faith?", http://www.jesusceo.com/profile/index.html.
55. Mission & Vision Statement of the Jesus, CEO Foundation, http://www.jesusceo.com/ourmission.html.
56. Laurie Beth Jones, *Jesus CEO: Using Ancient Wisdom for Visionary Leadership* (New York, New York: Hyperion, 1995), pp. 5, 8. See also, "Laurie Beth Jones: Is She a New Age Christian," Lighthouse Trails Research Project, http://www.lighthousetrailsresearch.com/lauriebethjones.htm.
57. National Board Members of Lead Like Jesus, http://www.leadlikejesus.org/templates/cusleadlikejesus/details.asp?id=21633&PID=88945&mast=.
58. Laurie Beth Jones, *Jesus CEO*, pp. 301, 295.
59. Ray Yungen, *A Time of Departing: How Ancient Mystical Practices are Uniting Christians with the World's Religions*, p. 61.
60. Alice Bailey & Djwhal Khul, *The Rays and the Initiations*, Part One - Fourteen Rules for Group Initiation, http://laluni.helloyou.ws/netnews/bk/rays/rays1111.html.

Chapter Twenty-One

1. Rick Warren meets with the S3K Leadership Network, Video Resources, Synagogue 3000, http://www.synagogue3000.org/video.html.
2. Transcribed from the video available at ibid., "Congregational Transitions," June 16, 2005.
3. Alice Bailey & Djwhal Khul, *The Externalization of the Hierarchy*, Section IV - Stages in the Externalization of the Hierarchy, The Subjective Basis of the New World Religion, http://laluni.helloyou.ws/netnews/bk/externalisation/exte1215.html.
4. Ray Yungen, *A Time of Departing: How Ancient Mystical Practices are Uniting Christians with the World's Religions*, p. 105.
5. "In Search of the Spiritual" by Jerry Adler, *Newsweek*, Aug. 29 - Sept. 5, 2005 issue, http://www.msnbc.msn.com/id/9024914/site/newsweek/, (page 2); quoting Alan Wolfe, director of the Boisi Center for Religion and American Public Life at Boston College.
6. "The Importance of Sound Doctrine" by A.W. Tozer, *The Best of A.W. Tozer*, Book Two, Compiled by Warren W. Wiersbe, pp. 174-176.
7. According to a search for the term "Lord" in the New Testament of *The Message: The Bible in Contemporary Language* by Eugene Peterson (USA: NavPress, 2002-2003), at http://bible.crosswalk.com/OnlineStudyBible/bible.cgi?new=1&word=lord&section=2&version=msg&language=en.
8. Ibid.

Chapter Twenty-Two

1. William M. Easum and Thomas G. Bandy, *Growing Spiritual Redwoods* (Nashville, Tennessee: Abingdon Press, 1997).
2. Lyle Schaller, as quoted on About Us, EBA Origins, Easum, Bandy and Associates, http://www.easumbandy.com/aboutEBA/origins.html.
3. Ibid., and also About Us, EBA Team, Bill Easum, Easum, Bandy and Associates, http://www.easumbandy.com/aboutEBA/team.html?b=Bill%20Easum.
4. About Us, EBA Team, Tom Bandy, http://www.easumbandy.com/aboutEBA/team.html?b=Tom%20Bandy.
5. About Us, EBA Origins, http://www.easumbandy.com/aboutEBA/origins.html.
6. For information on Leonard Sweet and the (New Age) New Spirituality, see http://www.crossroad.to/Quotes/Church/post-modern/leonard-sweet.htm; http://herescope.blogspot.com/; http://www.sliceoflaodicea.com; and http://www.lighthousetrailsresearch.com/leonardsweet.htm.
7. Book Look, Rick Warren's Ministry Toolbox™, Issue #83, 1/1/2003, http://www.pastors.com/RWMT/?ID=83.
8. As quoted in "What Christian leaders have to say about Tom Bandy," About Us, Easum, Bandy, and Associates, http://www.easumbandy.com/tomBandyB.html.
9. "Growing Spiritual Redwoods (Summary)" by Thomas G. Bandy, Free Resources, Easum, Bandy, and Associates, http://www.easumbandy.com/resources/index.php?action=details&record=1074.
10. Ibid.
11. Alice Bailey, *From Bethlehem to Calvary*, Chapter Seven - Our Immediate Goal, The Founding of the Kingdom, http://laluni.helloyou.ws/netnews/bk/bethlehem/beth1081.html.
12. Neale Donald Walsch, *Friendship with God: an uncommon dialogue*, (New York, New York: G. P. Putnam's Sons, 1999), pp. 376-377.
13. "Growing Spiritual Redwoods (Summary)" by Thomas G. Bandy, http://www.easumbandy.com/resources/index.php?action=details&record=1074.
14. "Obstacles and Opportunities for Congregational Mission in the 21st Century" by Thomas G. Bandy, Free Resources, Easum, Bandy, and Associates, http://www.easumbandy.com/resources/index.php?action=details&record=1073.
15. Ibid.
16. Ibid.
17. As quoted in "What Christian leaders have to say about Tom Bandy," http://www.easumbandy.com/tomBandyB.html.
18. "Dedicated. Motivated. Determined." About Us, Easum, Bandy, and Associates, http://www.easumbandy.com/about.html.
19. Alice Bailey & Djwhal Khul, *The Rays and the Initiations*, Part One - Fourteen Rules for Group Initiation, http://laluni.helloyou.ws/netnews/bk/rays/rays1042.html.

20. Alice Bailey & Djwhal Khul, *The Externalization of the Hierarchy*, Section II - The General World Picture, http://laluni.helloyou.ws/netnews/bk/externalisation/exte1040.html.
21. Ibid., Section III - Forces behind the Evolutionary Process, http://laluni.helloyou.ws/netnews/bk/externalisation/exte1178.html.
22. Alice Bailey & Djwhal Khul, *Problems of Humanity*, Chapter V - The Problem of the Churches, http://laluni.helloyou.ws/netnews/bk/problems/prob1052.html.
23. Neale Donald Walsch, in his essay in *From the Ashes*, Beliefnet Editors, p. 19.
24. "Growing Spiritual Redwoods (Summary)" by Thomas G. Bandy, http://www.easumbandy.com/resources/index.php?action=details&record=1074.
25. *Tozer on Worship and Entertainment*, A.W. Tozer, Selected Excerpts Compiled by James L. Snyder, p. 155.
26. As quoted in "What Christian leaders have to say about Tom Bandy," http://www.easumbandy.com/tomBandyB.html.
27. Alice Bailey, *From Bethlehem to Calvary*, Chapter Two - The First Initiation, The Birth at Bethlehem, http://laluni.helloyou.ws/netnews/bk/bethlehem/beth1022.html.

Chapter Twenty-Three

1. "Obstacles and Opportunities for Congregational Mission in the 21st Century" by Thomas G. Bandy, Free Resources, Easum, Bandy, and Associates, http://www.easumbandy.com/resources/index.php?action=details&record=1073.
2. "Association," Webster's New World Dictionary of the American Language; Second College Edition, (New York, New York: Simon & Schuster, Inc., 1984).
3. E.g., Bill Easum, "Sacred VS. Secular," Online Conversation, Free Resources: FAQs, Easum, Bandy, and Associates, http://www.easumbandy.com/resources/index.php?action=details&record=527.
4. Ceri, Pagan Network, forum, 15-05-2005, 12:42, http://www.pagan-network.org/forums/showthread.php?t=14410; quoting Craig Hawkins, *Witchcraft: Exploring the World of Wicca*, Baker Books, 1996, pp. 210, 21.
5. Warren Smith, *The Light That Was Dark: From the New Age to Amazing Grace*, Second Edition, (Magalia, California: Mountain Stream Press, 2005), pp. 163-165. (Available through various ministries on the Internet and Amazon.com.)
6. "The Once-Born and the Twice-Born" by A.W. Tozer, *The Best of A.W. Tozer*, Book Two, Compiled by Warren W. Wiersbe, p. 163.

Chapter Twenty-Four

1. Alice Bailey & Djwhal Khul, *The Reappearance of the Christ*, Chapter IV - The Work of the Christ Today and in the Future, http://laluni.helloyou.ws/netnews/bk/reappearance/reap1019.html.

2. Alice Bailey & Djwhal Khul, *Esoteric Psychology II*, Chapter III - Humanity Today, The World Situation, http://laluni.helloyou.ws/netnews/bk/psychology2/psyc2250.html.
3. Alice Bailey & Djwhal Khul, *The Reappearance of the Christ*, Chapter VII - Preparation for the Reappearance of the Christ, http://laluni.helloyou.ws/netnews/bk/reappearance/reap1049.html.
4. "A PLAN FOR PEACE" by Rick Warren, *Ladies' Home Journal*, December 2005 issue, p. 28.
5. Alice Bailey & Djwhal Khul, *The Reappearance of the Christ*, Chapter VI - The New World Religion, http://laluni.helloyou.ws/netnews/bk/reappearance/reap1042.html.
6. Ibid., Chapter III - World Expectancy, http://laluni.helloyou.ws/netnews/bk/reappearance/reap1018.html.
7. Aspen Ideas Festival, The Aspen Institute, July 6, 2005, "Discussion: Religion and Leadership," with David Gergen and Rick Warren, http://www.aspeninstitute.org/site/c.huLWJeMRKpH/b.901097/k.C0C7/Agenda.htm. Transcribed from the audio available at Lighthouse Trails Research Project, http://www.lighthousetrailsresearch.com/newsletternovember05.htm.
8. Alice Bailey & Djwhal Khul, *The Reappearance of the Christ*, Chapter IV - The Work of the Christ Today and in the Future, http://laluni.helloyou.ws/netnews/bk/reappearance/reap1025.html.
9. Interview with Rick Warren, CNN Larry King Live, Aired December 2, 2005, Transcript, http://transcripts.cnn.com/TRANSCRIPTS/0512/02/lkl.01.html.
10. United Nations, Interfaith Prayer Breakfast, September 2005, transcribed from the audio available at http://www.lighthousetrailsresearch.com/newmissiology.htm.
11. Alice Bailey & Djwhal Khul, *The Reappearance of the Christ*, Chapter V - The Teachings of the Christ, The Establishing of Right Human Relations, http://laluni.helloyou.ws/netnews/bk/reappearance/reap1033.html.
12. Alice Bailey & Djwhal Khul, *The Destiny of the Nations*, Christ and the Coming New-Age, http://laluni.helloyou.ws/netnews/bk/destiny/dest1065.html.
13. Alice Bailey & Djwhal Khul, *The Externalization of the Hierarchy*, Section III - Forces behind the Evolutionary Process, http://laluni.helloyou.ws/netnews/bk/externalisation/exte1213.html.
14. Ibid., http://laluni.helloyou.ws/netnews/bk/externalisation/exte1204.html.
15. Alice Bailey & Djwhal Khul, *The Reappearance of the Christ*, Chapter VII - Preparation for the Reappearance of the Christ, http://laluni.helloyou.ws/netnews/bk/reappearance/reap1054.html.
16. "The Mystic Plague: Catholicism sets a Spiritualist Agenda" by Richard Bennett (a former Roman Catholic priest), Berean Beacon, http://www.bereanbeacon.org/articles/Mystic_Plague.htm. This article contains information on the connections between Roman Catholicism, Mysticism, the New Age, and the coming false "Christ" and kingdom.
17. Alice Bailey & Djwhal Khul, *The Reappearance of the Christ*, Chapter III - World Expectancy, http://laluni.helloyou.ws/netnews/bk/reappearance/reap1018.html.

18. Ibid., Chapter VII - Preparation for the Reappearance of the Christ, http://laluni.helloyou.ws/netnews/bk/reappearance/reap1054.html.
19. For information on Kingdom Dominionism, see "Dominionism and the Rise of Christian Imperialism" by Sarah Leslie, Discernment-Ministries, Inc., http://www.discernment-ministries.org/ChristianImperialism.htm.

Chapter Twenty-Five

1. Rick Warren, *The Purpose Driven Church: Growth Without Compromising Your Message & Mission*, p. 356.
2. "Another Word Concerning the Down-Grade" by C. H. Spurgeon, from the August 1887 *Sword and Trowel*, The Spurgeon Archive, http://www.spurgeon.org/s_and_t/dg03.htm.
3. "Divisions Are Not Always Bad" by A.W. Tozer, *The Best of A.W. Tozer*, Compiled by Warren W. Wiersbe, pp. 71-73.
4. As written in their own transcript, Anderson Cooper, Anderson Cooper 360 Degrees, Aired June 17, 2004, CNN, Transcripts, http://transcripts.cnn.com/TRANSCRIPTS/0406/17/acd.00.html.

CPSIA information can be obtained at www.ICGtesting.com
Printed in the USA
LVOW12s0343170315

430850LV00001BA/83/A